The Letters and Journals of

JAMES FENIMORE COOPER

VOLUME V

The Letters and Journals of

JAMES FENIMORE COOPER

Edited by

JAMES FRANKLIN BEARD

VOLUME V

THE BELKNAP PRESS OF
HARVARD UNIVERSITY PRESS

Cambridge, Massachusetts

1968

Distributed in Great Britain by
Oxford University Press
London

Typography and design by Burton Jones

Printed in the United States of America by
Harvard University Printing Office

Bound by Stanhope Bindery, Inc., Boston, Massachusetts

Library of Congress Catalog Card Number 60–5388

ACKNOWLEDGMENTS

The cheerful, prolonged, self-effacing collaboration enabling the completion of this project has been the editor's best reward. This silent effort once more prompts his thanks. For members of the Fenimore Cooper family, especially for Mr. Paul Fenimore Cooper and Dr. Henry S. Fenimore Cooper, and for his Advisory Committee, ordinary expressions of gratitude are more than usually inadequate. Neither the Cooper family nor the Advisory Committee (Mr. Frederick B. Adams, Jr., Mr. Clifton Waller Barrett, Professor Julian P. Boyd, the late Professor Mark DeWolfe Howe, Professor Howard Mumford Jones, Dr. Louis C. Jones, Professor Kenneth Murdock, Professor Robert E. Spiller, Mr. Milton Halsey Thomas, and Professor Willard Thorp) have ever faltered in their interest or generosity. The editor notes with regret the passing of such friends of the edition as Professor Howe, Miss Clare Benedict, and Miss Dorothy C. Barck.

Collectors and institutions whose holographs have contributed texts of letters are fully listed in the Catalogue of Sources, Volume VI. Owners not listed in earlier volumes who have provided original or unique materials for Volumes V and VI are: Bibliothèque de Nancy, Nancy, France; Mr. Sampson P. Bowers, Cooperstown, New York; City Library Association, Springfield, Massachusetts; Colorado State Historical Society; Connecticut State Library; the late H. Gail Davis; Detroit Institute of Arts; J. K. Lilly Collection, Indiana University Library; Leningrad Archives; Professor Andrew Breen Myers, Flushing, New York; New Jersey Historical Society; New York City Chamber of Commerce; The New York Society Library; Mr. DeLancey R. Ober, Baltimore; Peabody Institute Library, Baltimore; University of North Carolina Library; the Rhode Island Historical Society; The Scheide Library, Princeton, New Jersey; Sleepy Hollow Restorations, Tarrytown, New York; Stadt- und Universitäts-Bibliothek, Frankfurt-am-Main; Robert Hull Fleming Museum, University of Vermont; Wadsworth Atheneum, Hartford, Connecticut; Mr. A. Pennington Whitehead, New York City and Cherry Valley, New York; and the Yale University Art Gallery.

Additional scholars and librarians to whom I owe thanks for assistance in locating letters or other materials are: Professor Harry B. Adams, Academician M. P. Alekseev, Mr. F. Clever Bald, Professor Warner Barnes, Mrs. Mina R. Bryan, Mr. Roger Butterfield, Mr. Edward Bryant, Mr. Henry Cadwalader, the late Professor William

Charvat, Mr. Jack B. Collins, Miss Joan Corbett, Mr. Malcolm Freiberg, Professor William M. Gibson, Professor Harrison Hayford, Mr. Harold Hazelton, Mr. George H. Healey, Mrs. Frank E. Hock, Mrs. Margit Holzinger, Miss Fanny C. Howe, Mr. Richard E. Jenkins, Jr., Mr. Frank N. Jones, Mr. John D. Kilbourne, Mrs. Miriam L. Lesley, Miss Sue Loubiere, Father Albert Mason, Professor James B. Meriwether, Mrs. Robert E. Morris, Mrs. John DeWitt Peltz, Professor Thomas Philbrick, Miss Doris M. Reed, Mr. Karl Remmen, Miss Caroline Rollins, Mr. Frank Rollins, Miss Margaret Rose, Mr. Howard L. Smith, Miss Mildred Steinbach, Mr. G. William Stuart, Jr., Mrs. Catherine Supinski, Miss Enid T. Thompson, Professor Frederick B. Tolles, Professor Warren S. Walker, and Father David J. Williams. For prompt response to frequent calls on their knowledge and resources, I am again and especially grateful to Mr. Roy Butterfield, Historian of Otsego County, to Mr. Paul Z. DuBois, Librarian of the New York State Historical Association, to Dr. Oliver W. Holmes, Director of the National Historical Publications Commission, to Mrs. Henry W. Howell, Jr., Librarian of the Frick Art Reference Library, to Dr. Donald C. Gallup and Mrs. Anne Whelpley of the Yale University Library, to Mr. Frank Wells of the Library of Congress, to Mr. Tilton Barron and Miss Marion Henderson of the Clark University Library, and to Mr. Marcus McCorison, Miss Avis G. Clarke, and Miss Mary Brown of the American Antiquarian Society.

The generosity of the John Simon Guggenheim Memorial Foundation made possible much of the basic research for this edition. It has also been aided, at intervals, by grants from Dartmouth College and from Clark University, and by "assists" from the Shell Oil Company. Most recently, Deans Dwight E. Lee and Saul H. Cohen of the Graduate School of Clark University considerately found resources to provide clerical assistance for the preparation of the Index. Much of the more onerous part of this considerable task was performed by Mrs. Virginia Varney, Mrs. Ethel Delaney, Mr. Stephen Hemenway, and Mrs. Jean T. Corbett.

Permissions to reprint copyrighted materials have been kindly supplied by Mr. Arthur H. Brook, II, for the Yale University Press, by Mrs. Nina M. Harkins for *The Sewanee Review*, and by Leroy D. Cross for *The New England Quarterly*.

JAMES FRANKLIN BEARD

Clark University
Worcester, Massachusetts

CONTENTS

ILLUSTRATIONS

FOLLOWING PAGE 100

FOLLOWING PAGE 228

canvas. Size: 29 x 36 inches. Courtesy of the New York Chamber of Commerce.

Plate VIII. Portrait of General Winfield Scott (1851) by Miner K. Kellogg (1814–1889). *Oil on canvas. Size: 25 x 20 1/2 inches.* Courtesy of The New-York Historical Society.

FOLLOWING PAGE 388

Plates IX–XI. *The Course of Empire* by Thomas Cole. Cooper considered this series of large canvases, which Cole executed for his patron Luman Reed between 1833 and 1836, "not only . . . the work of the highest genius this country has ever produced, but . . . one of the noblest works of art that has ever been wrought." Cole communicated his intention, perhaps for the first time, in a letter to Reed, dated Catskill, 18 September 1833:

"A series of pictures might be painted that should illustrate the history of a natural scene, as well as be an epitome of Man, — showing the natural changes of landscape, and those effected by man in his progress from barbarism to civilization — to luxury — to the vicious state, or state of destruction — and to the state of ruin and desolation.

"The philosophy of my subject is drawn from the history of the past, wherein we see how nations have risen from the savage state to that of power and glory, and then fallen, and become extinct. Natural scenery has also its changes, — the hours of the day and the seasons of the year — sunshine and storm: these justly applied will give expression to each picture of the series I would paint. It will be well to have the same location in each picture: this location may be identified by the introduction of some striking object in each scene — a mountain of peculiar form, for instance. This will not in the least preclude variety. The scene must be composed so as to be picturesque in its wild state, appropriate for cultivation, and the site of a sea-port. There must be the sea, a bay, rocks, waterfalls and woods.

"The first picture, representing the savage state, must be a view of the wilderness, — the sun rising from the sea, and the clouds of night retiring over the mountains. The figures must be savage, clothed in skins, and occupied in the chase. There must be a flashing chiaroscuro, and the spirit of motion pervading the scene, as though nature were just springing from chaos.

"The second picture must be the pastoral state, — the day further advanced — light clouds playing about the mountains — the scene partly cultivated — a rude village near the bay — small vessels in the harbour — groups of peasants either pursuing their labours in the field, watching their flocks, or engaged in some simple amusement. The chiaroscuro must be of a milder character than in the previous scene, but yet have a fresh and breezy effect.

"The third must be a noonday, — a great city girding the bay, gorgeous piles of architecture, bridges, aqueducts, temples — the port crowded with vessels — splendid processions, &c. — all that can be combined to show the fulness of prosperity: the chiaroscuro broad.

"The fourth should be a tempest, — a battle, and the burning of the city — towers falling, arches broken, vessels wrecking in the harbour. In this scene there should be a fierce chiaroscuro, masses and groups swaying about like stormy waves. This is the scene of destruction or vicious state.

"The fifth must be a sunset, — the mountains riven — the city a desolate ruin — columns standing isolated amid the encroaching waters — ruined temples, broken bridges, fountains, sarcophagi, &c. — no human figure — a solitary bird perhaps: a calm and silent effect. This picture must be as the funeral knell of departed greatness, and may be called the state of desolation."

— Louis L. Noble, *The Course of Empire, Voyage of Life, and Other Pictures of Thomas Cole, N.A., with Selections from His Letters and Miscellaneous Writings* (New York, 1853), 176–78.

Plate IX. *First Panel:* "The Savage State" or "Commencement of Empire." *Size: 61 1/2 x 39 inches.* Courtesy of The New-York Historical Society.

Second Panel: "The Arcadian or Pastoral State." *Size: 62 1/2 x 39 inches.* Courtesy of The New-York Historical Society.

Plate X. *Third Panel:* "The Consummation of Empire." *Size: 75 x 50 1/2 inches.* Courtesy of The New-York Historical Society.

Fourth Panel: "Destruction." *Size: 62 1/2 x 38 1/2 inches.* Courtesy of The New-York Historical Society.

Plate XI. *Fifth Panel:* "Desolation." *Size: 61 x 39 1/2 inches.* Courtesy of The New-York Historical Society.

Study (1827) by Thomas Cole, for the scene from *The Last of the Mohicans* shown in Plate XII. *Brown ink on cream paper. Size: 4 3/4 x 7 3/4 inches.* Courtesy of the Archives of American Art, Detroit, Michigan.

Plate XII. Two representations of *Cora Kneeling at the Feet of Tamenund,* a scene from *The Last of the Mohicans,* both painted by Thomas Cole in 1827.

The painting at the Wadsworth Atheneum, commissioned by Robert Gilmor of Baltimore, was acquired by Daniel Wadsworth, much to Gilmor's distress. It was bequeathed to Alfred Smith in 1848 and by him in 1868 to the Wadsworth Atheneum. A letter from Wadsworth to Cole, dated 5 November 1827, hints that Cole copied the painting, possibly for Gilmor. Entries in exhibition catalogues in 1831 and 1848 indicate the existence of one or more additional paintings of the same scene by Cole. It excited much admiration. *Oil on canvas. Size: 21 1/2 x 35 inches.* Courtesy of the Wadsworth Atheneum, Hartford, Connecticut.

The painting at the New York State Historical Association, certainly no copy of the first, is an original representation of the same scene. Unless it is the "copy" referred to in Wadsworth's letter, its history is completely obscure. *Oil on canvas. Size: 25 x 35 inches.* Courtesy of the New York State Historical Association.

ILLUSTRATIONS IN TEXT

Part Seventeen

"ANTI-RENT"

1845

"ANTI-RENT"

1845

When Cooper began his Anti-Rent or Littlepage trilogy in late 1844, the controversy between landlords and tenants [1] in New York State was nearing its climax. In 1839, after the death of Stephen Van Rensselaer III, the "Good Patroon," the novelist predicted: "No man can hold such an estate [about 750,000 acres] as Rensselaer's in this country, unless he is in a situation to be constantly conferring favors." Five years later, as if to defy the inevitable, he was employing his fiction to rebuke the militant discontent, stressed at intervals by violence, in which hundreds of farmers in Albany, Rensselaer, Delaware, Columbia, and the adjoining counties combined to repudiate payments currently and cumulatively due on their leases.

With increasing bravado during the early months of 1845, the Anti-Renters declaimed their independence and, wearing masks and calico, demonstrated in favor of their unorthodox concepts of justice. Convened at Moses Earle's farm near Delhi in Delaware County on 7 August 1845, a band of these "Injins" shot and killed Deputy Sheriff Osman Steele as he collected the farmer's cattle for a forced sale. Popular indignation was intensified, martial law was declared, ringleaders and demonstrators were arrested, and two suspected assassins were sentenced to hanging. Rebuffed and outnumbered though they were, the farmers still held a balance of power between Whigs and Democrats; and they used this leverage to obtain concessions in new legislation, constitutional revisions, and court decisions. Discouraged, the Van Rensselaers

1. The words do not indicate precisely the actual relationship between the parties. In general, the tenants held titles (under what was termed an "incomplete sale"), paid taxes, and could sell their interests in the property. The landlords exacted a yearly fee (payable in produce, labor, cash, or some combination); retained timber, mineral, and water rights; and, in a clause known as the "quarter-sale" (later declared unconstitutional), reserved to themselves one fourth of the sale price or full title to the property at three quarters of the market price whenever the tenant wished to sell.

and other landlords disposed of their holdings to tenants who could or would buy and then sold out to speculators, leaving less fortunate farmers to more intractable foes.

Whereas the Anti-Rent War is now remembered merely as the death-struggle of the landed gentry in New York State and as a link in the chain process by which incompatible colonial cultures were assimilated to each other or extinguished, it heralded for Cooper either "the commencement of a dire revolution, or the commencement of a return to the sounder notions and juster principles that prevailed among us thirty years since" (*Miles Wallingford*, preface, v). It seemed to epitomize the conflict in American life that was eroding the Republic he had known, loved, and hoped to preserve; and he set out ambitiously in *Satanstoe* (1845), *The Chainbearer* (1845), and *The Redskins* (1846) to chronicle through four generations of the Littlepage family the social, economic, and political forces operative in the local conflict, assuming that its national implications would be obvious. Parallels and contrasts maintained through chronological shifts of setting were intended to indicate the drift toward civil chaos.

Cooper was probably correct in supposing that the form of a relatively simple thesis novel like *The Bravo* would not have enabled him to show that the tendency of a society following uninhibited dictates of self-interest was self-destructive and that a society observing rules of civility, undergirded by firm legal and constitutional structures, was preferable. "A social fact," he noted in *Miles Wallingford* (450), "cannot be carried out to demonstration like a problem in Euclid, the ramifications being so infinite as to reduce the results to something very like a conclusion from a multitude of interests." But, regardless of the merits of portions of the Anti-Rent trilogy, Cooper misjudged the technical difficulty of controlling these ramifications in fiction. The quite special conditions in New York State resulting from the landholding practices were too atypical to represent the conditions of society at large. And the case *for* the landlords and *against* the tenants emerged in the novels as more equivocal than Cooper liked to suppose it. "If the patroons of the State have not hired him to write," stated *The Albany Freeholder*, an Anti-Rent organ, in a long review of *The Redskins* on 5 August 1846, "we would advise them to buy in the whole edition. Its circulation will certainly do them no good."

By making his narrators landlords, Cooper repeated unconsciously his strategic error in *A Letter to His Countrymen* and *Home as Found*: he identified himself and his personal associations too closely with his controversial materials. Though he and his whole circle of friends were sympathetic to the proprietors, Cooper was not a landlord; and his response to the Anti-Rent agitation transcended, by intention at least, the special interests of any group. *The Redskins,* the only one of the novels with a contemporaneous setting, should surely have had a disinterested or ambivalent narrator. When the reader finds him instead an excessively aggrieved character whose behavior is permeated by self-interest and self-pity, he is tempted to telescope author and narrator and regard the book as an elaborate, ill-considered apology for a caste. But the reader can never be certain how far the near-hysteria of the narrator should be attributed to Cooper's realism and how far it should be attributed to his need for a surrogate to express his own sense of urgency and frustration. The "argument proves too much," as the Anti-Rent reviewer suggested.

Fortunately, Cooper's attitudes can also be examined in the larger context of his thought when, during the middle and late 1840's, the Anti-Rent War, Abolitionism, and the Free Soil agitation all seemed symptomatic of a malaise in the body politic. What he feared in these movements was the implicit (and sometimes explicit) assumption that the means of reform were subordinate to the ends and that any resistance, including violence, was preferable to acquiescence. "What will be the result of this Free Soil Movement?" he asked in a postscript torn from a letter written during this period.[2] "As a *party* it can not succeed, since one half the country will oppose it, and consequently defeat it. As *Disunion* it may fill this country with desolation. Disunion would be civil war — or war with the South — American with American. I am as much indisposed to submit to extravagant slave-

2. The body of the text, including the date and the name of the addressee, is missing. The fragment is in the Clifton Waller Barrett Collection of American Literature, University of Virginia.

holding pretensions as any man in the country, but sectional parties is not the mode by which they can be peacefully put down. Personal pique and personal ambition have assumed the aspect of liberty, and are seeking to make the masses their dupes. The attempt will fail."

Hypersensitive to the slightest threat of disorder in the state, Cooper saw with withering clarity how the forces at work in modern republics could be as destructive as those in the classical republics. The only legitimate procedure for reform was in his eyes the application of reason to the problems within established legal and constitutional forms; and the only safeguard to these forms was the voluntary respect of citizens and, when necessary, the fearless constraint of authority. The forms themselves should remain inviolable except through self-prescribed mechanisms of change. Cooper could see in this pre-Civil War era, as clearly as Henry Adams was to see much later, that the concept of a constitution expressing "the Law of Nature and of Nature's God" was anachronistic in a society whose highest authority was the people's will; but he could still hope, despite the warning of his senses, that the majesty and grandeur of the earlier conception could somehow be restored. If he warred against time itself, as he must have suspected, it was because he insisted that reason as embodied in law was the only legitimate arbiter in human affairs and that the cost of violence was human life and happiness and, ultimately, the loss of freedom.

787. *To Richard Bentley*

Otsego Hall, Cooperstown, Jan. 22d 1845

Dear Sir,

I have this day, drawn on you, 90 days sight, for £123.4.s.10.d. in favour of Mr. [Robert][1] Edmeston, a gentleman of respectability, who resides somewhere in the North of England, or the South of Scotland. This bill is drawn against the forth coming work, which I call "The Family of Littlepage." The amount is to suit a neighbor, and I have gladly drawn from this place, as it saves me a long journey at this inclement season, and leaves me at leisure to finish the book, which is now far advanced, and will go to press in a few days. I should be very much chagrined to have any thing happen to this bill, most especially on account of the parties to whom it goes. Now for the work.

"The Family of Littlepage" will form three complete Tales, each perfectly distinct from the other as regards leading characters, love story &c, but, in this wise connected. I divide the subjects into the "Colony," "Revolution" and "Republic," carrying the same family, the same localities, and same *things* generally through the three different books, but exhibiting the changes produced by time &c. In the Colony, for instance, the Littlepage of that day, first visits an estate of wild land, during the operations of the year 1758, the year that succeeded the scenes of the Mohicans, and it is there that the most stirring events of the book oc[c]ur. In the "Revolution" this land is first settled, and the principles are developed, on which this settlement takes place, showing a book, in some respects resembling the Pioneers, though varied by localities and incidents — In the "Republic" we shall have the present aspect of things, with an exhibition of the Anti-Rent commotion that now exists among us, and which certainly threatens the destruction of our system — You know I write what I think, in these matters, and I shall not spare "The Republic" in all in which it is faulty and weak, as faulty and weak it has been to a grievous extent in these matters.

I think the Story of the Colony a very good one; the others remain to be written. These books will be perfectly distinct as Tales, and each will make an ordinary sized novel, though I hope the interest of one will be reflected on the others.

I should like to hear from you, when the bill has been accepted.[2]

Yours truly
J. Fenimore Cooper

Mr. R. Bentley.

You had abundance of time with Miles, and I shall take care of you in this particular.

ADDRESSED: Mr. Richard Bentley | Publisher | New Burlington Street | London. | To go by the Cunard Steamer from | Boston. POSTMARKED: COOPERSTOWN N. Y. | JAN | 23 [N?]O | 14 FE 14 | 1845 STAMPED: [*illegible*] LETTER
MANUSCRIPT: Cooper Collection, Yale University Library.

1. Cooper wrote "Andrew," though according to Bentley's reply (see below) the bill was drawn in favor of Robert Edmeston. The Edmestons were an English family who owned land in Otsego County. Andrew Edmeston (d. 1826) of Berwick-upon-Tweed, England, and Cooperstown, New York, had been a friend of Cooper many years earlier.

2. Bentley replied on 3 March:

"I had the pleasure of writing to you on the 18th Sept. 1844 informing you that I had accepted your Dft for £200 (dated August 29 1844, 90 days sight) *on general account, and not as a balance.* I also repeated, what I urged in a former communication, that it was not in my power to pay the same consideration for the second part of Miles Wallingford as I had agreed to give the first portion of that story, and which I certainly should not have ventured to offer, had I known at the time that there would be a sequel.

"The sale of both publications has justified unfortunately my anticipation of the result; the amount of copies sold of Miles Wallingford not being equal to that of your preceding works, and the sequel falling off in sale to the extent of more than 100 copies below the former. For this latter part I shall be willing to credit you for £250. This amount with the £350 paid for the first part of Miles Wallingford will make together £600, while my profit on both publications together does not exceed £170, and I regret to add that the sale has quite discontinued.

"This I trust will evince my earnest desire to act with liberality in the matter, which throughout our long connection has ever been my aim.

"I have recently been favored with your letter of [22 January] ult — advising me that you had drawn on account of the first portion of a new Work of Fiction to be composed in three parts the sum of £123.4.10 in favor of Robert Edmeston dated 22 Jany. last 90 days sight. This bill was presented a few days [ago], and duly accepted. I had much pleasure in honoring your Dft especially as you particularly requested it. I hope you will allow me to press upon you the desirableness of a mutual understanding as to the precise state of the account current between us, which I have endeavoured in my previous letters to make perfectly clear. It is the more necessary to call your attention to this, as your dft for £200 (29 Aug. 1844) before adverted to, was drawn as a *Balance*. This must have originated in your supposing £350 would be coming to you for the second Part of Miles Wallingford, but, as I have shown, it is not in my power to give this sum, £100 of this dft will therefore have to be debited against the forthcoming book; and as you have further drawn against this £123.4.10, I shall be in advance *£223.4.10* on account of this new work.

"Permit me to draw your attention also to the fact that the taste for Works of Fiction has been for sometime past declining in this country, and the number of copies printed has been consequently reduced. With regard to your own Works on reviewing the sale of your later productions, I find I must confine myself in future to an impression of 750 copies. And this limit is the more necessary when the subject is not at once completed — continuations never being so saleable as single works. This number of copies will not enable me to offer you (with every desire to give you the fullest market value for your Works) more than £250 for your next work in 3 volumes. Should I hereafter be encouraged to print more, I shall be most happy to increase the price.

"The aspect of public affairs seems likely from late accounts from [the] United States to become somewhat threatening. I trust there will be found sufficient calm minds to prevent a serious misunderstanding between two countries which ought always to be friends. It would indeed be deplorable even for a moment to contemplate a hostile collision." (MS: YCAL.)

788. *To James Knox Polk*

Otsego Hall, Cooperstown, Jan. 28th 1845

Sir,

The time having approached when it will become necessary to make a new appointment of a Marshall for the Southern District of New-York, or leave a Whig in office who was thrust into the place of a democrat, at the change in the government, in 1841, I am asked to address you on the subject.

Although I feel very reluctant to interfere, by application, in affairs of this sort, I cordially joined in the recommendation of Mr. Anthony J Bleecker, the displaced officer, at the time he was appointed by Mr. Van Buren, and I have the same disposition, in renewing the application, now that his original claims are stre[n]gthened by the manner in which he was sacrificed, purely on account of his political opinions. I can give no stronger recommendation, than by saying, did the restoration of Mr. Bleecker depend on me, it should be made without the smallest hesitation. I conceived the appointment a particularily good one, at the time it was first made, and it certainly does not weaken his just pretensions that he was removed solely because he was a democrat. When I speak of my own opinion of Mr. Bleecker's claims as the strongest recommendation I can urge, I wish merely to be understood that no higher evidence can come from any man with proper ideas, than to solicit others to do that, which under similar circumstances, he feels he would do himself.[1]

I take this occasion, Sir, to congratulate you on the unsought for proof of confidence you have recieved from your countrymen. It must greatly increase the satisfaction of being thus selected for the highest elective office in the world, to be conscious that the honour has been the fruit of no political intrigue, or calculated professions.

With much respect, and the best wishes for the complete success of your approaching administration,

I remain, | Sir, | Your Ob— Ser.

J. Fenimore Cooper

Ja's K. Polk, Esquire. | President Elect, | U. S. A.

ADDRESSED: Ja's K. Polk Esquire | President Elect | U. S. America

MANUSCRIPT: General Records of the Department of State (RG 59), Applications and Recommendations, 1845–1852, National Archives of the United States.

1. Bleecker (1799?–1884) was not reinstated. A well-known New York real estate auctioneer, he became a founder of the Republican party, a candidate for mayor of New York City in 1856, and an assistant internal revenue inspector during the Civil War. (*The* [New York] *Evening Post*, 18 January 1884.)

789. *To Mrs. Cooper*

Stevenson's, Sunday morning, while James has gone to church. [2 March 1845]

Dearest,

I never had a better time, thus far, than I had yesterday. We went to the Corners on wheels, thence eight miles on runners, when we found another open carriage waiting for us, changed the horses, and got down an hour and a half before the necessary time. I saw the oldest Miss Berthoud in the road, and learned that the family was well.[1]

[Jacob] Sutherland, his wife, James Wadsworth [2] and family were in the cars. We are all bound to Joe Head's. I dine here at one, and go down in the South America, at five this evening. The rest will follow in a day or two. Sutherland looks ill, but not as ill as I expected to see him.

I met Mrs. [George] Clark[e] at the station. Her face is full of wrinkles, her flesh is gone and she looks seventy — or, rather, she looks ill. There is an end of all coquetry in her *faute de moyennes.* She told me that Mrs. Jenkins has a daughter.[3] I understand Ben Wilcocks has another.[4]

I send, by mail, John Jay's pamphlet,[5] and a copy of Weed's paper.[6] The last is to be read by Paul, *and then kept for me,* as I wish to use it, in the new book. The Anti Rent speech is the matter I am in quest of.

The opinion, here, is all against the Bishop. Wadsworth told me of a case that occurred in the house of Fitz Hugh, the party insulted being a Miss Car[r]ol[l], a young lady of perfect purity of manners and character,[7] whom he had hardly seen before — The place, the stairs, part assailed the *legs,* and the young lady kept her room until he quitted the place. You will see that John Jay alludes in the plainest manner, to two more cases, in West Chester. It is supposed a hundred cases might be adduced.

Dr. [Horatio] Potter, I am told, is against, as is Stevenson. Chief Justice [Ambrose] Spencer is against; John R. Murray is against &c, &c.

The river is free from Ice. Mr. Wessels [8] met me on the steps of the tavern, Hannah having seen me from the windows of Stanwix Hall, as I left the cars, and sent him in pursuit. I stepped into a book-store, and he passed me. He is a very simple, quiet young man, of, I should think, no great force of character, or capacity, but who seems amiable. I am going to see them, between churches.

I shall go down in the South America — Love to all, and most of all to yourself. Most tenderly yours,

J. F. C.

ADDRESSED: Mrs. Fenimore Cooper | Cooperstown
MANUSCRIPT: Cooper Collection, Yale University Library. PUBLISHED, IN PART: *Correspondence*, II, 535–36.

1. Cooper referred to Matilda (b. 1820) or Emily (1822–1898) Berthoud, daughters of Charles Louis Henri and Louisa Berthoud, who emigrated from Geneva, Switzerland, about 1830 and settled near Fort Plain, New York. Cooper became acquainted with the family after Louisa Berthoud wrote him in 1838 to inquire about placing one of her daughters in his family as a governess. (Berthoud family Bible, The State Historical Society of Colorado; MS: Louisa Berthoud to Cooper, 26 March 1838, YCAL.) See Cooper to Winfield Scott, 3 January 1849.

2. A Civil War general mortally wounded in the Battle of the Wilderness, James Samuel Wadsworth (1807–1864, Harvard n.g.) devoted himself earlier to civic enterprises and to the management of his large landed estate at Geneseo, New York. He and his wife Mary Craig Wharton of Philadelphia had six children. (Henry Greenleaf Pearson, *James S. Wadsworth of Geneseo* [New York: Charles Scribner's Sons, 1913]; *DAB*.)

3. Jane, younger daughter of Amariah and Marion Gunn Storrs and sister of Mrs. Richard Fenimore Cooper, married Henry Jenkins of Rensselaer County, New York, and had Mary Cooper Jenkins, later Mrs. James D. Wasson of Albany, on 27 February 1845 (Storrs, *The Storrs Family*, 458).

4. Helen Julia Wilcocks (1845–1868), born on 20 January (Jordan, *Colonial Families of Philadelphia*, I, 218).

5. In *Facts Connected with the Presentment of Bishop Onderdonk: A Reply to Parts of the Bishop's Statement* (New York: Stanford and Swords, 1845), John Jay defended himself and a colleague employed by the presenting bishops from Onderdonk's accusation: "You have had your ears open to all the gossip and scandal, which men, reducing themselves to the low caste of informers and panders, could seek out and scrape together for the use of my inveterate enemies."

6. A pseudonymous article in the *Albany Evening Journal* of 18 February 1845 maintained that a change in the supreme power of a state should not affect contracts existing prior to the change. Cooper evidently referred to a reply, entitled "Manor Troubles," in the *Journal* of 25 February 1845, repudiating this argument and claiming, in addition, that leaseholds taken *since* the Revolution were "nul[l]ities, as they are destructive of equality and republicanism — and as much an invasion of justice as a usurious contract would be, and therefore voidable."

7. Dr. Daniel H. Fitzhugh (1794–1881) was a neighbor of Wadsworth near Geneseo, New York. Fitzhugh's son William Dana Fitzhugh married Anne Carroll, daughter of Charles H. Carroll of Groveland, New York. (James H. Smith, *History of Livingston County, New York* . . . [Syracuse, New York: D. Mason & Co., 1881], 353–54; *Biographical Review . . . The Leading Citizens of Livingston and Wyoming Counties, New York* [Boston: Biographical Review Publishing Company, 1895], 343–46.)

8. Lieutenant Henry Walton Wessells (1809–1889), who rose to the rank of brigadier general of volunteers in 1862, married Hannah Cooper, daughter of Mary Ann Morris and Isaac Cooper, in 1844 (Lefferts, *Descendants of Lewis Morris*, Chart E, II).

790. *To John Fagan*

Globe. New-York, March. 4th 1845

Dear Fagan,

By express to-day, I send you a few chapters of new book. Begin *at once*, as I am in a great hurry, and wish to save time. I shall be at Heads on Tuesday or Wednesday night, probably the last, and I hope to find a great bundle of proofs ready.

The running title must be, "Satanstoe."

You will find the name of the heroine printed "Aneke" — It must be altered wherever it occurs to "Anneke," or with two nn's — I add, when it is used the first or second time,[1] "Anne" — This must be altered in this way. "Anneke (Anna Cornelia, abbreviated)."

[*complimentary close and signature clipped*]

Mr. John Fagan | Stereotyper | Philadelphia

ADDRESSED: Mr. John Fagan | Stereotyper | Philadelphia
MANUSCRIPT: Cornell University Library.

1. Comma supplied.

791. *To Mrs. Cooper*

New York, March 5th 1845
St. Polks eve — Festival of Democracy [1]

Dearest,

I got here early on Monday morning, and have been hard at work since. I have discovered that the old books are worth something, and have actually sold the right to print 250 copies of each for $200. These books are likely to produce me two or three hundred a year, in future. I have been offered to day $1200 *in cash* for the right to print these books, Afloat and Ashore included, for the next ten years. I have offered to accept at *five* years, and there we stand at present. I have sold an edition *entire* of the New book, 3500 copies, for $1050. This is $100 better than what L[ea] & B[lanchard] gave me for 10,000. copies. The bargain now on the *tapis* may keep me here a day or two longer, but, if made, I shall not remain in Philadelphia more than a week, this time.

Ned [Myers] has his articles, and Lucy Sterling [2] will be duly christened –

The Bishop's affair grows worse and worse. Cases start up like mushrooms. I have heard of a dozen new ones in town. Two in West-Chester, one a sister of Mrs. Cha[ne?]y's. Ludlow Ogden's daughter [3] relates another. Rev. Mr. Johnson [4] of Long Island says openly, since Mrs. Beare's veracity is impugned,[5] he will give his own wife as a case just as bad. Mrs. Joseph Delafield [6] mentioned a case up the river, last evening. In short, there are so many one does not know how to count them.

There is to be a new pamphlet charging the Bishop home. He will be compelled to resign. I am sorry to say the dissenting bishops will and do suffer, though your brother will probably escape better than the others.

A case in New Rochelle this moment mentioned, and one, another, as recently as thirteen months. The feeling of the community is thoroughly aroused, and the man is lost.

Mrs. [Henry] Laight is well. Susy Watkins dying.[7] Mrs. [Samuel] Neale, gone south to join her mother [Mrs. Joseph C. Yates]. [John?] Jay has had scarlet fever, and Mrs. Jay looks like a girl – fat as a pig. Mrs. L[aight] *very* anti Bishop. The clergy are giving way in all directions – Gil – VerPlanck [8] shaking and David B. Ogden [9] also.

Tell Paul to make a neat package of your father's will, and to send it to Fort Plain, for express to New York, directed "John Jay Esquire, Counsellor at Law, Wall Street." It should come immediately.

This is a glorious May day – Bland, bright and exhilerating.

Love as usual, and most where most belongs,

J. F– C.

Mrs. C–

ADDRESSED: Mrs. Fenimore Cooper | Cooperstown POSTMARKED: NEW-YORK | MAR | 5
MANUSCRIPT: Cooper Collection, Yale University Library. PUBLISHED, IN PART: *Correspondence*, II, 536–37.

1. President Polk was inaugurated on 4 March 1845.
2. Myers' infant daughter.
3. Sarah (1800–1879) or Caroline (1820–1899), daughters of Thomas Ludlow Ogden (1773–1844, Columbia 1791) and Martha (Hammond) Ogden (1780–1853). T. L. Ogden had been a New York lawyer, active in Trinity Church affairs (Wheeler, *The Ogden Family*, 189–90).
4. Though Cooper apparently meant the Reverend Daniel Van Mater Johnson (1812–1890, General Theological Seminary 1835), rector of St. John's Church, Islip, Long Island, from 1842 to 1847, the reference is incompletely verified. In his letter to his wife of 29 April 1845, Cooper gives the maiden name of Mrs. Johnson; but her maiden name seems not to be preserved in records of the Diocese of Long Island. (Information supplied by the registrar of the Diocese of Long Island, Garden City, New York.)
5. Mrs. Charlotte E. Beare, wife of Henry M. Beare, rector of Zion Church, Little Neck, Long Island, was the chief witness for the prosecution. Onderdonk's attorney sought to defend his client by impugning her probity. (*The Proceedings of the Court Convened . . . for the Trial of the Right Rev. Benjamin T. Onderdonk . . .* [New York: D. Appleton & Co., 1845].)
6. Joseph Delafield married Julia (1801–1882), daughter of Maturin and Margaret (Lewis) Livingston, in 1833 (John Ross Delafield, *Delafield: The Family History* [New York: privately printed, 1945], I, 262 ff.).
7. Susan D. Watkins, daughter of John D. Watkins of Georgia and granddaughter of Governor Joseph C. Yates of New York, died in Charleston, South Carolina, on 4 March 1845 (*The* [New York] *Evening Post*, 18 March 1845).
8. Gulian Crommelin Verplanck.
9. David Bayard Ogden (1775–1849, Pennsylvania 1792), an eminent New York lawyer, served as counsel for the defense in the Onderdonk trial. He was a cousin of Thomas L. Ogden. (Wheeler, *The Ogden Family*, 194.)

792. *To Mrs. Cooper*

Head's, Friday. [March] 8th 1845.

Dearest,

Here I am at last, coming on last night. I was detained by an arrangement made with Burgess & Stringer, by which I sold them a right to re-print certain *old* books, for one thousand dollars in cash. They have paid me, and I might now return home, to-morrow, but, having come so far, I shall remain until next week, in order to save time next trip. I shall quit here about Thursday, and be home three or four days afterwards. So far, every thing has been done very favourably. A full edition of the new book is sold, and a good thing made out of the old ones. Something remains to be done with Afloat and Ashore, which B & S are anxious to get.

I have just met Mrs. [Elizabeth] Rush in the street. She is

looking well. Com. [James] Biddle sails for Liverpool, on the 25th with Mrs. Nicholas [Biddle], who goes to Europe for her health. She has connections in Ireland and intends to remain abroad some time, with three of her children.

I have also met Gurn[e]y Smith. He says the impression is very strong against both bishops, more particularily ours. Your brother's friends here, regret his mistake.[1] Every hour almost brings out some new facts. *Three* cases in West-Chester, a new one at New Rochelle. Quite twenty are openly named in New York and on Long Island. More all over the State.

John Jay says it is now believed he kept a mistress, and that the visit to the brothel was a fetch. Actual guilt is also spoken of, in a case in his own house. The determination is to drive him out of his chair, if a new trial be had. His friends desert him, and his foes increase. [*Ann Maria*][2] gives him up — Dr. Coit [3] d[itt]o, other clergymen the same. Don Cushman [4] also — these I have seen — Dr. C[oit] excepted, and of him I have heard directly.

Do not send any letter to me, *here,* after the reciept of this, but write to the Globe. After Thursday of next week, mail nothing for me.

I saw Alfred [Clarke] in New York, better, and looking well. [Joseph R.] Ingersoll is here, but I have not seen him. People begin to come north.

The weather is like May. I saw gardens making, and every sign denotes an early Spring. I am quite well, and every body tells me I look like a boy.

Adieu my best beloved, with tenderest regard to the children

J. F. C.

Shoes and trinkets, already in hand. I think I shall stereotype the Duchess,[5] and sell to B. & S.

ADDRESSED: Mrs. Fenimore Cooper | Cooperstown | New York POSTMARKED: NEW-YORK | MAR | 8 STAMPED: MANSION HOUSE | HEAD | PHILADELPHIA. PHILADA. RAIL ROAD

MANUSCRIPT: Cooper Collection, Yale University Library. PUBLISHED, IN PART: *Correspondence*, II, 550–51. (The date is incorrectly given as 8 August 1845 in the *Correspondence*.)

1. Bishop De Lancey voted "not guilty" at Bishop Onderdonk's trial, explaining his decision in a lengthy statement (*The Proceedings of . . . the Trial of the Right Rev. Benjamin T. Onderdonk . . .* [New York: D. Appleton & Co., 1845], 301–10).

2. The reading is quite uncertain.

3. Rector of Trinity Church, New Rochelle, New York, from 1839 to 1849, Thomas Winthrop Coit (1803–1885, Yale 1821) was a college president, biblical scholar, theologian, and seminary professor (*DAB*).

4. Beginning his mercantile career in Cooperstown between 1805 and 1810, Don Alonzo Cushman (1792–1875) became the head of a prosperous New York jobbing and importing house. He was active in the affairs of the Protestant Episcopal Church. (Henry Wyles Cushman, *A Historical and Biographical Genealogy of the Cushmans . . .* [Boston: Little, Brown and Co., 1855], 515–25; *The* [New York] *Evening Post*, 1 May 1875.)

5. "Duchess" seems to have been a pet name given to Susan Fenimore Cooper by her family. Cooper apparently referred here to her novel *Elinor Wyllys*, published by Carey and Hart in 1846.

793. *To Mrs. Cooper*

Head's, Friday [March] 14th/45

My Dearest Sue —

Here I am yet, and shall remain until to-morrow morning. I have just read the last proof of Vol. 1, and might leave this afternoon; and still get home on Sunday, but it is a bad day, and Mary Farmer wishes to go with me. I have, therefore named to-morrow at 9. A.M. for the start. This will keep me in New-York, most probably until Tuesday night, to be home Wednesday. I have done a great deal of business, and have gained so much as to leave me nothing further to do with the new book, than to stereotype two thirds of a Volume, when I come down, next time. As I shall have no concern with the publication, so far, well.

Mrs. Yates, and Mr. & Mrs. Neale are here, Susy Watkins having died on the 4th. Her body has gone to Schenectady.

I have seen nothing of Judge [Samuel] Nelson. He has probably passed through without stopping.

I am and have been perfectly well, this trip.

Head's affairs have been settled.[1] I have recieved $100 and he admits that he owes me $102, which I am to eat out. This will be done this season, and in all probability, and I shall lose nothing in the long run.

I did intend to purchase some dresses for a surprise, but suppose the girls would prefer doing it for themselves. I have a letter from Shubrick who thinks the first week in May, will be the time.[2] This will suit me exactly.

My plan is this — to bring the girls to New York and leave

them there for a week or ten days, while I finish my work here, and while they get their wardrobes in order. Then to proceed to Washington in company. A week at Washington must suffice, I should hope, for I cannot play all summer.

There is nothing new, my love being an old affair.

Tenderly Yours
J. F. C.

ADDRESSED: Mrs. Fenimore Cooper | Cooperstown | New York POSTMARKED: PHILADELPHIA Pa. | MAR | 14 STAMPED: MANSION HOUSE | HEAD | PHILADELPHIA.
MANUSCRIPT: Cooper Collection, Yale University Library.

1. Acting on behalf of fifteen persons of whom Cooper was one, William G. Cochran obtained an execution for $5,774.19 against Joseph Head, proprietor of the Mansion House, for the March term 1845 of the District Court for the City and County of Philadelphia. The sum mentioned as Head's indebtedness to Cooper was $186.87. On 28 February 1845, the creditors agreed to settle their claims against Head by disposing of his collateral to Wesley P. Hunt for $4,000 to be divided proportionately among them. Cooper was a signer of the agreement. Hunt effected the transfer on 8 March 1845. (MS of agreement: Roger Butterfield, New York City.)

2. Shubrick reported in his letter of 11 March 1845 from Washington, D.C., that the date for the marriage of his daughter Mary to Dr. George Clymer was not yet fixed, but that he believed it would be in the first week of May (MS: YCAL).

794. *To Carey and Hart*

Globe. New York. | March 17th 1845

Gentlemen,

I accede to the proposal that you are to have the right to republish the fifteen numbers of my naval biographies that have been and are to be published in Graham's Magazine, for the sum of $500 — I am to retouch, but not to rewrite these biographies, and you to pay $250 on publication of vol. 1, and $250 on publication of vol. IId —[1]

I shall retouch four or five of the biographies for vol. I, in time to deliver them in all next month.[2]

ADDRESSED: Carey & Hart | Philadelphia POSTMARKED: NEW-YORK | MAR | 18
MANUSCRIPT: Honeyman Collection, Lehigh University Library.

When the publishing firm of Carey, Lea, and Carey was dissolved in 1829, Edward L. Carey (1806–1845), the junior member, and brother of Henry C. Carey, established a new bookselling firm in partnership with Abraham Hart (1810–1885), an enterprising employee of the old house. Although Carey and Hart soon entered the publishing business, the only book they published for Cooper was *Lives of Distinguished American Naval Officers* (1846). Edward L. Carey, patron of the arts and president of the Pennsylvania Academy of Fine Arts, was too ill to be active in business for some years before his death. Cooper's correspondent was really Hart, who was prominent in the Jewish community of Philadelphia and who maintained the firm Carey and Hart until 1849, four years after Carey's death. (Henry Simpson, *The Lives of Eminent Philadelphians* . . . [Philadelphia: William Brotherhead, 1859], 184; *DAB*.)

1. Carey and Hart wrote Cooper from Philadelphia on 15 March 1845:

"We accept the offer made us yesterday, (The refusal of which you gave us till Monday) viz To sell to us the Entire Copy right to reprint the fifteen numbers of Naval Biographies now printed & to be printed in 'Grahams Magazine' for the sum of Five hundred Dollars, you to retouch them (not to rewrite them) so as to secure to us a Copy right on those which you omitted to take out a Copy right for originally.

"The 'Biographies' will be published by us in two Vols. (one of them as soon as you furnish us with Corrected proofs to print from) and on the day of publication of the 1st Vol. we are to pay you one half the above named sum ($250) in cash, and as soon as the last Biography is published in 'Grahams Magazine' we are to publish Vol 2d. On the day of publication of Vol 2, we are to pay you the remaining sum of Two hundred & fifty Dollars.

"Please acknowledge the rec't of this Letter by return of Mail, & at your leisure be kind enough to write us the few lines of Preface that you promised the writer." (MS: YCAL.)

2. The letter from Cooper is accompanied by a memorandum in his script itemizing the biographies to be published by Carey and Hart: "Will sell the right to reprint the fifteen numbers of Naval Biographies for $500 — Mr. C — to retouch but not to rewrite them. | Somers — 1. No. | Bainbridge 1. — | Perry — 2 | Jones — 2 | Shaw— 1 | Dale — 1 | Preble — 2 | Woolsey 1 | Shubrick 1 | Barry 1 | and four numbers to be written." (MS: Honeyman Collection, Lehigh University Library.)

795. *To Richard Bentley*

Otsego Hall, Cooperstown, April 24th 1845

Dear Sir,

Your letter, dated March 3d,[1] only reached me last night.

When I wrote you that I could no longer have the price of my books regulated by sales of editions, and that I must have a stated sum agreed on, for the future works, and you offered £350, although I thought the remuneration low, I acceeded to it, in preference to changing my publisher.[2] It is true, that in accepting the first bill on account of second part of Miles Wallingford, you said something of its being on account, as I remember the allusion, in consequence of an apprehension of not being able to publish in time.[3] As for the work, it is generally thought one of the very best of its series, by many persons as the very best, and I learn its success on the continent of Europe has been very decided. To my surprise I now learn your intention to curtail the price by £100, and a determination to give no more in future, than £250. for a tale.

In law, I am quite certain one of the parties to a bargain has no right to change the conditions, without the consent of the other. I have not the least doubt of my ability to insist on the payment of £350 each for 2d part of Wallingford, and for S[a]tanstoe, but I have no desire to separate from a house with which I have had so many transactions, in so hostile a manner. I shall therefore acquiesce in these changes, in order that we may part friends.

You credit me only £150 for the new book, after deducting £100, overpaid, according to your view of the matter. Now, I had drawn for £76 odd, to make up £200, on account of this book, and have actually sold another bill for £150, which I concieved, and still concieve was my due. The bill of £76 odd must have been accepted or protested some time since. If accepted, according to your views, I shall owe you £50, overdrawn. This money I will refund to you, that you may not have a shadow of ground of complaint. I shall have rather more than that sum to recieve shortly in England, and will take measures to see the £50 paid you, though I protest against its being due, according to our specific agreement. The last bill sold, I have repurchased, at some sacrifice. Of course, it will not be presented.

You have an unquestionable right to reduce your offers for new books to £250, though I do not think you have any right to change the price of a book that had been transmitted to you, in whole, or in part, under the last agreement. I must distinctly decline accepting this offer. Of course, each party is at liberty to act for himself, in future.

I shall send the remainder of Satanstoe, by the steamer of the 16th May, and, as has been said will see that you recieve £50, when I learn my bill for £76 odd has been accepted. If you have refused it, you will of course owe me the difference between £150, and the amount of the bill drawn in favour of Mr. Edmeston.[4]

I do not apprehend any serious difficulty between England and America. Newspapers are windy things, and seldom know much of any great question. As for Texas, it is a thing determined, and as to Oregon, its fate will be decided by its own inhabitants. In five years, it will be past reclaiming by any party but that which is approved of by its own people. I know nothing of the merits of the Oregon question, though I think America quite right as to Texas.

Respectfully Yours
J. Fenimore Cooper

Mr. Bentley.

You had better publish without delay.

ADDRESSED: Mr. Richard Bentley | Publisher | New Burlington Street | London | viâ Boston POSTMARKED: PHILADELPHIA Pa. | MAY | 13 WD | 1 JU 1 | 1845 STAMPED: PAID

MANUSCRIPT: Cooper Collection, Yale University Library.

1. See Cooper to Bentley, 22 January 1845.

2. See Cooper to Bentley, 9 January 1844.

3. A note, presumably Bentley's, on the holograph, states: "This was *not* the fact." The publisher's letters of 21 May and 18 September 1844 (MSS: YCAL) substantiate the note.

4. Bentley replied on 18 June:

"By your last communication I regret to find the view you entertain, of closing our connexion as author & publisher.

"With respect to our recent transactions it is due to myself to correct an erroneous impression that seems to exist on your part, that without any previous intimation from me, I departed from the terms I had offered as the fixed price for your Novels. The reasons compelling me to give less were stated as early as possible. I felt assured before the publication of the concluding part of Miles Wallingford that the sale of that portion would be less than the former part; & advised you that it would not bear the same price for copyright as a work complete in three volumes. Continuations I have always found to be heavy in sale, & the result on the present occasion has fully borne out my anticipation. The sale of the Second Part has not exceeded 570 copies. For the former portion of it I did not hesitate to credit you £350, although I should not have offered so much had I known it was to be continued. The same objection applies to Satanstoe.

"Throughout all the transactions I have had the pleasure of carrying on with you I have always endeavoured to act with liberality, and frankness. It is obviously my interest to retain at any reasonable sacrifice an author with whom I have been so long & so agreeably connected. I feel persuaded that no other publisher would give a larger consideration for more than one Work. I am sure you will concede that a publisher is entitled to some share of profit and I am quite willing to accede to any modification that can be proposed offering you a larger consideration than £250 in the event of success, but I really do not see my way in giving more than that sum in the first instance.

"I am very sensible of the friendly tone in which your view of the question between us is expressed.

"Before this will reach you, you will have learned that the Bill for £76.15.2 was honored by me on presentation." (MS: YCAL.)

796. *To Robert Campbell*

[24 April 1845]

Dear Sir,

I have been negotiating a new arrangement in England, by which I hope to add a couple £100s to my reciepts, per an. This arrangement involves a change of publisher, and last evening I got a letter, which renders this change almost, but not quite certain. Now, the effect of my letting the bill you hold go forward, would be to cause me to lose the advance on the present book, as it would put me under the necessity of including it under the old bargain. I consequently *may* wish to stop the bill — it is not absolutely certain, and I propose as follows: viz —

You now hold my bill for £150 at ninety day's sight, to go forward on the 11th May. It [will not][1] go before the 16th, however, as that will be steam-boat day. I propose that you hol[d it][2] until June 1st in order to give me time to determine finally, as to my arrangement, when it can either go forward as now drawn, I paying difference of time, or, should the new arrangement be made as I think will be the case, I will undertake to give you a good bill, *bought of a bank,* at Sixty days sight, which will put Mr. Edmeston in cash earlier by a forth night, than if the present bill should be sent by steamer of 16th May.[3]

I will see you on the subject to-day or to-morrow. I go below Monday next and shall not return much before the 20th May, when I will settle with you, one way or the other.

Yours &c

J. Fenimore Cooper

Robert Campbell Esquire.

ADDRESSED: Robert Campbell Esquire ENDORSED: Fenimore Cooper | April 1845
MANUSCRIPT: Sampson P. Bowers, Cooperstown, New York.

1. Manuscript torn. Text editorially supplied.
2. Manuscript torn. Text editorially supplied.
3. Cooper's bill on Bentley was a means by which Campbell, executor of the estate of the novelist's old friend Andrew Edmeston, sent funds to Edmeston's nephew and beneficiary Robert Edmeston.

797. *To Mrs. Cooper*

Globe. Tuesday, April 29th '45

Dearest,

Here I am, safe and well, after a less fatiguing trip than common. Canajoharie not very bad, and in nearly two hours sooner than necessary.

Imprimis, I heard two new cases *in the stage,* both coming from the females in our section of the country. Here O[nderdonk] is nearly given up, by all but a few. *There can be no doubt* of the man's guilt. Stanford [1] told me this morning that a Rev. Mr. Johnson, who married a Miss Nicoll of Long-Island,[2] had come forward in his shop, in presence of Dr. [Jonathan M.] Wainwright and defended Mrs. [Charlotte] Beare. He said—"I know Mrs. Beare and pronounce her as pure a woman as lives, and as for saying that none but a woman who had encouraged a man would be thus assail[e]d, I say, on the authority of my wife, that the Bishop made a very similar attack on her, less than two years since." There is a case of a Miss Marshall, that is said to be very strong, and her friends say she will testify if needed. She was alone with O[nderdonk] in a carriage, for half an hour, and he pushed matters very far. She locked herself in her room, when she reached home, but did not tell the circumstances to prevent violence.

Mrs. Laight is well, as Laight told me in the street. I shall go and see her this evening. Mrs. Brevoort was thought to be dying last night; but, there is a spark of hope this morning.[3] A Miss Delafield is just dead.[4] Fowler tells me Angelina Thorn lost a child some time since, and the effect has brought her husband into the church, and made a moderate man of him.[5]

I have seen no one else, but thought you would wish to hear of me, as soon as possible—I go South, tomorrow, and shall write from Philadelphia.

Adieu—Tenderly Yours

J—F—C.

ADDRESSED: Mrs. Fenimore Cooper | Cooperstown POSTMARKED: NEW-YORK | APR | 29

MANUSCRIPT: Cooper Collection, Yale University Library.

1. A New York merchant and bookseller, Thomas N. Stanford (1794?–1865) was from the 1830's to the 1850's a partner with James R. Swords in the Protestant

Episcopal publishing house of Stanford & Swords at 139 Broadway (Longworth and Doggett's New York directories; *The* [New York] *Evening Post*, 17 July 1865).

2. See Cooper to Mrs. Cooper, 5 March 1845.

3. Laura Elizabeth Carson, the wife of Henry Brevoort, died on 8 June 1845 (*The* [New York] *Evening Post*, 9 June 1845).

4. Caroline A. Delafield, the oldest daughter of Dr. Edward Delafield, died on 27 April 1845 (*The* [New York] *Evening Post*, 28 April 1845).

5. Angelina Jauncey Thorn, daughter of Colonel Herman and Jane Mary (Jauncey) Thorn, married Lewis Augustus Depau of New York City ([Joseph Outerbridge Brown], *The Jaunceys of New York* [New York: privately published, 1876], 22). No record of the death of their child has been located.

798. *To Jonathan Goodhue*

Globe, Tuesday Morning, April 29th [1845]

Dear Sir

Rev. Mr. [Joseph] Ransom, Rector of ⟨Christ⟩ Emmanuel Church, Norwich, Chenango Co, and a gentleman I have known for some years,[1] is desirous of getting a son placed in some permanent employment, as a sailor, where he may run the usual chances for preferment. The point is to get him into some *good* employment, after which it is understood the lad must stand or fall as he behaves.

If you can assist him, I should be glad, as his father has the usual earthly fortunes of a divine. If no situation offers in your own vessels, can you help him with any one else? Howlands [2] have been spoken of, and I have been requested to interest myself with them, but I prefer bestowing my patronage on *you*.

Yours very truly
J. Fenimore Cooper

Jo[n?]. Goodhue Esquire

ADDRESSED: Jonathan Goodhue Esquire | New York | Rev. Mr. Ransom
MANUSCRIPT: The New York Society Library.

Noted for his integrity, public spirit, and philanthropy as well as for his great wealth, Goodhue (1783–1848) was known as one of the "princely merchants" of New York. His wife was Catharine Rutherfurd Clarkson, sister of Mrs. Peter A. Jay and daughter of General Matthew Clarkson. (Jonathan E. Goodhue, *History and Genealogy of the Goodhue Family in England and America to the Year 1890* [Rochester, New York: privately published, 1891], 56–57; *ACAB*.)

1. See Cooper to Mrs. Cooper, 15 October 1840. The son to whom Cooper's letter later refers may have been William Ransom, with whom the father lived in East New York, Long Island, at the time of his death in 1871 (*The Church Journal*, 1 February 1872, The General Theological Seminary).

2. Gardiner Greene Howland (1787–1851) and Samuel Shaw Howland (1790–1853) were wealthy New York shipowners and merchants, not so well remembered for their charitable qualities as Goodhue (*DAB*).

799. *To William Branford Shubrick*

Head's, Friday, May. 2d '45

My Dear Shubrick;

Here I am, and have been since Wednesday night. [Joseph R.] Ingersoll and myself will be on in time for the ceremony, in company, and shall take care to do all things in order.[1] The Mayor told me, this morning, he could not quit his post.[2] So a colt must be provided. It may be well to hint this to the bridegroom.

I can not remain any time at Washington, on account of business connected with the sailing of the steamer of the 16th. Thursday will be the 8th. Saturday the 10th, we must quit you, remain here a day, and go on to New York, on Monday, or Tuesday, at latest. I shall man[a]ge to get to Washington, if I can, on the 7th, however. If I do, you are to let me stay to dine with Ingersoll on the 8th, unless he get an invitation somewhere else. I should think you would not much like to be bothered with company that day. At any rate, you know you can treat me just as [you] would one of yourselves. I had made up my mind to take a room at a tavern, ⟨and⟩ as I felt certain you would be run down.

For the ladies.

Mr. Fenimore Cooper will wear, either his black silk stockings with the hole in the toe, or the ribbed pair that have two holes in the heels. His pants will be black, but very glistening, French cloth died in the wool. His vest much the same. Over all he intends to wear his Elliott douillet[t]e,[3] which is of figured silk, wadded, and lined with flesh coloured silk. His face and hands will be washed, and he has brought on his sapphire ring expressly for the occasion. &c &c. &c.

Adieu — I doubt if you have a turn up with the Dons. What can they get by fighting us? They would lose California of course, with little chance of getting it back again. My love to the girls, and regards to all hands,

Yours, in a confounded hurry

Com — Shubrick J. Fenimore Cooper

ADDRESSED: Commodore Shubrick | Washington POSTMARKED: PHILADELPHIA Pa. | MAY | 3
MANUSCRIPT: Paul Fenimore Cooper, Cooperstown, New York.

1. Shubrick reported from Washington, D.C., on 28 April to Cooper at Philadelphia that the marriage of his daughter Mary to Dr. George Clymer would take place at 9 P.M. on Thursday, 8 May, and invited the novelist to dine with the family on 8 May. He also expressed the hope that Cooper and his daughters Caroline and Charlotte, who were already with the Shubricks, would remain with them for some time in Washington after the ceremony. (MS: YCAL.)

2. See Cooper to Paul Fenimore Cooper, 26 May 1846.

3. See Cooper's letter of 10 December 1847 possibly to George Palmer Putnam.

800. *To Mrs. Cooper*

Head's Sunday, May 4th '45.

Dearest,

Joe Ingersoll goes on with me, on Wednesday. I shall not be quite through here, before I leave, and may have to remain a day or two, on our return. I presume the girls will stay with Mary Wilcocks, or Mrs. [Harry] McCall, though nothing has yet been said on the subject. Mrs. Charles [Ingersoll] has been enquiring after them. Shubrick writes me the wedding *aura lieu* at nine o'clock. The happy pair will leave Washington next day, or Saturday at latest, and we shall probably remain until monday. This will leave me just time to reach New-York in time for the packet of the 16th.

I wish you to open all letters from New York, and ascertain if there be any thing touching the last bill, for £76 odd, and let me know by letter. This may be done at once, as soon as you hear of the arrival of next steamer at Boston. I wish to learn the result as soon as possible. No news will be good news. I shall expect to find a letter here, on my return from Washington.

I have little doubt of arranging here to my perfect satisfaction. In New York a good deal will remain to be done, and I may stay a week.

Tell Sue I have read some of her sheets, and sent on others that I have not read.

It is very warm here, and thin clothes will soon be in demand. I dined with [Benjamin] Wilcocks on Friday, and with Joe In[gersoll] on Saturday. The Bishop is to be elected here soon — this month, though some wish to defer. I hear Mr. [William H.]

Odenheimer wishes to bring back H[enry] U. O[nderdonk]! The man must be demented. The High Church party is fast cutting its own throat. They tell me Kemper [1] and Ives [2] are converted.

Mrs. Mac [Mrs. Harry McCall] is *grosse*—decidedly. The eldest Miss Henry is married, and gone to Scotland, pro tem. with her husband, a Mr. Wood, merchant of this place. He is a gentlemanly young man enough, with a strong accent. Emma is the bride's name.

There is nothing new here. I can find no more Johnstones, and suppose no more are to be found. I discovered a good many names connected with myself, and among others that of Hannah daughter of Wm. Carter, who must have been a sister of my great grandmother. Thence the name of Hannah on that side. My grand mother was named after *her,* doubtless. *Aunt* Hannah seems to have been an old maid.

Adieu, my love. I should like a report from the farm, touching the work, weather, and other matters. Let me hear as desired, and rest assured of all my love.

J. F—C.

ADDRESSED: Mrs. Fenimore Cooper | Cooperstown | New York POSTMARKED: PHILADELPHIA Pa. | MAY | 4
MANUSCRIPT: Cooper Collection, Yale University Library.

1. Missionary Bishop Jackson Kemper (1789–1870, Columbia 1809), who founded three colleges, numerous lower schools and academies, and seven dioceses which established the Protestant Episcopal Church in the Northwest, was a High Churchman respectful of ritualistic observances; but he never converted to Roman Catholicism (*DAB*).

2. Captivated by the Oxford movement, Levi Silliman Ives (1797–1867, Hamilton n.g.), consecrated bishop of North Carolina in 1831, announced his conversion to Roman Catholicism in 1852. Some years earlier he was arraigned for founding the Brotherhood of the Holy Cross in his diocese. Though he published his apologia, Ives became a teacher and never achieved prominence within the Roman Church. (*DAB*.)

801. *To Mrs. Cooper*

Head's. May 14th 1845

Dearest,

We got here safe and sound Monday, afternoon, and intend going on to-morrow. Your letter of the 10th, and the Detroit letter with the draft, both reached me yesterday. So far, well. You do not say, there is no New-York letter for me, but I infer it, from the context — All this is well enough, and should the draft be paid, as I presume it will, I shall be easy enough for several months.

We are all well — hot — hot — hot — sweltering hot. I shall be home at the end of this week I trust, whatever the girls may do. They have told their own story, so I need say nothing about them.

What a frightful rumour about George P —! [1] *Can* it be true. If so he must have absconded, and his mother will break her heart. I can only hope there is some mistake.

I have but a moment to write. All your requests will be attended to. As for Sarah, she will find that *his* people are not *her* people, like poor old Nanny.

The girls write a great deal, but the wedding was a weeping time for them.

Yours most tenderly
J. F — C.

ADDRESSED: Mrs. Fenimore Cooper | Cooperstown | New York POSTMARKED: PHILADELPHIA Pa. | MAY | 15
MANUSCRIPT: Cooper Collection, Yale University Library.

1. Cooper referred to his nephew George Quartus Pomeroy (b. 1815), cashier of the Howard Trust and Banking Company of Troy, New York, until the bank discontinued business in 1843 or 1844. Whether or not the "frightful rumour" related to the bank's failure is not clear, but all its liabilities were discharged. (Albert A. Pomeroy, *History and Genealogy of the Pomeroy Family . . .* [Toledo, Ohio: privately published, 1912], 456; Arthur James Weise, *Troy's One Hundred Years, 1789–1889* [Troy, New York: William H. Young, 1891], 149; *Tuttle's City Directory, for . . . 1844–5* [Troy, New York: N. Tuttle, 1844].)

802. *To Mrs. Cooper*

Globe. Friday 16th May. '45

My Dearest Sue,

We left Philadelphia, yesterday at 12, and got here at seven. The girls will tell you their own story. Peter and Abraham Schermerhorn,[1] with several of their children, were in the cars with us. Our passage was easy enough.

My money has been duly recieved, and I am $2200 better than I was. It came very apropos, as did the Philadelphia money. This makes $2830 recieved since I left home. Your carpet was paid for to-day, and I have ordered a new stock of wines.

The box has been opened, and contains some little matters,

which I have sent to the girls. Judging ⟨of⟩ by the superscription, I should think they were all for Fan, though I've a notion a purse is intended for me.

Poor Sutherland! He was three days dying, Chester tells me, had his senses to the last, and had all his family around him.[2] One of his lungs was nearly gone.

Dick's argument I hear, was strong, and [William H.] Sewards, on the whole, declamatory.[3] [Henry Walton] Wessel[l]s and [Horace H.] Comstock are both in town, and both at Astor House.

Dick tells me that he remembers to have heard a story, similar to these, to George [Pomeroy]'s prejudice, many years since. The matter was rectified by himself at the time, but not until the story reached his ears. Forgery was then imputed.

I learned to-day that Gil. Verplanck says the Bishop [Benjamin Tredwell Onderdonk] *must* resign. Tyng, it is said, will be elected to Pennsylvania, though he is unquestionably called to St. George's, as poor Milnor's successor.[4]

I magnetised Miss Sally Peters [5] at Shubricks, with a good deal of success.

I think I shall write to Nancy [Mrs. Pomeroy] before I come home. It will take off the edge of the meeting.

As the weather is bad, the girls wish to stay until Tuesday evening, which will keep me from seeing you until Wednesday, the 21st. They do not wish to stay longer, and it is best I should see them home. Otherwise, I should have left town this afternoon. Bentley must have accepted the draft.

Adieu — Yours as ever

J. F. C —

ADDRESSED: Mrs. Fenimore Cooper | Cooperstown POSTMARKED: NEW-YORK | MAY | 17

MANUSCRIPT: Cooper Collection, Yale University Library. PUBLISHED: *Correspondence*, II, 541–42.

1. Abraham Schermerhorn (1783–1850), brother and business partner of Peter Schermerhorn (see Cooper to Greenough, 26 February 1830), was a wealthy merchant prominent in New York society (Richard Schermerhorn, Jr., *Schermerhorn Genealogy and Family Chronicles* [New York: Tobias A. Wright, 1914], 166–69).

2. Cooper's friend Jacob Sutherland died at Albany on 13 May 1845. The novelist's informant was probably William Williams Chester (1786–1869), founder of a well-known New York carpet store, who married Sutherland's sister Hannah (1796–1863) (Dexter, *Graduates of Yale College*, VI, 156; Robert E. Chester-Waters, *Genealogical Notes of the Families of Chester* . . . [Leicester, England: Clarke and Hodgson, 1886], 22).

3. Richard Cooper argued the case of *Cooper* v. *Greeley and McElrath* before the Supreme Court at the May term (*Correspondence*, II, 540–41; Hiram Denio, *Reports of Cases Argued and Determined in the Supreme Court . . . of the State of New-York* [Albany, New York: Gould, Banks & Gould, 1846], I, 347–67).

4. Stephen Higginson Tyng (1800–1885, Harvard 1817) succeeded James Milnor (1773–1845, University of Pennsylvania n.g.) as rector of St. George's (Episcopal) Church, New York City, in 1845 and served until 1878 (John S. Stone, *A Memoir of the Life of James Milnor, D.D. . . .* [New York: American Tract Society, 1848]; *DAB*).

5. Sarah Robinson Peters (1785–1850), daughter of Richard (1744–1828) and Sarah (1753–1804) Peters and sister of Cooper's friend Richard Peters (see Cooper to Richard Peters, 2 December 1845), was a splendid conversationalist, much admired in Philadelphia literary society (Nellie Peters Black, ed., *Richard Peters, 1810–1889, His Ancestors and Descendants* [Atlanta, Georgia: Foote & Davies Company, 1904], 13, 117–18).

803. *To Edwin Croswell, for the* Albany Argus

Congress Hall, May 21, 1845.

Mr. Editor—

In passing through Albany this morning, I have seen an article in last night's Evening Journal, in which Mr. Weed, after once retracting all his libels on me, when published, has seen fit substantially to repeat them. For this article, he and I will again appear before a jury.[1] But, I will make no remarks here. Mr. Weed says he has always been ready and able to prove the truth of all he has ever said about me. Now, I am prepared to show, as an evidence of this person's accuracy, that *he has himself admitted, publicly in his Journal,* his inability to prove one of his libellous accusations; and I shall give him as early an opportunity as the law will allow, to prove some more of them. This admission was entirely disconnected from his retraction.

The pretence that our courts have ever ruled that the truth is not a complete defence in a libel suit, in the civil action, can only gain credit with the supremely ignorant.

Your ob't servant,
J. Fenimore Cooper.

Editor of Argus.

SOURCE: *Albany Argus*, 22 May 1845.

1. This new suit against Thurlow Weed was apparently never filed. Referring to Cooper's demurrer before the New York Supreme Court to Horace Greeley's plea to Cooper's latest declaration, Weed promised in his *Albany Evening Journal* of 20 May 1845 to reprint "sketches" of the arguments of Governor William H. Seward for the defendant and Richard Cooper for the plaintiff. Renewing in his article the complaint that he had never been permitted "to give the truth in evi-

dence," the editor repeated several libelous comments on Cooper. He had no desire to resume the combat in the courts, however; and, after reprinting the promised summaries from Greeley's *New York Tribune* in the *Evening Journal* of 22 May, he lapsed into silence.

804. *To Henry Phillips*

Otsego Hall, Cooperstown, May 23d 1845

Dear Sir,

Your letter, dated April 30[th?],[1] reached this place, while I was absent at Washington. This circumstance will account for the delay in answering it. I passed a face in Broadway, last week, that I remembered to be yours when it was too late to speak to you, and regretted that I did not sooner recollect to whom it belonged.

In reply to your questions, I have no remembrance of having written any thing on the subject of a Prairie on fire, unless it were in a book called The Prairie. It is quite likely you have never seen such a book, but it can be found in most libraries of such sort of works, and the passage, or chapter, will speak for itself. I question, however, if it prove of much use for your purposes. If I have written any thing else on the subject, it has escaped my memory. As I have forgotten the names of more than half my own personages, however, you are not to consider me as very good authority.

It [2] has not been my good fortune to meet you since our interview in Philadelphia. The world is so coming together, and getting to be so neighbourly that I trust we shall yet see each other again, before we quit the scene altogether.

Very Respectfully | Your Ob. Ser.
J. Fenimore Cooper

To | Henry Philips Esquire | New York

ADDRESSED: Henry Philips Esquire | City Hotel | New York POSTMARKED: COOPERSTOWN N.Y. | MAY | 24

MANUSCRIPT: The Henry W. and Albert A. Berg Collection, The New York Public Library. PUBLISHED: Henry Phillips, *Musical and Personal Recollections during Half a Century* (London: Charles J. Skeet, 1864), II, 124.

A popular British singer and actor, Phillips (1801–1876) left a colorful account in his *Recollections* (II, 104–208) of his tour of the United States and Canada in 1844 and 1845. Impressed by Cooper's appearance at Head's and then discovering his identity, Phillips wrote that he invited the novelist "to smoke a cigar with me in my bedroom, and received a most kind message in reply . . . He came, and we passed a couple of most delightful hours together." (*DNB; Recollections*, II, 122–25.)

1. On 30 April 1845, shortly before he returned to England, Phillips addressed Cooper from the City Hotel in New York: ". . . being in possession of a Number of Songs and Scenas to illustrate the different objects I have met with; amongst others is a descriptive Scena: *the Prairie on Fire*; I should feel exceedingly obliged if you would point out to me; that which you consider the best description of that subject in any of your works; from which I could make an extract." (MS: YCAL.) Phillips noted later in his *Recollections* (II, 205) that G. P. Morris had given him "some very clever lines descriptive of 'The Prairie on fire,' which I set to music, and which proved another valuable addition to my list of scenas."

2. The holograph has a superfluous "is" at this point.

805. *To Thomas B. Johnstone*

Otsego Hall, Cooperstown, May 26th 1845

Dear Sir,

I am fearful my long silence may have led you to think your case has been forgotten. So far from this, however, it has been the subject of my own personal enquiries, but I regret to say without any further success. I have examined the records of Christ Church pretty fully, for births and marriages, but can discover no John Johnstone whatever. Nor can I discover the *birth* of Andrew Johnston. His marriage, you tell me, took place at Jamaica.

I have also been over the tomb-stones, as yet without any success. The list of taxables, too, has been examined by myself, as well as the index of the records of wills. There is a John Johnston on the last, but he was evidently a common mariner who had little or no property, nor does the date correspond with what we want. I find Andrew Johnston on the list of taxables, rated about the same as the majority of the respectable people, though not among the highest.

The records of the deeds remain to be examined. There is also a family now existing in Philadelphia of the name of Johnstone, which is of some standing, and in which there was a Col. Johnstone, some twenty or thirty years since, who was sheriff.[1] I intend to enquire among these Johnstones for information.

Notwithstanding all these failures, there is a hope left. Were the Annandale family church people, then it is quite likely that John Johnstone, on the supposition that you are right, married a quakeress, such connections having been quite common in that early day, in Philadelphia. He may even have assumed the guise of a quaker himself, for the purposes of concealment. The root of the great Morris family, among us, had recourse to such an artifice, remaining a quaker in appearance some years. It is very possible your ancestor did not marry a church woman, and with us, the persuasion of the woman always determines the character of the officiating clergyman, at a wedding. It may be necessary, therefore, to look at the records of other denominations for the register of the births and marriages. If there ever was a John Johnstone in Philadelphia, who held real estate, however, the records of deeds *must* show it, and I shall next examine them.

There is a circumstance which renders it probable that if we succeed, it will be by examining other than church records. We have *proof* there *was* an Andrew Johnston in Philadelphia. The baptism of his son, and his name on the list of taxables show this. Still the baptism of Andrew Johnston is not to be found on Christ Church records. This renders it probable that his wife brought his family on those records for the first time. The record of deeds will be our great dependence, and I understand they are very complete.

While in Philadelphia, I met a Scotswoman, a Mrs. Crawford. Her husband is the brother of the British consul at Havannah. They were recently from ⟨Jamaica⟩ Cuba, themselves, and she told me Mr. Crawford had recieved a commission from some gentleman in Jamaica to make enquiries very similar to those I was then making.[2] Is this the act of a friend, or of an opponent?

There is an allusion in your last letter that renders it proper we should understand each other clearly. I mean where you speak of a poor man's thanks. I have no expectation of any pecuniary reward, whether we succeed or not. Under no circumstances could I accept it. Were I a professional man, it would be a different matter, but, situated as I am, my self-respect would preclude the idea of such a thing. If called on to pay any sum worth speaking of, I should expect to be repaid as a matter of course. At present my outlays are very trifling, a few dollars in fees, and these much increased by an oversight of my own. I shall ask you, when we end our searches, to bestow the amount in charity, on the poor of your own parish. The amount will not probably reach two guineas, including my own blunder. If however, it be of any moment to you, we will forget it. Of course, when professional men are employed *regularily*, they must be paid. I shall certainly incur no such expense without express authority; nor do I know it will be at all necessary.

I feel a good deal of interest in the inquiry, and have a pleasure in pursuing it. Several of my friends entertain the same curiosity, and will contribute their aid cheerfully. As for [Joseph R.] Ingersoll, though a lawyer, he is a childless widower, with a handsome income, and I can venture to say, the thought of a fee has not yet crossed his mind. He is an excellent fellow, of the highest character, a meek christian, and withal a member of Congress of standing. I entertain no doubt of his disposition to befriend you, disinterestedly.

I shall soon be in Philadelphia again, when I shall make further enquiries, and beg to remain until then in your remembrance.[3]

I am, dear sir, | Very truly Yours

J. Fenimore Cooper

To the Rev. Mr. Johnstone | Clutton | Near Bristol | England.

ADDRESSED: Rev. Tho[m?]: B. Johnston | Clutton Rectory | near Bristol | England | viâ Boston and English Steamer POSTMARKED: COOPERSTOWN N.Y. | MAY | 28 AMERICA | LIVERPOOL | JU 13 | 1845 BRISTOL | JU 14 | 1845 ENDORSED: Recd. June 14/45 STAMPED: PAID

MANUSCRIPT: The Henry W. and Albert A. Berg Collection, The New York Public Library.

The Reverend Thomas Bryan Johnstone (d. 1879?; Trinity College, Cambridge, 1811, M.A. 1815) was rector of the parish of Clutton from 1815 until he died or retired in 1879. His photograph and church papers are preserved at the Clutton Church and Rectory. The name, which Johnstone and Cooper seemed to spell both with and without the final "e," is correctly spelled with the "e." (*Crockford's Clerical Directory*, 1879; information at the Clutton Church.)

1. The reference is vague for positive identification.

2. Johnstone replied on 3 July 1845 that the inquiry was probably instigated by his older brother in Jamaica, who was much concerned with the investigation (MS: YCAL). The members of the Crawford family are unidentified.

3. Johnstone thanked Cooper profusely and supplied him with additional genealogical detail in a letter of 3 July 1845, but the correspondence apparently lapsed at this point (MS: YCAL).

806. *To William Branford Shubrick*

Hall, Cooperstown, May 29th 1845

My Dear Shubrick,

I was on the point of writing when I got your letter,[1] which raised a blush on my cheeks, a thing that has not been seen there for many a day.

Our journey home was pleasant, though hastened by bad news. [William Heathcote] de Lancey was thrown out of a waggon, on the 16th, and came very near being killed. He was standing erect, looking over the driver's shoulders to see what was the matter with the horses, one of which had a leg over the pole, when a desperate effort of the animals actually jerked the waggon from beneath his feet, and caused him to throw a summerset backwards, falling with his head towards the vehicle, and on his forehead, face and breast. The blow has been severe, nor have we been fully apprised of the extent of the injury until this evening, when it is mentioned in our letter, that Sunday last was the first day his mind has not wandered. He has been gradually mending, however, since the first twenty four hours. The danger is not entirely gone, as inflammation and water on the brain may follow, though the forehead is the strongest casing our brains possess.

I am much obliged to Mr. Bodisco, and I hope you told him I should have paid him my respects, but for the distance and the wedding. If I never see him until we meet in Russia, I fear we shall never meet. As for rumour, she is no longer a liar, being past that, never telling the truth.[2] I sincerely hope you will take the Congress,[3] and go to the cream of the earth in her.

I fell in with a large party of Schermerhorns on our return, and learned the sudden death of Sir John Chambers White, who was an uncle by marriage, of one of them.[4] I am not certain whether you ever met him here, or not. He was a New-Yorker by birth, and a distant relative of Mrs. Cooper's, besides being an uncle of Mrs. de Lancey's. He had got to be a Vice Admiral of the White, and had his flag flying at the Nore, when he died. I knew him very well, and liked him much. He was the officer who said [Isaac] Chauncey knew more of a ship than any man he ever conversed with. He stood high himself, in his own service.

Mrs. Cooper is, and has been very nervous on the subject of the Bishop, but is getting to [be] more composed. Still, our good news frightens her, since it lets her into the secret of the danger her brother has been in. Otherwise, we are all well, and the circumstance that Caroline and Margaret de Lancey (sister and daughter) have left the invalid, is quite encouraging.

I saw the Columbus,[5] looking very well, but did not get on board her. [James] Biddle and I exchanged cards, and extra visits, but did not meet. Paulding, they tell me, is not pleased with his command.[6]

I heard of the article in the S[outhern] Literary Messenger,[7] but have not see[n] it. Wilkes will live to put all this down, and to recieve the credit he deserves, and which he has so fairly earned. I met him in New York. He was in good spirits.

In Philadelphia, I passed an evening with the Peters', but was not as successful as at your house. At another party, I made a private experiment in a corner, and produced an immediate impression, though it was not thought proper to persevere. In New York, I failed entirely, on two new subjects.

The girls were much amused with all their visits, but were anxious to get home to their mother as soon as they heard of their uncle's accident. I must tell you of Elliott's gallantry. In addition to other civilities, happening to be coming home at two in the morning, he fell in with a party serenading, and he brought them to Ingersoll's house, and gave the ladies, as they assure me, a very delightful serenade. Next day he called, and when the young ladies attributed the serenade to some young Philadelphian, he came out and claimed his dues. I earnestly advised him to keep quiet at Washington, though he swears he made Bancroft Secretary.

Thank you for the biscuit,[8] which I shall certainly look after. You call them Wine Biscuit, and they will do to go with Elliott's wine, which promises to be really good.

The girls will write in a day, or two, and to them I must refer Mrs. Shubrick for all the gossip of the road. Mrs. Cooper and all hands send best regards, while it [is] unnecessary for me to say that I remain, as ever,

Most truly | Yours

Com. Shubrick J. Fenimore Cooper

ADDRESSED: Commodore Shubrick U. S. N | Bureau of Prov. & Cloth. | Washington POSTMARKED: COOPERSTOWN N.Y. | MAY | [29?]

MANUSCRIPT: Paul Fenimore Cooper, Cooperstown, New York.

1. Dated Washington, 27 May 1845 (MS: YCAL).

2. Shubrick reported a rumor, "quite current, that one object of your visit to Washington was to make final arrang[e]ments for your mission to Russia. Bodisco spoke to me about it, and seemed to credit it — he inquired if you spoke French and said your appointment would be very acceptable to the Emperor — after all it may be true and I know nothing about it — how is it? Shall I take you out in the

Congress, or would you prefer a Packet?" Alexandre de Bodisco was Russian minister to the United States from about 1837 until his death in 1854. (MS: Shubrick to Cooper, 27 May 1845, YCAL; *ACAB*.)

3. The fourth *Congress* was a 44-gun, 1867-ton ship, built in 1839 (GNR).

4. Sir John Chambers White, who died on 4 April 1845, was the uncle of Helen White Schermerhorn (1792–1881), Mrs. Abraham Schermerhorn (Richard Schermerhorn, Jr., *Schermerhorn Genealogy and Family Chronicles* [New York: Tobias A. Wright, 1914], 166; Burke's *Peerage*, 580).

5. A 74-gun, 2480-ton frigate, built in 1816 (GNR).

6. Captain Hiram Paulding (1797–1878) commanded the sloop *Vincennes* in the East Indies from about 1845 to 1847 (*ACAB*).

7. Shubrick's letter of 27 May referred to a particularly severe review of Charles Wilkes's *Narrative of the United States Exploring Expedition* (1845) in the *Southern Literary Messenger*, XI (May 1845), 305–22.

8. "A barrel of Baltimore Wine Biscuit," Shubrick wrote on 27 May, "will in a few days be in New York, at the office of the New York and Baltimore Packets, directed to you." (MS: YCAL.)

807. *To George Bancroft*

Otsego Hall, Cooperstown, June 5th 1845

My Dear Sir,

I wrote a little book a year or two since called "Ned Myers." It contains an account of the real career of an old shipmate of mine, and of a man who is deserving of some rewards for his sufferings and conduct in the last war. I refer ⟨to⟩ you to the book itself for those services, of the truth of which I have the strongest corroborative proof in addition to Ned's own account of himself. Ned is an experienced seaman, and has often been chief mate of merchant vessels. But, the fact that he was made captain of the forecastle of the Delaware, under Com. Crane,[1] is a sufficient proof of his qualifications. He recieves a small pension for an injury recieved on board the Brandywine, but could not obtain one for a serious hurt he got on board the Scourge when she went down on Lake Ontario, in 1813. He is partially a cripple from a fall on board a Dutch East Indiaman, but is quite able to perform the duty contemplated for him.

Com. Elliott informs me that the recieving vessel at Philadelphia is entitled to two passed midshipmen, but it is difficult to keep gentlemen of that rank on board such a craft, as much as is desired. Now, Ned is certainly just the man for a place of that nature, should there really be a vacancy. Sober, moral, religious, steady, and perfectly familiar with ships and seamen, I do not know where a better selection could be made for such a situation. Permit me to recommend him earnestly to your attention, if any opening of the sort exists, either at Philadelphia, or elsewhere — He is not fit to go to sea on account of his lameness, but admirably qualified for the place I have described. He is at present working hard in the gunner's crew, at New York, on a dollar a day when he works. He finds the pay close work, and the labour hard. His name is Edward R. Myers. I think it would have a good effect on the morale of the service to give such a man some moderate preferment, the book having made his claims familiar to the common men.[2] If you have never seen the work, I would advise you to read it, less as an author, than as a brother litterateur. Its whole merit in a literary sense, is its truth, but the book can give you some notion of a common sailor's career.

I hope Com. Shubrick has said a word to you concerning our mutual friend Neville,[3] whose claims to a small vessel are great, and who will take good care of her. I believe the Boxer is the craft he has his eye on.

As I do not inflict many letters, I will venture to make this a little longer. I have been writing some Naval biographies for Graham, and have taken a fancy to write the life of Old Ironsides among the rest of them. I may have occasion to ask for information from your department, and not having the powers of Congress, must take that as a favour, which the Honorables take as a right. I shall of course pay for extra time, should I require copying. My friend Shubrick will take charge of the duty for me, as long as he remains at Washington, though I am not without hopes you will send him off to sea, too.

As a farmer, I must add we have had a pernicious frost lately, and I have actually seen the ground covered with snow, since our walk under the Treasury Building.

With Great Respect | Very Faithfully | Yours
J. Fenimore Cooper

P. S. Lest I leave a false impression of our climate, it may be well to say the season promises well, after all.

ADDRESSED: Geo. Bancroft Esquire | Sec. Navy | Washington POSTMARKED: COOPERSTOWN N.Y. | JUN | 7
MANUSCRIPT: Cooper Collection, Yale University Library.

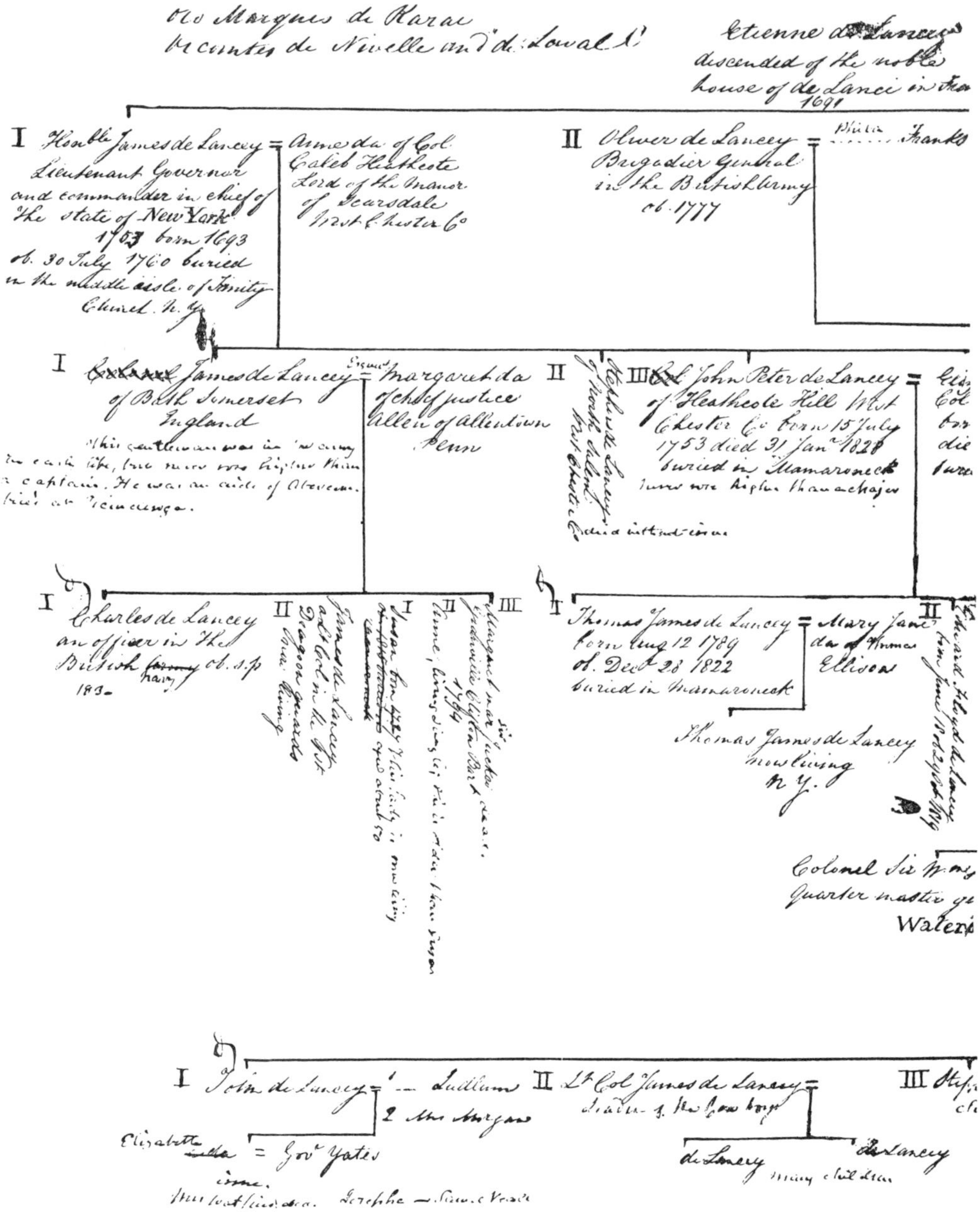

See Letter 808 to Robert Bolton, Jr.

This Courtlandt genealogy in the Landed gentry is fully ... as to collaterals, as I know

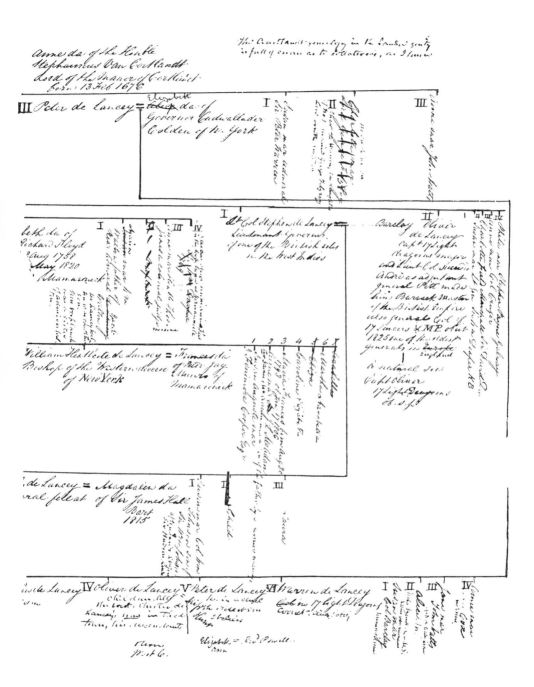

Anne da. of the Honble Stephanus Van Cortlandt Lord of the Manor of Cortlandt born 13 Feb 1676

III Peter de Lancey = Elizabeth da. of Governor Cadwallader Colden of N. York

I Susan m. Admiral Sir Peter Warren

II

III Anne m. John Watts

I Lt. Col. Stephen de Lancey = ... Barclay
Lieutenant Governor of one of the British isles in the West Indies

II Oliver de Lancey Capt 17 Light Dragoons major and Lieut Col. succeeded André as adjutant general Pitt made him Barrack Master of the British Empire also general Col of 17 Lancers & MP obit 1825 one of the oldest generals in England

a natural son Capt Oliver 17 Light Dragoons ob. s. p.

...beth da. of Richard Floyd ... Aug 1758 ... May 1820 ... Mamaroneck

I ... II ... III ... IV ...

William Heathcote de Lancey = Frances da. of Peter Jay Munro of Mamaroneck
Bishop of the Western diocese of New York

1 2 3 4 5 6 7
Caroline ... Eliza ...

...de Lancey = Magdalen da. of Sir James Hall Bart 1815
...ral ... feleat

I ... II Child III ...

IV Oliver de Lancey ... Children All the ... Charles de Lancey ... his descendants

V Peter de Lancey ...

Elizabeth = ... Powell

VI Warren de Lancey Cornet 17 Light Dragoons ...

I II III IV ...

1. As commander of the Mediterranean Squadron, Captain William Montgomery Crane (1784–1846) apparently assumed command of the *Delaware* in 1828 (*DAB*). See *Ned Myers* (Philadelphia: Lea and Blanchard, 1843), 172–73.

2. Bancroft indicated in his reply of 21 July that he found Ned Myers' case "difficult." "But I am turning that over in my mind and hope to have it in my power to meet your wishes. Yet I am not clear about it." (MS: PFC; *Correspondence*, II, 550.)

3. Cooper seems to have been referring to Frederick A. Neville, appointed midshipman in 1820, lieutenant in 1828, and commander in 1851. He was placed on the reserve list in 1855 and dismissed in 1861, probably for Confederate sympathy. (GNR.)

Bancroft replied: "Your young friend, the Commander shall have his claims considered with that respect, which your recommendation warrants. He is an applicant for either of two positions, & I hope to gratify him in the one or the other." (MS: Bancroft to Cooper, Washington, 21 July 1845, PFC; *Correspondence*, II, 550.)

808. *To Robert Bolton, Jr.*

Cooperstown June 2[6?] 45

Dear Sir,

I am afraid a letter I wrote in answer to this was never recieved. I have made a few annotations here,[1] to correct errors, and send it off at once lest you might suffer by the delay. I shall take measures to communicate with you again.

In great haste | Yours

Robert Bolton Jun Esq — J. Fenimore Cooper

ADDRESSED: Robert Bolton jun Esquire | New Rochelle | West-Chester | New York POSTMARKED: COOPERSTOWN N.Y. | JUN | 27

MANUSCRIPT: Paul Fenimore Cooper, Cooperstown, New York.

An antiquarian and local historian who entered the Protestant Episcopal ministry in 1869, Bolton (1814–1877) earlier farmed and taught in Westchester County. He was born and educated in England. (Henry Carrington Bolton and Reginald Pelham Bolton, *The Family of Bolton in England and America . . .* [New York: privately published, 1895], 363–68.)

Cooper's note appears on the first page of a letter from Bolton (29 March 1845, postmarked 1 April) requesting Cooper to annotate a genealogical table of the De Lancey family prepared from a letter the novelist had written to Miss Margaret? Munro. The inside leaves contain the chart. Bolton also requested Cooper to share with him any copies of monumental inscriptions pertaining to the De Lanceys obtained in France and to furnish the old French and the new coats of arms borne by the family.

1. See the chart reproduced on pages 38–39.

809. *To Cornelius Van Wyck Lawrence*

Hall, Cooperstown, July 3d '45

My Dear Sir,

A nephew of mine, Isaac Clason Cooper,[1] was in the custom house, until quite lately, in the humble station of a Night Watchman. He had been intemperate, but for several years, as I am told and believe⟨d⟩, has behaved himself perfectly well, and has been a sober man. Some time since he applied to me to aid him in being made a day inspector, which, besides giving him an easier life, would much increase his pay, but having no acquaintance with Mr. Van Ness[2] I could not assist him, though I tried — It was not that Mr. Van Ness was indisposed to attend to my recommendation, but because he never heard of my application, or, as I believe knew of the relation in which I stood to Mr. I. C. Cooper. I think this, as he made one appointment afterwards, in a case that I by no means urged, on my sole recommendation.

To night, I have been surprised by hearing from my nephew that he was removed by Mr. Van Ness, on the 15th June, without any charge against him, and that, on a representation, he was promised to be reinstated, which was not done. He wishes my interest in the case.

Now, I do not know the official standing of my nephew. If that be good, he is entitled by education, by the standing of both grandfathers, and by the losses of his father, to something better than the place he has lost. His father actually impoverished himself by building a floating battery — the predecessor of Fulton's first battery — on Lake Ontario. This battery he lost in a gale, in consequence of an eagerness to join [Isaac] Chau[n]cey before the boat was quite ready, and the debt he thus contracted subsequently ruined him.[3]

I repeat, you can ascertain the official conduct of Mr. Cooper. If it be not good, I have not a word to say. If it be good, however, I put the case before you for your decision, confident you will do what you think is right, and more than that I wish you not to do for me, or any man.

I hardly know whether to congratulate you, or not. The appointment is flattering, but if you do not sigh for the Bank parlour, I am mistaken.

Very truly | Yours

Cornelius W. Lawrence, Esquire J. Fenimore Cooper

If any thing is done in this case, let me beg it may be done at once. A reappointment would be very acceptable, though I present the claims to promotion, as the young man has a family, and is without means.

ADDRESSED: Cornelius W. Lawrence Esquire | Custom House | New York POSTMARKED: COOPERSTOWN N.Y. | JUL | 4 STAMPED: PAID
MANUSCRIPT: Paul Fenimore Cooper, Cooperstown, New York.

Merchant and banker, Lawrence (1791–1861) resigned his post as Jacksonian congressman in 1834 to become mayor of New York City for two terms. He was collector of the port of New York from 1845 to 1849. (*ACAB*.)

1. See the following letter.
2. Cornelius Peter Van Ness (1782–1852), former attorney, governor of Vermont, and minister to Spain, had just been replaced by Lawrence as collector of the port of New York (*ACAB*).
3. See Cooper to Peter Gansevoort, 3 January 1836.

810. *To Isaac Clason Cooper*

Hall, Cooperstown, July 3d 1845

Dear Sir,

Your letter has just reached me. I have written in your behalf to Mr. Lawrence this evening, and, if your standing in the Custom House be good, I think he will, at least, reappoint you — I think this, because I am on very good terms with Mr. Lawrence, and am of opinion he would wish to oblige me. If any thing is done, it will be done at once, and I beg you will let me know the result.

Very truly yours

Mr. I. C. Cooper J. Fenimore Cooper

You ought to know that Fenimore is spelt with one *n*.

ADDRESSED: Mr. Isaac Clason Cooper | New York POSTMARKED: COOPERSTOWN N.Y. | JUL | [3?]
MANUSCRIPT: The New-York Historical Society.

The third and youngest child of Cooper's brother William and Eliza Clason, Isaac Clason Cooper (d. 1848?) wrote from New York on 2 July 1845 to tell his uncle of his removal from a night inspectorship at the New York Custom House and to ask Cooper's intercession with Cornelius Lawrence, the new collector. Before receiving Cooper's reply on 21 July, he was restored by Cornelius Van Ness, the outgoing collector. He was again removed on 25 August 1845, apparently at the instigation of political foes, and again restored, evidently through Cooper's influence. He wrote again on 2 December 1847 to say that he had once more been removed in an economy drive and to bespeak Cooper's influence, through Governor William L. Marcy, with Secretary of the Treasury Robert J. Walker. The result of the novelist's application, if made, is not known; and Isaac Cooper and his family soon disappeared completely from the knowledge of the Fenimore Cooper family. (MSS: I. C. Cooper to Cooper, New York, 15 September 1845, 26 September 1845, 2 December 1845; Cooper to Mrs. Cooper, New York, 15 November 1850; YCAL.)

811. *To Mrs. Cooper*

Hall, Cooperstown July 4th 1845

Runaway,

You may have missed me at Syracuse, but you can not imagine how much you have been missed here. For a day, or two, I was about to call out "matie" every half hour, and your daughters were mistaken for you, at every turn.

It rained here, dearest, Monday, Tuesday, Wednesday, Thursday. At first we moaned about your decision, but when we found how long the storm continued, we were glad you went. To-day has been charming, a little cool, but no rain and a bright sun.

Wednesday the two fratelli Beach appeared.[1] The younger accepts, but asks leave to take off the wire edge of his wit, [upon?] his friends at Louisville. He appears in the parish next week, when we hope that the new broom will begin its work.

No news from Hadley. He is doubtless *from home*, busy, as he has been written to, and does not answer. By this time, I should think it done — Dow has answered, *is very grateful* and accepts.[2] The affair, however, is by no means terminated. I think the P[omeroy]s much easier on the subject. Mrs. P[omeroy] seemed quite relieved this evening and P[omeroy] really in good spirits.

I am sorry to say my unruly ox has done much damage to my very best corn. Some of it may recover, but many bushels must be lost.

Your cook has made a cream cheese which looks well, and as most of what she does *tastes* well, I live in hopes of success. A day or two will decide.

This day has been as quiet as last years 4th was the reverse — A great many boats on the lake, but that is all, with the exception of crackers and some most infernal bell ringing last night — even Napoleon could not have stood it.

No news of the Toe [*Satanstoe*]. I wait to hear from the publishers.

As yet no news from Detroit, and I may be compelled to go to New York. Opposition is so active, that we can leave home at 6 A.M, and reach Albany by 1. P. M. There are two lines on the Canajoharie road, and what is odd the old line thrives under it — The price, however, is very low, and will fall to 75 cents, I think, all round.

We had chickens to-day, but I shall pull up on them, for our company — Peas promise, as do cucumbers, and potatoes. We had potatoes in the soup yesterday. To-day, Paul and I emptied a pint of champagne to "the day and all who honour it."

Tiptongue was weighed this morning, and bore down 820 llbs. This is gaining 92 llbs in 84 days, not as well as he has done, but pretty well.

Eight of the youngest turkies have vanished at a swoop. These were on the hill, and with a mama turkey, who wandered too far. Forty is all I hope for.

I have written to Mr. [Foot?], and expect he will be here tomorrow morning.

I have nothing to add but love to your sisters, Fan, Mrs. de L —,[3] Mag [Margaret De Lancey] and all hands.

As for yourself, you need no assurances. The girls have just said they intend to have their bee, tomorrow.

Adieu,

J — F. C —

ADDRESSED: Mrs. Fenimore Cooper | Geneva POSTMARKED: COOPERSTOWN N.Y. | JUL | 5

MANUSCRIPT: Cooper Collection, Yale University Library. PUBLISHED: Cooper, *The Yale Review*, n.s. V, 825–26; *Correspondence*, II, 548–49.

1. The Reverend F. T. Tiffany resigned as rector of Christ Church on 12 May 1845, and Alfred Baury Beach (1821–1897, Trinity 1841, General Theological Seminary 1845) accepted the parish as his first pastorate. From 1848 to 1853 he was rector at St. John's Church, Canandaigua, and afterward at St. Peter's Church, New York City. (*NCAB*, IX, 163; Hurd, *History of Otsego County*, 275.)

Amos Billings Beach (1814–1885, Union 1832, General Theological Seminary 1836), brother of A. B. Beach and rector of Zion Church, Butternuts (Morris), Otsego County, in 1845, held pastorates also in Binghampton, Oswego, and Ithaca, New York (*The Ithaca Democrat*, 22 January 1885).

2. The Troy *Directory* lists Amos K. Hadley, a lawyer, at 21 First Street, and Joseph W. Dow, a grocer, at 96 Congress Street (*Tuttle's City Directory, for 1845–46* . . . [Troy, New York: N. Tuttle, 1845]). Evidently the Pomeroys and perhaps

Cooper were making efforts to extricate George Quartus Pomeroy from his embarrassing situation.

3. Comma supplied.

812. *To Mrs. Cooper*

Hall, Cooperstown, July 11th 1845

My Dearest Sue,

I have heard from Detroit, enclosing ⟨for⟩ $450 more, which make $2650 *rétirés du feu*. Mr. [George E.][1] Hand writes also, that the court decided the question about which Paul, Morehouse,[2] Dick and myself had so many consultations in my favour, which leaves every chance of getting the amount of the note ($3200) and puts the Ogden matter on velvet.

I have heard from Bentley, who comes partly to, but not near enough to carry me back to him. I shall wait another packet for his repentance, and then write to Colburn. Accept his terms, as they now stand, I will not.

I went to Worcester on Tuesday to attend Dick's law suit. He was beaten, but very moderately, and appeals. I have no doubt of his eventual success. The country is very pretty, abundantly wooded, and with less than common of the raw look of a new region. We got pork fried, floating in grease for dinner.

We are eating cucumbers, peas, new-potatoes &c, out of the garden. The peas are delicious. The chickens will be abundant, and I hear of no more losses at the farm. The milk house is finished, and is really a very pretty spot; cool, neat, and convenient. The turkies grow and already fly — As for your goslins, eight in number, they are already young geese.

I am glad to tell you that the corn that was bitten off continues to grow, and that the visit of the ox will only retard the harvest a few days. We have put a T on his nose, and cured him of his propensity to throw fences.

I think you will do well to press your brother to come with you. As for the fatigue, the roads are good now, and exercise will be good for him.

Mr. [Alfred B.] Beach is expected to-day, or to-morrow, and stays with us for a day, or two. Tiffany, I hear, goes through the land abusing us, me in particular, though I can not discover what he says. If he leave me opening, I will pounce upon him, and let the world have a taste of his quality, through a court of law, as well as an ecclesiastical one: I can easily get him suspended; if not unfrocked. One bounce John Duane[3] has told me. He said [William H.] Averill signed the letter *without reading it.* Now, Averill has attached to his name a written qualification, which shows he must have read the letter, since it refers directly to its contents. But truth is no check on that man's tongue.

We are all well, and shall be glad to see you.

Ever Yours —

Mrs. F. C. J — F. C —

ADDRESSED: Mrs. Fenimore Cooper | Geneva | New York POSTMARKED: COOPERSTOWN N.Y. | JUL | 12 STAMPED: 5
MANUSCRIPT: Cooper Collection, Yale University Library.

1. See Cooper to Hand, 9 June 1847.
2. A Cooperstown lawyer, Eben B. Morehouse (d. 1849) was elected in 1847 in the Sixth District to an eight-year term as justice of the Supreme Court of New York State (Franklin B. Hough, *American Biographical Notes* . . . [Albany: Joel Munsell, 1875]).
3. Unidentified.

813. *To Lewis Gaylord Clark*

Otsego Hall, Cooperstown, | July 12th 1845

Dear Sir,

In answer to your enquiry,[1] I can only say I remember *no work of fiction,* in which I could have made the allusion to Bunker Hill, that you name, unless it be Lionel Lincoln. It is so long since I read the book, that I will not take it upon myself to say it is there, but there is a good deal about Bunker Hill in that book, and I think there is something of the sort you name.

I have great pleasure in sending M. Dolgoroucki the specimen you ask.[2] You will see by the enclosed, I have made the opportunity useful in expressing a feeling that I have long entertained, and which is very sincerely felt. I am sorry that you should have had so much trouble about so unimportant a matter, but we are not left to be judges for ourselves in cases of this nature.

I remain, | Respectfully yours
J. Fenimore Cooper

L. Gaylord Clark Esquire | New York.

ADDRESSED: L. Gaylord Clark Esquire | New York POSTMARKED: COOPERSTOWN N.Y. | JUL | 14 STAMPED: 10
MANUSCRIPT: Clifton Waller Barrett Collection of American Literature, University of Virginia.

1. In his letter of 9 July, Clark wrote: "Will you have the kindness to inform me in which of your earliest works the description was given of the preparations at night for the battle of Bunker Hill? The *book* has done what the *scene* to which I allude never can — it has escaped my memory. I shall have occasion to refer to it in our August No., and shall feel obliged if you will indicate its source to me." (MS: YCAL.) Clark noted in his "Editor's Table" (*The Knickerbocker*, XXVI [August 1845], 184–87) that a poem "Bunker's Hill" by A. M. Ide, Jr., in the same issue of *The Knickerbocker* had reminded him of Cooper's "picture of that memorable battle," that he had been inspired to reread the novel, and that he was anxious that "readers should share the gratification which has been renewed to us." Declaring that Cooper's "description of the battle . . . has never been approached by any American pen," he quoted several passages from the novel in *The Knickerbocker*.

2. See the following letter. Clark's letter of 9 July contained a copy of a letter from J. P. Brown, an American resident and a correspondent of *The Knickerbocker* at Constantinople, requesting autograph materials by Cooper, Bryant, and Washington for Prince Dolgoruky's "already very rich collection." See also Cooper to Clark, 8 July 1846.

814. *To Prince Dimitry Dolgoruky*

Otsego Hall, Cooperstown | July 12th 1845

Sir,

I am asked to furnish a specimen of my hand-writing to a nobleman of the Russian family of Dolgoroucki. The compliment of making such a request would supply its apology, and the compliance might pass as a matter of course; but I shall profit by the occasion, to express to M. Dolgoroucki, and to all of his country, who may happen to read this note, the sense I entertain of the liberal and kind feeling that is so generally manifested in Europe, by Russians to Americans. My own introduction into European society was first owing to the attentions of Russians, for I had lived months at Paris, totally unknown and disregarded until I was recieved with polished liberality into a circle that included the names of various members of the family of Galitzin, whom I still remember with pleasure. Among the Galitzins I met various other Russians of breeding and intelligence, to most of whom I am indebted for acts of civility and kindness, recieved in a strange land.

But, on all occasions, did I find the Russians well disposed to us Americans. At Rome, I found the amiable and intelligent

Princess Volkonski; [1] also Prince Gagarin.[2] Every where, indeed, that I went, and met with Russians, I met with friends; and I have reason to believe that other Americans have experienced similar kindnesses from the same quarter. Ever since the noble interference of the just-minded Alexander, at the treaty of Ghent, Russia has proved herself the friend of America, and I am one of those who wish my nation to manifest a public preference to those who treat their country and countrymen, in and out of its own hemisphere, with liberality and justice.

I beg Prince Dolgoroucki to accept the assurances of my personal consideration and friendship.

J. Fenimore Cooper

A Mon[sieur] | Mons[ieur] Prince Dolgoroucki à Constantinople.

ADDRESSED: A Mons[ieur] | Mons[ieur] le Prince Dolgoroucki à Constantinople.
MANUSCRIPT: Leningrad Archives. PUBLISHED: P. A. and M. A. Golitzin, "Fenimore Cooper," *Neizdannyje Pisma Inostrannyx Pisatelei XVIII–XIX Vekov* (*Unpublished Letters of Foreign Authors of the Eighteenth and Nineteenth Centuries, from the Leningrad Manuscript Archives*), under the general editorship of Academician M. P. Alekseev (Moscow-Leningrad: U.S.S.R. Academy of Sciences, 1960), 272–76.

A poet, member of the Green Lamp, and acquaintance of Pushkin in his youth, Dolgoruky (1797–1867), son of the poet I. M. Dolgoruky, became a diplomat and served in Russian embassies in Constantinople, Madrid, London, Rome, and other cities. He was minister at the Persian Court from 1845 to 1854. An American enthusiast, Dolgoruky had many American friends, including Washington Irving; but he never fulfilled his wish of coming to the United States. (Golitzin, "Fenimore Cooper," *Unpublished Letters*, 272–73.)

1. Princess Zinaida Aleksandrovna Volkonskaya (1792–1862), author of works published in Russian and French and a friend of Pushkin, Gogol, and other eminent writers and artists. She went to Italy in 1829. (Golitzin, "Fenimore Cooper," *Unpublished Letters*, 273.)

2. Prince Gregoire Ivanovitch Gagarine (1782–1837), Russian minister at Rome during Cooper's residence there. He also served as minister at Munich from 1832 to 1837. (*Dictionnaire Diplomatique* [Paris, New York, etc.: Academie Diplomatique Internationale, n.d.].)

815. *To George Bancroft*

Hall, Cooperstown, July 27th 1845

My Dear Sir,

It is not an easy thing to give an opinion in a case like that you have mentioned.[1] I suppose the falsehood related to public matters, and certainly, it is a wise and safe principle to say that the officer who can not be depended on, in his reports and statement of matters of public moment, is not worthy of holding a commission.

A man may be guilty of "scandalous conduct" by telling falsehoods in private matters. In such a case, it strikes me the sentence of the court ought not to be disturbed, on the ground of expediency; nothing justifying the exercise of executive authority, *as against the accused,* but a very clear case that is directly connected with the public good. It is probable the mere point of honour would not satisfy the public mind, for an interference with the sentence of a court; but, falsehood, in an official act, is so obviously fatal to the confidence indispensable to public trusts, that I think I should feel a disposition to protect the government. An officer whose statements are not true, might even involve the country in a war. You take his reports as the foundation of your own action. Now, it is true, that he who will tell one lie, merely wants motive to induce him to tell another; but, in the administering of justice, there are gradations in murders, and ought there not to be in falsehoods.

I know nothing of the present facts, not even by rumour. In a clear, strong, case of public interest; I would at least, in a public order, ⟨to⟩ give increased weight to the punishment of the court. In some cases, I might dismiss; in all, I would never think of employing the offender again. Here, your half-pay system would fitly apply. I have no hesitation is saying that, in a clear case, of a public nature, the court ought to have cashiered; and in others not so flagrant, to have degraded.

The sentence of placing at the foot of the list, is a very useful one, judiciously used, and would have been a capital punishment for a private lie of the ordinary sort — I think, I have some where heard, that it has been pronounced illegal under our code. If so; it is a pity.

Of all human offences, lying is the most common. Many men lie, or seem to lie, because they are incapable of seeing the truth. It requires a clear head always to relate things as they happened, and, if I can guess the party implicated in this affair, he is a very weak man, though I never suspected him of being dishonourable. Exaggeration in discipline, in principles, in good, as well as bad, is apt to attend feebleness of mind, and sometimes exaggeration of facts. If the point relate to what has been said, some thing is due to the chance of misinterpretation. A man *may* tell the most deliberate lies, in this way, but others may also misunderstand him.

I fully appreciate the other parts of your letter.

By the way, *if you can get his opinion*, [Charles] Morris is a very safe adviser. *I* should say, be cautious. This country has not a very high appreciation of abstract integrity.

Very Truly | Yours

Geo. Bancroft Esquire J. Fenimore Cooper

ADDRESSED: Geo. Bancroft Esquire | Sec. U. S. Navy | Washington POSTMARKED: COOPERSTOWN N.Y. | JUL | 29 STAMPED: 10 ENDORSED: J. Fennimore Cooper. | opinion of Voorhees sentences. | Cooperstown | July 27th 1845 MANUSCRIPT: Massachusetts Historical Society.

1. Cooper's letter was prompted by the final paragraph of Bancroft's letter of 21 July 1845: "A recent event has given me much concern. A Naval Court-Martial has found one of its officers, a captain, guilty of scandalous conduct, & the specification is falsehood, and they have *not* dismissed him. Were you near me, I should take your advice as to the mode of relieving the navy from the disgrace of a sentence, which virtually declares immoral and dishonorable conduct to be no obstacle to a place of equality in rank, command, & emolument with the captains of the Navy." (MS: PFC; *Correspondence*, II, 550.)

In a court-martial convened on 2 June 1845, Captain Philip Falkerson Voorhees (1792–1862) was convicted and sentenced to reprimand and suspension for three years for improper interference at Buenos Aires between the Montevidean and Buenos Airean governments. In a second court-martial convened on 24 June 1845, he was found guilty and suspended for eighteen months on two charges: disobedience of orders and issuance of an order in the ship's log authorizing illegal flogging. The alleged "scandalous conduct" so disturbing to Bancroft was that Voorhees maintained in his official report that *wind* and *weather* prevented his docking at Norfolk according to orders, whereas the Secretary believed he had evidence that the violation of orders was premeditated.

Thinking Voorhees' second sentence too lenient, Bancroft reconvened the court on 5 August 1845 and obtained a new sentence of dismissal from the service, with a recommendation of merciful consideration. The President reversed this sentence, substituting suspension for five years, and in 1847 remitted the sentences altogether. Voorhees was restored to service and in 1849 to command, but his later years were clouded by further conflicts with naval authority. (*Defence of Philip F. Voorhees, before the Court of Inquiry, Convened at Washington City . . . May 11, 1857* [Washington, 1857]; *Memorial of Capt. Philip F. Voorhees . . . to the Senate and House of Representatives, December, 1860* [Washington, 1860]; *DAB*.)

816. *To William Branford Shubrick*

Hall, Cooperstown, August 19th 1845

My Dear Shubrick,

I have read your letter[1] attentively, and now sit down to answer it. As respects the Pacific Squadron, we are of the same mind. In the event of a war with Mexico, it will be the most responsible station afloat, and the most desirable one for a man capable of discharging its high trusts as they should be. How far the present incumbent [Captain John Drake Sloat] is that man, you know as well as I do. He will do better than half who have commanded in that remote sea, but one would not send him at such a time as this. Still I should have answered much as you have done, and I think the secretary right not to supersede him, unless he greatly increases the force. There is always a simple process of doing that, however, by sending orders to Biddle to hurry across from China,[2] and to remain on in command, on the western coast, on his arrival. This is as good a method of superseding as can be adopted. Biddle must now be in China, and in six months he might, probably will be on the west coast of America. It would probably take you that time to get your command together, were you to be ordered.

Conner ought not to be superseded.[3] He has had the awkward and delicate part of the service, and is entitled to see the more honorable and profitable — I am much mistaken in the man, if he be not quite equal to all his duties.

As for the bureau,[4] I think you ought to lay aside all sacrifice in order to keep a navy officer in it. You can not do it, if the government be really disposed to put in a civilian, since they can at all times make the change to please themselves. You will therefore be attempting that, which in the nature of things, you will be unable to accomplish. Rely on it they will appoint your successor, and not the navy. It is not your duty to see that such appointments are properly disposed of, and I question the wisdom of assuming responsibility that does not belong to your station. In the course of time, the failure will be ascribed to you.

As for the choice between the yard and the bureau, it is very much matter of choice. The allowances are something, and so is the command. Then that yard has peculiar duties, and familiarity with them may be of service to you. Nor do I see that accepting the yard ought to be regarded as lessening your claims to service afloat. An understanding might be had with *this* secretary on the subject, though *that* secretary might not abide by it.

I should consult my own wishes and pocket as between the

yard and bureau. *I* should prefer the first, I think, though I doubt not the last will give you most influence in the event of an opening for a command —

Does not the Sec —'s interest prove a desire to get the bureau vacant, and would it not be better to let him have it, if he so much wishes it? You, on the spot, can best judge of that.

I think Mexico will make such a war as will compel us to act on the defensive, though I think it questionable if she declare war openly. With Texas she is at war now, and on Texas she will probably wage her war, fighting our troops if they oppose her. This she may be silly enough to think will compel us to wait until Congress, here declares war, in order to act offensively at sea.

I am not sufficiently acquainted with the law to answer your question about seamen — There is no question that *one* party can declare war, Mr. Jefferson's theory in the case of Tripoli [5] to the contrary notwithstanding, and a war supersede the provision of a peace establishment law — Jefferson did this; the law of 1801, abolishing the grade of Commanders, and he appointing them anew, without any new law in 1804. War justifies a thousand things that can not be done in time of peace — If there is a war, however, Congress will undoubtedly be immediately convened, and vote for supplies &c recommended.

In the event of a Mexican war, I should think a great many small vessels would be useful — schooners and brigs, with a few heavy guns, and small crews, so as to float light and sail fast. A line of battle-ship or two to batter San Juan, might be wanted, and a few frigates; but small cruisers could best blockade and cut up privateers.

When I wrote Mr. Bancroft, I knew nothing of the facts of Voorhees' case.[6] I now think there can not be two opinions about it. I am sorry for him, and for his wife, but what can be done?

You send me news of Elliott. I had supposed him convalescent. Old officers, however, are some times killed off in the service before the breath has left their bodies.

With best regards to all at home, Yours as ever

J. Fenimore Cooper

You see what anti-rentism is about? It is the great American question of the day.

ADDRESSED: Commodore Shubrick | Bureau Pro. & Cloth. | Navy Department | Washington POSTMARKED: COOPERSTOWN N.Y. | AUG | 20 STAMPED: 10
MANUSCRIPT: Paul Fenimore Cooper, Cooperstown, New York.

1. Unlocated.

2. Commodore James Biddle commanded the East India Squadron (Navy *Register* for 1846, 4–5).

3. Captain David Conner commanded the Home Squadron in 1845 and 1846 (Navy *Register* for 1845, 4–5; Navy *Register* for 1846, 4–5).

4. The Bureau of Provisions and Clothing over which Shubrick presided.

5. In his Message to Congress of 8 December 1801, Jefferson maintained that his constitutional right permitted him to act defensively, but not offensively, without authorization from Congress. See Cooper's refutation of this point in his *History of the Navy* [Philadelphia: Lea & Blanchard, 1839], I, 446–48.

6. See the preceding letter.

817. *To Paul Fenimore Cooper*

Hall Cooperstown, Sept — 8th 1845

My dear boy,

Your train does not travel on Sundays, and your letter has just arrived. I send you $85, wishing you to have enough while you have not too much. The deposit[e?] money will come à propos in Jan.

Tiffany has been fool enough to sue me, and not cunning enough to draw up his declaration so as to give me any trouble, which he otherwise might have done.[1]

We are all well. I shall be in New York from the 22d to the 28th or 30th and at Philadelphia, afterwards. I wish you to be economical, but let me know when you want money in time.

Mother sends her best love, as would the girls if they were in — I think you would do well to call and see Mr. Dana and hand him the letter, though you will have no occasion to get his bond — Or you can call and say nothing about the letter —

God Bless You.

[*The close of the letter has been cut away.*]

MANUSCRIPT: Cooper Collection, Yale University Library.

1. Alfred H. Corning, Tiffany's lawyer, forwarded the clergyman's declaration with a note dated New York, 4 September 1845, reminding Cooper to file a plea at the Supreme Court of the City of New York within twenty days. Each of the eight charges of the declaration cited, with some variations, a general allegation by the novelist to the effect that Tiffany was a liar. (MS: YCAL.) Cooper evidently believed he would have little difficulty substantiating his alleged slanders.

818. *To Carey and Hart*

Hall, Cooperstown, Sept. 17th 1845

Gentlemen,

There has been some misapprehension between us on the subject of Old Ironsides.[1] I have been under the impression that it was to come into the second volume, and have been wondering I did not hear some thing of Vol. Ist. I have had no letter from you, that I have not promptly answered, and the proof chart has never reached me.

However, I leave home for Philadelphia on the 22d,[2] shall stay two or three days in New York, and see you shortly. I would advise Preble, a little retouched for vol. I. It will fill the vol. handsomely. But I will give you the other as soon as I can get all the facts, having agents at work at Washington now. I shall go to Washington when down.

Adieu

Messrs Carey & Hart. J — Fenimore Cooper

I was very sorry to see poor Carey's death,[3] having no notion he was so low. I got the news from Mr. Jos. Ingersoll, who wrote me just as he came from the funeral.

ADDRESSED: Messrs. Carey & Hart | Booksellers | Philadelphia POSTMARKED: COOPERSTOWN N.Y. | SEP | 18 STAMPED: 10
MANUSCRIPT: Ferdinand Dreer Collection, The Historical Society of Pennsylvania.

A note on the holograph, signed "F J Dreer," states: "given me by H C Baird Esqr. | January 6 1853."

1. Hart wrote Cooper from Philadelphia on 13 September requesting copy for "Old Ironsides" and corrected biographies of John Paul Jones and Richard Dale. He indicated that he had sent a reduced diagram of Tripoli Harbor to Cooper six weeks earlier to ascertain if the shoals were placed as the historian had directed, but that he had received no reply. (MS: YCAL.) The article called "Old Ironsides" was not included in *Lives of Distinguished American Naval Officers*, but was published posthumously in *Putnam's Monthly*, I (May 1853), 473–87, and I (June 1853), 593–607.

2. Comma supplied.

3. Edward L. Carey died on 16 June 1845 (Henry Simpson, *The Lives of Eminent Philadelphians* . . . [Philadelphia: William Brotherhead, 1859], 184).

819. *To Hooper Cumming Van Vorst*

Hall, Cooperstown – Sept. 19th 1845

D[ea]r Sir,

I am already under more conditional engagements to lecture the coming winter than I shall be able to meet. Under the circumstances, therefore, I feel compelled to decline the honour of addressing your association. Had the application been earlier made, I should have felt a peculiar pleasure in obliging you, as Albany has always been a town in which I feel great interest. I was a school-boy in it, forty five years since, and have many sincere friends still remaining there, whose acquaintance was then first made – This is not among the *young* men, as you may suppose, though it is among their fathers –

I remain, Sir, | Very Faithfully Yours
J. Fenimore Cooper

——— Van Voorst Esquire | Chair. Lec. Com. Y: M. Ass. | Albany.

ADDRESSED: ——— Van Vorst Esquire | Chair. Lect. Com. Young Mens Association | Albany POSTMARKED: COOPERSTOWN N.Y. | SEP | 21 STAMPED: 5
MANUSCRIPT: The New-York Historical Society.

Chairman of the Lecture Committee of the Young Men's Association for Mutual Improvement in Albany, Van Vorst (1817–1889, Union 1839) had written on 18 September 1845 to invite Cooper to address the association, consisting of "about one thousand young men," on a subject of his choice during the coming December or January. Van Vorst later became a prominent lawyer and jurist in New York City. (*Union College: Centennial Catalog*, 57; MS:YCAL.)

820. *To Richard Bentley*

New York. Sept. 23d 1845

Dear Sir,

I have delayed answering your last, in order to reflect on the contents.[1] In the meantime no offer or negotiation with any other house has been attempted by me. On the whole, I have determined that you shall have the three Books connected with the Littlepage Manuscripts for the £250 each, with the other conditions you name. Satanstoe you have with a credit of £50, towards "Chainbearer," which is the next work, now nearly stereotyped. This book is not a sequel, but a work in which the same scenes are used, and *some* of the old characters of Satanstoe are introduced, with new hero, heroine and love-story. The next book will be on the same plan, connecting one or two characters with the three books as Leatherstocking appears in different tales. My sole object in consenting to your terms, is to avoid the appearance of a misunderstanding by separating the Littlepage Manuscripts. I do not consider the £250 price as any way binding after the next book.

I shall send you half the book, or one American volume, by the middle of October, and the remainder about ten days later. I wish you to go to press at once, and to publish before Dec. 1st if possible.

I now draw on you at ninety days, for £200. This is the balance due on the Chainbearer, paying the £50 now due you, or making the £250 you name. I trust there may be no more difficulties with the bills. I draw now, because I am going through New York and shall not be here to draw when the sheets go. The difference in time, however, will be but about a fortnight or so.

Wishing you good luck with the books, | I am, yours

J. Fenimore Cooper

Mr. Richard Bentley | London

Excuse a blot.

ADDRESSED: Mr. Richard Bentley | Publisher | New Burlington Street | London | Viâ English Steamer | from Boston POSTMARKED: B[OSTON] | 25 | SEP | 5 cts [N?]O | 15 OC 15 | 1845 STAMPED: PAID
MANUSCRIPT: Cooper Collection, Yale University Library.

1. Bentley's letter of 18 June 1845. See Cooper to Bentley, 24 April 1845.

Part Eighteen

A TROUBLESOME CLERGY

1845–1846

A TROUBLESOME CLERGY

1845–1846

The Sixty-first Annual Diocesan Convention of the Protestant Episcopal Church of New York, at which Cooper and his friend Samuel Nelson represented Christ Church, Cooperstown, convened in St. John's Chapel, New York City, on 24 September 1845 in an atmosphere of crisis. On 3 January 1845, Bishop Benjamin Tredwell Onderdonk had been convicted and suspended by a Court of Bishops on "certain charges of immorality and impurity." According to the majority report of a Special Committee, this unprecedented calamity had compelled the diocese to "realize the solemn truth of the maxim, that there can be no Church without a Bishop. The churches, societies, and individuals of our communion, are daily suffering for the want of Episcopal acts. Our children cannot be confirmed, our edifices for worship cannot be consecrated, ministers cannot be instituted and settled, clergymen cannot be ordained, – in fine, the flock is without a shepherd, – a condition of disaster and peril which no words can magnify."

Had Bishop Onderdonk been deposed or forced to resign, the Convention could have elected another bishop. This normal procedure was frustrated by the sentence of indefinite suspension, for which there was neither precedent nor canonical definition. The General Convention, which held final jurisdiction, would not meet for another two years; and the Standing Committee of the diocese, which had already strained its canonical powers, required immediate guidance and confirmation of its authority. The Convention had to improvise. The Bishop's more loyal adherents argued that the sentence of the Court was invalid or so temporary that Bishop Onderdonk could at once be restored to his temporal and spiritual sway. Other delegates, convinced that he had forever forfeited the confidence of his diocese, urged measures to induce him to resign, though one alert delegate noted that his right to resign would have been included in his suspension. Resting on his plea of "not guilty," the Bishop maintained an aloof, unbroken silence above the clash of opinion and counteropinion.

Tracing the legal and metaphysical implications of the Bishop's status proved as futile as it was fascinating. The more than 350 lay and clerical delegates, many of them strangers to parliamentary ways, explored alternatives in six days of sometimes turbulent debate. The possibilities were labyrinthine. The Standing Committee had, of necessity, invited other bishops to perform essential Episcopal functions, relying on Diocesan Canon X, which authorized this procedure when there was "no Bishop." But, since the diocese was not *technically* "destitute of a Bishop," the Committee and invited bishops suspected that these ministrations, however necessary, were illegal. So hopelessly deadlocked was the Convention that it refused, at first, to emend the canon slightly to authorize these visitations; and it rejected a sane proposal for the election of an assistant bishop, with authority, to administer the affairs of the diocese. In 1847 the General Convention recognized the absurdity of the whole situation by forbidding indefinite suspensions; but it waited until 1852 to permit the election of a provisional bishop, Cooper's friend Jonathan Mayhew Wainwright. The diocese recommended the removal of Bishop Onderdonk's suspension in 1859, but he lingered on in his suspended state until his death in 1861.

Although Cooper was curiously reticent about his plausible solution to the controversy, the constitutional aspects of the debates assured his active participation. From the first day, when he requested the reading of the canon to settle a point of order, he was in close attendance, with such friends as John C. Spencer, Daniel D. Barnard, Luther Bradish, Hamilton Fish, Gulian C. Verplanck, John Jay, Jeremiah Van Rensselaer, and Samuel Nelson. When some delegates tried to stampede a permanent adjournment on Saturday, 27 September, he countered obstinately with a motion for temporary adjournment. When the Reverend Martin P. Parks of the West Point Military Academy categorically denounced public opinion as an evil force that had unjustly besmirched an innocent bishop, Cooper arose in some heat to distinguish between responsible and irresponsible public opinion (see pages 77–78). Though he believed that the diocese held the power to dismiss its Bishop, and though apparently Hamilton Fish and others shared his reasoning, he preferred not to urge it on the Convention. His solution was, briefly, that the status of the Bishop as bishop and as diocesan was separable: that the Bishop's function as diocesan, being essentially contractural, might be dissolved for cause by either party, whereas his position as bishop was *sui generis*. As Hamilton Fish pointed out to Cooper after the Convention, this eminently sane resolution of the difficulty was never clearly presented to the delegates.

Perhaps one reason for Cooper's silence was the thorough private investigation he was perforce conducting into the life and conduct of the Reverend Frederick Trenck Tiffany, former rector of Christ Church, Cooperstown. The novelist had befriended Tiffany on numerous occasions, and their difference developed chiefly from his having been one of Tiffany's sponsors when the clergyman was appointed chaplain of the House of Representatives at Washington in 1842–43. Sympathizing with him in his domestic afflictions and his erratic health, Cooper wrote unqualified recommendations. On the rector's return to Cooperstown, the novelist heard, evidently through Congressman Samuel S. Bowne, that on 12 December 1842 in an interview Bowne had arranged, Tiffany applied to President John Tyler for a military chaplaincy, though Tiffany was meanwhile assuring his Cooperstown congregation of his return. Cooper's curiosity was piqued; and, probably before Tiffany's application to the vestry for leave during a second Washington season, Cooper was making unsavory discoveries. These suggest that the clergyman was an incorrigibly weak and devious man rather than a malicious man, but the sharp contrast between his unctuous manner and his demonstrably peccant behavior roused Cooper's indignation. Eventually he cut Tiffany and began to comment somewhat freely to his fellow parishioners and vestrymen.

Tiffany apparently learned of this talk in his disfavor from Edwin Spafard, a friendly member of his congregation, in a letter dated Cooperstown, 8 July 1844. According to Spafard, the main charge was that Tiffany had "uttered a deliberate falsehood" in the matter of the application to President Tyler, informing some persons that it was contingent, telling others that it was made accidentally and jocosely, and denying to others that it was made at all. Spafard urged Tiffany, if there were truth in the charge, to go to Cooper, express his regrets, and promise to reform. "Mr. Cooper has his failings as well as the rest of us," Spafard noted, "but I have no hesitancy in saying he would be glad to have the matter settled, and would gladly forgive and forget." Replying on 12 July 1844, Tiffany denied any consciousness of wrongdoing and pointedly ignored the suggestion that he seek an accommodation with Cooper. Whether or not the novelist had the full sympathy of the congregation, his interpretation of Tiffany's conduct seems to have won general acceptance. Even the Phinneys, who were closely related to Tiffany by marriage, did not at once break with the Coopers. The rector's position in the parish became less and less tenable, and he resigned in May 1845. In September 1845 Tiffany's lawyer, Alfred H. Corning, forwarded to Cooper the declaration of a suit for $10,000 on eight counts of slander.

Cooper resolved to meet this disagreeable surprise directly by pleading the general issue or by justifying. Each of the eight counts recited the charge that Tiffany was a "liar," with additional charges in some counts as that he was a "scoundrel" and a "miserable preacher." To justify successfully required Cooper to gather overwhelming evidence, and he set about collecting every shred of pertinent information. The number of peccadilloes adduced in his pleas to the eight counts finally totaled seventy-six: they included repeated instances of Tiffany's failure to pay debts, demonstration of his failure to keep an accurate parish register, testimony concerning his plagiarism of sermons and parts of sermons, illustrations of his callous treatment of his parishioners, and many examples of his prevarication. Four times Cooper's burgeoning calendars of pleas in justification were carried to the New York State Supreme Court with petitions that the suit be barred, and four times these pleas were resisted in demurrers. The initiative passed back and forth for more than three years, with little or no possibility of victory for either side. If the stalemate had not already been recognized, it was obvious when, to Cooper's shock, his daughter Caroline Martha fell in love with Tiffany's nephew Henry Frederick Phinney and married him. The suit was fortunately forgotten.

821. *To Mrs. Cooper*

Globe. Thursday morning — [25 September 1845]

Dearest,

I have but a moment to say that I am quite well. Have done much business, and think I have got behind the curtain in the Tiffany business — Arranged the note, and am now engaged at all hours in convention.

The Clergy will be against us, probably by twenty to thirty votes. There is every prospect of our carrying the laity. Last evening laity stood on vote for President, which some think a test vote, 8 ahead.

Tell Dick Amos Beach gives material testimony, and so will [Samuel] Nelson I think, though he comes to the scratch reluctantly. He *can* tell a great deal, if he *will*. Others not yet seen, except Balch and Spencer neither of whom seems to know much, although the last has some indistinct notions on the subject.

I dined with [Peter G.] Stuyvesant, yesterday, in his new house, which is a fine dwelling, and much larger than the last.[1] John King,[2] Russel[l],[3] Hamilton,[4] [Luther] Bradis[h], Anne Rutherford,[5] Dr. Taylor[6] and Rufus Prime,[7] the party.

I never was better, and ate the first hearty meal yesterday, I have in a forthnight. I have no expectation of getting away from this place for several days. Mrs. Laight well. Girls much enquired after.

Yours as ever, with love to all.

Mrs. F. Cooper J. F. C.

ADDRESSED: Mrs. Fenimore Cooper | Cooperstown | N. Y POSTMARKED: NEW-YORK | 25 | SEP | 5 cts.
MANUSCRIPT: Cooper Collection, Yale University Library.

1. Stuyvesant, who had moved from 621 Broadway to a new house at 175 Second Avenue, corner of Eleventh Street, represented St. Mark's Church, New York City, at the Protestant Episcopal Convention. Most of his guests were delegates.

2. Gentleman farmer and politician, John Alsop King (1788–1867), son of Rufus King, served as state assemblyman, state senator, congressman, and, from 1857 to 1858, governor of New York State. He represented Grace Church, Jamaica. (*DAB*.)

3. Archibald Russell (1811–1871), son-in-law of Anna Rutherfurd Watts, represented the Church of the Ascension at Esopus, Ulster County. (Florence Van Rensselaer, *The Livingston Family in America and Its Scottish Origins* [New York: privately published, 1949], 170.)

4. Lawyer, politician, and writer, James Alexander Hamilton (1788–1878, Columbia 1805), son of Alexander Hamilton, preferred a secondary political role, helping President Jackson select his cabinet and giving advice freely in later years. He represented Zion Church, Greenburgh, Westchester County. (*DAB*.)

5. Anna Rutherfurd Watts (1794–1876), daughter of John and Helen (Morris) Rutherfurd and widow of John Watts (1786–1831) (Van Rensselaer, *The Livingston Family*, 128).

6. Thomas House Taylor (1799–1867, South Carolina College 1818), rector of Grace Church, New York City, and a well-known Low-Churchman (*ACAB*).

7. Rufus Prime (1805–1885), a wealthy New York merchant who delighted in literary pursuits (*ACAB*).

822. *To Mrs. Cooper*

Globe. Sunday morning, Sept. 28th 1845

Dearest,

Here I am yet, having been in close attendance on the convention, since wednesday, from nine in the morning until late. It is true dinners have occupied the evening. We have done no harm as yet, although we have failed [to][1] do all the good we might. My ink was detestable and I have changed it. We have authorised the standing committee to call in Episcopal aid, and that is something. But we are in a minority. All the dependant clergy stick by Trinity and the committees. They do not do this even decently, for they gather around the delegates of that church, in the pews, and vote with them like so many Swiss. We have gained, however, and shall continue to gain. I have not spoken yet, though much urged to do so. I may do it on Monday. If I do you will have no occasion to regret it. We had great difficulty in getting them to adjourn over to this week, the disposition being to finish off hastily in their own way, and break up last night. Had we done so, a scene of confusion would have followed that would have been disgraceful. I was instrumental in adjourning over. To-morrow things must be brought to a close.

I have done little in the way of business. Tiffany is here, but his reports have been met and are shaken. Mr. [Alfred B.] Beach got his seat but Mr. [Joseph] Ransom does not.

Tell Dick I have not seen Dr. [Leverett] Bush, but he is here, and I hope to see him to-morrow. Mr. Beach has seen him. He tells me that the doctor says he ⟨ha⟩ recieved $50 from the vestry and 9 more from John Tiffany.[2] This was for about four months salary. Now, at the time, Dr. B[ush] told me that T[iffany] had given him authority to get one half of T[iffany]'s salary from the treasurer, but it could not be had in consequence of T[iffany]'s having pledged it to other persons. The whole amount would be say $115, for which $59 only has been paid; he (T[iffany]) recieving *all his salary for two years for his own purposes.* The Dr. is a little savage I understand.

Don Cushman professes a disposition to tell every thing, but is prejudiced against, though he has been shaken. You may judge of the sort of influence to which he has been subjected by the following fact mentioned by Mr. Beach.

"Cooper lords it over you, at Cooperstown, and you are afraid of him," said Cushman. "Now he spoke of you lately, as '*my* clergyman.' "

"I know he did, Mr. Cushman, for I heard him. A friend of his asked him, by what right he sat in convention, in answer to Mr. Cooper's questioning his certificate, all in pleasantry, and the answer of Mr. Cooper was 'There is my clergyman and this is my colleague,' pointing to Judge Nelson and myself."

"Ah! but I do not mean any thing in the convention; it was a few weeks since, at a lake-party, at which [you][3] were both present."

"But I never was at a lake party with Mr. Cooper in my life, and *that* can't be true."

Now whence all this stuff? Can it have but one source? Certainly not.

Amos Beach says that Tiffany made two attempts to persuade him to prevent his brother from coming to us. Returning to the attack the *second* day, after having been repulsed the *first.* I shall show him up thoroughly depend on it.

Tell Dick the Secretary of the Convention can verify the accuracy of the reports in the journals.

I shall probably remain here until Wednesday; return in about ten or twelve days, and be home a few days after.

My next will be from Heads. I never was better, and eat heartily as of old.

With fondest love to all | Yours

Mrs. F. C. J. Fenimore Cooper

I write to Paul to-day. Tell Dick, Nelson distinctly recognises what his wife told me, and has intimated that he will converse with her on the subject as soon as he gets home. Still he plays 'possum.

ADDRESSED: Mrs. Fenimore Cooper | Cooperstown | New York POSTMARKED: NEW-YORK | 29 | SEP | 5 cts
MANUSCRIPT: Cooper Collection, Yale University Library.

1. The word is blotted out.
2. John Lathrop Tiffany (1793–1878), brother of Frederick Trenck Tiffany (Tiffany, *The Tiffanys of America*, 127).
3. The word is partly concealed by a blot on the opposite side of the paper.
4. See Cooper to Richard Cooper, 25 May 1831.

823. *To Paul Fenimore Cooper*

Globe. New York, Sunday, Sept. 28th 1845

My Dear Paul,

We have adjourned over to to-morrow, after four days of spirited, but good-natured discussion. Trinity Church has a majority, of course, the dependant clergy obeying her nod in all things. We are making an impression, and have already got a sort of compromise on one or two important points. The Standing Committee is re-elected to a man, but it has been obliged to abandon its coddling policy, and to treat the diocese as if vacant, and is directed to call in episcopal supervision. There we stand now, but to-morrow will be the test day. I shall probably say something to-morrow. We shall not triumph, but we shall make and leave an impression.

I have little else to tell you. The Tiffany business goes on and well. We have obtained forty additional days to plead in, and are using them to advantage. Much matter directly to the point has been obtained, and much will be added. The declaration is drawn up evidently on his representations, and very inartificially. The words are not laid as uttered, and those that are laid, are so laid as to give us a fair opening ⟨as⟩ to show what his clerical character truly is.

I wish you would write me a line, directed to Philadelphia, to let me know how you get on. I am perfectly well; all the better I fancy for the indisposition [I] had.

God Bless you, my dear boy, | Your Affectionate Father
J. Fenimore Cooper

P. Fenimore Cooper Esquire | Cambridge

ADDRESSED: Paul Fenimore Cooper Esquire | Cambridge | Massachusetts POSTMARKED: NEW-YORK | 29 | SEP | 5 cts.
MANUSCRIPT: Paul Fenimore Cooper, Cooperstown, New York.

824. *To Mrs. Cooper*

Globe. October 1st [1845]

Dearest,

Your letter has just reached me. Fortunately, I relied but little on Kate [Nelson], and I firmly believe the Nelsons mean to dodge. But, no matter. I can beat him [Tiffany] without the[m.][1] Dr. [Leverett] Bush's case will turn out important. Tell Dick to ask Henry Ernst [2] if T[iffany] did not leave an order for him to pay half his current salary to the Doctor. If so, he has been guilty of palpable dishonesty, for the Doctor did officiate, or got others to officiate four months, and was entitled to recieve $125; whereas he *has* recieved but $59, T[iffany] appropriating *all* the rest of the salary to himself. This will tell. Nelson distinctly admits that the salary was $700 and the house. *I distrust him however.* Don Cushman is to meet me in a few minutes, when we shall see how candid he will be.

Convention adjourned last night, harmoniously as to feeling, and beautifully as to form. It was the most solemn parting of the body I ever witnessed. In point of fact, the Bishop's men did nothing that we seriously opposed. Our lay majority towards the last compelled a compromise and they abandoned the salary ($2500 per an —),[3] the declaration that the diocese was not vacant, and the plan of an assistant Bishop. All the rest was well enough, and some of it was imperiously demanded. On the whole *we* are satisfied. The most extraordinary part of the proceedings, is the fact that not one person in five wishes to see the Bishop restored. It is all high and low church party feeling. On the whole, things stand much better than they did.

By the way, tell Dick T[iffany] has been here, and [Alfred B.] Beach spoke to him on the subject of his communicants. T[iffany] says his list is at the bottom of that box yet, but *he can recollect some ten names in addition to those already sent him by Mr. Beach,* and expects to get the remainder. Now *we* can enumerate about ten more, which makes 70 or 72, and no doubt these are all.

T[iffany] knows we are on the scent, and yet he finds only ten in addition to the sixty sent him.

[Don A.] Cushman has just left me, refusing to tell any thing, the moment I began to write down his answers, though he had come to do so.

J. L. White [4] answers like a man, and gives important testimony. His brother [5] wriggles but may be got to the scratch.

I am on the wing for P —. Tell Dick I am delighted, and shall write him in a few days. It is now three, and I go at five. Adieu.

Mrs. F. C. J. F. C.

A prospect of selling Elinor, with a small profit — from 1 to 200 dollars.

ADDRESSED: Mrs. Fenimore Cooper | Cooperstown | N. Y POSTMARKED: NEW-YORK | 1 OCT | 5 cts
MANUSCRIPT: Cooper Collection, Yale University Library.

1. Cooper's pen exceeded the margin of the paper.

2. Henry B. Ernst (1809–1868), jeweler and silversmith, son of John Frederic Ernst, Jr. (Hurd, *History of Otsego County*, 260; Gertrude A. Barber, *Records of Christ Church, Cooperstown, Otsego County* [Manuscript, 1932], 42. Carbon copy at American Antiquarian Society).

3. Comma supplied.

4. Joseph Livingston White (d. 1861), born in Cherry Valley, Otsego County, New York, served from 1841 to 1843 as Whig congressman from Indiana. He subsequently practiced law in New York City. (*BDAC*.)

5. David L. White, a lawyer in New York City at 14 Wall Street from 1845 to 1857 (*Doggett's New-York City Directory, for 1845 & 1846* [New York: John Doggett, Jr., 1845]).

825. *To Richard Cooper*

Head's, Philadelphia, Oct. 2d 1845

My Dear Dick,

Here I am at last, after eight days detention in New York, during seven of which, I was not able to quit the Convention, even for an hour. I saw [John C.?] Spencer, Balch,[1] [John] McVickar, and [Don A.] Cushman, however, in the Convention, and questioned them. The three first knew nothing. Cushman made an appointment with me, for 12 [N.?] Wednesday, and kept it. I had told him what my object was, and he came with a fair profession of a readiness to answer, admitting my right to have the benefit of the truth. He told me when his daughter was married, Oct. 26th 1843, but did not know when Tif[fany] came or went —

I asked another question, and he answered it — I proceeded to write down his answer, when he wished to know what that answer had to do with the matter. I told him it had, as I might show T[iffany] had made different representations to others. He then said, he believed he might be mistaken, and made a different statement, which I proceeded to write down. "But how can this do you any good?" "I believe I can show that Mr. T[iffany] has made different representations from this too — I care not which you swear to, as either will answer my purpose." "Then I'll answer no more — put me on the stand — good morning," and he walked out of the room!

I next found J. L. White, and told him my business. He recognised my right to interrogate him and said he would answer me frankly. I began my questions, when he objected, saying that he could only answer to pertinent matter. He understood I had charged T[iffany] with lying in reference to the chaplaincy, and I ought to confine myself to the matter in hand — I told him generally how matters stood, when he shrugged his shoulders, and said "go on, sir — I'll answer." On the whole, he behaved well, and after we had talked the matter over a little, and heard what I had to say about my interview with T[iffany] it was evident his mind underwent a great change, and he called me back to state one of the most important items he revealed. The substance of his testimony will be this.

He went to Washington with T[iffany]. On the way there, or while there, T[iffany] told him his people would raise his salary, *but for me,* but my influence prevented it. This is true neither way. No one thought of the thing, and never hearing of a project so wild I did not have any occasion to oppose it.

He said T[iffany] told him *he did not wish to quit Cooperstown, that he had been there a long time* and was much attached to the place, but was advised to apply for the chaplaincy, and to take it, if he found his health getting worse. After a while, he said his health was worse, and he had applied, and thought he should get what he wanted on his own terms. When he was going to see Mr. [John] Tyler, he told White of the fact, saying he meant to apply for some particular place that was vacant, or soon would be, he forgets which. *T[iffany] wished ⟨him⟩ earnestly to conceal the application from his congregation.* This is what W[hite] called me back to tell me. He said that T[iffany] had related to him a conversation he had held with me, to this effect. I came to the rectory one Sunday morning, and said "So T[iffany] you want to be made a chaplain I hear. Why did you not let me know it, and I would have got the chaplaincy for you." "I told Cooper, I did not want the chaplaincy — *my health was better and I did not wish to go.*" To this Mr. White will swear, I make no doubt. The last admission is important, as, by connecting it with his subsequent services, applications, letters &c we may prove that he was cajoling us. In addition to the above, W[hite] told me the story of the loan from his father's estate, in reference to which he and his brother David, both think T[iffany] behaved ill. He expressed a wish to David White to get a chaplaincy a long time ago, but whether it was before he went to Washington he cannot swear, though he evidently thinks it was. [Joseph] Ransom told me, D[avid] White had told him it was before. I shall see both the Messrs. White, on my return to New York.

To Edwin Spafard [2] I have written, and also to Com. Shubrick to search the Department.

On the subject of the declaration, we need have no concern. I have never said he was a liar in direct connection with the chaplaincy application, so he cannot lay the words, unless generally. That is the reason no words have been laid, in that express connection — All I ever said directly was said to Johnson,[3] and nothing was said of particulars, unless it was to add that he had abused his parish calling it "cold and heartless and selfish."

Dr. [Leverett] Bush's affair is serious too. Ask H[enry] Ernst if T[iffany] did not give the Dr. a right to recieve one half his current salary while the latter officiated, and, if, under this agreement he, Ernst did not pay B[ush] $50, declining to pay any more on account of the other demands on him. I think the answers will be yes. B[ush] got $9 more from John Tiffany. This is all he ever recieved for four months services. Now, it will not do to say B[ush] did not earn or deserve his money, for T[iffany] has since drawn every dollar of his salary and not paid B[ush] what is due to him out of it. This smells rank, and must be enquired into. It may be well, to save time, to write to Dr. B[ush] propounding queries.

You will remember that T[iffany] has often admitted to Amos Beach that his salary was $700 and the house — [Samuel] Nelson says the same —

I make no doubt of getting more facts from J. L. White, and possibly some from his brother. J. L. W[hite] answers like a man, and I make no doubt will be found true.

Alfred Beach says T[iffany] told him *he* could add about ten to the list that B[each] sent him. So can we, and they make about 70 communicants, or certainly less than 75, when he reported 89, after an addition of 14, previously to which he had reported 88! I had thrown out some general hints to [Don A.] Cushman the day before our appointed interview, and I make no question T[iffany] is sorely troubled. It is my opinion he will bolt, if [Ambrose] Jordan will let him — T[iffany] told J. L. White, Jordan had volunteered.

I have much to tell you, and take notes, which I have in a book — but this much I thought it best to let you know as early as possible. Joe Ingersoll thinks, the "if I have an enemy on earth I forgive him," a conclusive fact he was "unfit to preach." He also thinks the fact of having preached another man's sermons a clear fact in answer to the charge.

White says T[iffany] owes his father's estate about $1000, $650 lent near ten years since. He himself offered to take T[iffany]'s mare and wagon for the debt, but T[iffany] said he must sell them and use the proceeds for the support of his family. What did he do with that horse and wagon. Did he not sell them for western land. Enquire — I think he sold one or both to Daniel Comstock,[4] who gave a note in part payment, and T[iffany] passed away the note. Perhaps [Henry] Scott can tell you.

I shall neglect nothing in this quarter.

Let them know at the Hall that I am here and well — have left the box for Miss [Sarah R.] Peters but have not seen her. Ingersolls all well, as is Mrs. [Harry] McCall, who says her child resembles a monkey.

The weather is delightful — so are the peaches.

Yours truly

Richard Cooper Esquire. J. Fenimore Cooper

White told me Cushman was a man that he knew was not to be relied on.

ADDRESSED: Richard Cooper Esquire | Cooperstown | New York POSTMARKED: PHILADELPHIA Pa. | OCT | 3
MANUSCRIPT: Paul Fenimore Cooper, Cooperstown, New York.

1. The Reverend Lewis Penn Witherspoon Balch (1814–1875, College of New Jersey [Princeton] 1834, General Theological Seminary n.g.), who married Anna, daughter of Cooper's friend William Jay, was rector of St. Bartholomew's Church, New York City. He also held pastorates in Pennsylvania, Maryland, Georgia, Rhode Island, Michigan, and Canada. (Galusha B. Balch, *Genealogy of the Balch Families* [Salem, Massachusetts: Eben Putnam, 1897], 470–72.)

2. Spafard (1814–c. 1884), son of Dr. Ariel and Percy (Williams) Spafard of Cooperstown. His occupation in 1845 is unknown, but he was later a teacher in Brooklyn. (Dr. Jeremiah Spofford, *A Genealogical Record, Including . . . Descendants of John Spofford and Elizabeth Scott . . .* [Boston: Alfred Mudge & Son, 1888], 171, 317.)

3. Parley E. Johnson, a Cooperstown pharmacist and physician during the 1830's and 1840's (Hurd, *History of Otsego County*, 36; Livermore, *A Condensed History of Cooperstown*, 91–92).

4. Daniel Dexter Comstock, son of William and Friday (Hawkins) Comstock and brother of Horace H. Comstock (John Adams Comstock, *A History and Genealogy of the Comstock Family in America* [Los Angeles: The Commonwealth Press, Inc., 1949], 130).

826. *To Mrs. Cooper*

Heads, Oct. 3d 1845

Dearest,

Dick will have told you that I got on here, wednesday night. We are hard at work on vol. II, vol I being done. As for Tiffany, Dick can tell you something of him, too. Don Cushman has behaved extremely ill, refusing to answer my questions the moment he found his answers were to the point. But, J. L. White has communicated important facts — important as to honesty, and as to truth. He gives T's version of the conversation with myself, which is no more like what passed than if it related to another matter. Rely on it, we use him up.

Here all are well. Mrs. [Harry] McCall says her child looks just like a monkey, to begin with. Miss [Mary] Wilcocks is well. Mr. Ben Wilcocks was thrown from his wagon, about three weeks since, and much hurt, and he has since had influenza. The effect of both has been to render him nervous and low spirited, and apprehensions have been felt that he might fall back into the state from which he emerged only six, or eight years ago. I saw him this evening, when he was said to be better than he had been.

He has let his large house for $1500, and removed into a smaller one, though sufficiently large, for which he had no tenant.

In other respects, I hear no news. The fair promises to be a great matter, many things having been forwarded from New York. It is to be held in the room of the Chinese museum which it is expected to fill, once certainly, if not twice.[1]

In convention, I saw our old friend Rev. [Theodore B.] Bartow, who is strongly anti-bishop. I also saw Mr. Bourns[2] who is ditto. The clergy did not behave well. Most of them think [Benjamin T.] Onderdonk guilty, and yet they voted, looked and talked, as if they thought him innocent. It will take ten years of exemplary behaviour in the clergy of the diocese to recover lost ground. Men insist on something more than the observance of forms — they require a little of the substance of religion. The whole will terminate in new charges, and a deposition. When that occurs, there will be a party to dispute the sentence, and to maintain that deposition from orders does not infer deposition from the diocese.

The close of the convention, nevertheless, was harmonious and respectable.

The peaches *here* are good yet, and I do wish you could eat some of them. I shall try to get a basket for preserves — October peaches, which are hard and keep a good while.

I have hopes of disposing of Elinor [Wyllys], though it will cost $600 to stereotype it. $200 more than one of my books. Still I ask $800 for three years — which with the $200, or $250 from England, will make $3 or 400 profit. All this, however, is only in hope, though a reasonable hope. Chainbearer is a good book I think, and Satanstoe has been a good deal read. The edition of 3600 is nearly sold, and Burgess is negotiating for more.

I shall be home between the 15th and 20th. Tell Dick to be active and inquisitive, as I can hope for very little more here. Something from the Whites, but not much. As for his [Tiffany's] application for the chaplaincy that can be proved by fifty people.

I am perfectly well, and have not touched a melon since I left home. Indeed, I have seen none here.

With tenderest love, your

J. F. C.

ADDRESSED: Mrs. Fenimore Cooper | Cooperstown | New York POSTMARKED: PHILADELPHIA [Pa.] | OCT | 4 STAMPED: ⟨5⟩ 10 [*inserted by hand*]
MANUSCRIPT: Cooper Collection, Yale University Library. PUBLISHED IN PART: *Correspondence*, II, 551–52.

1. Preparations were in progress for the Ladies' Fair to assist in the restoration of the Philadelphia Academy of Fine Arts which had been damaged in two fires in June 1845.

2. The Reverend Edward Bourns (1801–1871, Trinity College, Dublin, 1833) taught Latin and Greek at Geneva College from 1839 to 1845 and at Brooklyn College from 1845 to 1849. He served as president and professor of Latin and Greek at Norwich University from 1850 to 1871. (*Hobart College: General Catalogue*, 49.)

827. *To William Branford Shubrick*

Head's, Sunday, Oct. 5th 1845

My Dear Shubrick,

So far, well.[1] Gen Jones is quite right. Tiffany did call on him, or some one else in the war department, in the winter or spring of 1843, accompanied by Dr. Hawley, to ask a chaplaincy in the army. I know the fact, by his admission to others, though to me he denied having made any application at all. The chaplaincy he wanted was that of Governor's Island. Tiffany, at the time, was chaplain of the House of Representatives, which may aid Gen. Jones in recalling his identity. What I wish now to learn is whether any conditions were annexed to the application. Tiffany says he applied conditionally — that is to say, that he was not to take the chaplaincy if his health enabled him to remain at Cooperstown, and to take it, if it did not. Was any thing said of his health, at all, in that interview? Would he be apt to apply to any one else, in the department?

I want such answers as the party can swear to.[2] So far, we have had great success in collecting testimony, and are preparing a dose for the reverend gentleman, who will repent the course he has taken. To me, he distinctly denied ever having made any serious application for a chaplaincy. He now admits that he did. But, it's a long story, and I must defer it.

Who is to have the Home Squadron? [3] There will be something to be done there, this winter, depend on it. Does Bancroft go to Germany? [4]

Bring your answers here, yourself, by Thursday next.[5]

Adieu, with best regards

Com. Shubrick. J — Fenimore Cooper

MANUSCRIPT: Paul Fenimore Cooper, Cooperstown, New York.

1. Responding to Cooper's inquiry of 30 September 1845 (unlocated), Shubrick had learned that no written applications from Tiffany for a chaplaincy were on file at the Navy or War Department. However, Shubrick reported in his letter of 3 October, General Roger Jones (1789–1852), the adjutant general, recalled distinctly "that some time in the winter of 42–3, a gentleman who he is sure was named Tiffany was introduced to him at his office by the late Revd. Mr. [William] Hawley [(d. 1845), rector of St. John's Episcopal Church in Washington, D.C.] with the view of getting an appointment as chaplain, but on the explanations given by the adjutant general as to the manner in which such appointments are made the application was not pressed — " (MS: YCAL; *ACAB*; Alexander B. Hagner, "History and Reminiscences of St. John's Church, Washington, D.C.," *Records of the Columbia Historical Society*, Washington, D.C., XII [1909], 98–103.)

2. In a subsequent letter, dated Washington, 7 October 1845, Shubrick reported General Jones's unwillingness to testify on oath about so seemingly "unimportant" an interview so long past. According to the General's recollections, "it was rather an interview of inquiry than of application, something was said about his (Mr. T'[s]) connection with the parish of Cooperstown, and the uncertainty whether his health would make it necessary for him to leave that place, and how his parishioners might like his making inquiries about the matter — something was also said about the post of Governors Island." (MS: YCAL.)

3. Shubrick replied that Matthew C. Perry was to succeed David Conner in command of the Home Squadron, but that Conner would retain command as long as he wished or "as long as there is the least chance of there being any thing to do." (MS: Shubrick to Cooper, 7 October 1845, YCAL.)

4. Shubrick wrote on 7 October that so far as he could learn Bancroft had not the least intention of leaving the Navy Department (MS: YCAL). The historian was appointed minister to England on 9 September 1846.

5. "I cannot leave the city just now, suppose you take a run thus far" (MS: Shubrick to Cooper, 7 October 1845, YCAL).

828. *To Paul Fenimore Cooper*

Head's, Philadelphia, Oct. 5th 1845

My Dear Boy,

Your letter reached me yesterday. As for the Argus, do as you please,[1] though I believe your sisters intend to forward to you our own daily papers, which you will recieve a little late to be sure. It is so important at your time of life, however, to get early and practical information that I am quite willing you should look for it, where you can best obtain it.

I will bear the subject of a library in mind, and commence getting the books you require. By the time you are admitted we can have made some progress in the business.

As for the convention, I found it very laborious, but the newspapers exaggerated our disorder. There was only one scene of disorder, and that came from the confusion of the president, rather than from any confusion in the house. Good temper prevailed, very generally, though a few hits were exchanged. We did no harm, passing nothing to which the minority was seriously opposed. We had preferences, but were willing to accept the first few resolutions of the committee, if we could do no better. We did not pass the resolution giving the Bishop his current salary, that recognising him, or that requesting an Assistant Bishop. In a word, we did nothing, about which we cared any thing.

I spoke once — twenty minutes perhaps,[2] but the papers did not like to say much of me. I believe I spoke quite as well as most of them, and certainly had a merit that was a little rare in the body, that of stopping when I was done. The house was attentive, and I think what was said was not thrown away.

But, this convention has greatly lowered the clergy in my opinion, as I believe it will in the estimation of the public. They evidently cling to party more than they do to principles. I did not hear the remark of Mr. Forbes that you quote,[3] or I might have been [tempted][4] to answer it.

I am getting on famously with Tiffany. Three fourths of that which he has laid, I never said, and the rest we can effectually dispose of. He is sadly frightened, and one of his friends has proposed an arrangement — whether with his knowledge or not, I do not know. My answer was, Mr. T[iffany] can drop his suit when he please, but, as for myself, I shall do nothing but justify. I have obtained important facts from J. L. White, late M. C. from Indiana, and shall get more on my return to New York.

Let me have another letter, by this day week, at the Globe New York. I shall not be home before the 20th. My last accounts are favourable, and say that Fan is better.

Very affectionately | Your Father

Paul Fenimore Cooper Esquire. J. Fenimore Cooper

ADDRESSED: Paul Fenimore Cooper Esquire | Cambridge | Massachusetts POSTMARKED: PHILADELPHIA Pa. | OCT | 6 STAMPED: 10

MANUSCRIPT: Paul Fenimore Cooper, Cooperstown, New York.

1. In his letter dated Cambridge, 2 October 1845, Paul indicated his intention of subscribing to the *Albany Argus* for six months if his father had no objections. He requested his father's assistance also in beginning the collection of a law library. (MS: YCAL.)

2. Cooper's speech to the convention on Monday evening, 29 September, was reported as follows by Robert A. West:

"James Fenimore Cooper, Esq., said that for thirty years he had sat in that house at different periods, but this was the first time he had ever attempted to mingle in its debates. He had been urged, he said, to take part in the discussion that had now for some days been going on, but he could not overcome his feelings, the natural reluctance that sprang up in his heart against mingling in this controversy, until he had heard the clerical gentleman from West Point [the Reverend Martin P. Parks, chaplain and professor of moral science in the United States Military Academy]. When he had heard that gentleman express himself upon 'public opinion,' an irrepressible impulse seized him to obtrude himself before this convention, — an impulse he could not wish and did not wish to control — and, therefore, he had struggled for the floor. Few are less subject to the influence of public opinion than I am, the speaker went on to say: few care less for it, as all know who know any thing of me will admit. Senseless clamor has little effect on my mind; and I am willing to admit that it is the duty of a christian, particularly of a minister of God, to turn a deaf ear to its cries, when it is in opposition to the mandates of God himself. But nevertheless there is a public opinion which it is the duty not only of the christian, but every member of society, to respect.

"The course of his argument, he continued, would require him to take a short review of this whole controversy, which he would do in a few words, (and they would be but few,) and in a spirit of such impartiality as would command, he hoped, the candid attention of all present. First, then, he would speak of the character of the charges which had been brought against the late Bishop of this diocese. He would not express an opinion upon his guilt, or upon his innocence, but he earnestly begged the members of this convention to reflect seriously upon the character of these charges. As for himself, when revolving these charges in his own mind, and debating upon them there, he had found a summary so apposite, and so much in his own views, that he would not trouble the convention with the conclusions to which he had come, but he would read the opinions of one of the members of the court.

"(Mr. Cooper here read the conclusions of the Bishop of Delaware, as given in the report of the trial of Bishop Onderdonk. The Bishop of Delaware gave seven reasons why a clergyman guilty of the conduct proved against Bishop Onderdonk should no longer be permitted to exercise the functions of a bishop, the substance of which was, that his conduct indicated an impure and unholy state of mind that unfitted him to lay down the rules and morals of the Church.)

"Mr. Cooper then went on to say, whether Bishop Onderdonk be guilty or not, he would not undertake to decide; but he would ask every christian member of that convention to say, if, with charges of this character against him, Bishop Onderdonk could ever be restored, so as to be useful in this diocese?

"Mr. Cooper then examined the proceedings and organization of the court that had tried Bishop Onderdonk. First, the canon required a presentation. That had been complied with. The canon required a trial. That had been complied with. The court of seventeen bishops met in convention. The house knows the result. The vote for condemnation stood ayes 11, noes 6, a fraction less than two to one. The court thus had pronounced him guilty. Of the sentence itself, he would not here undertake to speak, but upon the expression of the opinion of the court, it was enough for him to rely, to show the gentleman from West Point that the opinion was not the senseless clamor of a public, but the sober, solemn opinion of the highest authority of the Church. To prevent cavilling, however, Mr. Cooper said, he would further state the case as impartially as he could.

"We all know, continued Mr. C., that this trial has been alleged to proceed from party spirit, and that the prosecution was the result of party in its inception, and in its prosecution. It so happened that he (Mr. C.) did not belong to any party, neither to the high church nor to the low church, for he was neither very high nor very low. To form his opinion, he had sat down with the book reporting the trial in his hand, and had given it all the attention and examination in its principles and in its parts that his ability permitted. The publication of the book of the trial enabled the whole public to form their opinions as well as the court itself. But if there was a low church party, is there not a high church party too? And is there not a probability that one may err as well as the other? Again, it is alleged that there were persons in the Court of Bishops who, from their principles or impressions, were unfit to be there. Their party predilections, it is said, disqualified them from acting as impartial judges. This is said on account of differences in their theological opinions. Now, if in such an allegation there is any good reason, it might destroy, and probably would destroy, every tribunal and every jury in the land; for it is next to impossible to constitute a court that may not have in it party men. And on this principle, too, it would be impossible to constitute a court in the Church, for men differ in it as to certain principles, as much as men of the world. But apart from this, there have been advanced objections to certain members of the court. One of them, he must confess, would have acted more wisely if he had withdrawn from the court. Strike him off, and the vote would have stood 10 to 6. Another member of the court so committed himself, (I will tell you why I was led to ascertain this by and by,) as to become an inmate of the dwelling of the person whom he had on trial — a sharer of his bread and salt. (He was understood to mean Bishop [George Washington] Doane.) Now if the bishop just alluded to had not been in the court, the second should not have been, and so the vote would have been the same. What induced him to make an investigation, was that a connexion of his [Bishop W. H. De Lancey] had been charged with being this inmate of the Bishop's dwelling, during the time of the trial. He had denied it with some warmth, and when it had been insisted upon that it was so, he had examined and found that although the inmate was not the connexion of his, yet that the charge was true of another bishop. He condemned this intimacy then as dooming the trier to the bold and ready manifestation of a foregone conclusion. Both of the bishops, in his opinion, should have been struck off the court, and in a court of law, they might have been challenged as jurors for cause; but strike them off and the result would have been 10 to 5.

"Now as the book of the trial had been published, and all the facts of the case had been put into the hands of every man that desired it, *ceteris paribus,* the people were as good judges, or as capable of judging as the court. Well then, with this public, how stood opinion? None would dispute his statistics, he thought, when he said there [were] as many who thought the Bishop guilty, as thought him innocent. Judging from his own observation, and what he had heard, he thought that opinion stood as three to one, but say two to one, or if not two to one, say man to man. Now, then, take this division of man to man, how comes the application of the remarks of the gentleman from West Point, or which of these two divisions of public opinion, in such a case as this, is bound to yield — that which is sustained by the canon and the court, or that sustained solely by private opinion?" (Robert A. West, *Records of the Proceedings and Debates at the Sixty-first Annual Convention of the Protestant Episcopal Church, in the Diocese of New-York . . .* [New York: Stanford and Swords, 1845], 98–100.)

3. Paul Cooper quoted a report that the Reverend John Murray Forbes (d. 1885, Columbia 1827, General Theological Seminary 1830) had said " 'men of the world got their consciences so scar[r]ed they couldn't understand the nice moral distinctions drawn by clergymen' " (*CUOA*; MS: Paul Fenimore Cooper to Cooper, Cambridge, 2 October 1845, YCAL).

4. Cooper wrote "attempted."

829. *To Mrs. Cooper*

Heads, Saturday, Oct. 11th 1845

Dearest,

I believe I will send another tinpinny before I quit this place, to let you know how I get on. In the first place it is as warm as summer, and I have had to buy some cotton vests. In other respects it is very pleasant. My book will be finished this afternoon, and I shall go to New York to-morrow night. One week in town, and then for home.

Tell Sue I have her $100, in *gold galore*, for her. The book will appear in November, as will my own. I shall bring her the new preface, and shall send the sheets to Bentley with my own.[1]

The fair does pretty well. It had recieved $4500 at the end of the second day, and it closes to-night — though there will be a raffle on monday. The raffles are numerous and illegal. I have put in $2.50 one chance in thirty, in hopes to get some law books, though without any expectations of succeeding. Miss [Sarah R.] Peters had take[n] $400 the ⟨second⟩ third evening, divided into $200 — $130 — $70 — resembling a lady's waist.[2]

Mr. [George] Bancroft is here, with his family. I believe one of his children is unwell. I have been asked by [Joseph R.] Ingersoll to meet him at dinner, but could not on account of clearing off my work. He is to pass an hour with me to-morrow morning.

Bishop Potter [3] is at work, but opinion is suspended. To own the truth, the clergy have lost so much ground in this affair of ours, that no one seems disposed to bestow unnecessary faith. It will take years of good behaviour for them to recover their lost ground. Ingersoll has not yet been to see his new bishop.

What do you think of Tiffany! By what I can learn, he is getting Billy [4] ready to swear that, in our interview, he told me, ⟨he⟩ in answer to an offer of mine TO GET THE CHAPLAINCY FOR HIM, that *he did not wish* it — *his health was better, and he did not NOW wish to quit Cooperstown*! There's a saint for you! J[oseph] L[ivingston] White will swear he told him this. ⟨This⟩. By the way, desire Dick to write to Parson [Hugh?] Smith,[5] to inquire what he *knows* concerning T[iffany']s preaching other men's sermons. He probably *knows* something positively.

I am sorry to say the peaches are gone, so I can bring you none home. I shall try, however, in New York. I have written to Dr. [Leverett] Bush, and desired him to send his answer to C[ooperstown]. Horseneck Post [*illegible*] [6] Dick can open it — or you can do it. I know what the bargain was, however, from his own mouth, and I believe from T[iffany]'s letter to him.

I have had an interview with a Mr. Granville Vernon, M. P. a son of the Archbishop of York, and the cousin of various great persons. A niece of his, a Miss Harcourt, is married to Lord Norreys. He gave me all the gossip of London, knew every body I knew, and knew all about them.[7] He says Lord Abingdon *had* about £15000 a year, but, without any vices, and by pure negligence has suffered himself to get so much involved that his estate is at nurse, and he lives on £2000 a year. Norreys he says is a veritable monkey, being the greatest mimic he knows and a perfect chatterbox, though good natured, and not bad principled. He will be cut down to the entailed estates, or about £7000 a year, which is quite as much as I supposed the father to have.

Old [Samuel] Rogers is well, and very little altered. Lady William [Russell] has gone to join her husband at Berlin, though he keeps the beautiful Jewess openly, to the great scandal of the pious King and Queen.

Lord Kerry's widow was the admiration of all London, for a few years, but has given way at last, and become the wife of a certain Charles Gore, as roué a second son as England contains! [8]

None of the Greys has a child, until they reach a parson, who with a parson's luck has a house full. My pretty Mrs. Grey — the young Duke — has got nothing from her banker father, and doubtless writes as we all do to help feed the household. The present Earl is married but childless.[9]

Mr. Vernon says that [Edward] Stanley was in love with his present wife when he came here, but was thought too young to marry,[10] that [Henry] Labouchere was in love with the lady Wortley has since married; [11] Wortley in love with the present Lady Grey,[12] and Denison [13] in love with somebody else.

God Bless you all — with tenderest love

J. F — C.

ADDRESSED: Mrs. Fenimore Cooper | Cooperstown | New-York POSTMARKED: PHILADELPHIA Pa. | OCT | 11 STAMPED: 5 10

MANUSCRIPT: Cooper Collection, Yale University Library. PUBLISHED, IN PART: *Correspondence*, II, 552–54.

1. Bentley published *Elinor Wyllys* in London on or about 1 December 1845; Carey and Hart, in Philadelphia on or about 1 January 1846 (Blanck, *Bibliography of American Literature*, II, 311).

2. The Philadelphia Academy of Fine Arts was twice damaged by fire earlier in 1845, and the Ladies' Fair was one of several efforts to collect funds for its restoration and repair.

3. Alonzo Potter (1800–1865, Union 1818) was consecrated bishop of Pennsylvania in 1845, after the premature retirement of Henry U. Onderdonk. Potter was an author, teacher, and college administrator as well as a parish priest. (*DAB*.)

4. Possibly William Holt Averell.

5. See Cooper to Mrs. Cooper, 14 October 1845.

6. The word, which may be "Unadilla," is squeezed into the end of the line.

7. Cooper met Granville Harcourt-Vernon (1792–1879), of Grove Hall, Notts, whose father Edward Vernon (1757–1847), third son of the first Baron Vernon and archbishop of York, adopted the surname Harcourt on succeeding to the Harcourt estates. The niece Elizabeth Lavinia (d. 1858), daughter of George Granville-Harcourt, married in 1835 Lord Norreys (1808–1884), who succeeded his father as Montagu, sixth Earl of Abingdon in 1854. (*Burke's Peerage*, 64–65, 2002–03.)

8. William Thomas (1811–1836), Earl of Kerry and heir of the third Marquess of Lansdowne, married in 1834 Lady Augusta Lavinia Priscilla Ponsonby (d. 1904), daughter of John, fourth Earl of Bessborough. The Countess of Kerry took as her second husband in 1845 Charles Alexander Gore (d. 1897). (*Burke's Peerage*, 1192.)

9. Henry George (1802–1894), third Earl Grey, succeeded to the title in July 1845. Charles (1804–1870), Cooper's "young Duke," next in succession in 1845, was married to Caroline Eliza (d. 1890), daughter of Sir Thomas Harvie Farquhar, Bart. She wrote novels under the name Mrs. Elizabeth Caroline Grey. The parson referred to was apparently the fifth son of the second Earl, the Reverend John Grey (1812–1895), who had two or three children in 1845. (*Burke's Peerage*, 926–27.)

10. Stanley, who succeeded as fourteenth Earl of Derby in 1851, married in May 1825, shortly after his visit to the United States, Emma Caroline, second daughter of Edward Bootle Wilbraham (Wilbur D. Jones, *Lord Derby and Victorian Conservatism* [Athens, Georgia: The University of Georgia Press, 1956], 10).

11. John Stuart-Wortley (1801–1855), who succeeded as second Baron Wharncliffe in December 1845, married in 1825 Georgiana Elizabeth, daughter of Dudley, first Earl of Harrowby (*Burke's Peerage*, 2075).

12. Henry George, third Earl Grey, married Maria, daughter of Sir Joseph Copley, Bart., in 1832 (*Burke's Peerage*, 927).

13. John Evelyn Denison (1800–1873), later Viscount Ossington, spent most of his political life in the Commons, serving as its speaker for almost fifteen years. He married Lady Charlotte Cavendish Bentinck, daughter of William, fourth Duke of Portland, in 1827. (*DNB*.)

830. *To Richard Bentley*

New-York. Oct 13th 1845

Dear Sir,

By the Cambria (16th instant) you will recieve the sheets of Chainbearer, complete. My letter by the last packet[1] will have prepared you for their reception. We shall publish here, late in Nov, or early in December.

I also send you the sheets of a novel called Elinor Wyllys, written by a female friend, and which I hope you will publish. It is a good book and a first book, and may lead to something better. I appear as its editor but with explanations. I shall name no price for these sheets, but trust you will pay such a consideration as the book may be worth. You had better publish this book also in November, or December, as it will be published here, about the same time as Chainbearer.

I beg you will write me on the subject of Elinor as soon as you have any thing to communicate. The third book on the Anti Renters, will be ready in the spring. I think it will attract attention on the other side of the water, as well as here.

In haste, | yours,

Mr. R. Bentley | London. J. Fenimore Cooper

ADDRESSED: Mr. Richard Bentley | Publisher | New-Burlington Street | London
POSTMARKED: NEW-YORK | 13 | OCT | 5 cts [M?]B | [24] OC 24 | 1845
STAMPED: PAID

MANUSCRIPT: Cooper Collection, Yale University Library.

1. Cooper's letter of 23 September.

831. *To Mrs. Cooper*

Globe. Tuesday. Oct 14th 1845

Dearest,

Your letter and Dick's [1] of Sunday have both been recieved.

You will be surprised and a little concerned to hear the Laights are seriously talking of sailing for the Mediterranean, on the 1st Nov. It is not yet absolutely determined, though the probability is that they will go. His health is the cause, and the plan will be to sail in the Prince de Joinville, a Marseilles packet, land at Gibraltar, and go to Malta on a steamer, thence pass by Palermo &c to Naples and so back to Havre, avoiding the winter merely. Hamilton Wilkes will probably take their house. I have just left them, and dine with them to-morrow.

My business here will soon be finished. One of the Whites is absent, or I might leave this Thursday evening. It is possible I shall leave Friday. I have sold Chainbearer, but expect to return to town next month for a few days.

Tell Dick as follows. I have not yet seen Col. Bankhead,[2] but shall see him to-morrow. Tiffany has been at him, wishing to know what he has to say against him, to which Bankhead answered nothing! If all his questions are as pertinent as this, he will not effect much. I saw D[avid] White to-day, and he is evidently better disposed to communicate than at first. I shall see him to-morrow, company interfering this morning. Bankhead wishes to see me, I hear. I have also a little scent from Dr. Hugh Smith,[3] which may lead to some thing. I shall attend to the loan.

Good luck threw Dr. [Leverett] Bush in my way, yesterday. He thinks he has T[iffany']s letters and has promised to send them to me by mail. His story is this. T[iffany] was to give him half his salary for the time he officiated. He officiated about four months, and was paid $50 by vestry, and $9 by John Tiffany, $5 in cash and $4 in books. He wrote to T[iffany] for the balance, and got an answer saying that he (T[iffany]) *thought he had been paid by the vestry*. The Dr. wrote explaining, and never got any answer. Supposing T[iffany] did not mean to pay him without a controversy, he had said no more about the matter. The Dr. is better, and evidently much improved. In his answer T[iffany] said he had no money. But, it must be remembered that he took all the salary himself, and if he supposed the vestry had paid the Dr., it infers a right in the vestry so to do. The reason he was not paid, was the fact that T[iffany] had left more demands on his salary than could be met. Now that salary was paid because the services were performed, and the man who performed them got only half his wages. The Dr. actually paid Mr. Griswold [4] $6 for officiating for him, and sent Mr. Burnham [5] over at considerable expense &c. He felt bound to perform his part of the contract, and did perform it. I think the letters may show something.

Edwin Spafard refuses to give a copy of the letter,[6] and is evidently in Tiffany's interest. No matter – White and others make us strong on the material point, and I remember enough of the letter to enable us to plead. I have Spafard's letter to me,[7] too, to show his animus.

I have seen all the journals, 1836 & 37 excepted, that tell any thing. In 1835 there were 68 communicants — In 1838, 88. These 88 hold out until 1844; when they become 89! It is very evident he was afraid to go higher than ⟨184?⟩ 88, and he would not go lower. He never had 75 in his life, at any one time. I think it evident he got his communicants in this wise. Until 1835, he was a missionary, and he reported *all* his communicants — Westford, Cherry Valley &c. When he dropped these parishes, and other clergymen took them, he held on to the communicants. There are many material points connected with these reports. I think Dick had better get 1836 & 37 through Mr. [Alfred B.] Beach — his brother having them. Dick himself ought to have 1837 or 1836, he and I being delegates at Utica together. Perhaps I have them. I shall do all that can be done here.

I shall attend to the shawl. The other things, Mrs. [Peyser?] excepted are bought. I have a letter from Paul, who is [in] want of a little money, which I shall send him from this place.

There is a report in town the Great Britain has been ashore off Nantucket, and some apprehensions are felt on her account. She is like to prove a failure I fear.[8]

The opinion here is that the Bishop's party has lost ground by the convention. I think he will give up ere long. [Samuel] Seabury's crowing recoils on himself.[9] Were the thing to be done over again, we should get the parishes. As it was, we got them on the two last votes, though we lost more than they did. My respect for the clergy, as a body, is entirely gone. I do not believe they are as fair, or as much to be relied on, in a matter of principle, as most educated laymen, with or without religion. Their influence in this diocese is weakened for years. With me, they never can stand where they did.

I shall leave this letter open until to-morrow noon, it being now bed time. You will be surprised to learn that Miles [Wallingford] has not sold as well as Satanstoe. I have several hundred of the first edition of Miles on hand, with little prospect of ever selling them for as much as they cost to make.

Mrs. [John Stuart?] Skinner is here, and I shall go and see her this morning. I am finishing this letter before I go out, and consequently have nothing new to say. I shall not write again, unless detained beyond Saturday, which I do not at all expect. I *may* be home Saturday, but probably not. My speech in convention appears to have made some impression, as every body who heard it speaks to me of it. The report in Churchman is absurd.[10]

Yours most tenderly
J. F. C.

ADDRESSED: Mrs. Fenimore Cooper | Cooperstown | New York POSTMARKED: NEW-YORK | [13?] | OCT | 10 cts. NE[W-YORK] | 15 | OCT | 5 [cts.]
MANUSCRIPT: Cooper Collection, Yale University Library.

1. Richard Cooper's letter, dated Cooperstown, 12 October 1845, addressed to Cooper at the Globe Hotel, New York, related mainly to their efforts to collect evidence for *Tiffany* v. *Cooper*. Richard urged his uncle to obtain more explicit testimony, if possible, concerning Tiffany's debt to the estate of David White's father and concerning any expressed intention by Tiffany prior to his departure for Washington of obtaining a chaplaincy at Governor's Island. (MS: YCAL.) Mrs. Cooper's letter, like most of her letters to her husband, was presumably destroyed.

2. Tiffany had applied to Colonel James Bankhead (1783–1856), commander of the military installation of Governor's Island, for the post of chaplain (*ACAB*).

3. The Reverend Hugh Smith (1795?–1849, Columbia 1813), rector of St. Peter's Church, New York City (*CUOA*; *The* [New York] *Evening Post*, 26 March 1849).

4. Probably Asa Griswold, Deacon, a missionary at Harpersville and Windsor in Broome County in 1843 (*Journal of the Seventh Annual Convention of the Diocese of Western New-York* . . . [Utica, New York: printed for the Convention, 1844], 4).

5. Probably the Reverend Richard F. Burnham, from the Diocese of Pennsylvania, who in 1843 assumed charge of the missionary stations of Guilford and Mount Upton in Chenango County (*Journal of the Seventh Annual Convention of the Diocese of Western New-York*, 3).

6. Spafard's letter to Tiffany, dated Cooperstown, 8 July 1844, acquainting him with the charges circulating against him and urging him either to instigate a public investigation to prove his innocence or to admit his guilt privately to Cooper and seek an accommodation (MS copy: YCAL).

7. Unlocated.

8. The S.S. *Great Britain*, a huge iron vessel of 3270 tons introduced by the Great Western Steamship Company in 1845 and equipped with a screw propeller driven by "the most modern, powerful and economical steam engines," was wrecked on the Irish coast in 1846 and piled on the rocks for eleven months. She was eventually repaired and employed in the Australian service. (William Armstrong Fairburn, *Merchant Sail* [Center Lovell, Maine: Fairburn Marine Educational Foundation, Inc., 1945–1955], II, 1324.)

9. Seabury seems to have made no speeches at the convention, but he labored on Bishop Onderdonk's behalf as editor of *The Churchman*.

10. *The Churchman* of 11 October 1845 contained a brief, inaccurate digest of Cooper's speech of 29 September 1845.

832. *To George Bancroft*

New York. Oct. 16th 1845

My Dear Sir,

The Count Holinski, a Polish Gentleman who has brought a letter to me from a much esteemed friend in Paris, and whose acquaintance will be the best recommendation I can give him, desires to be introduced to you.[1] In recommending M. Holinski to your kindness, I am persuaded you will find a sufficient gratification in his society, to more than justify the liberty I am taking.

May I ask that you will place M. Holinski in the way of seeing the President, and some of the other gentlemen of the capital, who will naturally suggest themselves to your mind.

Beli[e]ve me very t[r]uly | Yours
J. Fenimore Cooper

Geo. Bancroft Esquire | Washington

ADDRESSED: Geo Bancroft Esquire | Washington ENDORSED: J. Fennimore Cooper | N Y. Oct 1845 | introducing Count Holinski
MANUSCRIPT: Massachusetts Historical Society.

1. Count Alexander John Joachim de Holynski or Holinski (c. 1814–1887) brought a letter of introduction dated Paris, 5 June 1845, and two books from Captain J. Tanski, a Polish refugee whom the Coopers met and befriended in Paris in 1831. In New York on 14 October 1845, Holinski wrote to inform the novelist of his errand, express a desire to meet a writer as celebrated in Poland as in the United States, and request an interview. Himself a traveler and author, eventually a United States citizen, Holinski published: *Coup d'Oeil sur les Asturies* (Paris, 1843), *La California et les Routes Interocéaniques* (Brussels, 1853), and *L'Équateur Scenes de la Vie Sud-Américaine* (Paris, 1861). (MSS: YCAL; The Reverend Francis Bolek, ed., *Who's Who in Polish America* [New York: Harbinger House, 1943].)

833. *To Paul Fenimore Cooper*

New York. Oct. 16th 1845

My Dear Boy,

I have never supposed that you were in the least pulmonary.[1] You have no indication of any such disease, though your constitution is not strong enough to allow of trifling. Temperance in all things, and early rising, with exercise, are all you require.

I shall go home to-morrow or next day. There is no good report of my speech, though that of the Express was much the best.[2] I said very little, however, and spoke mainly to one point.

I enclose a note, and shall remit to you again from Cooperstown. Contract no debts, but write me frankly when you want money, while economy is not only a virtue, but, in our case, a duty. We should never forget your sisters.

We are strong in our facts, in the slander case, and shall probably be stronger. My last letter from home was of the 14th, when all were well.

Adieu

P. Fenimore Cooper Esquire J. Fenimore Cooper

ADDRESSED: Paul Fenimore Cooper Esquire | Cambridge | Massachusetts POSTMARKED: NEW-YORK | 16 | OCT | 5 cts.
MANUSCRIPT: Cooper Collection, Yale University Library.

1. The letter to which Cooper replied is unlocated.
2. See Cooper to Paul Fenimore Cooper, 5 October 1845.

834. *To John Fagan*

New-York. Oct 17th 1845

Dear Sir,

After all I came off without the Title pages of Chainbearer and Elinor. As I have given an order to Burgess and Stringer to recieve the plates of the first, it may be out of your power to send them to me, but I wish you to do so if you can, and to send the Title page of Elinor also. Just enclose them [in] a letter to my address at Cooperstown.[1]

[Cowperthwaite][2] did not send me their account [*of the abridged* History of the Navy]. If you can get that, I wish it forwarded also.[3] I beg there may be no delay with the Titles as I have not yet entered the Copy Rights —

Yours &c
J. Fenimore Cooper

Mr. John Fagan | Philadelphia

ADDRESSED: Mr. John Fagan | Stereotyper | Philadelphia POSTMARKED: NEW-YORK | 17 | OCT | 5 cts.
MANUSCRIPT: Slack Collection, Marietta College Library.

1. Fagan acknowledged Cooper's letter and forwarded the title pages on 18 October (MS: YCAL).
2. Cooper wrote "Cowpertwhaite."
3. "I asked Thos., Cowperthwait[e], & Co. for an account; and they desire me to say that they have printed up the full number (3000) of their contract, and have on hand unsold about 650. They assure me, that they make every exertion to push its sale, and supply the Trade Sales liberally.

"I have been requested by a firm here (who desire their name not to be mentioned,) to ask you what price you would take for the Stereotype Plates (*including your Copy-Right*) of this Naval History — that is, what you would sell it to *me* for, I transferring it to them." (MS: Fagan to Cooper, 18 October 1845, YCAL.)

835. *To Curtis Guild, Jr.*

Hall, Cooperstown. Oct. 20th 1845

Sir,

Your letter, *postage paid*,[1] would have been promptly answered, but I was in town, at the time it arrived. I only got home last evening, and you will see that I now lose no time in complying with your request. In addition to the autograph I will tell you a story.

A year or two since, a letter arrived at this place — I am sorry to say it came from Boston, — charged '37½ postage. The double charge was owing to the fact that the letter had first been sent to New York, and thence to this place. The writer, unlike Mr. Curtis Guild Junr, had *not* paid the postage.[2] As I thought the omission a little pointed, I determined to take no notice of the application. But, the next month, came letter the second, viâ New York, and away went another three shillings in postage. This new assault compelled me to strike my colours, lest what was then only six shillings might soon get to be twelve.

I remain, Sir,

Your perfectly satisfied friend

Mr. Curtis Guild Jr J— Fenimore Cooper

MANUSCRIPT: Massachusetts Historical Society.

Cooper's letter is mounted in a specially-bound, interleaved copy of James T. Field's *Yesterdays with Authors*, III, 305.

After his apprenticeship as a shipping clerk, Guild (1827–1911) became a journalist and newspaper publisher, achieving reputation as manager and editor-in-chief of the Boston *Commercial Bulletin*, which he controlled from 1859 to 1898. A well-known Boston author, bibliophile, and antiquarian, he was the father of Governor Curtis Guild of Massachusetts. (*DAB*.)

1. Guild wrote Cooper from Boston on 30 September 1845 to request an autograph, stating, in part: "I have read all your novels and should like to gaze upon the signature of the writer. I have *unlike autograph seekers paid my postage*. I count on this as one thing in my favor." (MS: YCAL.)

2. The culprit was J. G. Jarvis, Jr., whose two letters were dated Boston, 11 July and 4 August 1842. See Cooper to Jarvis, 7 August 1842.

836. *To Paul Fenimore Cooper*

Hall, Cooperstown, Oct. 22d 1845

My dear boy,

Your letter has naturally alarmed me. I know the influence of the weather, and such weather as is to be found at Boston, too well, not to see that you may have written under its effects on your nerves, but I can hardly suppose you would say so much without some cause. I attach great importance to the opinion of intelligent physicians, who use the newly invented instrument, in pulmonary cases — If three such men have examined you, and unite in saying your lungs are sound, the symptoms must be favourable. Disease can not have proceeded so far as to produce any material affection. This is the time to treat it, and the climate of Boston is a very bad one for a person so situated. I wish you, therefore, to write me distinctly what your symptoms are. And *all* of them. The mere taste in the mouth, of which you speak, is far more likely to come from the stomach, or even the head, than from the lungs. It seems the physicians could make nothing of ⟨the⟩ it. Have you fever, night sweats, stricture of the breast, or any other decided symptom? I should think not, or your physicians would have thought either of them worthy of notice. Write *me* distinctly; not in general terms, at once, on this subject, and leave Cambridge at once, if you entertain any serious doubts, and find the climate bad. The spring is the w[o]rst time, however, and it may not be necessary to come away this term, unless the reasons are clear.

At all events, take care of yourself. Use exercise in good weather — on horseback if you like it — and avoid exposures. Exercise, dry feet, warm clothing, generous food, no stimulants, and care have carried many a decidedly pulmonary patient through a long life — You have not the least of a pulmonary appearance, though your constitution is not robust — The five or six years that are to follow, are all important to you, in the way of health — Dr. Mutter was a decided case — his parents died of it, and he had the look of a consumptive person — lucid eye, high colour, bright teeth &c &c, yet he has reached forty, and now considers himself as past the Rubicon, on the side of safety. He has done all this by taking care of himself.

Your habit of stooping might well give you symptoms; that should alarm you, without having any real connection with tubercles of the lungs — The attitude often produces a sense of stricture that is relieved by exercise — The real difficulty of breathing is best ascertained by exercise and running, which relieves one of these sensations while it heightens the truly bad one. Your cousin William first betrayed to me the feebleness of his lungs in ascending Mount Vesuvius — He is the only one of my family that I can recall who has died of consumption. This is a great deal in your favour. Then William had the appearance of a poitrinaire, in eyes,[1] teeth, colour, whereas you are just the reverse — Nevertheless, the disease may attack any one, but rarely, unless as the consequence of exposure, except in decided cases, of which I do not believe you to be one.

I enclose a Boston note for $10, and will continue so to do, from time to time, to keep you supplied. I leave your sisters to finish the letter.

J. F— C.

ADDRESSED: [*not in Cooper's hand*] Paul Fenimore Cooper | Cambridge | *Mass*: POSTMARKED: COOPERSTOWN N.Y. | OCT | 22 Unpaid | 5 STAMPED: PAID

MANUSCRIPT: Paul Fenimore Cooper, Cooperstown, New York.

The holograph contains a note from Mrs. Cooper thanking Paul for his disclosure of his symptoms and suggesting that his difficulties were the result of overexertion or a stomach upset. It also contains affectionate notes from Paul's sisters consoling him and offering good advice.

1. Comma supplied.

837. *To Paul Fenimore Cooper*

Hall, Cooperstown, Oct 24th 1845

My Dear Son,

Come home at once. I wrote you ⟨yester⟩ day before yesterday to this effect, but now write again lest you should hesitate. Do not go by New York, unless for your own amusement, and the weather be good. Stay a day or two in New York if you think proper, but do not trouble yourself with consulting so many physicians. They will certainly insist your lungs are affected, if you persevere in asking them. The symptoms must determine the point.

Next month, I shall go down, when you can accompany me, and we will decide where you shall winter. Perhaps it may be well to send you to sea, somewhere. Every thing depends on checking such a disease, if it really exist, at once. But come home. You must have plenty of money, since your pledged money will be principally returned to you.

[*The remainder of the letter has been cut away.*]

ADDRESSED: Paul Fenimore Cooper Esquire | Cambridge | Massachusetts [*readdressed in another hand:*] Cooperstown — | Otsego Co | N Y POSTMARKED: COOPERSTOWN N.Y. | OCT | 25 CAMBRIDGE Ms. | OCT | 28 [*The postage totaled at 10¢, is indicated, once in script and once by stamp, as 5¢ each way.*]
MANUSCRIPT: Cooper Collection, Yale University Library.

838. *To Ephraim Ward Bond*

Hall, Cooperstown, Oct 30th 1845

Sir,

It will be entirely out of my power to deliver the lectures that you name,[1] all or one, during the ensuing winter. I did promise to deliver one lecture in Boston, and another in Salem, in the event of my visiting your portion of the country next winter, but, my son having been compelled to quit the Law School of Cambridge, on account of his health, it is almost certain I shall not go into that part of Massachusetts at all. My object would have been to see him, but it is now more probable that I may accompany him south, than that he will return to Cambridge. You will therefore see that it would be improper for me to make engagements there is little likelihood of my ever being able to meet.

I am, Sir, | Your Obe. Ser.
J. Fenimore Cooper

[*addressee's name clipped*]

MANUSCRIPT: The City Library Association, Springfield, Massachusetts.

Bond (1821–1891, Amherst 1841, LL.B. Harvard 1845), a lawyer who became vice-president and then president (1867–1886) of the Massachusetts Mutual Life Insurance Company and president of the Springfield Five Cent Savings Bank, was an officer and guiding spirit of the Young Men's Institute of Springfield. Founded in 1843 for the purpose of "moral, intellectual and social improvement," the Institute numbered about 300 members in 1845, maintained a small library, and sponsored a lecture series. (R. S. Fletcher, M. O. Young, W. J. Newlin, *Amherst College. Biographical Record of the Graduates and Non-Graduates* [Amherst, Massachusetts: Trustees of Amherst College, 1939], 56; *The Springfield Almanac, Directory, and Business Advertiser, for 1845* [Springfield, Massachusetts: V. W. Skiff, 1845], 43.)

1. Bond wrote from Springfield on 27 October requesting Cooper to address the lyceums at the nearby villages of Cabotville and Chicopee Falls and the Young Men's Institute of Springfield on the evenings of 23, 24, and 25 December 1845. If the time suggested were inconvenient, Bond invited the novelist to choose another week before 1 February 1846 or, if his engagements permitted him only one evening, to address only the Institute. (MS: YCAL.)

839. *To Richard Henry Dana*

Hall, Cooperstown, Oct 30th 1845

My Dear Sir,

I was on the point of writing to thank you for the politeness manifested to my son, and at his suggestion, when I got your letter last night.[1] Paul is now at home, and in better health than I had hoped for. Six months of idleness and travelling will quite restore him, I think, but I question if he will so soon dare to encounter your climate, which *makes* robust people, if you will begin in it, ab origine, but plays the deuce with us delicate mountaineers, who live twelve hundred feet above that ocean in which you bathe.

I am in a little embarrassment as respects ⟨to⟩ an engagement made to lecture the coming winter before The Mercantile Library Association of Boston. I intend to disburthen my mind to you, on the subject, and ask a little advice. The facts are these: — An application was made to me by a Mr. Whiston of Boston, who has an uncle resident in this village,[2] in visiting whom he had ascertained that I had delivered certain extempore lectures on points of Naval History, among ourselves, which it doubtless struck him would be equally well recieved in Boston, as they had been by my own neighbours. I answered that writing a lecture would be out of the question, but, as I intended to visit my son in the course of the winter, if the association would accept an extempore address on the Battle of Plattsburg Bay, or the Forty days before Tripoli, or the Battle of Lake Erie, I might be able to give it one. Now, I sent to Tappan & [Dennet] [3] of Boston, two years since, several hundred copies of my answers to various assaults, that had been made on me, by Messrs Burgess, Mackenzie, Duer &c, in which I think that triumviri is pretty effectually used up. Mr. Mackenzie has affected to answer me,[4] it is true, but he has carefully avoided all the graver points, and has dealt with *facts* in a way that will irretrievably disgrace him, when his mistatements shall be exposed. But the merits are of no moment in the case I am putting. I had been the assailed party in the controversy about Lake Erie, had been rudely and publicly attacked, and had a moral right to be heard in answer. My pamphlet contained that answer, and was offered to the public of Boston, as it had been elsewhere. Just before he quitted Boston, my son applied at Tappan's to learn the fate of the pamphlet. He was told, and a little coarsely I should judge by his account, that not a copy had been sold; that the people of Boston had made up their minds on the merits of the matter in discussion, and that they did not wish to read any thing about it.

To be frank with you, I have no wish to lecture before such a community, if this statement be true. There is not a man in Boston who has the smallest idea of the merits of the Lake Erie controversy, unless he has read that pamphlet, for it is the only publication that contains an approach to the truth, unless my own life of Perry and Jarvis' Life of Elliott [5] be excepted. But, let which side be right, or which wrong, I have a claim to be heard, and as this statement makes out things, I am not considered even worthy of a hearing. Is this – *can* this be the condition of public opinion in Boston, on any question? Write me frankly, I beg of you, in reply.[6] I have been so long accustomed to be treated with injustice, have got to be so familiar with ill treatment from my own countrymen, that they can no longer hurt my feelings. The utter disregard of fact that is exhibited in all public statements in this country, renders its opinions so valueless that it would be altogether contemptible but for its power to injure. This is nearly all that remains to public opinion in this country, and it is a power that is far oftener exercised against the deserving than against the undeserving.

At all events, you will see I can have no wish *to appear* to court the attention of a community that treats me as Messrs Tappan has represented. Now, that my son has quitted Cambridge, probably never to return there, I could only go to Boston at a sacrifice of time and money, and this lessens the inducement to stand up and talk to people who have made up their minds to think I am dealing in fiction when I profess to deal with fact. I have often been told your people are very parish-like in their notions but this is going much farther than I could concieve possible.

As for my son, he would very gladly have cultivated your acquaintance, but his health required the sacrifice he has made, and I believe he was quite right. He thinks well of the school, and regrets being obliged to leave it. He knew no one, and, being for the first time in his life, thrown entirely among strangers, I make no doubt he viewed his case more on the dark side than was necessary. Still he was quite right to come home, and I shall take him off of Kent & Blackstone, for a few months.

What has become of your chap? [7] I think I see him backing hides at Monterey, at this moment — His back might have suffered more from a contact with hides, while his head appears to have escaped. I do not know whether the compliment is to me, or to himself, but many persons asked me if I had not written his book, when it first appeared.

With much regard | Yours

R. H. Dana Esquire J. Fenimore Cooper

ADDRESSED: Richard H. Dana Esquire | Boston | Massachusetts POSTMARKED: COOPERSTOWN N.Y. | NOV | 1 ENDORSED: J. Fenimore Cooper, | Oct 30/45 — Ans. | Nov[embe]r 10th —

MANUSCRIPT: Clifton Waller Barrett Collection of American Literature, University of Virginia.

1. Dana's letter of 25 October. An earlier letter from Cooper to Dana, misaddressed to Cambridge, had been retrieved by the novelist's son from the Cambridge post office and presumably destroyed because, Paul Fenimore Cooper explained to Dana, "it simply related to a matter which had been adjusted." Dana had been prevented from entertaining Paul in his home by absences from Boston and by the redecorating of his house, but he visited Paul in his room shortly before Paul left Cambridge. (*Correspondence*, II, 555–56; MS: YCAL.)

2. Francis G. Whiston, a Boston clerk and a member of the Boston Mercantile Library Association, apparently made the application while visiting the Reverend O. Whiston (1804–1881), a Universalist minister in Cooperstown. (Mrs. C. L. F. Skinner, ed., *The Universalist Register* . . . [Boston: Universalist Publishing House, 1882], 91–92. This publication was an annual pamphlet.)

3. Cooper wrote "Bennett." Charles Tappan and Charles F. Dennet, booksellers, 114 Washington Street (*Stimpson's Boston Directory* . . . [Boston: Charles Stimpson, 1844]).

4. See Cooper to Shubrick, 27 October 1844.

5. Russell Jarvis (1791–1853, Dartmouth 1810), an editorial writer for the Philadelphia *Public Ledger* who lived in New York, was the author of the anonymously published *Biographical Notice of Com. Jesse D. Elliott; Containing a Review of the Controversy between Him and the Late Commodore Perry; and a History of the Figure-head of the U. S. Frigate Constitution* (1835), an important source for Cooper's writings on the Battle of Lake Erie (*ACAB*).

6. Replying on 10 November, Dana advised another subject. Quite aside from the merits of the controversy, he argued, Perry's great popularity and Elliott's exceeding unpopularity in New England made the Battle of Lake Erie too inflammatory a topic. Dana thought that the Bostonians held "very slight," if any, ill feeling toward Cooper and "that should you come here & lecture on any subject upon which you & they can meet upon common ground, you will be received with every attention, & be most gladly listened to." (*Correspondence*, II, 556–58; MS: PFC.)

7. Richard Henry Dana, Jr., the father wrote on 10 November, "is doing well

in the Law. He has a good constitution, though not the Boreas face, & timber-hard arm that he brought home from sea. He is much confined to business, & exercises too little. I warn him, but it does no good." (*Correspondence*, II, 559; MS: PFC.)

840. *To Carey and Hart*

Hall, Cooperstown, Nov. 1. /45

Dear Sir,

I had mailed Perry and Paul Jones before recieving your letter.[1] They are both corrected and a little enlarged, and it will be necessary for me to see proofs. I shall be in Philadelphia in about three weeks, and in New York in two, so you can govern your movements accordingly. The other numbers shall be sent in a day, or two, though you can print Dale & Woolsey, if you see fit from Graham. They will contain no changes of moment.

As for Old Ironsides, it will be impossible for me to do justice to the subject I find, without going to Washington. You must give me time, for your own sake – Can we not fill a second volume without it, and put it in a third? [2] But we shall see each other so soon it is not worth while to discuss by letters.

My son has been obliged to quit Cambridge on account of his health, and the uneasiness and diversion from my ordinary pursuits, has occasioned me some loss of time. I have also had my plea to prepare in the case of my priest, and must say if you[r] rabbis give as much occupation to an honest man, god help you.

Yours truly

Carey & Hart. J. Fenimore Cooper

If your proofs be ready a forthnight hence, or ten days hence, send them to me at the "Globe Hotel, New York" – [3]

ADDRESSED: Carey & Hart | Booksellers | Philadelphia POSTMARKED: COOPERSTOWN N.Y. | NOV | [*illegible*] STAMPED: 10 ENDORSED: A. 11. 6
MANUSCRIPT: Boston Public Library.

1. Unlocated. The biographies mentioned in this paragraph were included in the second volume of *Lives of Distinguished American Naval Officers.*

2. *Lives of Distinguished American Naval Officers* was extended only to two volumes, and "Old Ironsides" was published posthumously. See Cooper to Carey and Hart, 17 September 1845.

3. Volume I of *Lives of Distinguished American Naval Officers* appears to have been published in March 1846, Volume II in May 1846 (Blanck, *Bibliography of American Literature,* II, 298).

841. *To Mrs. Cooper*

Globe Tuesday, afternoon, Nov. 18th 45

Dearest,

I left Paul with Ned [Edward F. De Lancey], who was at the Cars to meet us. As the weather is fine, I suppose the boys will have a comfortable day of it. Young Johnson [1] is in the house, from Utica, and hopes to catch Paul to-morrow before he leaves Albany for New Haven. Paul is to join me here, on Thursday, or Friday—Thursday was agreed on, but he can not come until Friday, if he remain a day at New Haven, which was the plan on parting.

I have been all day hunting for [Dr. John Wakefield] Francis and the other doctors, without seeing them. I have written to Francis, however, and to-morrow will make thorough stitch.

Elinor is not published, but will be in a day or two.[2] The notice spoken of must refer to a bookseller's copy. Hart was on, a few days since, and exchanged 500 copies with Burgess & Stringer, as against my book; which makes 500 sold, at any rate. If 3000 sell, the author gets another $100. Hart told Stringer it was a good book, and beautifully written. So far, well. But finis coronat opus.

Chainbearer will be published early next week, and not before.[3]

It is may weather, here; positively pleasant without fire. Last night was one of the pleasantest I ever passed on the river. My berth was wide, and [I] slept it out until eight o'clock, the first time I ever did so. Craft the Hendrick Hudson, a boat as much superior to any thing you ever saw, as the best boat you ever saw was superior to the [second?] boat on the river. Every way a noble vessel, and as swift as a balloon.

With tenderest love, | Yours

Mrs. F— C. J— F— C.

Alas! How I miss the [Henry] Laights.

ADDRESSED: Mrs. Fenimore Cooper | Cooperstown | N. Y. POSTMARKED: TROY N.Y. | NOV | 19 STAMPED: STEAM

MANUSCRIPT: Cooper Collection, Yale University Library. PUBLISHED, IN PART: *Correspondence*, II, 559–60.

1. Charles Adams Johnson (1826–1891, Geneva [Hobart] n.g.), classmate of Paul Fenimore Cooper at Geneva College and son of Alexander B. Johnson, president of the Ontario Branch Bank in Utica, New York. A law student in Utica in

1845, young Johnson became a professional army officer. (*Hobart College: General Catalogue,* 66.)

2. Bentley published Susan Fenimore Cooper's *Elinor Wyllys* in London on or about 1 December, but Carey and Hart apparently delayed publication until late December or early January (Blanck, *Bibliography of American Literature,* II, 311).

3. Burgess, Stringer and Co. evidently published *The Chainbearer* on 21 or 22 November (see the following letter), and Bentley on 19 November (Spiller and Blackburn, *Bibliography,* 141).

842. *To Mrs. Cooper*

Globe. Friday 21st Nov. 1845

Dearest,

Paul came on last night, looking very well, and not much tired. He passed one day with Ned, and another in New Haven. To day, after attending to a little business in his new character of Trustee,[1] he went off with Jim [Thomas James De Lancey, Jr.], and, though it is now dark, I have not seen him since. There will be about $250 to recieve on your account, which will furnish him with the ways and means for his excursion. $140 of this money, however, must come from the Salem farm, and I shall send him and Jim into West-Chester, in quest of it, next week, if the weather continue good. Thus far, it has been excellent, and I am now writing without a fire.

Stevens[2] declines purchasing, on account of wanting money. I have written to Mr. Lenox[3] on the subject, and shall probably get his answer next week early. He is out of town just now. Neither book is yet published, though Chainbearer will appear to-morrow. No news here of Elinor [*Elinor Wyllys*]. She will appear next week I suppose, though Hart may keep her back a few days on account of the other book.

I do not think I shall go to Washington. Paul can do my business there, and that will save me the trouble and the expense.

I cannot say I have done much business as yet, but next week I shall be prompt. The great difficulty is to get people together, in this bustling, rambling town.

Last night I saw [Dr. Edward] Delafield. He told me that he did not regard Paul's symptoms as at all alarming, and by no means as decided even as far as they went. He thought the young man nervous and alarmed about himself, but thought plenty of exercise in the open air, with such food as he best digested and which sat lightest on his stomach, would set him up. Cigars he concieved might have done all the mischief, coupled with inactivity.

Bishop McCoskry is here. They say he is a bishop's man and high church.[4] He is not well looked upon by the opposition, I find. He told me he saw your brother at Rochester, where he had just been confirming. That he was well, seemed as well as ever, and thought himself well. Ned told Paul that his father was as well as ever.

We are waiting here for John C. Jay to come down with his father's accounts, in order to settle with Paul, as Trustee. I never was better. With tenderest love

Yours

J. F. C.

Chainbearer published. Elinor not.

ADDRESSED: Mrs. Fenimore Cooper | Cooperstown | N — York POSTMARKED: NEW-YORK | 22 | NOV | 5 cts.

MANUSCRIPT: Cooper Collection, Yale University Library.

1. Paul Fenimore Cooper succeeded Peter Augustus Jay as trustee of the estate left to Mrs. Cooper and her children under the will of John Peter De Lancey. William Jay's son John and Peter A. Jay's son John Clarkson assisted in this transfer of the trusteeship.

2. Possibly John Austin Stevens (1795–1874, Yale 1813), president of the New York Bank of Commerce, although Cooper may have been referring to one of several other persons of that name (*DAB*). He eventually sold Greenough's *Chanting Cherubs* (MS: A. Storrs to Cooper, New York, 3 August 1848, YCAL) to a Mrs. Stevens, whose identity is otherwise uncertain.

3. James Lenox (1800–1880, Columbia 1818), the financier, book collector, and philanthropist (*DAB*).

4. Samuel Allen McCoskry (1804–1886, Dickinson 1825), Protestant Episcopal bishop of Michigan from 1836 to 1878, had been ordained deacon and priest in 1833 by Bishop Henry U. Onderdonk. Like the Onderdonk brothers, he was formally relieved of his ecclesiastical duties when charges of moral misconduct became public knowledge. (*ACAB*.)

843. *To Mrs. Cooper*

Head's, Nov. 26th 1845

Dearest,

I got here yesterday, having left Paul at the Globe. He wished to remain there a few days longer, on account of Jim [Thomas James De Lancey, Jr.], John Nelson and his other acquaintances. I can see no change in him, though he says he feels better. The bracing weather may do that, however, of itself. He certainly seems no worse, and his cough is less in cold bracing weather, than in any other; though it is very trifling at any time. He is careful of his throat, and does pretty well as to diet.

My book is published, but Elinor is not. Hart told me that Pocket Handkerchief was ascribed to one of my daughters, and this book to the same person. I gave the prescribed answer, and carried matters off well. As yet, no opinion has been given of the book, for no one has read it. Not even Hart. It must stand, or fall, on its own merits. Hart has sold 1000 copies to two dealers, in advance. Burgess had sold about 2500 of Chainbearer. But the sale af all such books, if copy right, is heavy.

I have not had a syllable from home. I trust you have written, and that I shall hear to day. Paul has recieved the $116 due you for Fire dividends, and is now acting as trustee. He was a little awkward in transacting business, at first, but is so quick as readily to comprehend a thing. He does not go into West-chester, on account of the weather, but employs John Jay to collect the rent, which will be only $87.50, instead of $127, as I wrote you before.

As yet, I have seen no one, though I learn that the fair cleared $9500. On the 4th, there will be a great ball of all Philadelphia,[1] and I shall try to get Paul to it, that he may see a little of the world. As yet, he has visited no one. He takes very good care of himself in going into the air.

I have nothing further to say, except to send my tenderest love to all.

Yours as ever
J. F. C.

ADDRESSED: Mrs. Fenimore Cooper | Cooperstown | New York POSTMARKED: PHILADELPHIA Pa. | NOV | 26 STAMPED: 5
MANUSCRIPT: Cooper Collection, Yale University Library.

1. The Ladies' Fair for the benefit of the Philadelphia Academy of Fine Arts was followed by a Bazaar Ball on the evening of 4 December 1845.

844. *To Mrs. Cooper*

Head's Sunday, [November] [1] 30th 1845

My Dearest Sue,

Paul did not join me until last evening, overstaying his time one day. He improves in appearance, and says he is decidedly better in feelings. His cough diminishes, as does the pain, and his bowels have now been quite regular for a week. In short, I see no reason for supposing his lungs at all affected. I shall consult Jackson,[2] however, so that we shall have his opinion. I have been reading a short treatise on diseased cravings of the stomach, with a desire for stimulants, particularily tobacco, seasoned food &c, and I think I find Paul in every line. That craving, which is connected with bodily apathy, is at the root of all his maladies. He eats sparingly enough now, and seems disposed to take care of himself. He is amused with what occurs around him.

I supped with old Mr. [John Quincy] Adams and Kit [Christopher] Hughes, at Joe Ingersoll's, last friday. The old man was in good spirits, and well disposed to talk, but also disposed to listen. On the whole, I was pleased with him, though I think he is very wrong headed. I did not name Mrs. de Wint [3] to him.

Shubrick has written me he shall be compelled to be absent at Norfolk, for a week, very soon,[4] and I scarce know whether to go on, or not. I want information, and want to see him. If I go, I cannot be home before the middle of the month. Paul thinks he shall return with me. Home is so much home, that he tires of taverns. Perhaps it may be well for him to make another excursion in March, and pass January and February with us. Cold air has no apparent effect on his feelings, he says.

I wish you would open the New York letters, and write me from whom they are. A letter sent at once, would find me here. Paul brought me your letter of the 25th. As for myself, I am perfectly well, with a good digestion, and I live as usual. My two attacks have probably saved me a bilious fever, of which there have been much this year. Many persons have died of them.

Elliott is here, and in an advanced dropsy, not only of the body and limbs, but of the heart and chest. He cannot survive, I should think, though he seems to think he may. I have seen his wife, and thanked her for the "few little matters." Elliott, himself, believes he is getting better.

[Captain George C.] Read is going to the coast of Africa, and the Mediterranean, with a broad pennant —[5] This is the service for which [William Compton] Bolton was designed, and I fear a reason has induced the secretary to change his mind.

We have had sharp weather, and a light snowstorm. The

1. Elliott medal of Cooper.

11. Lake Otsego, looking north, toward the "Sleeping Lion."

III. Cooper's Chalet Farm, seen from the western shore of Lake Otsego.

IV. Christ Church, Cooperstown, from an old photograph.

streets are now white, and I dare say you have sleighing. I wish Peter [6] spoken to, on the subject of the potatoes; they will freeze unless cared well for. Has he bought any hay, and, if so, at what price?

I was wrong in saying no one has read Elinor [Wyllÿs]. [Abraham] Hart himself has read the last half, and likes it much. He has not published, but has sold in advance 1000 copies in New York, and has printed his last 1000 copies, so as to have a supply on hand, in the event of a demand. I think the other $100 will come. The book may clear $3 or 400, after all, and that is a good deal for these times.

Griswold, to my surprise, is still here, though his name, he tells me, is on a door plate in Savannah or Charleston, I forget which — His wife is with the door plate. How long he will remain here, is more than I can say, though some time, I fancy. It is, altogether, a queer operation.[7]

I have seen no lady but Mary Wilcocks, and my kinswoman Mrs. Vincent,[8] who is a nice little body; handsome and the picture of health, though the mother of a house full of children, and very fine children, too. I shall make a sally with Paul, however, tomorrow, or as soon as the weather will permit.

I can hear nothing of Chainbearer. The papers are mum, as usual, but I know it sells pretty well. They cannot put me down entirely, though they do me infinite harm. A precious set of dishonest knaves are they!

Every body is on the qui vive for the message — Oregon or no Oregon — Peace or war.[9] The reports are a little more peaceable than they have been — As for Mexico, that point is essentially settled. There will be no war with her, and I suspect the difficulties with France are at the bottom of her moderation.

Douw, *the* Van Rensselaer's husband,[10] is staying in the house. He spoke to me of Otsego, and of Cooperstown in particular, without my knowing who he was. Is there not a suit for a divorce pending?

Bishop [Alonzo] Potter is making a little talk, by consenting to lecture before the Mercantile Library Association. The Philadelphians are not used to such scholastic escapades in a prelate. But the episcopal character stands low just now.

Elinor will be published in a few days. I have given the quietus to the Pocket Handkerchief story, by saying firmly that I wrote the tale myself, and would not have allowed my name to be affixed to any thing I had not written. I have spoken to [George R.] Graham about the Autograph,[11] and he has asked for the manuscript to look it over. I shall ask at least, $25 for it, and I think he may take it.

I was sorry to see that Dick was at work at his plea, the last hour, but that would be the fact if we had a year to plead in. I do not know whether I told you that Tiffany paid his physician in New York, $5 — The vast sum that exhausted his funds. He is a precious chap!

I saw Ned [Myers] in New York, grumbling and laughing, as usual. He thinks he has been neglected by the government, and I think so too.

Do not fail to write me immediately, for I was quite uneasy at not hearing from you, for twelve days. Paul I think decidedly improving, and, as for myself I am as ever,

And yours in the bargain,
J. F. C.

Paul is too lazy to write, but sends tenderest love to all.

ADDRESSED: Mrs. Fenimore Cooper | Cooperstown | New York POSTMARKED: PHILADELPHIA Pa. | NOV | 30 STAMPED: ⟨5⟩ 10
MANUSCRIPT: Cooper Collection, Yale University Library. PUBLISHED, IN PART: *Correspondence*, II, 560–62.

1. Cooper wrote "Dec."
2. Dr. Samuel Jackson (1787–1872, M.D. Pennsylvania 1808), a distinguished Philadelphia physician and teacher of medicine, was a founder of the Philadelphia College of Pharmacy, an associate in the Medical Institute of Philadelphia, and a professor at the University of Pennsylvania (*DAB*).
3. See Cooper to A. T. Goodrich, 12 July 1820.
4. Shubrick's letter was dated Washington, 28 November 1845 (MS: YCAL).
5. Read had been appointed to command the African Squadron (Navy *Register* for 1846).
6. Peter Gill, Cooper's farm assistant.
7. On 20 August 1845, Griswold married Charlotte Myers, a wealthy Jewess of 5 Aiken Row, Charleston, South Carolina. Both partners had ambivalent feelings toward the marriage; and, when Griswold found that his bride could be a wife only in name, they separated, continuing briefly to observe outward forms. (Joy Bayless, *Rufus Wilmot Griswold: Poe's Literary Executor* [Nashville, Tennessee: Vanderbilt University Press, 1943], 104–13.)
8. Mrs. Vincent may have been the wife of Frederick Vincent, an attorney and counselor from Norfolk, Virginia, admitted to practice in Philadelphia on 27 Sep-

tember 1845 (John Hill Martin, *Martin's Bench and Bar of Philadelphia . . .* [Philadelphia: Rees Welsh & Co., 1883], 320).

9. President Polk's first Message to Congress, delivered on 2 December 1845.

10. Margaret Van Rensselaer (1819–1897), the oldest surviving daughter of Stephen Van Rensselaer IV, married John de Peyster Douw (b. 1812) in 1837. She divorced Douw and married Wilmot Johnson of Baltimore. (Florence Van Rensselaer, *The Van Rensselaers in Holland and in America,* [New York, 1856], 54–55, 71.)

11. Cooper may have referred to Susan Fenimore Cooper's short story "The Lumley Autograph." See Cooper to G. R. Graham, 14 September 1850.

845. *To Richard Peters*

Mansion House — Dec 2 | 1845

My Dear Sir,

I was not at home when your kind invitation was recieved. "I accept" as Mr. Clay said, "I accept," and I shall endeavour to bring my son with me too. He is shy and not very well, but good company, if not attended with too high living, does him good. It was with great difficulty I got him in, last evening, but he confessed afterwards, he was glad he had complied with my request.

I am about to sit down to Mr. Polk's *lengthiness,*[1] and must wish you good night.

Very truly yours

Richard Peters Esquire — J— Fenimore Cooper

MANUSCRIPT: Peters Papers, The Historical Society of Pennsylvania.

Great-grandnephew of the well-known colonial minister Richard Peters and son of the Richard Peters who was Revolutionary commissioner of war, Cooper's friend Richard Peters (1779–1848) was a lawyer, a legal reporter, and an indefatigable compiler of United States Circuit and Supreme Court records. He married Abigail Willing, daughter of Anne McCall and Thomas Willing in 1804. (*ACAB*; Nellie Peters Black, ed., *Richard Peters, 1810–1889, His Ancestors and Descendants* [Atlanta, Georgia: Foote & Davies Company, 1904], 118.)

1. The President's Message.

846. *To Mrs. Cooper*

Head's, December 3d '45.

Dearest Sue,

We have seen [Dr. Samuel] Jackson this morning. I told him the story, and Paul made his annotations. The chest was then tried. The ⟨right⟩ left lung was pronounced good, on tapping, which is the first experiment. The right the same. Jackson said, after several trials, he could detect no difference, or any defect by that experiment, which I understand is considered proof that disease is not at all advanced, even when it actually exists. The ear was next applied. The left lung was pronounced perfectly good. The right gave a weaker sound, thus showing that the physician knew what he was about. This was without his having been told which lung had been thought suspicious by the two other physicians. But Jackson, who is a prince of physicians, said at once, the difference [in] sound did not denote pulmonary disease. On the contrary, it was opposed to the usual symptoms in such cases. In pulmonary disease, the difference in breathing, or the defect commonly, nay invariably in early stages, was local, almost always on the upper part of the lobe, whereas in Paul's case, it was the whole lung which sounded alike. He said we had double organs, and they frequently differed in powers. A thickening of the [mucous membrane] [1] might produce the difference in the sound he heard, and he did not believe there was any tubercular disease in the case. We were with him a good while, and he appeared quite steady and clear in his opinion. Of his own accord, however, he added that he did not like to decide, or to advise on a single examination, and desired us to come again, which we shall do to-morrow or next day.

Jackson pronounced Paul's disease to be nervous, principally, and said he wanted exercise. He thought a southern climate of no particular importance, and evidently saw that the discomforts of taverns might be more injurious than a little cold weather. *Our* climate, however, he thought might interfere with exercise, but, on the whole attached quite as much importance, I thought, to cheerful company, and occupation of the mind, as to any warmth of climate. He examined the throat, and showed me that it was still inflamed. He advised generous food, meats in particular, but wished first to get rid of the inflammation of the throat. The blood vomited, and all Paul told him of that, he disregarded. Also the pain — He attached no importance to either. He said Paul did not make red blood enough, and that must be remedied. He advised boneset tea, every day, and is to prescribe some tonic for the stomach, if he retain his present opinion after seeing him again.

I am greatly relieved by this opinion, and I can see that Paul is, too, though he seems to hunt for unfavourable symptoms. As for the symptoms, themselves, they continue to improve. The bowels are quite regular, the pulse is better, the appetite stronger, the cough nearly gone, and clearly comes from the throat. I think he looks better in the face.

To-day we both dine with Mr. Peters, where Paul went with me a night or two since. He enjoyed himself, and I am getting him gradually out into the world.

Poor [Benjamin Chew] Wilcocks[2] died last Monday and is to be buried to-morrow. I have heard no particulars.

Elinor is not yet published—Chainbearer I can tell you nothing of. I shall not be home until the middle of the month, and I now think Paul will come with me. He will go to Washington on Friday and rejoin me in about a week. I shall not wait for him, however, unless he return in time.

I can get $600 for a sale of Naval History, but ask a $1000. The price offered is so low, that I do not like to accept it. It is not for copy right, but only for the right to print from my plates, the abridgement for 10 years. I may take it, however, though I now think not.

Paul is desirous of passing the holidays with us, and I rather think will do so. But nothing is yet decided. I shall write as soon as Jackson has seen him a second time.

All sorts of stories are circulated about Wilcocks' estate, which, I make no doubt, will be found to be very respectable in value.

Adieu until next day after to morrow, | Tenderly yours,

J. F. C.

Paul got Charlotte's letter this morning. I have had but one in 16 days.

ADDRESSED: Mrs. Fenimore Cooper | Cooperstown | New York POSTMARKED: PHILADELPHIA Pa. | DEC | 4 STAMPED: 5

MANUSCRIPT: Cooper Collection, Yale University Library.

1. Cooper seems to have written "mucuous membrance."
2. See Cooper to Mrs. Cooper, 10 January 1843.

847. *To Mrs. Cooper*

Head's, Dec. 5th 1845

Dearest Sue,

We have just paid our second visit to Jackson, whose opinion is confirmed and who said the right lung had sensibly improved.

He thinks that the difference between the lobes will disappear entirely, and, if not, that it is not in the least serious. He thinks home, with care not to catch cold, will be better than taverns, or boarding houses, in any climate. In a word, he does not seem to think the climate material. The pain he treats as nervous and common, and evidently thinks the lungs sound. I have now little concern on that head, and Paul, I can see, is much relieved. Hitherto, he has shown an ingenuity in trying to make out the case against himself. He has confessed to me that he was often stupid from excessive smoking, and that sometimes his hand shook like an old mans. Tobacco would have killed him, in a year or two, and he is now suffering under the reaction of ceasing to use the stimulant.

Jackson prescribes boneset made with *cold* water. He thinks that and exercise will set him up. The throat is better, too, but he has given him some ammonia lozenges for the cough. Beyond this, he sees nothing necessary to be done. He has directed Paul to eat generous food, any thing which sets best on his stomach, naming boiled in preference to roasts, chops &c &c, but any thing he can digest. He says he wants generous nourishment. To-day, he found the pulse much better, and so it has been.

I think I can see an improvement in Paul's appearance. His face is filling a little, and I make no doubt he weighs more than he did.

We dined with the Peters' on Wednesday, and Paul took a little wine and ate canvass backs in moderation, with no bad, but rather with a good effect. To-day, he and I dine with Dr. [Robert] Hare, and to-morrow *he* goes to Washington, in company with the two Ingersolls, who came on to attend poor Wilco[c]ks' funeral. We buried him yesterday, in the midst of rain, but caught no colds. I have not heard how he has left his affairs, but I hope comfortably.

Poor Elliott can not last long.[1] I went to see him to-day and found him sensibly weaker. It was plain that his family consider his case desperate. He made some allusions again to his end, and I believe he thinks he has no chance in this world. He looks like an emaciated, white-headed, old man of seventy.

Elinor not yet published. Of Chainbearer, I can tell you

nothing, though Griswold does not think it as interesting as Satanstoe. It has a fault which he pointed out, but it is a more interesting book than Satanstoe. Dus Malbone [*the heroine*] he likes.

I shall quit Philadelphia, in a day or two, and be at home by the 13 or 14th.

Tenderly Yours
J. F. C.

Paul send[s] love.

ADDRESSED: Mrs. Fenimore Cooper | Cooperstown | New York STAMPED: 5 (*The part of the address sheet containing the postmark has been cut away.*)
MANUSCRIPT: Cooper Collection, Yale University Library.

1. Jesse Duncan Elliott died on 10 December 1845.

848. *To Mrs. Cooper*

Globe, New York, Dec — 9th 1845

Dearest,

Although I wrote you so lately, I have thought a letter letting you know I am on my way north will be acceptable — I might leave town to-morrow, if I saw fit, but intend remaining here a day or two, to look at men and things. Paul you know is at Washington, nor do I expect to see him until he reaches home. I shall write him this evening to say he can pass a month at Head's if he see fit, having made an arrangement to keep him there, as long as he may see fit to remain — Nevertheless, I expect to see him at Christmas. I wrote you that Jackson thinks his case not pulmonary, or, rather said so to me, in a private conversation. When I told him you had hereditary asthma, he immediately said that accounted for the peculiarity of the breathing of the right lung, which was *not pulmonary* breathing. I also sent you his opinion on the Pomeroy case. He is an excellent physician, of great experience, and stands as near the head of his profession as a man can, when he has so many able competitors —

Enclosed is a reciept, which I wish you to send to the Bank, in order that [Henry] Scott may use it, if he see fit.

I shall attend to all the commissions. I have two copies of Elinor, but the book is not yet published. I can tell you nothing of Chainbearer, as I have not yet been to the publishers — I only came on this morning, having a fine day, and a good time. I expect to return via New Haven, though it is not absolutely certain.

Two small boxes have just come in with Fanny's name on them. I see Miss Louisa Jay, scratched out on the [paper?] envelopes, from which I infer that they come from that source.

I have also just received a note from Capt — Breese, accompanied by a leaf cutter, made on board his ship the Cumberland, at Tripoli, out of a fragment of the wreck of the Philadelphia frigate — [1] This is a very agreeable remembrancer, and it is really very neatly made —

As yet this is all I have seen. It is not probable I shall write again, as I intend to leave here as early as Saturday, at the latest — possibly on Friday.

I can tell you nothing of the cherubs, or the picture, but doubt eithers selling. I have got a few hundreds by a partial sale of Naval History. Business *may* keep me here into next week, but I do not think it [at] all likely — In that event I shall write again.

Adieu, with tenderest love

J— F— C—

ADDRESSED: Mrs. Fenimore Cooper | Cooperstown | New York POSTMARKED: NEW-YORK | 10 | DEC | 5 cts
MANUSCRIPT: Cooper Collection, Yale University Library.

1. Samuel Livingston Breese commanded the frigate *Cumberland* of the Mediterranean Squadron in 1845. On 31 October 1803, in a memorable episode of the Tripolitan War, the frigate *Philadelphia,* Captain William Bainbridge, was run aground in the harbor near Tripoli and partly destroyed by Tripolitan gunboats. See Cooper's description of the action in *The History of the Navy* (Philadelphia: Lea & Blanchard, 1839), II, 12–19.

849. *To Paul Fenimore Cooper*

Globe. New York, Dec. 9th 1845

My dear boy,

Before I left Philadelphia, I made an arrangement with Messrs Head & Hunt,[1] to enable you to stay there as long as you please, without paying them — leaving that for me to do. Now, on your return, if Jackson advise your remaining, or if you wish to remain a week or a forthnight, for your own amusement do so, laying by cash enough to bring you home. Fifteen dollars would be rather short commons, but twenty will do it genteel[l]y. I could wish you to pass the holidays with us, if you think it prudent, but not otherwise. I do not believe you have pulmonary affection of the lungs, but do not wish to incur any unnecessary risks. Jackson, the instant I mentioned to him that there was hereditary asthma in the family, said that accounted for the peculiarity of the breathing of your right lung, which sounded exactly as such lungs do sound with slight affections. He told me the pain was of no moment whatever, and thought it might proceed from the cold which produced the peculiar breathing. This was in a conversation which took place when I went to consult him about George's case. You will see him of course, when you are in Philadelphia.

If you stay in Philadelphia, you had better call at the [Richard] Peters' and Dr. [Robert] Hares, if you only leave cards. If Gen. [Thomas] Cadwalader call on you, contrive to see him, and if you meet Joe Mil[ler,][2] tell him I tried to find him, but could not having quite forgotten his address, and was not able to discover any one who knew it. If you could see him, by hook or by crook, I should like it. Do not let the Holidays bring you home contrary to your wishes, and I can send you money if necessary. I wish you to be economical, but to benefit by your excursion.

My last letters make all well, and they write there is capital sleighing, which I fancy we shall keep all winter.

Do not fail to write at least twice a week while absent.

Very affectionately your father

Paul Fenimore Cooper Esquir[e]. J. Fenimore Cooper

ADDRESSED: Paul Fenimore Cooper Esquire | Mansion House | Philadelphia POSTMARKED: NEW[-YO]RK | 10 | DEC | 5 cts
MANUSCRIPT: Paul Fenimore Cooper, Cooperstown, New York.

1. William P. Hunt and Joseph Head became associated in the management of the Mansion House, 122 1/2 South Third Street, in 1845 (*McElroy's Philadelphia Directory for 1846* . . . [Philadelphia: Edward C. & John Biddle, 1846]).

2. The bracketed letters overran the margin.

850. *To William P. Jones*

Globe. Dec. 12th 1845

D[ea]r Sir,

The asking price of the Cherubs is $1000, and they are worth the money. I think they will bring that much if properly managed.

I will take $750 cash, however, if the transaction can be closed to-day.[1] I leave town to-morrow morning early, and must leave the affair with Mr. Jenkins,[2] unless it be concluded to-day.

If you accept, a line left at the Globe will find me at 12 o'clock.

Respectfully | yours

Wm. P. Jones Esquire. J. Fenimore Cooper

ADDRESSED: Wm. P. Jones Esquire | Box 625 | Lower Post Office | New York POSTMARKED: NEW-YORK | DEC 12 | 2 cts

MANUSCRIPT: Clifton Waller Barrett Collection of American Literature, University of Virginia.

Jones was listed as a grocer in New York City directories from 1841 to 1849. His establishment in 1845 was at 46 Front Street and his home at 178 Henry Street. He may have been the William Parkinson Jones of Connecticut and New York City mentioned in John H. Jones, *The Jones Family of Long Island* (New York: Tobias A. Wright, 1907), 386, 388.

1. In a letter dated Globe, 12 December 1845, Jones replied that he considered "the arts too 'sacred for traffic'" and would not make an offer for Greenough's *Cherubs.* He nevertheless observed that he had thought of paying $600 since the wings were not perfect and the marble contained obstinate finger marks. Later, on 23 February 1846, he offered 15 shares of a copper stock reputed to be worth $50 a share but assigned no fixed market value. A letter from Amariah Storrs to Cooper, dated 3 August 1848, reported delivery of the statuary to a Mrs. Stephens, who presumably bought it. She may have been the wife of the merchant and yachtsman John Cox Stephens; but the present ownership of the *Cherubs,* if it survived, is unknown. (MSS: YCAL.)

2. Probably Edgar Jenkins, auctioneer, 8 Wall Street (*Doggett's New-York City Directory, for 1845 & 1846* [New York: John Doggett, Jr., 1845]).

851. *To John Walker Brown, for* The Protestant Churchman

Hall, Cooperstown, Dec. 19th, 1845.

Mr. Editor, —

A communication in the last number of your journal, may render it proper for me to take some notice of it.[1] In alluding to that Bishop of the majority, who, in my opinion, ought not to have sat on the trial of Dr. Onderdonk, I did not refer to the Bishop of Ohio. I am aware of no circumstance that should have excluded Dr. McIlvaine from his seat, nor have I ever intended to be so understood. As for any disqualifications growing out of a difference in opinion on theological subjects, I am greatly mistaken if a portion of my remarks did not go directly to say that I could see no propriety in admitting such objections.

If Dr. Onderdonk had his theological or controversial opponents on that Court, he had also his theological or controversial supporters. One would be as liable to objection as the other. I have never thought so ill of any prelate in the Church, as to believe he would acquit or condemn a brother in the pure spirit of party.

I am afraid you have been unnecessarily severe on the editor of The Churchman, in connection with this little matter. He was not the first, by a dozen, to impute my allusion to Dr. McIlvaine. As for the reports of the speeches that appeared from day to day, they were scarcely worthy of notice in any point of view, and for that reason I did not think it necessary to correct this mistake; if, however, I felt disposed to complain of the report of The Churchman, as respects myself, it would not be for imperfectly or confusedly reporting me, or for falling into an error that others had fallen into before it, but for attributing to me not only that which I did not say, but positively the reverse of that which I did say. I am far from ascribing this to design. My own experience has taught me that I am not to expect to be reported accurately, either in public or in private, and I believe few men in this country are. But, the building in which the Convention assembled was so ill adapted to debating, that, for one, I did not hear a fourth of that which gentlemen who sat higher up the Church said. I hope the suggestion will not be thought impertinent, if I venture to add that many think Trinity could not do better than to erect a hall for the meeting of the Convention, and which might be used generally for the purposes of the Church.

Before closing this communication, suffer me to say a word on another subject. The report of the delegates of St. Peter's, Albany, would appear to answer the arguments of those who believe that the legal and just effect of a sentence of suspension, is to vacate a Bishop's Diocesan jurisdiction.[2] I am one of those who believe that such is, and must be, and will be the consequences of a suspension, but I am not willing that the report of the delegates of St. Peter's should be taken as containing any answer to my reasons for so thinking. It will be remembered that one of the resolutions that was finally abandoned, distinctly recognized the principle, that the jurisdiction was not vacated in consequence of the suspension, and it struck me *that* was the resolution on which the question should properly have been debated. Had that resolution been pressed, it was my intention to have spoken on it, when arguments that were at least more consonant with my own views, than those met in the report, would have been offered. I dare say, others could give the same reply to this part of the report of the lay delegates in question.

It is very evident, Sir, that the question of jurisdiction is to be seriously argued before this Diocese. Much has been already said that goes beyond any thing that was urged in Convention, and it is probable that much more will be offered to the consideration of the laity and clergy, previously to the meeting of the next council of the Church. The more the point is discussed, the better it will be understood.

With much respect, yours, &c.,
J. Fenimore Cooper.

SOURCE: *The Protestant Churchman*, 27 December 1845 (The General Theological Seminary).

A native of Schenectady, New York, Brown (Union 1832, General Theological Seminary 1836) edited *The Protestant Churchman*, the organ of Low Church opinion in New York, for a brief period in the mid-1840's. He lived in Astoria, New York, and died at Malta on 9 April 1849. (*The* [New York] *Evening Post*, 19 May 1849; *Union University: Centennial Catalog*, 41.)

1. Introduced by an editorial notation that Cooper had disclaimed any intention of referring to Bishop Charles Pettit McIlvaine (1799–1873, College of New Jersey [Princeton] 1816) in his speech on the convention floor on 29 September and that the editor of *The Churchman* had taken "the unwarrantable liberty" of affixing this interpretation to the speaker's words, the "communication" read:

"Sir, — I have just received the record of the speeches, &c., at the late Convention of the Diocese of New York, and have just read the speech of Mr. Fennimore Cooper. That gentleman spoke of two bishops — who in his opinion, ought not to have sat on the trial of Bishop O[nderdonk], and 'should have been struck off the Court, and in a court of law, might have been challenged as jurors, for cause' — (*p.* 100 *of the Record.*) One of those bishops, the speaker said, was of the six who voted *not guilty*; and he made it perfectly manifest, which of the six he alluded to. The other was of the eleven, on the other side; but Mr. Cooper gave no intimation as to the individual in his mind. It was published, however, in The Churchman, soon after, that he referred to Bishop McIlvaine. Why to him, more than to several others, who, as much as he differed in theological matters, from Bishop O[nderdonk], and had as much taken official ground against his official doings, is not easily to be understood. It has, however, been denied in private ways, that Mr. Cooper referred to Bishop McIlvaine. Were it not for the published declaration of The Churchman to the contrary, there would be no need of asking any questions about it. But as it is, the friends of Bishop McIlvaine, and of the course he has taken in the late troubles and perils of the Church, will be obliged, if you will state in your paper, what you may happen to know, or may be able to learn, as to the correctness of the interpretation put in The Churchman, upon Mr. Cooper's allusion. | Veritas." (*The Protestant Churchman*, 13 December 1845.)

2. Cooper referred to John C. Spencer's pamphlet *Report to the Vestry of St. Peter's Church, Albany, of the Lay Delegates . . . Who Attended the Diocesan Convention . . . at the City of New York . . .* (Albany: Erastus H. Pease, 1845). Spencer maintained that Bishop Onderdonk's suspension amounted to a technical disqualification without producing a vacancy in the diocese. Cooper distinguished between Onderdonk's status as bishop and as diocesan, arguing that the suspension terminated the bishop's contract as diocesan without destroying his status as bishop. See Cooper's letter (no. 860) to an Unidentified Editor, November — December 1845?.

852. *To Luther Tucker, for* The Cultivator

Hall, Cooperstown, Jan. 6th 1846

[Mr. Editor,] [1]

Facts being the very foundation of science, it has struck me that the following might assist some inquirer into the causes of the "potatoe-cholera."

In 1843, the disease among the potatoes showed itself in this country. That year, in many parts of the country, the potatoes rotted in their bins, and it was found necessary to remove them. In 1844 the disease was more prevalent, while in 1845 it was much less extensive. In my own case, very little of the disease appeared among the potatoes raised, in either year. Still, there was a little of it, among the pink-eyes, in particular. Having observed that potatoe-balls were very scarce in my own fields, and indeed in all this region, and being confident that the potatoes now raised in this country are much inferior to those raised five and thirty years since, I sent to England for seed. A friend was kind enough to obtain for me twenty four hampers of fine Lancashire potatoes, last spring, which reached me just in time for planting. I had them placed in new ground, on the side of a field in which were planted pink-eyes, trout and orange potatoes. The yield of all the potatoes was light, on account of the drought, but the Lancashire did as well as could be expected. Four and twenty bushels of the English potatoes were put away, for seed, in a cellar, under a hay mow, where the temperature is barely above freezing; as good a place for the preservation of vegetables as could be selected. A quantity of the trout and orange potatoes were put in another corner of the same cellar. Fearful that the weather was getting too severe for my seed potatoes, as the mow grew thinner, I ordered them to be removed, last week, to another cellar. On opening the straw that covered the heap, more than half the potatoes were found to be far gone, with the disease. As the rot has appeared in none of the other sorts that were grown in the same field, including pink eyes, I am left to infer that the English potatoes were infected, while the others were not.

I merely state the fact. The disease existing so extensively last year in England, may possibly have some connection with this loss; though to connect the circumstances it is necessary to believe that two seasons are required to develop the rot.

I will only add, that I had brought into my house, some of all the varieties that were grown, the English ⟨potatoes⟩ excepted; and I cannot find that a single potatoe has been affected. I know of no difference in the culture, or land, that should have produced this result. No manure was carted on any part of the field, though plaster was used throughout. As piles of logs and stumps had recently been burned on the land, it is possible the ashes may have reached to these English potatoes, though not more so than to the others, as the log heaps extended over all parts of the field. I do not think, moreover, that the vines ever looked thrifty.

Yours &c
J. Fenimore Cooper

P.S. It may be well to say that the English potatoes, diseased as they are, have been fed to store hogs, with perfect impunity. What is left of them seems to be as nourishing as the sound potatoe. They are affected with the black, cholera-looking disease, and appear to moulder away, rather than turn into a semi-liquid putrid substance, as was the case with some grown in my garden, in 1844.

ADDRESSED: Editor of Cultivator | Albany POSTMARKED: COOPERSTOWN N.Y. | JAN | 18 STAMPED: 5

MANUSCRIPT: Honeyman Collection, Lehigh University Library. PUBLISHED: *The Cultivator*, n.s. III (February 1846), 59–60.

An agricultural publisher who began life as a journeyman printer, Tucker (1802–1873) in 1840 consolidated his *Genesee Farmer*, founded in 1831, with *The Cultivator*, published in Albany (*DAB*).

1. Cooper wrote "Messrs Editors."

853. *To Richard Bentley*

Hall, Cooperstown, Jan. 7th [1846][1]

Dear Sir,

I have this day drawn on you, at ninety days, in favour of Robert Edmeston, for One Hundred and Fifty pounds. This is drawn as against "Ravensnest, or the Anti-Renters," the last of the Littlepage Manuscripts. When this bill shall be paid, it will leave me £100 to recieve in full for the work, under our last arrang[e]ment — I trust there will be no difficulty with the bill, as the book will be ready early in the Spring. As for the bill, you may not see it until the middle of February though that will depend somewhat on circumstances.

So much is said of War, just now, that you may like the opinion of one who has favourable opportunities of judging for this side, at least — I believe Congress will give the Notice to terminate the treaty. This may be done, in the course of the next three or four months, but I think not sooner.[2] This will leave one year, *from that time*, for the two parties to make up their minds in. I am of opinion this country will sustain the President in not yielding the mouth of the Columbia, but that the 49th degree will be yielded, whenever asked for, as already offered.

No one wishes war here, but the country will fight at any time, if asked to do so, in what it concieves to be a good cause. The commercial papers are no guides to any great political facts here, since the merchants cannot even control the election[s?] of their own communities. With the country at large, they count for very little, in a political point of view.

War will not be declared directly by either party, even should war come, which in my opinion, will hardly be the case. Neither party can act, beyond preparation, until the termination of the time mentioned in the Notice, and should collision come, it will probably come between detachments and vessels sent to take possession.

As I see you published Elinor Wyllys, I hope something will accrue to its author.[3]

Begging there may be no difficulty with the bill, I remain

Yours Truly

J— Fenimore Cooper

Mr. Richard Bentley | London.

ADDRESSED: Mr. Richard Bentley | Publisher | New Burlington Street | London | England | By the mail Steamer | viâ Boston POSTMARKED: COOPERSTOWN N.Y. | JAN | [8?] VR | 15 FE 15 | 1846 STAMPED: PAID 5

MANUSCRIPT: Cooper Collection, Yale University Library.

1. Cooper wrote "1845."

2. The Anglo-American Convention of 1818, which permitted joint occupation of the disputed Oregon Territory, stipulated that the occupation agreement might be unilaterally terminated on one year's notice. President Polk gave the expected notice on 21 May 1846 in accordance with a joint resolution of Congress.

3. "I am sorry to inform you that the result of the publication of Ellinor Wyllys is very unsatisfactory. The number of copies sold does not exceed 150. I regret this much, but assure you that it has not been without my best exertions to prevent such a disastrous result." (MS: Bentley to Cooper, 1 May 1846, YCAL.)

854. *To Richard Bentley*

Hall, Cooperstown, Jan. 14th 1846

Dear Sir,

To accom[m]odate both parties, I have drawn on you for £150, as against the new book. This will leave £100 to be paid, when the work is complete. It is in a fair way, and will be ready in March to go forward altogether. I shall take care of it as usual. I wrote you on the subject, with the first set of bills more fully, and send this by way of precaution.

I do not think war will come out of our difficulties. At any rate there can be nothing done for more than a year, and a year is a good while to reflect on [the?] [1] consequences, on both sides. What will be the end of it all, it is hard to say, for I think it very evident both sides want the waters of Puget Sound, and both certainly can not have them.

Have you any news for me, on account of Elinor Wyllys.

Yours in haste

Mr. Richard Bentley. J. Fenimore Cooper

ADDRESSED: Mr. Richard Bentley | Publisher | New Burlington Street | London | To go by | The Queen of the West | packet of the 21st Jan | viâ New York POSTMARKED: COOPERSTOWN N.Y. | JAN | 18 VR | 15 FE 15 | 1846 STAMPED: PAID 5

MANUSCRIPT: Cooper Collection, Yale University Library.

1. Manuscript torn.

855. *To William Branford Shubrick*

Hall, Cooperstown, Feb. 1st 1846

My Dear Shubrick,

This being Sunday, and my family kept at home by the death of Mrs. Richard Cooper, who died on the 28th, and is to be buried to-day, I have given the intermediate time to yourself. As I suppose Charlotte has written Mrs. Clymer concerning her cousin's illness, I shall not dwell on that event, one we all deplore, and which is a most sad thing to poor Dick.

I begin to think the Oregon affair may become very serious. England will avoid war to the last, but collision *in* the territory, and war as a consequence, are very likely to follow. The difficulty seems to be here. – [Charles] Wilkes tells us that the earth has no equals to the waters of Fuca and Puget's Sound.[1] The possession of the last, is what England aims at, and what she will not give up, if she can help it. If this government were to act with dignity and wisdom, give the notice with an air of calm resolution, arm and manifest an intention to maintain its rights, and, at the same time, let it be known that the 49th is her standing offer, as in fact I suppose it to be, England would not meet the crisis. She would not *now* fight for Puget's Sound, though she is very likely to be put in a position from which there will be no retreat, and all through the [pusillanimity] [2] and ignorance of members of Congress. As in the French business, in 1835, Congress, or the Senate, will t[hw]art the administration, until they force the country to the verge of war.

It is not easy for one who has not lived on the spot, to comprehend the extent of the apprehensions of England, on the subject of the Democratical tendencies of this country to aggressive war. They were so completely taken by surprise in 1812, that they have not yet recovered from it. While I was abroad, hundreds of Englishmen, men of mark, Lord Ashburton [3] included, made allusions that betrayed the existence of this feeling. England has been dreading aggressive war on our part, and the moderate tone of her papers, on the reciept of the Message,[4] is the result of agreeable surprise. The suspension of the negotiation, and the withdrawal of our offer, were known in England, and all taken together, great apprehension of what might occur existed, and the facts prove a relief.

But, all this leaves the true matter at issue, just where it was. The nation that should possess *all* the waters around Vancouver, would unavoidably command the North West coast, and the Pacific as far south as the islands. The division by the 49th would divide these advantages, but the mere possession of the Columbia, would be a mockery in a nautical point of view. I see a harbour laid down on Wilkes' map,[5] at the mouth of the Straits of Fuca, *on* Vancouver, which would fall to us by the line of the 49th and I conceive it would be of the last importance, as a man-of-war harbor. The straits can not exceed ⟨two⟩ eight miles in width, if as wide, and that port would be a second Gibraltar, as to position. But for this consideration, I would yield the whole island, though I think the harbour ought to be looked into. I see that Mr. Gallatin proposes to run a line *through* the straits, until he reaches the main and then to follow the coast to the 49th [parallel],[6] and so to the Mountains.[7] This would be a good arrangement, enough, for a time of peace, but would give the English an undue advantage in a time of war; while, on the other hand, the English might go to sea by the Northern passage, admitting the Americans to command the Straits of Fuca. I suppose the government is aware of all these points; if not you sailors should drop it some hints.

I do not admire your Secretary's report.[8] In some respects it is downright bad. I am surprised, indeed, it has not been openly and vigorously attacked. It is in the worst spirit of small economy. A man is to be sucked of his marrow, so long as he can be used, and then thrown away. I admit the old system has been a bad one, in very many respects, but this is not the way to mend it.

Is there any truth in the report that [Henry W.] Ogden is to be promoted over [Charles] Gau[n]tt, [Henry] Henry & [William] Rams[a]y.[9] Is there any positive objection to the first? Then as to the others, it seems strange to pass men who are given the finest ships in the service, without direct charges. If unfit to be promoted why leave them in their ships? Should Henry be passed, he will be passed by the very secretary who has left him in charge of the finest sloop employed, for a whole year! There is contradiction in this. I do not say that two of these men ought to be promoted, though I do say that mere private morality is a delicate thing to meddle with, on such occasions. The continence of sailors, forsooth! One might as well lay stress on the continence of a Bishop. How many Scipios are there in the service besides Scipio Shubrick? There's Scipio [Charles] Stewart, Scipio [Charles G.] Ridgeley, Scipio Harry Ballard, Scipio Charley Morgan, and Scipio a hundred others. Why might not the first be objected to, as well as these two men? I wish you would send me a line with the gossip, on these points — My own principle is that every man should be promoted, in his turn, unless a good *professional* objection offer. Immorality to a degree to impair professional respect, might be an objection, but not short of it. A man should be able to take care of a ship, at all events, to entitle him to the rank of even a commander. On that point, I should insist.

But, what an assault on the marine corps! [10] A man is to serve a whole life in that corps, for the honour of commanding a two-decker's guard! This is a detestable spirit, in which to govern. No recommendation of admirals, but plenty of recommendations to depress. A navy can never be built up in this spirit. You'll have to come to my plan of breaking up the inferior grades and rendering promotions more frequent, making the ordeals severe as to professional knowledge and professional habits, at these promotions, and higher rank —

If Mexico give any trouble, it will be through English influence — I wish our quarrel with our neighbour were as clear a matter as that with our cousin. I know that the people of Texas had a good moral and legal right to revolt. No people is bound to adhere to a government of military revolution, nor do I believe that the result has been matter of calculation originally. Nevertheless, these Texans are our own people, and the whole thing has a suspicious look, and we might so easily have bought off the Mexican right — There is our mistake — money would have done it, and money we have and might so easily have paid.

I have just returned from the funeral of Mrs. Richard, with the thermometer near zero — We were in sleighs, and the distance short, the church comfortable, but it was intensely cold — Most of our funerals [are] in the winter, and almost every funeral produces another.

Paul saws wood by way of exercise — My wood-house is warm but airy, open to the south, and there he works sometimes two hours a day. I think he improves, though he will not get rid of the inflammation of the bronchitis until warm weather come. His constitution has recieved a severe shock, and all from smoking. He confesses that at one time, he was smoking nearly the whole time.

The newspapers will tell you the court of errors has given them a triumph, as respects the law of libel. This is their usual ignorance, or usual lying. The decision does not touch the principles of the law at all, even if any body did respect our Court of Errors, which is shortly to be struck out of existence, by common consent. All that has been decided is that *our* declaration wanted a certain technicality, which we shall supply and sue the other partner. The Chancellor has given a singular opinion. He says, in substance, that it does not bring a man into discredit by accusing him of being a shaver, because the brokers of Wall Street [include][11] acts that are legal in their definition of shaving.[12] This is saying that the brokers of Wall Street can pervert the English language at their own pleasure. The dictionaries defend, and men in general, understand by shaving, extortion, and extortion is discreditable. As to the *fact*, that you know has nothing to do with settling a question of law. Stone admitted, publicly in his paper, that he had no reason to suppose I had ever been guilty of any transaction to justify a charge that he endeavoured to explain away as a joke! Yet, the public is willing to uphold such rascals. This Stone, moreover, though vulgar, and malicious and false, was a Saint compared to half the New York editors, who are certainly the worst in the country.

I see Owen has just made a strong speech on the Oregon question.[13] His logic is good, if the facts be fairly stated. More men fail in statements than in reasoning; or men do not *reason* before making their statements, but afterwards, though reason has commonly as much to do with the one as the other. Take Wilkes' Oregon, and examine Fuca and Puget's Sound for yourself. When you see Wilkes ask him if he knows any thing of the port he has laid down *on* Vancouver's, near the mouth of the Straits, and which is called St. Juan.[14] If a good man-of-war harbour, as I take all the deep bays of that coast to be, it is all important to possess it, for it will give its owner, cæteris paribus, an immense advantage in the event of a war. But for the ports along the shore of the island I see no other objection to letting England own down to the Straits [of Juan de Fuca], but the fact that she has no right to own any part of the country, or any part south of Nootka.

Let me hear in your answer, what is said of Mexico. I have always doubted the wisdom of our appointment to that country, though I knew but little of the man, of late years.[15] Still he may have acted prudently and the Mexicans ill. The fact of his waiting for instructions [is] in his favour, at any rate. He might have returned, and put $11000 in his pocket, clear.

So you go to the yard,[16] which I think is altogether a good exchange for you. You will be at least a $1000 a year better, in pocket, will be acting more in the line of your profession, will be just as much on the spot for all useful information, and more independent.

I do not believe the Oregon business will be got along with, as easily as some suppose. England clearly wants all the available waters, and will bully a long time before she will give them up. Our people know so little of John Bull, who is a better actor than we make, and blusters most when she seems to be only determined. If met firmly, she will give up; but she will not give up so long as our opposition feed her hopes as they are now doing. Rather than fight, England would abandon all below the 49th could she do so before committed to the world, by being led on by the opposition, here. I hope the government at Washington will not fall into the feebleness of any way connecting the tariff with the treaty about Oregon. A weaker, or indeed a falser policy could not be adopted.

For myself, I am very uncertain as to how, or where my future life is to be passed. I am afraid this climate is too severe for Paul, and I think all but myself would be better could they take more exercise in the open air in winter. If I could afford it, I would return to Europe for a few years, at least, but I cannot afford that, now. My pen, which added so largely to my income when abroad before, now produces nothing worth naming in this country, and would produce literally nothing [were] [17] I absent. It is true, that the difference, might and probably would be made up by the additional reciepts in Europe, but there ⟨was⟩ would still be a large deficiency in means to encounter the cost of movements with a family so large — I am obliged, therefore, to abandon that hope. If I quit my present home, there is no one to hire the house, and some $20,000 invested here, would become useless to me; or nearly so. Sell it, I do not like to, nor do I believe I could, if disposed, at half its value. These considerations give me great uneasiness at times, for I really begin to think the winter climate will affect all the children, in the end; Paul certainly can not pass next winter here, unless there is a great improvement in the course of the ensuing summer. We have great advantages, it is true, in the size of this house, which is airy and admits of a good deal of exercise. We can live in it, too, without the use of stoves, which destroy thousands as used in this part of the world. The country is not unhealthy of itself, though working and sitting over stoves, and going out into severe cold, brings many to their beds, and some to their graves. Five young persons have been buried in this village, within a few days, and nearly all from colds thus taken. If I could get a tenant here, I think I would try a change for a few years.

Lest you should suppose I am dumpish from just seeing poor Mrs. Richard buried, I will explain that I am now finishing this letter just one week after it was commenced, and just one week after I witnessed that melancholy ceremony. Since then Dick has been out with me, and to the eye is tranquil, though he feels much.

Is the Lt Jones who resigned last year, old Jacob's son? [18] If so will it not be odd that a boy who commenced on the deck of a ship, as a child, has never been able to make a sailor.

I suppose they will leave Conner in the gulf as long as there is any chance of there being any difficulty. The change contemplated, would be an absurdity at such time as this.

What will [James] Biddle, [Robert F.] Stockton and [John D.] Sloat all do together,[19] on the other side? If there should be trouble with John Bull, it will be very likely to commence on the North West Coast. When Biddle gets there, as I suppose he will, our force will be respectable, especially should the Savannah[20] be kept out. You do not like Biddle, but there is a good deal in him. I do not believe he is a man for a happy ship, but he is an honorable man and an exceedingly clever one.

Well, adieu – My best regards to all hands – your *son* and daughter, and for ought I know grand children. I rather think I shall look at you in March, for a day or two. The magnificent distances of Washington form its curse, or one might like to pass more time in it. You stay there by year, do not feel how much the stranger is oppressed by being obliged to go forty miles of a morning. Adieu –

Commodore Shubrick. J. Fenimore Cooper

MANUSCRIPT: Paul Fenimore Cooper, Cooperstown, New York.

1. "Nothing can exceed the beauty of these waters, and their safety: not a shoal exists within the Straits of Juan de Fuca, Admiralty Inlet, Puget Sound, or Hood's Canal, that can in any way interrupt their navigation by a seventy-four gun ship. I venture nothing in saying, there is no country in the world that possesses waters equal to these." (Charles Wilkes, *Narrative of the United States Exploring Expedition, during the Years 1838, 1839, 1840, 1841, 1842* [Philadelphia: Lea & Blanchard, 1845], IV, 305.)

2. Cooper wrote "pusillinamity."

3. See Journal XXIV, 28 June 1833. Alexander Baring, first Baron Ashburton, had negotiated the Webster-Ashburton Treaty in 1842.

4. President Polk's Message of 2 December 1845 claimed the whole of the Oregon Territory for the United States, recommended to Congress the required year's notice terminating joint occupation under the Convention of 1827, and requested extended protection for United States settlers in the territory (Richardson, *Messages and Papers of the Presidents,* IV, 392–98).

5. Wilkes's map of the Oregon Territory is bound in the sixth volume of his *Narrative.*

6. Cooper wrote "paralell."

7. See Albert Gallatin, *The Oregon Question* (1846), reprinted in Henry Adams, *The Writings of Albert Gallatin* (Philadelphia: J. B. Lippincott & Co., 1879), III, 512–13.

8. Among the economies recommended in Secretary of the Navy George Bancroft's report, dated 1 December 1845, were a reduction in the number of officers and a substitution of merit for seniority as a criterion for promotion. Shubrick's attitude, expressed in his letter of 17 February, agreed with Cooper's: "Our Secretary's report meets with favor no where[;] fortunately neither himself nor his report nor his opinions have much weight – his notions on navy matters are of the worst kind[;] he ridicules the idea of Admirals, makes it a rule to ask every young officer who visits him, his opinion of the conduct and character of the superior officers and is doing much to break down the little discipline that the canker of a too long peace has left to us." (Document Two, *Executive Documents, First Session of the Twenty-ninth Congress,* I, 645–54; MS: YCAL.)

9. In seniority, Gauntt, Ramsay, and Henry stood at the head of the list of commanders in this order; Ogden ranked fifth. The first three were promoted in 1847. (Navy *Register* for 1845, 1846, 1847, and 1848.)

10. Bancroft recommended no increase of men or officers in the Marine Corps and explicitly deplored the manpower waste among its personnel (Document Two, *Executive Documents, First Session of the Twenty-ninth Congress,* I, 649).

11. Cooper wrote "including."

12. Agreeing that the word "shave" might be used in a defamatory sense, Chancellor Reuben H. Walworth stated: "The word shave is also used to denote the buying of existing notes and other securities for money at a discount beyond the nominal amount of the debt and interest due or to become due on such notes or securities. And this court has decided that shaving of that description is a legitimate and legal business, and does not come either within the letter or spirit of the usury laws." (Hiram Denio, *Reports of Cases Argued and Determined in the Supreme Court . . . of the State of New-York* [Albany and New York: Gould, Banks & Gould, 1847], II, 300–01.)

13. On 28 January 1846, Congressman Robert Dale Owen (1801–1877) of Indiana had stressed in the House of Representatives the practical importance to the United States of the navigational resources south of the forty-ninth parallel and argued from parliamentary sources that the British could advance no legitimate claim to this territory (*The Congressional Globe, First Session of the Twenty-ninth Congress,* I, 268–72; *DAB*).

14. "Wilkes says," replied Shubrick on 17 February, "the harbor laid down on Vancouver island, St. Juan, is not a man of war harbor being open to South West winds[;] indeed the only good harbors are in Puget Sound, in the part of the territory from which England in all her offers proposes to exclude us — The line proposed by Mr. Gallatin, as I understand it, would give us all the good harbors, but I should greatly prefer to run down the 49th parallel to the ocean, as that would give us the whole of the str[ait] (ten miles wide Wilkes says) and force Mr. Bull to go out by the northern passage, but the ultra democrats here say we must go to 54°: 40′." (MS: YCAL.)

15. John Slidell, brother of Alexander Slidell Mackenzie, had been commissioned Envoy Extraordinary and Minister Plenipotentiary of the United States to Mexico on 10 November 1845 and "intrusted with full powers to adjust both the questions of the Texas boundary and of indemnification to our citizens." General Herrera's government refused on 21 December 1845 to accredit Slidell, who protested but remained in Mexico awaiting instructions. On 12 March 1846, the government of General Paredes, Herrera's successor, also denied Slidell accreditation. (Richardson, *Messages and Papers of the Presidents,* IV, 438–40.)

16. Shubrick was assigned to command the Washington Navy Yard.

17. Cooper wrote "where."

18. The son of Jacob Jones (see Cooper to Shubrick, 2 August 1840) was Richard A. Jones (d. 1846), appointed midshipman in 1812, lieutenant in 1820, and commander in 1844. The Jones who resigned from the Navy on 13 May 1845 was William A. Jones, appointed midshipman in 1831, passed midshipman in 1837, and lieutenant in 1841. (GNR; MS: Shubrick to Cooper, 17 February 1846, YCAL.)

19. Biddle commanded the East India Squadron and Sloat the Pacific Squadron. Stockton served under Sloat. (Navy *Register* for 1846.)

20. The *Savannah,* 44, Sloat's flagship, was a 1475-ton frigate built and launched in 1842 (GNR).

856. *To Samuel Seabury, for* The Churchman

Hall, Cooperstown, Feb. 3, 1846.

Mr. Editor, —

After admitting to your columns a communication, as personal and objectionable in its statements and tone, as that of the correspondent who caricatures the Christian temper, simplicity and good faith of the imaginary divine, known as "Parson Grant," and whose name he has assumed, I have an entire right to ask an insertion of a reply.[1] Four objections to the communication in question arise in my mind, and they affect its honesty, its logic, its accuracy as to facts, and its knowledge.

I object to its honesty, because this *soi disant* "Parson Grant" manifests a virtuous indignation at what he calls my "dark insinuation," "thrust in the dark," &c. &c., when all that I have said and done in the premises, has been said and done in the face of day. This particular objection is increased by the fact, that this very "Parson," who in substance imputes to me not only meanness but improper motives, writes anonymously, himself; a mode of making attacks that is usually stigmatized by the very reproaches he wishes to heap on me!

I object to his facts, because he accuses me of attacking all the bishops of the majority, Dr. [Charles P.] McIlvaine excepted, when I have attacked neither. Advancing an opinion that a juror ought to have been excluded for cause, is not attacking that juror, unless the cause is named, and conveys reproach. I apprehend that, in this matter, your correspondent has transferred the judgment of the public, concerning the disqualification that *was* mentioned in the case of one of the six, to the case of the bishop alluded to as one of the eleven, in whose case the disqualification was *not* named. Simple affinity might have been a cause for excluding the expression of an opinion on the merits, and various other reasons that your correspondent appears to have overlooked. My allusion was proper for my argument, and no reflection being cast, I had a right to stop where I pleased in my statement. The very party who ought not to have sat, in my opinion, may have been totally unconscious of his disqualification. I hope that "Parson Grant" is unconscious of his motives for making his charges, but I very much doubt it.

I object to the logic, because, in imputing my course to "party," your correspondent is guilty of the absurdity of making me "thrust in the dark" at the men of my own side! I further object to this imputation, that it is unworthy of any "Parson," as indecent and untrue. Of its decency, it is unnecessary to speak, being entirely unprovoked, unless presuming to have an opinion of my own, on a matter in which it was a duty to form one, can be so received. The untruth is matter of record, as can be seen not only by the journals of the Convention, but by the columns of your own paper.[2] In 1843, I voted with the supporters of the bishop, on the question of the [Arthur] Carey Ordination; and still think he was right in his decision, though I begin to fear we were wrong in our opinion of the tendency of Puseyism; while I condemned his course in connection with the request of Mr. [John] Duer to place his protest on the journal. In this last matter, I have stated in your paper, that Mr. Duer had no right to ask that the journal should be made the record of his particular opinions, while the President of the Convention had no right to decide farther than that the request was out of order; the Convention alone having the control of its journal. My condemnation of both the request and the decision was open and unqualified. Now, sir, all these opinions may have been wrong; but they are not the opinions of one who acts, or thinks, on party grounds.

In the Convention of 1845, I voted against those who manifested a disposition, as it struck me, to support the late bishop of this diocese, through thick and thin. I may have been wrong in this, too, but the fact proves, at least, a certain independence of opinion, which it is not usual to find in a rabid "party" man, according to my notion of the matter. It is my right to state these things, when calumniated as a mere "party" man, and that too in Church matters; and it is also my right, under the circumstances, to ask that you should publish them.

I object to the knowledge of your correspondent who evidently confounds "Theology" with the principles that are to determine the "question of vacancy." Your correspondent affirms, it would seem, that I am about to "stir up my theology" on this "question of vacancy," and concludes his letter with a magnificent sort of menace, which, fairly interpreted, means that *he* is there to meet me! "Let him try it," he cries, in the true "Ercles vein."

Sir, I understand "theology" to mean the "science of religion," whereas the enjoyment of Church benefices, I am sorry to say, is connected with a science of a very different sort, in the eyes of some among us. I can easily conceive that "Parson Grant" fancies it a dogma of the faith that a priest should be paid, and well paid, too, though he did no duty; but it will be found, in the end, that the laws of the land have a voice in this matter.

Nothing was easier than for me to have referred to the case of the bishop of the minority, who, in my judgment, ought not to have had a seat in the late trial, and held my tongue on the subject of the bishop of the majority, who, I also thought, ought not to have sat. The allusion to the last, while I entertained the latter opinion, ought therefore to be ascribed to a love of fair-dealing, though I make no question it was quite thrown away on "Parson Grant." I might have been expected to sustain my objection in the case of the bishop whose opinion I opposed, while a man is easily credited when he makes an admission that appears to weaken his own side; as was the fact in the objection stated against the bishop whose opinion I approved. I had also a private motive, in a wish to disabuse some of an error on a subject that was named, by saying what I did in the case of the bishop of the minority.

It will be time enough to reflect on the necessity of answering "Parson Grant's" question, when he gets so far over his own propensity to "thrust in the dark" as to come out like an honest man, when he makes accusations, under his own name.

Your obedient servant,
J. Fenimore Cooper.

Editor of the Churchman.

SOURCE: *The Churchman*, 14 February 1846.

Introducing Cooper's letter, Seabury wrote: "It is hazardous for an editor to interpose between two correspondents, lest he may destroy the balance which he is bound to preserve. Our respect, however, for Mr. Cooper leads us to say one word in self-defence; and that is, that we did not understand 'Parson Grant' to deal in any improper personalities. Personal he certainly was; for how could he be otherwise when a person and personal acts were the professed subjects of his communication? But it was Mr. Cooper in his public character and Mr. Cooper's public acts to whom alone he referred and from which alone his inferences were drawn. Such at least was our impression. That the 'Parson's' inferences about *dark thrusts*, &c. were correct we do not say; but only that they were suggested by Mr. Cooper's published speech. That his allusion to Mr. Cooper's date [*sic*] was in good taste we would not affirm, but only that there was a published letter of Mr. Cooper to suggest it. So in regard to other matters; the allusions were suggested (whether authorized or not is another thing) by public acts; and it does not seem to us that such allusions are personal in any improper way. We do not make these remarks to shield 'Parson Grant,' who must take care of himself; but we offer them merely with the wish to convince Mr. Cooper that if we have admitted any thing unduly personal, it has been from no worse cause than an infirmity of judgment."

1. In a long anonymous letter, published in *The Churchman* of 31 January 1846, "Parson Grant" attacked Cooper rather savagely for stating in the late convention that two of Bishop Onderdonk's judges "should have been struck off the Court" and then failing to specify the bishops meant. Cooper had, "Parson Grant" charged, revealed with sufficient clarity and in a partisan spirit that Bishop George W. Doane was the judge favorable to Onderdonk who should have been excluded; but, beyond his denial that Charles P. McIlvaine of Ohio was the bishop of the majority to whom he referred, Cooper's second candidate for exclusion was unspecified. This vagueness, said "Parson Grant," made Cooper "still the assailant in the dark of ten of our bishops." The letter concluded: "Mr. Cooper seems to promise to stir up his theology on the question of vacancy. Let him try it."

2. See Cooper's letter for *The Churchman*, 7 – 21? October 1843.

857. *To Mrs. Cooper*

Globe. April 1st 1846

Dearest,

An hour after I wrote you this morning, I effected a sale of literary property, to the amount of $1500,[1] which will enable me to return home at the close of the week. I have the Cherubs, Picture, and $500 in England in reserve, amounting in all to $1600 more. This will pay off Ogden and other demands, leaving all my affairs in a small compass, and perfectly manageable. I am happy enough to get through with that western affair, leaving what remains of it to come in, and not to go out.

As I wish to press a bargain with [George R.] Graham of Philadelphia,[2] I shall stay here until Friday evening and be at home on Saturday – *possibly* a day earlier.

I met young Phil Kearny this morning. He resigns in a day or two, in the intention to push for a Majority should there be a war; a project that will probably succeed.[3]

With kindest love to all, I remain | Yours tenderly,

J. F. C.

Every body speaks well of Elinor [Wyllys], but its price kills it.

ADDRESSED: Mrs. Fenimore Cooper | Cooperstown | New York POSTMARKED: NEW-YORK | 2 | APR | 5 cts.

MANUSCRIPT: Cooper Collection, Yale University Library. PUBLISHED: *Correspondence*, II, 563.

1. See Cooper to J. K. Paulding, 9 May 1846.

2. Cooper probably wished to negotiate for the serialization of *Jack Tier*, which appeared in installments in *Graham's Magazine* from November 1846 to March 1848.

3. Philip Kearny resigned his lieutenant's commission on 2 April 1846 only

to be reinstated, at his own request, on 15 April 1846 to his former rank and assignment (J. Watts De Peyster, *Personal and Military History of Philip Kearny* . . . [New York: Rice and Gage, 1869], 124–25).

858. *To John Pendleton Kennedy*

Hall, Cooperstown, April 22d 1846

My Dear Sir,

Will you pardon my giving you a little trouble? It is of some moment to me to ascertain who and where a Mrs. Oldfield is, who visited this part of the country, in 1843. The object of these inquiries is to ascertain through her the circumstances connected with an exchange that she endeavoured to effect between the clergyman of our parish, a Mr. Tiffany and a Mr. Berry of Choptank.

I do not mean to trouble you any further, however, than to ascertain who Mrs. Oldfield is, where she is, and the best mode of obtaining the facts from her. These facts I understand to be as follows, viz. While here Mrs. Tiffany, the wife of our late clergyman, begged her to endeavour to obtain a parish for her husband, somewhere south — She proposed an exchange with this Mr. Berry, who came here, or to New York, had an interview with Mr. Tiffany, who declined the exchange. If you will ascertain and let me know all that is pertinent about Mrs. Oldfield, and about Mr. Berry, you will greatly oblige me.

Should your answer be written before the 7th May, have the goodness to direct to me here; if after at Head's Philadelphia.

As it is possible chance may put it in your power, while asking a question or two, in order to ascertain some thing else that will be of use, I will briefly state what I wish to learn, with the understanding you are to give yourself no trouble beyond the facts first mentioned unless the others fall in your way.

Did Mrs. Tiffany make such an application and when?

What is the value of Mr. Berry's living?

Had *Mr.* Tiffany any direct connection with the application?

Why did he decline the exchange?

As I think it probable these enquiries will cause me to go to Baltimore myself, should your answer let me know that Mrs. Oldfield and Mr. Berry (who is an Englishman, I am told) are to be found there, I will defer thanks and apologies until then.[1]

In the mean time, with my respects to the ladies and Mr. Gray,[2] I remain very truly yours

J— Fenimore Cooper

J. P. Kennedy, Esquire

Are you of my way of thinking, in believing that John Bull has no notion of accepting the 49th, or any thing that does not give him the waters of Pugets Sound? Webster's demonstration to the contrary will bring things nearer to a head than all that had been previously said and done. They regard him as a friend.

MANUSCRIPT: Peabody Institute Library, Baltimore, Maryland. PUBLISHED, IN PART: Killis Campbell, "The Kennedy Papers," *The Sewanee Review*, XXV (April 1917), 200.

Remarkably congenial for all their differences of temperament and opinion, Cooper and Kennedy (1795–1870, Baltimore College 1812), congressman (1838–1844) and secretary of the navy (1852–1853) as well as novelist, met on many happy occasions, including the journey from New York to Philadelphia on 6 September 1843 with William Gilmore Simms (see Cooper to Simms, 5 January 1844). When the Kennedys visited Otsego Hall in August 1845, the exuberant Cooper conducted them to "The Vision" and then, despite threatening skies, to a still higher vantage point, "The Prospect." The whole party was drenched in a cloudburst, and the Kennedy's joined in the later festivities at the Hall attired perforce in Cooper clothing. (Charles H. Bohner, *John Pendleton Kennedy: Gentleman from Baltimore* [Baltimore: The Johns Hopkins Press, 1961].)

1. With the playful salutation "*Fenny More* Cooper," Kennedy wrote from Baltimore on 15 May: "I have delayed this reply to your letter of the 22nd ult. until to day, from the want of opportunity to procure the information you wish in regard to Mr. Berry. Mrs. Oldfield, I know very well, as a lady of this City, the daughter of the somewhat celebrated Mary Chase of the old time. — I have not seen her of late, and am rather inclined to believe that she is not here at this time. To day I saw [the Reverend] Dr. [William E.] Wyatt, of St Paul's in this City. He tells me that Berry was in the diocese a year or two ago — but at present, he supposes is not attached to it. I understand he is an eccentric person, not in the highest odour of sanctity, and not likely to conduce much to your comfort in the matter of an exchange. Choptank is perhaps the most unhealthy part of the Eastern Shore of Md. and must be much more highly qualified as a *dying* than as a *living* for a clergyman. The stipend must be very small in such a parish, and I should think would put all the saintly virtues of Tiffany to their trial if he should be persuaded to give up Cooperstown for a trial of the experiment. Arguing therefore *à priori* I should conclude that neither Mr. Tiffany nor his wife — if they had their wits about them — ever made an application to exchange with Berry. — This will answer three of your questions. The 4th is, Why did he decline? — Answ. In the name of Heaven why should he accept?

"Now if these answers, do not serve your purpose, the best thing you can do is to come to Baltimore — or rather to Ellicott Mills — for we move to our cottage there in a few days — and stay with me until I can put you in the way of Mrs. Oldfield who with the help of the bishop may settle the whole matter.

"Our family — you saw the whole roll — unite in kindest regards to you and in the hope of seeing you." (MS: YCAL.)

2. Edward Gray (1776?–1856), Kennedy's father-in-law and a wealthy cotton manufacturer, was a member of the Kennedy household (Bohner, *John Pendleton* Kennedy, 63–67, 121, 204, 217).

859. *To James Kirke Paulding*

Hall, Cooperstown, May 9th 1846

My Dear Sir,

I am very sorry to say that my pecuniary benefits, in this country, amount to nothing worth naming.[1] I own so much literary property, and so many plates, that in the whole they amount to something, though far less than you would suppose. The cheap literature has destroyed the value of nearly all literary property, and after five and twenty years of hard work, I find myself comparatively a poor man. Had I employed the same time in trade, or in travelling as an agent for a manufacturer of pins, I do not doubt I should have been better off, and my children independent. The fact is, this country is not sufficiently advanced for any thing intellectual, and the man who expects to rise by any such agency makes a capital mistake, unless he sell himself, soul and body, to a faction.

My last bargain with B & S. was a complicated one, including the use of plates of no less than three old books, besides the new one. The price paid was $1500. The two preceding books, however, sold each an edition of 3500 for $1050, the plates at my cost. I do not think the three last books will nett me much more than $500 a book. B & S. say they have not sold the first editions of Satanstoe and Chainbearer.

I make no doubt you can do much better, as the press is a solid phalanx against me, and I am unpopular with the country, generally — Indeed, were it not for the convenience of correcting proof sheets, I would not publish in this country at all. I have a work in contemplation, that will be secured here, to cut off the profits of pirates, but which I do not mean to publish in America, at all, any farther than may be necessary to secure the copy right. If they will not pay, they ought not to read.

If I were fifteen years younger, I would certainly go abroad, and never return. I can say with Woolsey,[2] "if I had served my god with half the zeal I've served my *country*" it would have been better for me. You and I have committed the same error; have been American — whereas our cue was to be European, which would have given us success at home. The time was, when these things pained me, but every interest seems so much upside down, here, that another feeling has taken the place of even regret.

Yours very truly

J. K. Paulding Esquire. J. Fenimore Cooper

MANUSCRIPT: The Henry W. and Albert A. Berg Collection, The New York Public Library. PUBLISHED: James Fenimore Cooper, *Satanstoe*, Robert E. Spiller and Joseph D. Coppock, eds. [New York, etc.: American Book Company, 1937], opposite page 62.

1. Cooper here replied to Paulding's letter dated Hyde Park, Duchess County, 4 May 1846:

"Having lately purchased a little place here, and having plenty of leisure, it is my design to resume my Pen, both as a resource for Killing Time, and making the Pot Boil. Hitherto I have been a prey to the Bookselling Craft, and have made a good many bad Bargains. My desire is to avail myself a little of your experience and sagacity in future, and I have troubled you with this letter, for the purpose of requesting of you — provided you are at liberty to communicate them, and will do me the favour — to state the precise terms of your agreement with Burgess & Stringer for the publication of your work. I shall only use it for my own special direction. They tell me they will give me the same terms, but decline stating what they are — which is very satisfactory.

"I thank you for the pleasure your late publications have given me; and beg you to pardon this trouble." (MS: YCAL; published in Ralph M. Aderman, *The Letters of James Kirke Paulding* [Madison, Wisconsin: The University of Wisconsin Press, 1962], 432–33.)

2. In Shakespeare's *King Henry the Eighth*, III, ii, Cardinal Thomas Wolsey (1475?–1530) is made to exclaim:

"O Cromwell, Cromwell!
Had I but serv'd my God with half the zeal
I serv'd my king, he would not in mine age
Have left me naked to mine enemies."

860. *To an Unidentified Editor*

[November — December 1845?]

[*The beginning and the close of this letter or draft are missing.*]

. . . of this opinion is the point here at issue.

In forming their opinion on this subject, I apprehend many have confounded the old notion of the indelible character of orders, with some imaginary principle that establishes a supposed indissoluble connection between the diocese and its diocesan.

I think an intelligent inquiry will show there is nothing of this indissoluble nature, as between the diocesan and his diocese, whatever there may be as between the Bishop and the man.

In the first place it has always been held that orders, themselves, can be lost, by discipline. Now, that for which we contend is merely the legitimate consequence of discipline, and, if we are to have the thing we are to take it with its just consequences.

Some object to this, reasoning that the sentence says nothing on the subject of suspension from the diocesan function — If this objection be good for any thing, it is good for all; and Dr. Onderdonk, though a suspended Bishop, is not a suspended diocesan, and can claim all diocesan authority that is not strictly spiritual. But the vote of eight of the bishops was for deposition, and there are the words of their sentence, in which nothing is said of the diocese. It will scarcely be pretended that a deposed Bishop could remain a diocesan. Now, this brings us directly to the principle that leaves the diocese vacant under the present state of things. A deposed bishop ceases to be a diocesan, on con[s?]tructive and not on Statute, or canon law, because he could not continue a diocesan without doing violence to a paramount duty to the church; without gross injustice, & without admitting absurdities into the polity of the American church, and giving to discipline a character of rewards rather than one of punishments. The diocese becomes vacant as the diocesan loses his power to be useful. ⟨In⟩ For a case in which this power is lost, by a visitation of Providence, the church has made a just provision, which protects the rights of all parties; but in a case like that before us all the rights belong to the diocese, and, in the nature of things, they must be protected.

The diocesan is appointed by the diocese, under a *covenant.* The consent of the party chosen is necessary to complete the arrangement. This makes the appointment a contract. Many presbyters have been chosen bishops, by conventions, in the American church, who have declined the office. This, of itself, would show that the connection is of the nature of a contract, to which there are distinct parties. Men now living among us have declined accepting certain dioceses, when they have subsequently accepted others; all of which shows the connection is one of expediency and contract. It is, in fact, just like any other contract between men, that is of a theological nature; the connection of a bishop with the church being a very different thing.

On the part of the diocese, the vote of election is the evidence of the contract; on the part of the diocesan his acceptance. We will suppose that A were chosen as what is called Bishop elect, of this diocese. In that choice the diocese has exhausted its power. A— accepts, and so far as the parties are concerned, the contract is complete. But the polity of the church, for obvious purposes, requires the consent of the American branch of the church, ere the union be consummated. A goes to the church (in general convention assembled) asks for consecration, and it is refused to him. Is he then diocesan of New York, an incumbent who must die, or resign, ere another can be called to his place. Every one will deride the idea. He can not be a diocesan because he is not a bishop; or, if a bishop, he can not become a diocesan without the approval of the branch of the church that is in connection.

MANUSCRIPT: Paul Fenimore Cooper, Cooperstown, New York.

This fragment of a letter or a draft was a part of Cooper's response, obviously written for publication, to John C. Spencer's *Report to the Vestry of St. Peter's Church, Albany, of the Lay Delegates . . . Who Attended the Diocesan Convention . . . at the City of New York.* (Albany: Erastus H. Pease, 1845). (See Cooper's letter of 19 December 1845, for *The Protestant Churchman.*) No printed text of the full letter has been discovered, though Hamilton Fish, a fellow delegate at the convention, wrote Cooper on 12 December 1845: "I most earnestly hope that you have not abandoned the idea of publishing your reply to Spencer — [William] Jay's review does not meet the *main* argument — the great strength of *our* side of the question, is the distinction which you take between a 'Bishop' & a 'Diocesan' — I pray you not to omit your publication — for even if Jay does look to it, he does not state it as forcibly as it might be put — & it is a point which will bear being presented in different modes." (MS: YCAL.)

Part Nineteen

THE MEXICAN WAR

1846–1847

THE MEXICAN WAR

1846–1847

Even after the Mexican government replied to the annexation of Texas by severing diplomatic relations with the United States on 28 March 1845, Cooper supposed a war with England far more likely than a war with Mexico. His supposition was natural. President Polk's elaboration of the Monroe Doctrine and the expansionist aims of the new Democratic Administration, immortalized in the slogan *Manifest Destiny,* challenged directly the British and French policy of containment. The President spoke firmly on the Oregon and Texas issues, and his hope of obtaining California was easy to infer. Great Britain was the powerful rival whose interests and intrigues seemed significantly threatened; Mexico seemed disorganized, too weak politically and militarily to be a serious menace to the United States. These expectations, however natural, were soon dashed by the skirmishes at Matamoros which led to the Declaration of War against Mexico on 12 May 1846 and the Senate's approval of the Oregon Treaty on 15 June 1846. Also dashed was the general expectation that General Zachary Taylor's brilliant exploits in the northern provinces of Mexico would bring the unprepared Mexicans quickly to their knees.

Though the war was obviously to be fought mainly on land, Cooper was much gratified by Commodore Shubrick's assignment, on 9 July 1846, to relieve Commodore John D. Sloat as commander of United States naval forces in the Pacific. Arriving on 19 August in Boston where Shubrick a week earlier had hoisted his broad pennant on the newly renovated *Independence* 54, Cooper visited the Commodore and Mrs. Shubrick until 24 or 25 August, when the novelist escorted Mrs. Shubrick to Baltimore. For the next three years, Cooper followed his friend's movements as closely as possible through the press and through the mails.

Shubrick was the ranking naval officer in Pacific waters from November 1846 to July 1848, except for five months when conflicting orders and naval etiquette induced him to yield the command to Commodore James Biddle. By 31 December 1846, the sociable Commodore was complaining that for two weeks he had seen nothing "except two uninhabited islands, and now and then a flying fish – It is dreary in the extreme, and if I had had any idea of what I should suffer, from being so long a time without hearing from my family[,] no prospects of professional advantages would have induced me to come on such service – Think of being five months *at sea,* alone, in the isolation of a commander in chief. Why nothing can equal it except solitary confinement in a state prison." His chief professional opportunity was to be the unexciting task of maintaining the blockade. San Francisco, Monterey, and Los Angeles, the important points in Upper California, were already occupied; and, after visiting these posts, Shubrick evolved plans for taking key towns along the Mexican coast: Guaymas, Mazatlán, Acapulco, and San Blas. Captain Lavalette captured the first on Shubrick's order; and, after taking San José, a principal mart of Lower California, Shubrick's entire fleet converged on the fortified harbor of Mazatlán. Here the Commodore used such excellent tactics in surrounding the peninsula on which the town was located that it fell almost without a blow; and, according to a local historian, he administered the government so effectively that after six weeks the Mexican merchants formally invited him to remain. A shortage of men forced him to neglect Acapulco and San Blas, though the effects of his blockade were generally felt along the western coast. On 16 July 1848, about six weeks after the peace was arranged, Shubrick took leave of his fleet to return home by way of the Sandwich Islands and Hawaii.

As his letters to Shubrick suggest, Cooper was sufficiently acquainted among the military to follow dispatches from the more active eastern fronts in terms of personalities as well as armchair strategy. He was a friend of General John Ellis Wool, who assisted Taylor in the North; and he had known General Winfield Scott, who led the all-important thrust from Vera Cruz to Mexico City, since Bread and Cheese Club days. Captain Phil Kearny, who lost an arm and won a brevet at Churubusco, was related to Mrs. Cooper, as was his uncle General Stephen W. Kearny, who commanded the Army in California. Among numerous lesser figures whose fortunes Cooper followed with special interest was his niece's husband Captain Henry W. Wessells of the second infantry. Cooper apparently used his influence in Washington on Wessell's behalf; but the wounded captain wrote from Tacubaya, Mexico, on 2 March 1848, that candidates for brevet promotion abounded, holding claims dating "from the field of Buena Vista, to the entrance of our columns into the capital of Mexico, and it is a long list, or as [General Gideon J.] Pillow perhaps would say, a perfect 'Stream of heroes.'" About Scott, whom Cooper was soon to know better in New York City, Wessells' feelings were ambiguous. "There are times," he continued, "when Scott exhibits all the qualities of a great commander, and from the organization of his fleet at Lobos island a year ago, until the occupation of Perote in April, I do not believe there can be found one single error — but from that time until now — I will refrain from expressing an opinion — The balance power is incomplete, a cog, or wheel is wanting, for at times the whole machinery seems to run perfectly wild. God grant that our citizens may never be so deluded as to consent to place either him or [General William J.] Worth, in the highest seat of our glorious republic . . . Gen Taylor will be safe as regards the true interests of his country, being a man of incorruptible integrity."

Of the so-called "inner war," the web of intrigue and backbiting among generals and politicians, Cooper was not fully cognizant; nor did he share the professed reservations of the Whigs about the "rightness" of the war. "Texas was independent *de facto*," he wrote in the posthumously published continuation of his *History of the Navy*, "and she had become so by a marked breach of faith on the part of the central government of Mexico." Being sovereign, independent states, Texas and the United States had every right, he reasoned, to treat for annexation. Like his friend William Jay, Cooper preferred dollars to bullets as instruments of negotiation; but he would not have agreed with Jay's thesis, ingeniously argued in *A Review of the Causes and Consequences of the Mexican War* (1849), that the slave interests created the war to serve their selfish purposes. He did, however, object to efforts to extend slavery into the new territories. Practically, the war turned Cooper's attention to the Gulf of Mexico and smuggling in a new nautical novel *Jack Tier* and resulted in his dictating, at about the time of Shubrick's farewell visit at Cooperstown in July 1851, a dozen new pages for the proposed third volume of his *History of the Navy*. Psychologically, it seems to have renewed, in part, his confidence in the spiritual strength and unity of the Republic.

861. *To Mrs. Cooper*

Head's Friday [May] 22d 1846

Dearest Sue,

Here I am; arrived last night, and have found near forty pages ready for me, and have just read them. I think I shall not be detained here much after the 1st June — At New York I may be kept a little longer.

As yet, I have done nothing, beyond law business. Here are all the news —

The [Henry] Laights are in Paris, to be home in August. Laight does not get any stronger. I am afraid his time is nearly up, though these frail weak men often hold out surprisingly.

[Morse?] [1] is married, though to whom I have not learned. The bride has been pardoned, great youth.

Your brother was not at the consecration — sick head ache, interposing.

Boxes and bundles all delivered.

I sent Paul the last news papers, just before quitting New York. Nothing new from the South.

I saw the [William C.] Maitlands — all well; but Mrs. [Banyer?] [2] is suffering under one of the worst attacks she has ever had.

The Mexican war will produce great changes, or peace will be made at once. Every thing is at a stand. Men are uncertain what they ought to do. Money easier, though difficult to move.

Let Paul tell this to Dick — I believe it will be found that Tiffany gave [Joseph L.?] White a mortgage on his books — including those offered to be returned to [Thomas N.] Stanford. It is true this offer was not made until after the service of our plea, but another plea might be so framed as to get at the evidence.

Dr. Wyatt [3] of Baltimore describes Mr. Berry,[4] as a hard character, an English priest — Chop[tank?] is *not* more than $500 a year, in the western part of the State, and not very healthy. Otherwise well enough.

[John P.] Kennedy says the same in substance.

If we can show T[iffany] was actually negotiating an exchange with such a man, it will be some thing.

I have broken my spectacles, and write without any, so must conclude.

Kindest love to all. Tell Paul, I hear wonders of Hydropathy, in cases like his. Lebanon must be his spot, I think — where one or two of the girls might go with him for change.

Adieu

J. F. C.

ADDRESSED: Mrs. Fenimore Cooper | Cooperstown | New York POSTMARKED: PHILADELPHIA [Pa.?] | MAY | 22

MANUSCRIPT: Cooper Collection, Yale University Library.

1. If the reference was to S. F. B. Morse, Cooper was repeating rumor; for the inventor was married two years later.

2. Cooper was writing rapidly without spectacles. He may have intended to write "Banyer," but omitted the "n."

3. Ordained priest in the Protestant Episcopal Church in 1813, William Edward Wyatt (1789–1864, Columbia 1809) passed his entire ministry as associate rector and rector of St. Paul's, Baltimore (*ACAB*).

4. The Reverend Philip Berry (d. 1857) held scattered parishes in the United States. He moved to Esopus, New York, in the early 1850's and, before his death, to New Kent County, Virginia. (Obituary file at The General Theological Seminary.)

862. *To Mrs. Cooper*

Head's, May, 23d 1846

Dearest,

I wrote you on Friday, in great haste, and now write again to say that the letters of Paul and Richard have both come to hand, and that I am perfectly well. The book is going on famously, I having read eighty pages since I got here. I expect to be in New York, by the 3d or 4th and home before the 10th.

We have news of important successes on the Rio Grande, which will probably produce an influence on the duration of the war. [Zachary] Taylor is safe enough, as [David] Conner has offered him 2000 seamen and marines, should they be required. But the lightening so far ou[t]strips the mail, that you must have all the news.

As yet I have done nothing beyond printing, though I have an appointment for to-morrow. I have strong hopes of effecting a good arrangement to keep me occupied for the next six months.

Neither the statues nor the picture is sold, nor do I believe either will be, by the man who has them in hand. He has done nothing. I must move in the matter.

I have seen Charlotte McCall, but Mary Wilcocks is with her uncle at Washington. Uncle Jo [Joseph R. Ingersoll] is flirting away, but makes no signs of a matrimonial character.

I have paid no other visit, as yet, but one to Mrs. McCall. This evening, however, I intend to break ground.

Paul appears to have attended to his duty, and he ought not to forget to ask for the money for the calf, else he will not get it, until my return. In his next let him say whether there has been a frost and how much harm it did — How the meadows and pastures look &c — &c.

The water-cure must set him up, and do it, I make no doubt it will. The best old school physicians admit it is excellent in certain cases; especially in those in which the constitution requires a change. So far as I can learn, in no case where it is properly used, does it cause colds, which is all Paul has to fear.

Tell Dick his matter shall be attended to. [Edwin] Spafard's affair has gone so far, it had better go on. Perhaps useful facts may be obtained, as to Tiffany's statements to him; then the original letter may differ from the copy. Dick had better not plead to any of those matters until my return.

It is very warm, here, and I am shortening sail. Should it be warm to-night, I intend to take of[f] my flannel, and try a cold bath in the morning.

Tell Paul not to spare Pumpkin, and to *drive* him in the wagon, if he think it safe — Safe it is, with common care and daily work.

I have nothing more to say, my letter being sent merely to let you know that I am well and in good spirits. No attempt made as yet for Susy — Nothing done, indeed, in that way for even myself.

With tenderest love to all,

I remain yours the most of all

J— F. C.

Poor Ring[g]old, whom I knew very well, is dead of his wounds. I was talking to his brother about him, after he was dead and buried, though neither of us knew the fact.[1]

ADDRESSED: Mrs. Fenimore Cooper | Cooperstown | New York POSTMARKED: PHILADELPHIA Pa. | MAY | 24 STAMPED: 10
MANUSCRIPT: Cooper Collection, Yale University Library.

1. Samuel Ringgold (1800–1846, West Point 1818), soldier and military inventor, died on 11 May of wounds received on 8 May in the battle of Palo Alto, Texas. Cooper presumably referred to Samuel's brother Lieutenant Cadwalader Ringgold (1802–1867), commissioned midshipman in 1819 and promoted to rear admiral on the retired list in 1866, who accompanied Charles Wilkes on his exploring expedition. (*ACAB*.)

863. *To Paul Fenimore Cooper*

Heads, Tuesday, 26th May, 1846

My Dear Paul,

As I have written to your mother twice, this letter shall be sent to you. No doubt you have got all the military news, which is highly favourable. Gen — [Taylor] [1] seems to be perfectly master of his movements, and knows what he was about. He is clear-headed and cool, and made his call for volunteers at precisely the right moment. Notwithstanding the alarm that existed here, he appears to have been under no apprehensions. As early as the 6th April, he informed the government of his intention to build a fort that 500 men could defend, when it would leave the rest of his command free to act. Every thing has turned out, as he foresaw. The 500 men have, so far, defended the fort, with a loss of 13 in killed and wounded, and the remainder of his force has proved sufficient for all his exigencies. The volunteers are wanted for a forward movement. Near 2000 of them had arrived on the 14th, and Conner could reinforce with as many more. Our [people?] must now be in Matamoros, unless the Mexicans have reinforced very largely.

The important feature is the course of England. If she secretly sustain Mexico, we shall certainly have an English war; if she be wise, she will endeavour to persuade Mexico to make peace. I think the issue doubtful. The war is well sustained, though the Whigs dislike the popularity it may give the administration.

Yesterday, I had a conversation with a respectable physician concerning your case. He is an old school practitioner, and a youngish man. His remarks were these.

The pulse, the irregularity of circulation, and the loss of muscular power, are all direct consequences of the narcotick influence of tobacco. He suffered in the same way himself, and to an extent as to make his heart appear enlarged. He cured himself by throwing aside tobacco, in all its forms, as he says you may do. The inflamed throat and chest, to my surprise, he refers to the same cause. Tobacco has the effect to leave the mucous membrane in a state liable to chronic inflammation. He says that hydropathy is the best specific ever known. There is but one question to be ascertained in your case, and that is the power of reaction. If you have force sufficient to produce reaction, your cure would be rapid, but that power must exist to render the application safe.

I consider the result of this conversation very satisfactory, so far as your ultimate recovery is concerned. The time will depend on circumstances. The taste of blood, is the taste of blood in very small quantities from the inflamed blood vessels of the throat. The complaint is very common, in cases in which tobacco has not been used, though tobacco greatly disposes to it. Several persons whom I had thought in robust health tell me they have suffered in the same way.

I am strongly in hopes Peak [2] will help you. Homeopathy is slow, you will remember, and patience is a very necessary companion in such a cure. Avoid night air and getting wet, take plenty of exercise and look into your books of practice, by way of relaxation, and [easy?] toil. My doctor said the diet ought to be carefully attended to, especially if the bowels or digestion indicated any such necessity.

I am getting on very well, and shall leave here early next week. Yesterday I dined with Gen. Tom Cadwalader. Major [Samuel] Ring[g]old was his kinsman, his mother having been a Cadwalader, a sister of Gen. [John] Cadwalader of the revolution.[3] The poor fellow was shot through both thighs, the shot going through his horse and killing him dead. Mary Farmers old beau Col. Payne [4] is among the wounded. She must volunteer to nurse him.

Tell the girls Peter McCall is engaged to a Miss Mercer of

Maryland; a daughter of Major John Mercer, an old acquaintance of mine — [5] She is a belle and twenty two. As Peter is thirty eight, he will not wait a great while.

The Capt. McCall in the army,[6] is of the Philadelphia family and Peter's brother. Mrs. H[arry] McCall's little girl was christened in St. Peter's church, yesterday afternoon.

It is intensely hot here, and you can tell your mother I keep in the house, using cold baths. I got happily rid of the flannels night before last, and now do not miss them, unless it be by being more comfortable.

Write a letter to me next Sunday, and direct it to the City Hotel New York. I shall get that of Thursday here, and the other on Tuesday morning.

I shall leave this letter open until the arrival of the Southern mail, in order to send you the latest news. In the mean time say to your mother that I never was better, that the cold baths relieve my skin, and give me new force. The kindest love to all. I am writing on Gen Jackson's desk.[7]

Wednesday Morning, 27th

The southern mails merely confirm the good news from Point Isabel. A great many letters are in town, from officers of the army and navy, to their wives and friends. Among others, Lt. Mead[e], of the Topographical E[n]gineers, who is married to the Miss [Sergeant] [8] who looks like Sue, has written to his wife, and Harry Ingersoll to his.[9] [Harry] Ingersoll is the first lieutenant of [David] Conner's ship, and was sent up to the camp, with communications for the general. I heard his letter read last night. He boasts largely of his own exploits *on horseback*, flattering himself that none of the army people could have done much better, than riding sixty miles in two days, though he hints that his seat of honour is none the better for the exercise. But the material part of his communication is this — [Taylor] and Conner are certainly arranging a joint expedition against Matamoros. The letter was dated the 13th, and, unless the Mexicans have been largely reinforced, or the general should choose to wait for the volunteers, the attack was probably made by the 18th — [10] If so we must get the result in a day, or two.

I think the Mexicans have left the left bank of the river, entirely. So Gen. [Taylor] reports, and so the result will show, I make no question, unless large reinforcements are sent, to Arista. The opinion is general, that the war will be short, it being thought that a revolution will supervene. I am not so certain of this. Outward pressure usually has the effect to suspend internal revolutions. Then our government will wish to compensate itself for the expenses of the war, by some signal advantage. California must fall into our hands in the next sixty days, and I think our people will wait for that result. I expect to hear it is sold to England.

I got your mother's letter last night, and was glad to see her hand once more. Do you make your farm report whether she write again, or not.

I forgot to mention that poor Ringgold sent for Ingersoll, and died with his own hand in that of the last. He was quite free from pain, and had his senses to the last. His troop was commanded by a Lt. Ridgely [11] in the last battle, and appears to have behaved in the noblest manner. All our artillery behaved in the best possible manner. As Major [John] Erving's name does not appear, I fear he is on the sick list, he having been left behind at Corpus Christi, on account of his health. Still, he may have joined. The Mexicans have probably lost a thousand men, in the two affairs.

There is a report here, that Capt. Thornton [12] showed no judgment in his affair, while Hardee [13] behaved very well. Capt. May [14] has highly distinguished himself. The Mexican lancers charged Ridgely's guns, but he drove them back with canister. They also charged the 5th Infantry, which received them in square, and set them to the right about with a rattling fire of musketry.

[Taylor] will doubtless be made one of the new Majors General. Scott, it is said, will be kept back, though it is difficult to see how. The Whigs complain, for they wish to use him as a candidate and float into office on his glory. But all this is nonsense, popular feeling being so very capricious. One mishap would lose him all the popularity purchased in the war of '12.

Adieu — love to all.

P. Fenimore Cooper Esquire — J. Fenimore Cooper

ADDRESSED: Paul Fenimore Cooper Esquire | Cooperstown | New York POSTMARKED: PHILADELPHIA | MAY | 27 | 5

MANUSCRIPT: Paul Fenimore Cooper, Cooperstown, New York. PUBLISHED, IN PART: *Correspondence*, II, 543–46. (The date given in the *Correspondence* is 27 May 1845.)

1. Cooper wrote "Taylour" here and elsewhere in this letter.

2. Dr. James M. Peak (1808?–1855), a member of the American Institute of Homeopathy, practiced in Cooperstown in the late 1840's and early 1850's (*Institute Proceedings*, 1846–1853; Hurd, *History of Otsego County*, 261).

3. Major Ringgold's mother was Maria, daughter of the Revolutionary soldier General John Cadwalader (1742–1786) and first wife of Congressman Samuel Ringgold (*DAB, ACAB*).

4. Cooper's friend Lieutenant Colonel Matthew Mountjoy Payne (d. 1862), commissioned first lieutenant in 1812, was breveted colonel on 9 May 1846 for gallant and distinguished service in the battles of Palo Alto and Resaca de la Palma, Texas (*Historical Register and Dictionary of the United States Army*).

5. Peter McCall (1809–1880, College of New Jersey [Princeton] 1826), a distinguished Philadelphia lawyer who studied with Joseph R. Ingersoll and served as mayor of Philadelphia in 1844, married Jane Byrd Mercer, daughter of John Mercer (d. 1848, St. John's College, Annapolis), on 9 July 1846 at Cedar Park, West River, Arundel County, Maryland. Commissioned major by President Monroe, Mercer, the son of John Francis Mercer, the Revolutionary hero and governor of Maryland, accompanied General Winfield Scott on his inspection of European military fortifications in 1815. (James Mercer Garnett, *Biographical Sketch of Hon. James Mercer Garnett . . . with Mercer-Garnett and Mercer Genealogies* [Richmond, Virginia: Whittet & Shepperson, 1910], 53–54, 59; *NCAB*, IV, 374; *American & Commercial Daily Advertiser*, Baltimore, Maryland, 15 July 1846.)

6. Captain George Archibald McCall (d. 1868), commissioned second lieutenant in 1822, was breveted major and lieutenant colonel on 9 May 1846 for gallant and meritorious conduct in the battles of Palo Alto and Resaca de la Palma (*Historical Register and Dictionary of the United States Army*).

7. Jesse D. Elliott willed to Cooper the desk presented to Andrew Jackson by the citizens of Boston and to Elliott by Grenville Temple Winthrop (MS: Washington Lafayette Elliott to Cooper, 4 January 1846, YCAL).

8. Cooper wrote "Sargeant." George Gordon Meade (1815–1872, West Point 1835), still a second lieutenant in 1846, married Margaretta, daughter of John Sergeant (see Cooper to Mrs. Cooper, 27 May 1844), in 1840 (*NCAB*, IV, 66–68).

9. Lieutenant Harry Ingersoll was married to Sarah Emlen Roberts (Lillian Drake Avery, *A Genealogy of the Ingersoll Family in America, 1629–1925 . . .* [New York: Frederick H. Hitchcock, 1926], 221).

10. Matamoros was evacuated by the Mexicans and occupied by General Taylor's forces on 18 May.

11. Lieutenant Randolph Ridgely, accidentally killed on 27 October 1846, was breveted captain on 9 May 1846 for gallant and distinguished conduct in the battles of Palo Alto and Resaca de la Palma (*Historical Register and Dictionary of the United States Army*).

12. On 25 April 1846, Captain Seth Barton Thornton (d. 1847) had led a reconnoitering party which was routed by General Mariano Arista above Matamoros, with eleven killed, five wounded, and the remainder captured. General Taylor regarded this action as the commencement of hostilities in the Mexican War. (*Historical Register and Dictionary of the United States Army*.)

13. Captain William Joseph Hardee (d. 1873, West Point 1834), twice breveted for gallant and meritorious conduct during the Mexican War, became a general in the Confederate Army (*Historical Register and Dictionary of the United States Army*).

14. Captain Charles Augustus May (d. 1864), commissioned second lieutenant in 1836, was breveted major on 8 May 1846 for gallant and distinguished service in the battle of Palo Alto and lieutenant colonel on 9 May 1846 for gallant and highly distinguished conduct at the battle of Resaca de la Palma (*Historical Register and Dictionary of the United States Army*).

864. *To Richard Bentley*

Philadelphia, May. 28th 1846

Dear Sir,

Your letter of the 1st of the Month [1] has been sent to me, here, where I have come to finish off, as fast as possible the new book, the name of which I have changed to "The Redskins, or Indian and Injin." You can call it Ravensnest, if you please; though the first name is the most apposite.[2]

The delay has been caused by illness in my family. Mrs. Cooper and my son have both been much indisposed, and I have lost two nieces this winter.[3] For a month I was kept at home by the illness of my wife, and two days after she left her room I came here, to hurry the work.

We are getting on very fast, forty pages a day, but I can send you no more than vol I, and about a third of vol. IId by the steamer of the 1st. By the *packets* of the 8th you shall have the remainder, or by the ⟨Britannia⟩ Great Britain should she sail earlier.

By going to press at once with the two English volumes I now send you, there will be so much time gained.

I am negotiating here to publish a nautical tale in a Magazine — Graham's and I should like to know what could be done with it, on your side of the water. The magazine is printed so much in advance of the publication as to allow of its being sent over in good season. Will you drop me a line, as early as you can, on this subject.[4] I have offers from Europe, but wish to hear from other parties before I close.

This work closes our arrangement. I shall draw for the balance due me on Redskins, (£100) most probably before I quit Philadelphia, and without farther advice. The bill may arrive five or six days before the remaining sheets, but you may rely on the packages being duly attended to and on duplicates being sent.

For a remunerating price, I am ready to give as strong a

nautical tale, as any body going, but the publishers pay so little now, as almost to induce me to turn to some other pursuit. I do not like change, but shall be driven to something of the sort, without an increase of price. I can not write a book for the sum I recieve, and do justice to any one.

At all events, have the goodness to send me an early answer on the subject of the Magazine story. Here I am offered a liberal inducement, though not enough of itself, to induce me to accept it without an arrangement in England.

Our Mexican war will be a short one, unless England interferes, and takes sides with Mexico. This nation is roused, and goes into it, with great good will.

In haste, | Yours &

Mr. Bentley | Publisher | London. J. Fenimore Cooper

ADDRESSED: Mr. Richard Bentley | Publisher | New-Burlington Street | London | England | By the steamer of the 1st May | Boston. POSTMARKED: PHILADELPHIA Pa. | MAY | 2[8?] AA | 15 JU 15 | 1846 STAMPED: PAID 10
MANUSCRIPT: Cooper Collection, Yale University Library.

1. In the letter of 1 May, Bentley expressed concern about the uncustomary delay of the manuscript of the new novel. "I have for some time announced it as in the press," he wrote, "and have spent a considerable sum upon it, which unless I soon receive the MS will be in a great measure spent in vain." (MS: YCAL.)

2. Bentley retained the title *Ravensnest*.

3. Cooper was apparently thinking of his niece by marriage Mrs. Mary (Storrs) Cooper, wife of Richard Cooper, and of Mrs. Sarah Sabina (Cooper) Comstock, wife of Horace H. Comstock. The first died on 28 January and the second on 15 February. (Cooperstown *Freeman's Journal*, 31 January and 28 February 1846.)

4. See Cooper to Bentley, 20 July 1846.

865. *To William Heathcote De Lancey*

Hall, Cooperstown, June 9th 1846

My dear sir,

Understanding you intend to come and see us, en route for town, I write to make the following statement —

Mr. Beach, our clergyman, is a deacon, and very desirous to be ordained priest in his parish. We hear the money has given out, and point d'argent point de Suisse meaning no money no bishop. As well as other things, your visit will offer the only chance of having things as we wish. I hope, provided that he get the regular documents from our standing committee, you can ordain him, and write that you may not have the excuse of having left your pontificals at home. If you say *yes*, be good enough to send a missive ahead, a day or two before your own arrival, that preparations may be made.[1]

I saw Ned on my way up, looking as if he might occasionally study.

I am glad to say Paul is improving. He is losing precious moments in consequence of the abuse of tobacco, which not only deranged his whole nervous system, but actually stupified him, and kept him asleep half his time. In addition, it predisposed the mucous membrane of the throat and chest to inflammation, and a chronic disease has followed a sharp cold. Exercise on horseback, treatment, and relaxation are beginning to bring him round, though I do not think less than a year, or two, will completely set him up. I wish him to try water-cure, which works miracles. It will almost set a leg, and washes a good many people who might otherwise go foul all their lives.

With kindest regards to all,

I remain very truly Yours

Dr. de Lancey. J. Fenimore Cooper

ADDRESSED: The Rt. Rev. Dr. de Lancey | Geneva | New York POSTMARKED: COOPERSTOWN N.Y. | JUN | 10 STAMPED: PAID 5 ENDORSED: J. Fenimore Cooper | June 15/46

MANUSCRIPT: Cooper Collection, Yale University Library. PUBLISHED, IN PART: *Correspondence*, II, 564.

1. Bishop De Lancey ordained the Reverend Alfred Baury Beach and the Reverend Edwin Harwood priests in the Protestant Episcopal Church at a special service in Christ Church, Cooperstown, on 21 September 1846 (*Journal of the Tenth Annual Convention of the Diocese of Western New-York* [Utica, New York: printed for the Convention, 1847], 21).

866. *To Elliot C. Cowdin*

Hall, Cooperstown, June 30th 1846

Sir,

Your letter of the 24th has just reached me. In reply, I beg to say that it was not my wish to advert at all, to the reasons why I did not deliver the lecture before your association that I had partially promised Mr. [Francis G.] Whiston to deliver, and which, at one time, it was fully my intention to deliver; [1] but, since your own allusion to the subject, I concieve it will be more respectful to your association, and more just to myself, to make a brief explanation, rather than attempt to avoid one.

You may probably know that my integrity as a man, and my fidelity as a historian, were coarsely and brutally called in question, by certain persons who were, or fancied themselves to be the friends of the late Commodore Perry, in connection with my narrative of the Battle of Lake Erie. By proceeding against the late Mr. Stone for a libel, I compelled him, in order to save his money, the only consideration that had much influence with *him*, to make an issue involving not only all the legal, but all the moral ⟨facts⟩ principles of the case, including as a matter of course the facts. This issue was publicly traversed before distinguished arbitrators in the City of New York, two of whom were of Mr. Stone's own selection, and all of whom were of his political party. The result was a triumphant award in my favour. After this award was made, I published a pamphlet on the subject, completely vindicating my own history, as I concieve, and unanswerably proving the falsehood[s?], folly and frauds of those who had assailed me. This pamphlet I sent to Boston, to be sold, in common with other places.

You will remember that the subject was of a nature to interest the public, that I had been assailed, and that the award of the arbitrators was a pledge that my case merited attention. My reputation is as dear to me and my children, as any other man's reputation can be dear to himself and family. If I had any literary merit, as you are pleased to intimate, it was an additional reason why my appeal should at least recieve some notice, in every part of the country where it appeared.

About the time our correspondence took place, last year, and quite two years after the publication of my pamphlet, my son went to the Law School at Cambridge. I availed myself of his being there to desire him to call on the booksellers to whom the pamphlet had been sent, to enquire after the sales. The answer was contemptuous, not to say rude. My son was told that the people of Boston did not wish to be enlightened on the subject of the Battle of Lake Erie, that their minds were made up, and that not a copy was sold; or if any were sold the number was so insignificant as to render any account out of the question.

Astonished to hear such a reply given to a writer, who, to say the least, was accustomed to meet with ordinary respect from the largest publishers of Europe and America, I wrote to a distinguished literary friend in Boston, to enquire if it were possible that the state of feeling in your town was really such, that, under the circumstances named, no notice would be taken of a pamphlet which discussed an interesting point in history, and that too under circumstances which made a strong appeal to the sense of justice of every right-thinking community. I do not feel at liberty to go into details on the subject of the reply I recieved, but it was of such a character as to satisfy me that I should lecture to an audience that was much too self-satisfied to render it at all agreeable for one whose only motive in lecturing at all, was to oblige others and [in?] a love of truth.[2] I knew that the libels on me, in reference to this very matter, had been extensively circulated and widely believed in Boston, and if I could not obtain a hearing even, in my own defence, what motive could I possibly have to wish to obtain a hearing on any other subject?

Sir, I shall not affect reserves that I do not feel. The opinion of no community on earth, would be respected by me, after I knew it condemned ignorantly. I care very littl[e,][3] therefore, what is thought in Boston about my account of the Battle of Lake Erie, but I do care too much to preserve my self-respect, to appear voluntarily before any portion of a community, with a demand on its reliance on my intellect and truth, after this clear demonstration how I stand with it, previously. It is very true I might convince the people of Boston they have been mistaken, as I have convinced thousands in my own community, that were just as well satisfied they knew all about the Battle of Lake Erie, as would seem to be the case in your part of the country; but the attempt would be attended with a sacrifice of feeling, with no commensurate object, that will induce me to decline making it. If a quarter of [a] century's knowledge of my opinions, capacity and integrity is not sufficient of itself to obtain for me a hearing, when I ask it, on a subject in which the public has as much interest as I can possibly have ⟨myself⟩, I shall not humble myself so far as to ask it even of the people of Boston. I shall, therefore, never appear before them, in the character of a lecturer.

I am aware this is a long, and quite possibly to you, an uninteresting explanation. I should never have volunteered it, but your own letter seems to call for some sort of reply, and I know of none so proper as the truth —

I am quite sensible of, and truly grateful for the compliment conveyed in the reiterated requests of your association, that I should lecture before it. They certainly argue a ⟨certain⟩ degree of respect and interest, though, it would seem not enough to induce even your members to give me a hearing on a subject deeply affecting my own character, at the very moment it is, or ought to be of interest to every American — of interest to learn the *truth,* not the senseless concern that certain minds are eager to manifest in support of opinions once imbibed. We shall not quarrel about this, however, and one of my pleasantest associations with Boston, will be the recollection of the repeated wish, [which?] your association has manifested that we should become acquainted. Although I can never lecture before it, you will permit me to retain this agreeable recollection.

And now, sir, asking your forgiveness for occupying so much of your time, permit me to conclude with my best wishes for the success of your laudible efforts to acquire information. You will ever be a little deficient, in my view of the case, on the subject of the Battle of Lake Erie, and I do honestly think it would be in my power to enlighten you; but there are so many things on which you might instruct me, that I feel no disposition to value myself on some little advantage in this one particular. It is merely the result of the responsibility of a historian, close investigation as a consequence of that responsibility, and a professional education. It would be a little remarkable, if I did not understand this one subject better than those who have obtained their information from either loose statements made by looser news-paper writers, ⟨and⟩ or from the allegations of those who have taken up the subject to sustain one side of the question, rather than the truth. In my own case it is known to all who have any precise knowledge in the matter, that so far from having written in the interest of friends, I have lost old and attached friends by preferring the truth even to their favour.

But, I am wearying you with a subject, in which probably you feel no interest. I desire to thank you personally for the kind expressions of your letter, and make no doubt you are sincere in all you say. You will readily understand however, that no man can have a very lively wish to appear before a public that has treated him, in an important issue, in as indifferent a manner, as the Boston public has treated me, and in this, you will find the simple solution of my decision.

I might add, as respects last year, that my son, to visit whom I intended to go to Boston, was compelled to return home, on account of his health, as early as November, and that it is questionable after that, if it would have been in my power to see you at all.

Repeating my wishes for the success of your institution

I remain, Sir, | Very Respectfully | Your Ser.

Elliott C. Cowdin Esquire. J. Fenimore Cooper

MANUSCRIPT: Houghton Library, Harvard University. PUBLISHED: Dorothy Waples, "A Letter from James Fenimore Cooper," *The New England Quarterly*, III (January 1930), 123–32.

Partner in a Boston millinery firm, Cowdin (1819–1880) was a leading promoter of the Boston Mercantile Library Association, which sponsored an excellent library for merchants' clerks and the most popular lecture series in Boston. He chaired the Lecture Committee. Cowdin transferred his business and civic activities to New York City about 1853. (E. P. Whipple and others, *A Memorial of Elliot C. Cowdin* [privately printed without place or date].)

1. Cowdin's cordial letter of 24 June 1846 (MS: YCAL; printed by Waples with Cooper's reply) renewed an invitation extended by Cowdin on behalf of the Mercantile Library Association on 24 August 1845 (MS: YCAL) and delivered to the novelist in person by Francis G. Whiston, a member of the association, Cowdin acknowledged Cooper's provisional acceptance, written on 2 September 1845 but unlocated, on 23 September 1845 (MS: YCAL). The letter of 24 June 1846, to which Cooper here replied, offered him his choice of dates in the series beginning on 15 October and continuing for eighteen successive Wednesday evenings, indicated that the fee would be $50 if he wished to claim it, and assured him that his "reception would be as cordial as could be extended to any American." Indeed, Cowdin continued, there was "a very strong wish in our community to see one who has been so long and pleasantly known by his writings, and whose works are part and parcel of the intellectual treasures of the nation."

2. See Cooper to R. H. Dana, 30 October 1845.

3. The script is lost at the fold.

867. *To Lewis Gaylord Clark*

Hall, Cooperstown, July 8th '46

Dear Sir,

I have desired one of my daughters to translate the letter of Prince Dolgoroucki, and I enclose the original of Mr. Brown, both as you have requested.[1]

I am very sensible of the civility you have manifested in taking so much trouble, on my account, and desire to thank you.

I have had several letters from Constantinople, in my time, but never one so completely Asiatick, as this from Téhéran, which I shall place among my family archives, too, on account of its singularity, as well as on account of its amiable language. I have ever found the better class of the Russians among the most accomplished people of Europe, and it has been my good fortune to know a great many of them. In saying what I did to Prince Dolgoroucki I was perfectly sincere, and I would go out of my way sooner to oblige a Russian, than any man I know, on the mere ground of nationality. To myself, personally, English, French, Italians & Russians, were equally civil — all nations, indeed, but the Germans — but the Russians manifest consideration for the American name, which no other European people do — unless, indeed, it may be the Swiss.

Very Respectfully | Yours

Mr. Gaylord Clark. J. Fenimore Cooper

MANUSCRIPT: Cooper Collection, Yale University Library. PUBLISHED: *Correspondence*, II, 590–91. (The date is incorrectly given as 8 July 1848 in the *Correspondence*.)

1. Clark wrote Cooper on 6 July: "I enclose you a note received a day or two since from our old friend and correspondent at Constantinople, Mr. Brown, U. S. [Draftsman?] and now our only representative at the Sublime Porte, covering a letter from Prince Dolgorouki to yourself.

"Will you have the kindness to return again the note of Mr. Brown; and if it be not asking too great a favor, I should like exceedingly to know what M. Dolgorouki says in reply to the admirable letter from yourself, which you were good enough to leave open for my perusal." (MS: YCAL.)

The letter of J. P. Brown is unlocated. For the translation of Prince Dolgoruky's letter by Susan Fenimore Cooper on the manuscript with Cooper's letter to Clark, see *Correspondence*, II, 591–92.

868. *To Richard Bentley*

Hall, Cooperstown, July 20th 1846

Dear Sir,

Your letter reached me yesterday.[1] I do not object to the offer, though it must be qualified, in one or two particulars. A statement of my bargain with Mr. Graham will show in what. I am to give him a nautical tale, in ten parts, each part to make ten pages of his magazine. Now, I know from experience, that sixteen pages of my manuscript, will make rather more than ten pages of Graham. Consequently, I shall give him ten numbers of sixteen pages of manuscript each, or 160 p.p. Man. 240 pp. Man. make a common novel. It follows, that this tale will fall short of a common novel just one third; or it will make only two, instead of three volumes in England. This is the present arrangement with Mr. Graham. I am willing to extend the story to three volumes, and think I can make a better story by so doing, but I do not know whether he wishes such a change, or not. I propose therefore, that you pay me one third less than £350, for the tale as now settled, or the £350, if I can effect a change with Graham, in the length of the story. The price for the smaller amount would be, say £233.10, or thereabouts.

Graham expects to publish in ten months, after he commences. If one third be added to the story, it would be in fifteen months of course. You can settle your own mode for drawing, after you know these facts, though I should prefer £100 drafts to £50. If I draw at 90 days, now we have so many boats it can make no great difference to you.

Graham publishes on the 1st of each month, and intends to bring out the first number I believe in Nov, possibly in Oct. Of course you must publish simultaneously. Graham says he can let you have the printed sheets to print from, with perfect regularity, if you wish it, and I know he has his matter in type fully a month before he issues. My bargain with him binds me only to prevent any issue before his.

It is necessary to understand each other, and to do that at once. If you write me immediately, I can get your answer before I deliver Graham any part of the Manuscript, the day for which is Sept. 1st. I beg therefore, an immediate answer. Graham is acquainted with your mode of publishing, and assured me that there could not be the smallest difficulty in arranging the periods. He publishes in fact, on the 24th I believe; that is issues, though the magazine comes to the subscribers about the 1st. I see you do the same thing. He is well disposed, and will do all he can to oblige me. If he publish in Oct. I should have to send you the first part in manuscript, but I do not think he *can* publish before Nov. After we begin, of course we must go on.

I do not like the failure of the sheets, by the steamer of the 1st. I paid to have them go in that steamer, and know they left Philadelphia in time. It is of no consequence, I presume, as the book has been published but a few days, here, I understand, owing to some delay in New York. But it is important to me to be certain of my conveyance, especially with periodical publication.

On the whole, I shall not object to £50 drafts, making the last one the odd £33, or £100, if the price rise to £350.

On looking over your letter I see there is a fatal objection to the whole arrangement. I can not let you have the last 100 p.p. to publish before Graham publishes. My bargain with him forbids it. It may be published simultaneously with him, but not, as you say, three or four weeks, before him. Unless you can yield this point, I must send the work to a friend to be disposed of, as best he can. You will see, therefore, the importance of writing me immediately.

The times of drawing must be changed to meet the time the work will be in going through the magazine, and the right to publish the last 100 p.p. before Mr. Graham cannot be granted. You can have a number so as to publish in a book, about the time the work is finished here, but not so much in advance as you mention — very little, if any advance, and none at all without my arranging with Graham for it, which might be done for a few days, in my opinion.

Let me urge an immediate answer.[2]

Yours truly

Mr. Bentley J. Fenimore Cooper

As for Mexico, she will cost us a great deal of money, and it is not unlikely we shall dismember her. The northern provinces, or states, are ripe for revolt, and this country is much bent on taking California. I presume it is effectually in our hands now, in which case it will not be easily given up. The mines, too, seem to be in a bad way! Oregon, you know, *is* settled.

MANUSCRIPT: Cooper Collection, Yale University Library.

1. Bentley had written on 25 June:

"I received in the course of yesterday at the same time the two packets containing the whole copy of The Redskins. The first portion of the Work did not arrive, as I was led to expect by your letter, by the Steamer which left New York on the 1st. I have therefore lost an entire week by this delay. I take it for granted, however, that you have arranged the publication in [the] U. S. so as not to jeopardize my copyright here. I feel at present somewhat uneasy on this point as you do not mention the time of publication on your side of the water. Your bill for £100 drawn from Philadelphia at 60 days was accepted by me yesterday.

"In reference to the new naval Story which you propose to me, I assume that it will be of the usual extent of your other novels, that is, of such amount as to make three fair volumes. I gather from your letter that you mean to make this 'a strong nautical tale.' Relying upon your carrying out this notion, and to convince you that I am anxious to preserve a connection of so long standing, I am willing to advance £100 upon the price of the last novel.

"In making this offer I stipulate that I shall receive the monthly portions of the story in sufficient time to publish in my Miscellany of the same month, say, at latest, by the 24th of each month; and the last 100 pages to be supplied so as to enable me to publish the complete work three or four weeks before its completion in my monthly Miscellany. You do not say how much will be given in each Monthly of Graham, or in other words, over what period the whole will be spread. I conjecture that it may be about 18 months. The following will, I think, be a fair mode of distributing the payment, viz. On your transmitting the first portion you should draw on me for £50, and at intervals of 3 months to follow up these drafts by others of the same amount, but making the last £100. The total being £350. These drafts to be at 90 days." (MS: YCAL.)

2. Bentley accepted Cooper's proposals in a letter of 14 August on condition that the procedure followed be one which would safeguard his English copyright and permit him to publish the novel complete two weeks before the last installment appeared in his *Miscellany* (MS: YCAL).

869. *To Joseph Salkeld, for* The Evergreen

Cooperstown, N. Y. [August? 1846]

Mr. Editor: —

The explanations of the clerical appellations of the English Church, which are contained in a late number of the Evergreen,[1] will be found useful to the general reader. Many persons fancy that the clerical grades that have been established in that country are innovations on the scriptural orders of the ministry, when in truth they are in existence merely as the fruits of polity. Every branch of the Church Catholic must admit of some little departure from primitive usages to adapt its canons to times and countries, and since these are the facts of the English system, it is well to know them. The question how far these facts are theologically expedient, is another matter; whether wise or the reverse, however, they belong to Ecclesiastical History.

I wish a similar explanation could be given of the distinctions which exist in the Church of Rome. We have not the same interest in the practices of the Papal system, it is true, that we have in those of our Mother Church; but we are no more likely to imitate the latter, by creating arch-deacons and deans, than imitate the former by creating Cardinals. The facts in each case are desirable simply as facts connected with ecclesiastical polities.

I once resided in Rome for several months, and endeavored to obtain on the spot an accurate notion of these details of polity, but with no great success. I learned enough, however, to be certain that many popular errors exist on the subject, and some prejudices. It is an error, I believe, to suppose that the Pope must be taken from the Holy College. As I understood from no less an authority than Cardinal Fesch,[2] any person may be elected to the holy See; a Protestant and a layman for instance. Of course in the event of so improbable a selection, the party chosen would have to receive Romish baptism and Romish orders before he could be enthroned.

The very vulgar opinion that none but an Italian can be chosen Pope, is refuted by the known history of the Papacy.

The Cardinals compose a very anomalous body. I am under the impression that a Cardinal need not belong to the priesthood at all. Most of them do, certainly; but I think it will be found that some do not. I question if Cardinal Albani,[3] late Secretary of State to the Papal Court, was ever in orders.

There are distinctions among the Cardinals, which are termed Cardinal-bishops, Cardinal-priests, and Cardinal-deacons. I see by the Almanack de Gotha, for 1840, that there were then six Cardinal-bishops, all of whom were Bishops of Sees; forty-four Cardinal-priests, of whom twenty-one are not Bishops of Sees, while the remainder are — principally as Archbishops and Patriarchs; and eleven Cardinal-deacons, not one of whom is a Bishop. With one of these Cardinal-deacons I had a personal acquaintance in 1830. He was then what is called a Monsignore, (a my Lord,) and had been employed as a legate in one of the provinces. He wore the tonsure, and appeared in society even in a sort of gown, and was esteemed an *ecclesiastic*; but I was distinctly told he was not in holy orders. The duties of this gentleman, who is now a Cardinal, were altogether of a political nature, and I presume so continue to be.

Many of the Cardinals have been married, but as no ecclesiastic is permitted to marry, this was before they were received into the Church. Cardinal Weld,[4] the first English Cardinal for ages, unless Cardinal York [5] could be considered one, had been married, and his daughter by that marriage, Lady Clifford, was living at Rome when he was appointed.

Cardinals, in particular cases, have been permitted to marry, but this is also done to priests, by dispensation. In all such cases I believe the party lays aside the character of an ecclesiastic.

These distinctions are of interest, and a knowledge of them, in many cases, might prove useful to the scholar. I hope these hints may induce some one more competent than myself to explain the usages of the Church of Rome, as those of the Church of England have already been explained in your pages.[6]

J. F. C.

SOURCE: *The Evergreen, or Church-Offering for All Seasons; A Repository of Religious, Literary, and Entertaining Knowledge, for the Christian Family*, III (September 1846), 280–81.

Founder of *The Evergreen* and editor from 1844 to 1850, the Reverend Salkeld (d. 1850), a classical scholar and teacher of languages, also published *Classical Antiquities* (1844), a book on the Greeks and the Romans, and *A First Book in Spanish* (1848). Writing to Cooper from his home in Naugatuck, Connecticut, on 13 November 1846, Salkeld declared: "I am desirous that the C[hurc]h should gain a hold upon the literature of the day & it was my design in establishing the Evergreen to promote this object by making a sort of 'Blackwood' in the Church of it. The Evergreen is now circulated in every state in the Union: yet its circulation does not much exceed four thousand. Had I lowered my standard of Churchmanship a little & joined the *rabble* Churchman (excuse the expression) in keeping up the panic about Puseyism [&c?] the list of subscribers might have been doubled – but I am determined to avoid both extremes – to adhere to the plain principles of the Prayer-Book." A professed admirer of Cooper's "fearless Churchmanship," Salkeld had, in July 1846 apparently, directed his printers to send Cooper *The Evergreen* gratis. When the novelist refused the first six or seven issues of Volume III at the post office because he had not subscribed, an explanation from Salkeld, Peck, and Stafford, dated New Haven, 30 July 1846, was forthcoming; and, evidently in appreciation, Cooper sent his first letter. (MSS: YCAL; *The Connecticut Courant*, Hartford, Connecticut, 7 September 1850.)

1. III (January 1846), 6–7.
2. Joseph Fesch (1763–1839), half brother of Napoleon's mother, was created cardinal in 1803 and banished to Lyons from 1810 to 1814. He lived at Rome, where Cooper knew him, from 1814 to 1839. (*GE*.)
3. See Cooper to Charles Wilkes, 9 April 1830.
4. Thomas Weld (1773–1837) married in 1796 Lucy Bridget Clifford, granddaughter of the third Lord Clifford, and had a daughter Mary Lucy (1799–1831), who married in 1818 her second cousin, later the seventh Baron Clifford. Weld's wife's death in 1815, left him free to take holy orders, and he entered the College of Cardinals in 1830. (*DNB*.)
5. Henry Benedict Maria Clement, Cardinal York (1725–1807), was the last

of the family of James II. Made cardinal in 1747, he was known to his Jacobite followers as Henry IX. (*DNB*.)

6. Salkeld appended his comments on Catholic idiom and usages to Cooper's letter and, on 2 September, sent it to an unidentified Catholic authority for information of the kind Cooper requested. The editor published the reply, with a supplement of his own, in *The Evergreen*, III (November 1846), 325–27. The Catholic cleric pronounced Cooper's letter "liberal and honest" in spirit and "correct" in substance, though he was puzzled about "what Mr. Cooper means (as he believes in the Apostolic succession) by *'Romish' orders*, in contradistinction to Protestant orders."

870. *To Mrs. Cooper*

Tremont House, Boston, August 20th 1846

Dearest,

I got here last evening at ½ past seven. Mr. [Alfred B.] Beach and Miss Dwight were in the stage. He was for the springs; she, poor girl, for a new school, at Little Falls. We had a pleasant morning. At Albany, I saw no one, but in the cars I met an acquaintance, or two, and the day passed well enough.

I found here, Mrs. Jaffray,[1] and Miss Lewina Wethered,[2] who sends her regards to the girls and expresses a wish to know them. The ship will sail next week; as early as Wednesday Shubrick says. I shall stay here until monday, and then go on with Mrs. Shubrick and Miss Wethered.

I have been all ⟨in⟩ the morning looking at the ship and Bunker Hill &c.

Boston is certainly a very fine town, and the bay is particularily striking. There is a vast improvement since I was last here, in all respects. Charlesto[w]n, in one sense, is created, as is East Boston, which was formerly Noddle's Island.

I have seen no one, but Frank March, that I knew, navy men excepted. The ship is already in beautiful order. Ogden[3] has been obliged to give up, on account of his health, and [Elie A. F.] Lavalette goes after all. The midshipman of the boat, was little Ochiltree,[4] who was in the Macedonian.

The ladies all send regards, and I send my love. I shall write again next Sunday. A letter written after you get this, would find me at the City Hotel. Let Paul ask Dick if there be any news, and let me know the answer —

Adieu; with tenderest regard,

J. F. C.

MANUSCRIPT: Paul Fenimore Cooper, Cooperstown, New York.

1. Matilda Wethered (b. 1790), an older sister of Mrs. Shubrick, married George Jaffray of Portsmouth, New Hampshire (Wethered, *Genealogical Record of the Wethered Family*, 12).

2. Lewina, daughter of Samuel and Eliza (Yates) Wethered, was Mrs. Shubrick's niece (Wethered, *Genealogical Record of the Wethered Family*, 11).

3. Henry W. Ogden (d. 1860), appointed midshipman in 1811, lieutenant in 1817, commander in 1838, and captain in 1848 (GNR).

4. David Ochiltree, appointed midshipman in 1839, passed midshipman in 1846, and master in 1855 (GNR).

871. *To Mrs. Cooper*

Tremont House. Boston. Sunday. Aug 23. '46

Dearest,

Here I am yet, but Mrs. Shubrick and myself shall leave to-morrow, or on Tuesday, at the latest. This delay may prevent my getting back quite as early as I expected, but not more than two or three days.

I have had a return of my attack of cholera morbus. It commenced Friday after noon, and was accompanied by fever. I vomited this time, pretty severely, and was *"exercised"* in all ways. I took no medicine, however, but *iced water*. Finding the water too much for my stomach, though I did not vomit at all, after I began to take it, I resorted to ice alone, and certainly reduced the fever by means of ice, while *I believe* I restored the tone of my stomach. It is all over now, and I shall be well enough to travel to morrow.

I wish you would let Paul give Harry Clark the substance of what follows —

"I have seen the Dr. Warren who performed the operation. He says that man is cured. The expense of living out of the hospital, will vary from $3 to $10 per week, as Harry shall choose for himself. The expense of the operation itself, will depend on the means of the party. In Harry's case, it will not be much; I should think under $100. The whole expense I should think would be under $300 —

If Harry goes into the hospital, he will have to be operated on by the surgeon there, whomsoever he may happen to be. If he take lodgings out, he can employ whom he pleases. The hospital will doubtless be the cheapest, but it is a great deal to have a surgeon who has operated in a similar case.

Dr. Warren thinks, and I agree with him, that Harry had better come here. Until he sees him, he can give no definite answer as to his case. As he would prefer to operate in cooler weather, say October, I think he had better make his arrangements, and come on early in October, prepared to be operated on, when Dr. Warren can determine what is best to be done." [1]

You must not be uneasy on my account, for I have no doubt this last attack will do me good. I think the first attack stopped too suddenly, and that the second was necessary. There has been a sudden change of weather, however, and it may be owing to that. At all events, it is over, and I am careful in diet. The fruit here is bad; not better than with us.

I shall be disappointed if I do not find letters at the City Hotel. Let me know also, wh[at] letters come for me. I shall probably go as far as Baltimore with Mrs. Shubrick, and return the next day.

I hope Paul uses Pumpkin every morning. He has now the best opportunity for exercise and a new bridle can be bought at Kipps',[2] if he wants one.

I am writing in Shubrick's parlour, amid a crowd, and must conclude.

Ever most tenderly yours, and our childrens

J. F. C.

ADDRESSED: Mrs. Fenimore Cooper | Cooperstown | New York POSTMARKED: BOSTO[N] | [24?] | [AUG?] | 5 cts
MANUSCRIPT: Cooper Collection, Yale University Library.

1. See Cooper to Dr. Jonathan Mason Warren, 10 and 31 October 1846.
2. Benjamin F. Kipp operated a saddle and harness establishment in Cooperstown (Livermore, *A Condensed History of Cooperstown*, 91).

872. *To Mrs. Cooper*

Head's, [Thursday],[1] 27th [August] '46

Dearest,

We got here last night, Mrs. Shubrick a good deal fatigued. Our passage from Providence was not "rough and ready" but rough and rainy. Dr. and Mrs. [Thomas Dent] Mutter were on board, as were several other persons of our acquaintance. Newport is breaking up, for the season. Thousands have been there. It very fairly rivals Saratoga.

Boston is a very fine town, and has charming environs, I can easily believe, nevertheless, that the climate is infernal. I was not the only person, by a hundred, to whom it gave the cholera morbus. At present I am doing pretty well, and should do very well if I could be quiet, but this evening I take Mrs. Shubrick to Baltimore, to return to-morrow. The loss of time is of no moment, as [George Rex] Graham is absent, and will not return until next week, Tuesday. I shall be home next week, but not until near its close. All nausea has now left me several days, and I have [but?] one or two passages daily, and those far from bad. But good weather would set me quite up. I feel strong, and indeed, one day excepted, was not much enfeebled.

I wish Dick to let me know, by a letter mailed Monday night, if any thing has been done. That letter would reach me *here,* if mailed in time. And one mailed next day would reach me at New York. I got his and your letter at the City Hotel. I shall endeavour to see Mrs. Oldfield, at Baltimore.

Mrs. Shubrick sends quantities of love, as I do myself. She had a bitter moment, at parting, and in thrusting her head out of the cars to look after him, came near having it knocked off by a post. For an hour she was silent, after which she revived, became conversible, and has been in very good spirits since. Her mind now turns to Mary, and she is impatient to reach her. Adieu my best love. Ever yours most tenderly,

J. F. C.

Redskins is making quite a sensation, in the high set, to my surprise! [2]

ADDRESSED: Mrs. Fenimore Cooper | Cooperstown | New York POSTMARKED: PHILADELPHIA Pa. | AUG | 2[7?]

MANUSCRIPT: Cooper Collection, Yale University Library. PUBLISHED, IN PART: *Correspondence*, II, 564–65.

1. Cooper wrote "Friday."

2. Bentley published *The Redskins* in London on 6 July 1846 under the title *Ravensnest; or, The Redskins*; Burgess and Stringer published the work in New York in July or early August 1846 (Spiller and Blackburn, *Bibliography*, 145).

873. *To Mrs. Cooper*

Head's Sunday, August. 30th 1846

My dearest Sue,

Here I am again, well and sound. We left here Thursday afternoon, and reached Baltimore at eleven that night. I bethought me of the telegraph just as we left the house, and sent the enclosed note to Mr. Lewin Wethered,[1] who got it, just as you see from the office, a few minutes later. In consequence, young Wethered was on the wharf ready to take charge of his aunt. Asa Fitch [2] and Moncure Robinson [3] were among the passengers, and rendered the trip pleasant.

I was too lazy to come back on Friday (having no motive, since [George R.] Graham will not be here until Tuesday at soonest) and passed the whole day at Baltimore. I did not see [Michael R.] McNally, who I rather think is out of town. One of his daughters is married to a Mr. Chatard,[4] who is second lieutenant of the Independence. He was a widower, when he married her.

I did see Mrs. Oldfield,[5] who tells a straight story. Both Tiffany and his wife, begged her to help him to a parish. The climate was the reason he gave. This was in October 1843. He admitted that his health was then much better than it had been. She says that he named his salary, $700 or $800 per an. she forgets which, *"with the house free."* These were her own words. She says Mr. [Philip] Berry did go to Cooperstown the succeeding spring, and that he told her Tiffany frightened him away by an account of the sickliness of the place. That a fever raged, my family was sick of it (Sue was a little indisposed you will remember in the spring of 1844) and that he saw no one, not even Mrs. [George] Clark[e], but hurried off, as fast as he could! This is the substance of her account, which Paul can give to Dick. To Mr. Berry I shall write, before I quit this, his address being, Rev. Philip Berry, Clearspring, Washington Co.,[6] Maryland. I got it from the Bishop. He must be examined of course, as his account of the sickliness of Cooperstown may be of interest.

I left Baltimore yesterday morning, at nine, and got here at three. I found Comm. [Charles] Stewart and Gov. [James] Hamilton of South Carolina, at table, and the old set. In New York I saw Col. [Matthew M.] Payne, who is waiting to have the ball extracted from his back. It went in just over the hip bone, and lodged near the back bone. He continued on horse-back to the end of the fight, and this nearly cost him his life. He is now much better, however, can walk with a cane, and once rid of the lead will do well enough.

Joe Ingersoll is re-nominated for Congress, but Charles' success is doubtful. *He* is strongly opposed by democrats. Joe was nominated unanimously. Joe will get in, as a matter of course.[7] Miss Virginia looks interesting when he is mentioned, but there is no engagement talked of. Poor, laughing Annie Payne has been at death's door, but is convalescent.

Gurny Smith told me your sister's were at Mrs. Welch's, a little out of town. I will manage to see them, to-morrow, if possible.

Mrs. Clymer is expecting in all next month. Oct. 1st the Commodore said, but at Baltimore I heard sooner. Mrs. Shubrick left for Washington, yesterday.

I shall leave here, Tuesday afternoon, if Graham arrive, and pass one day in New-York, and think I shall see you in all the week, certainly.

I am quite well, with no remains of the Cholera Morbus. Every thing regular, and a good long snooze, last night, has quite refreshed me, though I went to bed much fatigued, with the eternal shaking of a bad rail-road. They tire me, much more than the old carriages.

I hope Paul uses the horse, much, and daily. Did I tell you that Redskins is in great favour with the better classes. The praise I have heard of it, has been warm, and is, I doubt not, sincere. Its time is just coming. The common sense of the book tells.

With best love to the girls and Paul, | Yours most tenderly

J. F. C.

ADDRESSED: Mrs. Fenimore Cooper | Cooperstown | New York POSTMARKED: PHILADELPHIA Pa. | AUG | 30 STAMPED: 10

MANUSCRIPT: Cooper Collection, Yale University Library. PUBLISHED, IN PART: *Correspondence*, II, 565–66.

1. Lewin Wethered (1834–1883), eldest son of Peregrine and Louise Maria (Wickes) Wethered (Wethered, *Genealogical Record of the Wethered Family*, 18).

2. As state entomologist of New York from 1854 to 1870, Fitch (1809–1879) conducted valuable pioneering studies of insect damage (*DAB*).

3. A civil engineer and financier, Robinson (1802–1891, William and Mary n.g.) achieved such renown as an engineer of railroads that Czar Nicholas I tried to employ him. He was especially noted for his tunnels, bridges, grades, and curvatures. (*DAB*.)

4. Frederick Chatard, appointed midshipman in 1824, lieutenant in 1834, and commander in 1855. He resigned in 1861. (GNR.)

5. Evidently the wife of Granville S. Oldfield, a Baltimore commission merchant who served as agent for Lloyd's.

6. Punctuation supplied.
7. Both Ingersolls were returned to Congress.

874. *To Mrs. Cooper*

Head's, Tuesday, Sept. 1st 1846

My Dearest Sue,

As [George R.] Graham is not expected until to-morrow, I have nothing to do but to write letters. Your sisters are here, and I saw them to-day, looking very well. Penn has paid, all in good money, and now they are trembling for next February. There is little question, however, that the state will maintain its credit.

I have seen most of the Ingersolls. Mrs. Charles and her husband have just returned from Saratoga. She tells me Mrs. Tom Willing was at Sharon, and was cut dead by every body, one lady excepted, who was under obligations to her. Mrs. Ellen Willing is *not* married, though they talk of such an event.[1]

Your sisters are with Mrs. Welch, out of town, but dine to-day with Mrs. Evans in Pine Street.[2] I am asked, but have declined.

If a letter come from England by the next packet, too late to reach me by Thursday night, or Friday morning, in New York, you had better keep it.

I shall leave here Thursday morning, and be at home Saturday. Graham has written he will be home on Wednesday, or to-morrow.

I find Joe Ingersoll looking very well, and half disposed to pay us a visit. If he do come, however, it will not be until October. We shall talk the matter over together.

I suppose Shubrick has sailed, though I have not seen it announced. Our news to-day, is, that California is annexed. This will leave him very little to do.

The fruits here are delicious. I eat freely of them, but they do me good rather than otherwise. My health is quite restored, and I perspire freely; the one thing needful. I keep myself quiet, and remain as philosophical as possible. I shall take home some peaches, which are dog cheap — 50 cents a basket, for delicious. Grapes, too, will be very abundant, though it is early for them. Adieu — Tenderest love — tell Paul to ride —

J. F. C.

ADDRESSED: Mrs. Fenimore Cooper | Cooperstown | New-York STAMPED: 10
MANUSCRIPT: Cooper Collection, Yale University Library.

1. Ellen Willing (d. 1872), the divorced wife of James H. Schott, Jr. (see Cooper to Mrs. Cooper, 9 April 1844), subsequently married Count Blondell von Cuellbroeck, Envoy Extraordinary from Belgium to Spain (Jordan, *Colonial Families of Philadelphia*, I, 129).

2. *McElroy's Philadelphia Directory, for 1846* lists Joseph R. Evans at 103 Pine Street and Joseph R. Evans, Jr., at 101 Pine Street. Both were commision merchants at 31 South Wharf.

875. *To William Adee Whitehead*

Hall, Cooperstown, Sept. 18th 1846

Sir,

Your letter apprising me of my election as a Corresponding Member of the New Jersey Historical Society, has been recieved.[1]

I accept this compliment with peculiar satisfaction, as I happen to be a native of your State, and have some claims, on account of my predecessors, to feel more than a common interest in her annals. Although I was taken from New Jersey an infant, some of my earliest school boy days were passed within her limits, and I have never lost the impression then made in her favour.

I shall not probably prove a very profitable correspondent, though I beg you will not hesitate to employ me in any inquiry, or other business, in which it may be thought I might be useful. I shall not consider labour expended in behalf of New Jersey as time thrown away, but as a simple exhibition of natural filial piety. May I ask of you to make my acceptance known in the proper quarters, with my acknowledgements for the honour done me.

I am, | Sir | Very Respectfully | Your Obli. Ser

J. Fenimore Cooper

W. A. Whitehead Esquire | Newark, N. J.

MANUSCRIPT: The New Jersey Historical Society.

After spending his young manhood in Key West, Florida, as collector of the port, Whitehead (1810–1884) moved to New York City in 1838 and, somewhat later, to Newark, New Jersey, where he was a prolific historian and treasurer of various corporations, including the American Trust Company. Between 1837 and 1882, he published about 600 articles and letters in newspapers. (Samuel I. Prime, "Sketch of the Life and Character of William Adee Whitehead," *Proceedings of The New Jersey Historical Society*, VIII Second Series [1885], 183–202; *ACAB*.)

1. As corresponding secretary, Whitehead wrote from Newark on 5 September 1846 to inform Cooper of his election on 3 September as a corresponding member

of the New Jersey Historical Society. A copy of the constitution and bylaws were forwarded with the letter. (MS: YCAL.)

876. *To Richard Bentley*

Hall, Cooperstown | Sept. 22d 1846

Dear Sir,

I enclose you Part 1. of the Tale for the Magazine. A duplicate will go by the "Sheridan" to Liverpool. The story will be in ten parts, and for the short price, of course. It is nearly written, and I will take care of your rights. You will see that you must publish this part in your November number, after which we shall have more time.[1] The end will be looked to by me, in such a way as to give you a good margin as to time.

I have drawn for the first £50 in favour of my stereotyper Mr. John Fagan — The bill is to go forward the beginning of Oct. not until the 3d I believe. You will probably see it, a few days after you get this.

Yours &c
J. Fenimore Cooper

Mr. Richard Bentley | London

MANUSCRIPT: Cooper Collection, Yale University Library.

1. *Jack Tier, or, The Florida Reef* appeared as *The Islets of the Gulf; or, Rose Budd* in *Graham's American Monthly Magazine of Literature and Art,* XXIX (November 1846), 205–15; XXIX (December 1846), 277–87; XXX (January 1847), 49–81; XXX (February 1847), 121–32; XXX (March 1847), 181–92; XXX (April 1847), 217–28; XXX (May 1847), 301–13; XXX (June 1847), 349–60; XXXI (July 1847), 37–48; XXXI (August 1847), 85–96; XXXI (September 1847), 133–45; XXXI (October 1847), 181–92; XXXI (November 1847), 241–52; XXXI (December 1847), 288–93; XXXII (January 1848), 42–48; XXXII (February 1848), 93–98; XXXII (March 1848), 159–64. The novel appeared as *Captain Spike; or, The Islets of the Gulf* in *Bentley's Miscellany,* XX (November 1846), 429–46; XX (December 1846), 533–51; XXI (January 1847), 8–28; XXI (February 1847), 121–41; XXI (March 1847), 227–46; XXI (April 1847), 365–84; XXI (May 1847), 471–91; XXI June 1847), 596–615; XXII (July 1847), 68–86; XXII (August 1847), 126–46; XXII (September 1847), 218–38; XXII (October 1847), 360–80; XXII (November 1847), 490–510; XXII (December 1847), 564–73; XXIII (January 1848), 77–88; XXIII (February 1848), 192–201; XXIII (March 1848), 375–83.

877. *To John Esaias Warren*

Hall, Cooperstown, Oct. 10th 1846

Dear Sir,

I can not now engage to deliver the lecture,[1] as it might embarrass my movements in the course of the winter. You will therefore be so good as to make your arrangements without reference to me, though I *may* find a leisure moment to [cut it?], and stop a gap, in the order of nature. I have a strong disposition to oblige you, but do not like to encumber myself with an engagement that it might be inconvenient to fulfil. I trust your association will be kind enough to receive this conditional answer, and I rely on you to make out my case for me.

I am very sensible of the politeness of your father and mother, in the invitation which you have sent me. Should I go to Troy, I may profit by it. I beg you to make my acknowledgements to them, and to offer my best respects.

For yourself, I wish you to accept the assurance of my wishes for your health & happiness

I am, dear sir | Resp. Yours
J. Fenimore Cooper

John E. Warren Esquire | Troy

MANUSCRIPT: Cooper Collection, Yale University Library.

Littérateur and world traveler, Warren (1827–1896, Rensselaer Polytechnic Institute n.g.) was a son of Mary, daughter of Cooper's neighbor J. M. Bowers, and George Bouton Warren (1797–1879), a prominent businessman of Troy, New York. He published in 1851 *Para; or, Scenes and Adventures on the Banks of the Amazon* and *Vagamundo, or the Attaché in Spain . . .*, narratives of his youthful experiences as a sight-seeing attaché of United States legations in Brazil and Spain. When Cooper and Warren became friendly as stagecoach companions in July 1848, the novelist read the text of *Para* and advised Warren on its revision as a book. Warren later lived in St. Paul, Minnesota, where he was mayor in 1860, and in Chicago, though he was frequently in Europe pursuing his literary interests. (MS: Warren to Cooper, Troy, New York, 23 October 1848, YCAL; information in the Troy Public Library.)

1. As a member of the Executive Committee of the Young Men's Association of the City of Troy, Warren wrote on 3 October 1846 to invite Cooper to lecture before the association during the coming winter at his own convenience and to offer the hospitality of his father and mother, as old family friends, during the visit (MS: YCAL).

878. *To Dr. Jonathan Mason Warren*

Otsego Hall, Cooperstown, Oct. 10th 1846

Dear Sir,

You may possibly remember having been spoken to, by a stranger, at the Massachusetts Hospital, in August last, on the subject of a lip affected by an erectile tumour, or a case similar to that in which you operated, as reported in the magazine of Dr.

[Isaac] Hays.[1] I was that stranger, and though I remembered your countenance when we accidentally met at the Hospital, I did not make myself known to you, in consequence of seeing how much you were engaged.

My neighbor Mr. Clark now goes to consult you in person, and prepared to submit to an operation should you advise it. I feel much interest in his success, having known him all his life, and no small portion of my own. Mr. Clark is the son of a very respectable builder who was much employed by my family, in his day, but was not able to leave this son more than a respectable support.[2] The latter, however, as he tells me has the means to pay for his nursing &c, and to make some compensation for the services of the medical gentleman who shall have the charge of his case. I have advised him to be frank with you on this subject, and trust he will a[c]quit himself with candor on a point that ought ever to be clearly understood. I ask leave to commend Mr. Clark to your care.

I enclose the statement made by Dr. King,[3] and which you saw when I had the pleasure of meeting you in August. I hope that accidental meeting may not be the last. You Bostonians sometimes get into this neighborhood, in quest of Sharon Water, and occasionally one finds his way to this house. Should you ever be tempted to make such an excursion, it would afford me pleasure to recieve you, and to renew the acquaintance formerly made in Paris.

I am, dear Sir, Very Resp. | Yours

Dr. J— M— Warren. J. Fenimore Cooper

MANUSCRIPT: Massachusetts Historical Society.

A versatile surgeon and voluminous contributor to medical literature, Warren (1811–1867, M.D. Harvard 1832) was one of several young doctors, students at the Hôtel Dieu, Paris, entertained by the Coopers in the early 1830's. Dr. Warren's operation on Harry Clark, performed on 16 October 1846 at the Massachusetts General Hospital, proved historic; for it was the first public operation under ether. (J. Collins Warren, "Jonathan Mason Warren," *Surgery, Gynecology and Obstetrics,* XLIII [February 1927], 273–79.)

1. Cooper referred to an article by Dr. Warren, "Ligature of Both Carotid Arteries for a Remarkable Erectile Tumour of the Mouth, Face, and Neck," *The American Journal of the Medical Sciences,* XI (April 1846), 281–91, also issued as an offprint. Warren later sent Cooper a copy of the offprint.

2. Harry Clark was evidently a son of Cyrenus Clark.

3. Dr. Consider King, a physician in Cooperstown (Livermore, *A Condensed History of Cooperstown,* 92.)

879. *To William Cullen Bryant, Theodore Sedgwick, Jr., and George F. Thomson, for the Committee of Arrangements for the Dinner to Edwin Forrest*

Otsego Hall, Cooperstown, Oct. 15th, 1846.

Gentlemen:

Your favor of the 12th, but mailed the 13th, did not reach me until last evening.[1] It would have required me to leave home, on this short notice, at daylight on the 15th, in order to reach town to attend the dinner, given to Mr. Forrest on the 16th. These circumstances will of themselves, explain one reason why I cannot accept of the compliment you have paid me. My affairs here, however, would in all probability have prevented my having the pleasure of being present on this occasion, as an absence from home, just now, would have been attended by great personal inconvenience.

I never saw Mr. Forrest but twice, and each time he was on the stage, and in the character of Othello. I certainly thought him a great actor, and I agree with you fully in thinking him entitled to receive all merited distinction from his countrymen. My mind has long been made up to attend no more public dinners, if I could well avoid it, but if disposed to depart from a rule prescribed to myself, I am disposed to think it would be done as cheerfully in honor of this gentleman as any other person among us. Messrs. Forrest, Hackett and Placide,[2] as Americans who have raised an honorable art to something near its just estimation, are each and all entitled to our consideration, and from certain peculiarities connected with ancient prejudices, probably possess more claims on us for public manifestations of our respect than men of almost any other class. The artist of any sort, or the literary man, has a hard time in this country, at the best; but it requires a great deal of moral courage, as well as rare talent, for an American to make such a reputation as that enjoyed by Mr. Forrest, in his particular branch of intellectual effort.

I have the honor to be, gentlemen,
Your obedient serv't.
J. Fenimore Cooper.

Messrs Bryant, Sedgwick, Thomson, &c, committee of arrangements for dinner to Mr. Forrest.

SOURCE: *The* [New York] *Evening Post,* 21 October 1846.

Variously listed in New York directories from 1844 to 1866 as merchant, editor, and clerk, Thomson was in 1846 an assistant appraiser at 12 Broad Street (*Doggett's New-York City Directory, for 1846 and 1847* [New York: John Doggett, Jr., 1846]).

1. Cooper's invitation, bearing the names of Bryant, Sedgwick, Thomson, and W. M. Beckwith, read: "The friends of Mr Forrest, desirous of showing their Respect and Admiration for his professional genius and private Character, have asked him to a Dinner at the New York Hotel on the 16th Octbr. at 7 o'c P M & we are instructed to ask the Honor of your presence on that occasion." (MS: YCAL.)

In setting the date 16 October for the dinner in a letter dated 12 October, Forrest gave his friends too short notice for the invitation of out-of-town guests. His letter and the invitation from his friends, dated 10 October, were published in William Rounseville Alger, *Life of Edwin Forrest, the American Tragedian* (Philadelphia: J. B. Lippincott & Co., 1877), I, 416–17. The occasion was Forrest's return from Europe.

2. The most celebrated member of a famous acting family, Henry Placide (1799–1870) sustained his reputation in roles ranging from broad farce to delicate comedy from 1823 to 1865. He was a particular favorite on the New York stage. (*DAB.*)

880. *To Frederic Oxnard*

Hall, Cooperstown, Oct. 26th 1846

Sir,

I have the greater pleasure in sending you an autograph,[1] because I have supposed you to be a relative of the late Commodore Preble. I am sorry the name is not worth more than it is, but such as it is, it is at your service.

I am, sir, | Your Ob. Ser—
J. Fenimore Cooper

Frederic Oxnard Esquire | Portland Maine

MANUSCRIPT: McGill University Library.

A grandnephew of Commodore Edward Preble (1761–1807), hero of the Tripolitan War, Frederic Oxnard (1828–1899) became a Congregationalist minister. He died at Derby, New York. (George Henry Preble, *Genealogical Sketch of the First Three Generations of Prebles in America . . .* [Boston: privately printed, 1868], 149; John M. Comstock, *The Congregational Churches of Vermont and Their Ministry, 1762–1942, Historical and Statistical* [St. Johnsbury, Vermont: The Cowles Press, 1942], 209.)

1. Oxnard's request for Cooper's autograph is dated Portland, Maine, 22 October 1846 (MS: YCAL).

881. *To Dr. Jonathan Mason Warren*

Hall, Cooperstown, Oct. 31st 1846

Dear Sir,

I regret with yourself, the fatal termination of Harry Clark's case,[1] though I had my apprehensions, from the beginning, that he had waited until it was too late. I feel persuaded that his friends here think all was done for the best, and that it was one of those events that human knowledge could not prevent. One of the most sensible of his relatives, told me yesterday that he believed Harry had made up his mind that he could not long survive, unless he got relief. I was ignorant that the disease affected the tongue, though I now well remember having been often struck, of late years, with the size of his tongue, and of a certain difficulty he had in speaking; or, it would more clearly express my meaning, were I to say that one had his attention drawn to the tongue, when the poor fellow was speaking.

We were quite touched at the distress poor Harry must have felt, at finding himself rejected at the inn. It was quite natural, however, for such a face could hardly be introduced at a public table. We have been so accustomed to seeing him, that his appearance had ceased to produce any disagreeable effects, but on strangers it must have been otherwise.

[Dr. Benjamin] Brand[r]eth,[2] of pill memory, had a son at school in this village. The first time the boy met poor Harry, he clasped his hands and exclaimed — "Oh! See that man — poor man! Stop, boys" — addressing two of my nephews, his schoolfellows, one of whom related the anecdote to me, — "Stop boys — I must go home and get him a box of pills."

I am very sensible of the attention you have paid me, by writing, and beg to thank you. A pamphlet also arrived, last night. Harry had shewn me the substance of the pamphlet in Lea & Blanchard's publication, but I was not sorry to possess a copy, for reference, in case of inquiry. We must console ourselves for the result in this case, by remembering it was God's will, and the conviction that the deceased could not longer have survived, if he survived at all, without becoming an intolerable burthen to himself.

I am, dear Sir, very faithfully | Yours

Dr. Warren, | Boston. J. Fenimore Cooper

MANUSCRIPT: Massachusetts Historical Society.

1. In a letter dated Boston, 28 October 1846, Dr. Warren explained to Cooper the circumstances of Harry Clark's arrival in Boston, of the apparent success of the operation, and of the death of the patient on the night of 26 October from unexpected complications. Warren attributed the result to diseased tissue penetrating

the brain. Though he noted that the operation was almost painless, he neglected to tell Cooper that it was performed under ether. (MS: YCAL.)

2. See Cooper to Paul Fenimore Cooper, 18 September 1840.

882. *To Gilbert Robertson, Jr.*

Hall, Cooperstown, Nov. 9th 1846

Sir,

I dare not authorize you to place my name among the certain lecturers of the winter.[1] If you will accept an extempore address on some subject that is quite familiar to myself, and an occasion should offer in the course of the winter to deliver it, I feel disposed to gratify you, but cannot do so on other terms, than its being convenient to myself.

I am much obliged to the Trojans for their good wishes, and think I may see them in the course of the winter; but do not feel authorized to say yes, either as to the lecture or the time, with certainty.

With many good wishes for your success

I remain, Sir, | Your. Ser.

G. Robertson Jun. Esquire J. Fenimore Cooper

MANUSCRIPT: Clifton Waller Barrett Collection of American Literature, University of Virginia.

A young lawyer in Troy, New York, Robertson (1815–1896, Union 1837) served as trustee of the public schools of Troy, justice of the Justices' Court of Troy, recorder, county judge of Rensselaer County, United States assessor of internal revenue, and postmaster of Troy. (Information in the Troy Public Library.)

1. Robertson wrote on 6 November 1846, as corresponding secretary of the Young Men's Association of Troy, to renew the request of J. E. Warren (see Cooper to Warren, 10 October 1846) that the novelist address the Young Men's Association during the coming winter (MS: YCAL). Cooper did not deliver the address.

883. *To Mrs. Cooper*

Hamilton Fish's office | Tuesday morning —
[24 November 1846?]

My Dearest Sue,

The morning was windy, but not cold. Half way between Cherry Valley and Canajoharie, the pole dropped in the middle of the road. It was then 11 o'clock. We got out and walked two miles, and thanks to your stockings, without getting my feet wet — Had I taken the boxes, I must have abandoned them in the highway.

A little before twelve, a lumber waggon overtook us, and we got in. At the village they told us the cars had not passed, and I persuaded the driver to hurry. We got to the bridge, I alighted, walked into the house, paid my fare, came out and lo! the cars. We were in time by somewhat less than five minutes — perhaps three.

I came down in the Isaac Newton — certainly a magnificent boat. We had a tolerable supper and a good night.

I shall go to-morrow — probably in the morning — My package is in the Great Western's Letter Bag, and that matter is disposed of.

[James De Peyster] Ogden stays at our house, and I saw him this morning for a moment. I have no news, and, as yet have done no business. But am now going out.

[Hamilton] Fish says there is no news. I have not seen [William C.] Maitland or Jim [De Lancey].

Adieu — with best love to all. Tell Paul, to ride Pumpkin, for the sake of both —

Yours tenderly
J. F. C.

MANUSCRIPT: Cooper Collection, Yale University Library.

1. The date is conjectural, but the evidence converges on the date assigned. The steamboat *Isaac Newton*, on which Cooper traveled from Albany to New York City, first appeared on the Hudson River on 8 October 1846. A floating palace of 1332 tons, she was replaced for the remainder of the season by a smaller boat on 25 November 1846. (John H. Morrison, *History of American Steam Navigation* [New York: Stephen Daye Press, 1958], 81, 124–25, 143.)

884. *To Mrs. Cooper*

Head's, Saturday. 28th [November] 1846

Dearest,

I got here on Wednesday, in a most inclement night. Frederick Prime and Lewis Rogers were my companions — The last told me that Madame la Marquise de Lavalette [1] had abandoned every thing else for politics. She had been at work all summer to get the Marquis into the Chamber, and had succeeded by one vote. He left Paris in June and returns next month.

I suppose you have seen the death of poor Dr. [Lyman] Foot.[2] All I know about it, is a sentence in a letter from Matamoros, which announces that Drs. Foot and Wharton[3] were both dead at Levacca. Poor Mary! She has a hard time before her.

[Lieutenant Henry W.] Wessel[l]s had arrived at Matamoros, a month since, and will no doubt be sent to Tampico with his regiment. Young Chapman[4] was at Camargo, at the same time, on his way to join the 2d Dragoons, at Monterey. Phil Kearny was at Matamoros with his troop, and would probably be employed to keep open the communications.

My affairs look pretty well. The manuscript is gone, and an arrangement is on the tapis that I find to my liking. It will give me a $1000 at no great trouble. I shall not complete it until next week, when I turn my face north. I hope to be home at the end of the week.

I got a slight cold in coming down, but hope to get rid of it without the old *suites*. The weather has been cold here, but is delightful now.

The Ingersolls are well, and make all sorts of inquiries. I saw Peter McCall's young wife, there, night before last. She is like her father, and is very lady like. Pretty too.

Adieu, with best love to all.
J. Fenimore Cooper

ADDRESSED: Mrs. Fenimore Cooper | Cooperstown | New York POSTMARKED: [PHILADELPHIA Pa.?] | NOV | 29

MANUSCRIPT: Cooper Collection, Yale University Library. PUBLISHED, IN PART: *Correspondence*, II, 562–63. (The *Correspondence* gives the date as 28 March 1846.)

1. Adeline, the former Mrs. Samuel Welles. See Cooper to Mrs. Cooper, 17 September 1843.

2. Dr. Foot died on 24 October 1846 (*Historical Register and Dictionary of the United States Army*).

3. Dr. William Lewis Wharton, appointed assistant surgeon in 1828 and major surgeon in 1837, died on 4 October 1846 (*Historical Register and Dictionary of the United States Army*).

4. Orren Chapman (d. 1859, West Point 1846), appointed second lieutenant in 1846, first lieutenant in 1853, and breveted first lieutenant in 1847 for gallant and meritorious conduct in the action at Medelin, near Vera Cruz, Mexico (*Historical Register and Dictionary of the United States Army*).

885. *To Charles Étienne Arthur Gayarré*

Hall, Cooperstown, Dec. 14, 1846.

Sir—

Quite recently, while I was in town, Messrs. Burgess and Stringer gave me the copy of the book that you did me the favor to send to their care, together with your obliging letter. This delay in the receipt of the communication and the history will explain to you the delay in my acknowledging the compliment.

It happened that Mrs. Cooper was much engaged in reading a work on Louisiana that had been given to me in Paris, by Mr. de Marbois, and the moment she saw your history, she seized it, and has been reading it since. Consequently, I have had no opportunity to look over your work, but shall do so on some early occasion.

There is little probability, sir, of my ever venturing so far from home in literature as to attempt the sort of work you mention. It properly falls to the share of Southern writers. My time, moreover, is nearly done. At 57 the world is not apt to believe a man can write fiction, and I have long seen that the country is already tired of me. Novelties are puissant in this country, and new names take the place of old ones so rapidly that one scarcely learns to distinguish who are in favor before a successor is pointed out. My clients, such as they are, are in Europe, and long have been, and there is no great use in going out of my way to endeavor to awaken a feeling in this country that has long gone out.

I am, notwithstanding, very sensible of the honor you have done me. Should you ever come North you will find me at no great distance from some of the most celebrated of our waters, and ever ready to offer you the hospitalities of my roof in the modest manner that my means will permit. I am, sir, your most obliged,

J. Fenimore Cooper.

Charles Gayarre, Esq., Louisiana.

SOURCE: *The* [New Orleans] *Times-Democrat*, 29 April 1883. PUBLISHED: *Correspondence*, II, 567–68.

A distinguished Louisiana historian, novelist, and politician, Gayarré (1805–1895, College of Orleans [Louisiana] 1825) wrote from New Orleans on 17 September 1846 as Secretary of State of Louisiana to explain that he was sending Cooper the first portion of his *Histoire de la Louisiane* (1846–1847) and that he hoped the work would encourage Cooper to write a novel with Louisiana as its setting. "Your pen," he wrote, "has consecrated and hallowed many a spot in our country and thrown the glow and charm of romance around many an incident of our national history. It is in your power to do for this southern region what you have done for more favored parts of the United States and to render Louisiana still more interesting in the eye of the world. By so doing, you would encrease your fame, conquer to your self a home in the heart of every one of the enthusiastic sons of this land, and by setting in bold relief the merits of the first French adventurers in this country, produce a work of national interest not only for the United States, but also for France where your works are so extensively known and so well appreciated." Gayarré later wrote a similar letter to William Gilmore Simms. On 25 April 1883, he sent Cooper's letter and an excerpt from Simms's letter to the editor of *The Times-Democrat* with an explanatory note. ([C. E. A. Gayarré?], *Biographical Sketch of Hon. Charles Gayarré, by a Louisianian* [New Orleans: C. Eden Hopkins, 1889?]; *DAB*; MS: YCAL.)

886. *To Joseph Salkeld, for* The Evergreen

[January 1847?]

Mr. Editor —

You have a correspondent who writes from Italy. As I passed years, formerly, in that part of the world, the word rarely passes before my eyes without arresting my attention. I think this is the case with all who know much of Italy — a region that we get to love, in the course of a few months, as one loves a dear friend. Its delicious climate, its stupendous ruins, its noble past, all contribute to render its sleepy present moment agreeable, if not very profitable. I like the people of Italy, too. They are full of feeling, and grace, and poetry, and a vast number are filled with a piety that their maligners would do well to imitate.

In looking over the communication of your correspondent, I have met with a remark that to me was new. He intimates that King Gioacchino (Joachim Murat) was betrayed by those who accompanied him on the occasion of his landing in Italy.[1] I shall neither confirm nor deny this statement, being ignorant of the facts; though a long experience in Europe has rendered me somewhat incredulous on the subject of such charges. I can repeat a tale in connection with this unfortunate sovereign, however, that I know to come from high authority, and which may have interest with your readers.

It is now near twenty years that I was passing an evening in the casino Aldobrandini, at Florence, in company with its master and mistress, the Baron P[oerio][2] and Mademoiselle K[autz], now

Comtesse de Lacépède, the wife of the son and successor of the celebrated naturalist. The Prince Aldobrandini was the brother of the Borghese who married Pauline, the sister of Napoleon, and succeeded to his titles and estates. The present Prince Borghese is his son. The Princess Aldobrandini was a French woman of the illustrious family de la Rochefoucauld, being a grand-daughter of the Duc de Liancourt, afterwards Duc de Rochefoucauld, whose travels in America were once so well known. This lady's mother was a de Tascher, through which family she was a relative of Josephine. She survives, under the title of the Dowager Princess of Borghese.

Owing to the connections just mentioned, it was natural that a portion of the company should feel an interest in all that related to the fate of one so nearly connected with Napoleon, as Murat. The Baron P[oerio] had filled an office which corresponds to that of our Attorney General, under King Gioacchino, and recounted many anecdotes of his reign. At length he spoke of his death, of which he gave the following interesting particulars, which I do not remember ever to have seen published.

According to the Baron P[oerio], Murat was captured near a town that had a garrison, and which was the head-quarters of a general officer who had formerly served under himself. The ex-king and his two aids were conveyed to the citadel, where the general treated them with due respect and delicacy. He communicated the capture to his superiors at Naples, by telegraph, and then bethought him of the best mode of making the time pass agreeably to his captive.

An English frigate had come into the port a day or two before, under the pretence of wanting to fill up her water. The captain of this frigate was invited to meet the ex-king, and towards evening they all sat down to dinner together. The meal passed off in pleasant and easy discourse, the ex-king himself leading. While thus engaged, the general was notified that the telegraph of the station next in the direction of the capital was at work. "That must relate to me," exclaimed Murat; and as the general made his excuses, and withdrew to ascend to the tower where signals were made and read under the old system of telegraphs, he promised Joachim to send down the sentences of this communication as each was interpreted. In a few minutes the following words were handed to Murat, written by the general in pencil. *"Consegnate il Generale Murat, senza"* — "consign the General Murat, without" — "Ah!" exclaimed the ex-king, "this refers to me, sure enough; I am to be consigned without — whom, or what? Wait a moment — a little patience will let us know."

In a minute or two another part of a sentence was sent down. It read as follows: *"gli uffiziali suoi, alla"* — "his officers, to the" — the whole communication, thus far, reading — "Consign the General Murat, without his officers, to the" —

Now it may be well to explain, that in Italian, as in French, and all languages of Latin roots, the articles, adjectives, etc. must agree with their nouns in gender. *"Alla"* in Italian, like the *"à la"* in French, infers that a feminine noun is to follow. Had it been intended that a masculine noun was to follow the words quoted, *"al"* would have been used instead of *"alla."* Immediately after the second portion of the communication reached the dinner-table, the general appeared to say, that it had got to be so dark the next signal could not be read. This left the ex-king to make his own conjectures as to what ought to have followed. *"Alla, alla,"* he repeated two or three times, in search of a feminine noun. "Ah! I have it — *alla fregata Inglese* — to the English frigate. So, captain, I am to have the honor of being your guest, and I doubt not of meeting with a hospitable reception." The English officer made a suitable reply, and Murat rose from table, talking the whole time of his approaching voyage in the frigate, and of his intentions for the future.

When it was time to retire for the night, the ex-king and his two aids were put in the same room. Murat had a cot, and mattresses were laid on the floor for the aids. The ex-king was very talkative, saying that he now renounced ambition altogether, and that he intended to pass the remainder of his days in some tranquil retreat, in the bosom of his family. After a time he dropped asleep.

The aids did not feel the same security as their chief, but lay awake, communicating with each other in whispers. About midnight they heard the trampling of horses in the court, and rightly judged that a courier had arrived. One of them arose and left the room to inquire the news, promising his companion to return as soon as he could learn it. There was a sentinel at the door, who saw the aid go out without speaking to him. After ascertaining that a courier had arrived, this gentleman endeavored to reënter the chamber, but was stopped. The sentinel was ordered to let the aids come out, but was commanded not to let them return. In a few minutes the second aid appeared, and was treated in the same way.

The telegraphic order had been, *"Consegnate il Generale Murat, senza gli uffiziali suoi alla commissione del morte"* — "Consign the General Murat, without his officers, to the *commission of death.*" In other words, send him before a court-martial to be condemned, agreeably to previous instructions furnished to all the commanders on that coast. This was done, and the ex-king was shot early that morning.

I do not vouch for the truth of this story.[3] I only say that it was related, substantially as here given, by a distinguished Neapolitan, in the company I have named. It is possible that the story of the aids having betrayed Joachim, may have arisen from the fact of their being thus separated from their chief, and being spared. But the Neapolitan government had nothing to gain by causing the death of two inferior officers of this class. If I am not mistaken, the Baron P[oerio] said these aids were French, or Corsicans.

[F]irenze [4]

SOURCE: *The Evergreen, or Church-Offering for All Seasons; A Repository of Religious, Literary, and Entertaining Knowledge, for the Christian Family,* IV (February 1847), 34–35.

On 13 November 1846, Salkeld wrote from Naugatuck, Connecticut, acknowledging a commendatory letter (unlocated) from Cooper, explaining his hopes for *The Evergreen,* listing its contributors, and requesting occasional contributions from the novelist. "I am induced to make this request the more earnestly," he urged, "because I am inclined to think from reading your works, that in regard to American & especially Yankee self-boastings; party-spirit in the Church; our civil institutions, &c we should agree exactly." (MS: YCAL.) Cooper's letter, published under the heading "AN INCIDENT CONNECTED WITH THE DEATH OF MURAT," was evidently his response.

1. In a sketch entitled "NAPLES — ITS PEOPLE," Salkeld's anonymous contributor had given from a Neapolitan source the following account of Murat's execution: "All the household of Murat were bought, and he was decoyed, by forged letters, to land in Calabria, where he had been made to believe that every thing was prepared for his reception. He marched a short distance into the country, and finding the peasantry cold to his cause, and no arrangements made for a revolt, retreated again to the shore. There he stood, and made signals in vain. The captain

of the ship which brought him set sail and left him to his fate, and he was seized and shot. All his most trusted servants were immediately *pensioned by the Neapolitan government.*" (*The Evergreen*, III [November 1846], 334.)

2. Giuseppe Poerio (1775–1843), an eloquent republican lawyer, was appointed *procureur général* of Naples by Murat in 1808 (*GE*). For other persons mentioned in this paragraph, see Cooper to Mrs. P. A. Jay, January–February 1829?, and Plate XII, Volume I.

3. Poerio's account, as narrated by Cooper, differs markedly from other accounts of Murat's death, though it may not be entirely irreconcilable with them. See, for example, R. M. Johnston, *The Napoleonic Empire in Southern Italy and the Rise of the Secret Societies* (New York and London: The Macmillan Company, 1904), I, 386–407.

4. The source has "Tirenze."

887. *To Kate, Mary, and Lucy Hosmer*

Otsego Hall, Cooperstown, Jan. 1st 1847

Young Ladies,

I was absent from home when your letter [1] reached this place, and since my return have been suffering under a cold that has so occupied my time with coughing, that I have been able to do little else. Seriously, I have never before had so ⟨serious⟩ prolonged and painful an attack of the same character in the seven and fifty years I have been permitted to exist. This, I trust, will be accepted as a sufficient apology for the seeming neglect of your communication.

I am always pleased to know that others [have] [2] some feeling for my labours, and particularily so when the feeling is awakened in the intelligent of your sex. The allusion in the post[s]cript,[3] however, is lost on me, though that would not surprise you if you knew how completely the contents of a book pass out of the recollection of an author after he has written a good deal. It was only last week, that a bet was referred to me to decide, in connection with one of my own [vessels?] [4] called the "Alacrity," and I had no more idea in what book this Alacrity is to be found, than I have of the Hebrew Points.[5]

In the use of names I commonly take the first that offers, though some little fitness is to be observed, as a matter of course. On this subject of names, I question if one could be invented, that does not belong to some one. I have made two efforts of this sort, and both failed. In naming Natty I dubbed him Bumppo, thinking I had invented an uncouth appellation that no one certainly could covet, and that no one would claim. Six months did not go by, before I learned there was a man of that very name living within five miles of me!

⟨In⟩ The other instance was in the Two Admirals, in which I called Sir Jarvey's steward Galleygo, because it was his business to go to and from the galley. On this name I felicitated myself, fancying it was wholly mine. I bragged of it, in the family circle, until my pride was lowered one day, by being shown an advertisement in a New York paper, in which Galleygo & Co offered some thing for sale. Since that time I have given the matter of names up.

As to anti-rentism, in my judgment it is to be the test of the institutions. If men find that by making political combinations they can wipe out their indebtedness, adieu to every thing like liberty or government. The[re] will be but one alternative, and that will be the bayonet.

Be pleased to accept my thanks, and have the kindness to excuse the tardiness of this answer for the reason I have given.

Your [Most?] Obe. Ser—
[J. Feni]more Cooper

To Mesdemoiselles | Kate, Mary & Lucy.

ADDRESSED: To | Miss K. Hosmer | Avon Springs | New York POSTMARKED: COOPERSTOWN N.Y. | JAN | 3 STAMPED: [5?]
MANUSCRIPT: J. K. Lilly Collection, Indiana University Library.

Daughters of George and Elizabeth Hosmer of Avon Springs, New York, Katharine F. (b. 1822), Mary E. (b. 1816), and Lucy Evans Hosmer were sisters of William Howe Cuyler Hosmer (1814–1877, Geneva [Hobart] College 1837), the poet of Seneca Indian life. Kate, who in 1871 lived in Villa Ridge, Illinois, married John G. Stoddard in 1849 and Captain Willis B. Edson in 1867. Mary married I. Wells, and Lucy married John Sears. (John Pierson, W. H. C. Hosmer, S. Amanda Whitbeck, *Genealogical Records of the Pioneer Families of Avon, N. Y.: Pierson, Waterous, Hosmer, Martin, Etc., and Their Descendants* [Rochester, New York: Express Printing House, 1871], 24–25; *DAB*.)

1. The "sister trio" wrote from Avon Spa on 26 November 1846 to express, in the idiom of an outmoded sensibility, the admiration and extreme delight with which they read Cooper's romances of the forest and the sea. They admired also the "irrefutable" logic of the Anti-Rent novels. (MS: YCAL.)

2. Cooper wrote "having."

3. In a postscript, the sisters remonstrated with Cooper for the use made of "a name identified with the patriots of Seventy-Six and illustrious in English History." They referred apparently to a quite unimportant character named Major Hosmer, a victim of Jason Newcome's wiles in *The Chainbearer* (134–35). The sisters sweetly forgave Cooper but expressed a mild hope that the character alluded to would not achieve the currency of Natty. (MS: YCAL.)

4. The manuscript is torn here and elsewhere.

5. William J. Radford, a former seaman and an enthusiastic reader of Cooper's nautical fiction, wrote from New York City on 26 December 1846 to ask whether the cutter *Alacrity* in *The Pilot* was a sloop, a schooner, or a square-rigged craft. Radford had, he said, always considered the *Alacrity* a sloop; but his opinion had been challenged and could not be confirmed or refuted with certainty by the most elaborate scrutiny of the romance. (MS: YCAL.)

888. *To J. B. Lee*

Otsego Hall, Cooperstown, Jan 14th 1847

Sir,

I greatly fear this Mexican war will turn out to be a much more serious business than was anticipated. There is great obstinacy in the Mexican, or Spanish character, and should we even reach Mexico, I do not see that the war will be any nearer to a close. I really think the project of fortifying and holding what we have got, avoiding all the sickly points, a very sensible one, and that which will cost the least while it will give all the advantages we desire. The coast can be blockaded, and Vera Cruz might be taken and the castle blown up, but all attempts at further conquest strike me as unwise.

I do not know whether these are your sentiments, but I thought I would communicate them, as the opinion of

Sir, | Your Ob. Ser.
J. Fenimore Cooper

J. B. Lee Esquire | Maysville, Ky.

MANUSCRIPT: American Swedish Historical Museum, Philadelphia, Pennsylvania.

In a letter to Cooper, dated Maysville, Kentucky, 31 December 1846, Lee described himself as an admirer of the novelist and requested an autograph. No information about Lee has been found in the local records of Maysville or of Mason County, Kentucky. (MS: YCAL).

889. *To William Branford Shubrick*

Hall, Cooperstown, Jan. 17th 1847

My Dear Shubrick,

According to my calculation you must now be at Callao, or off Panama, ready to abuse such of your friends as have not sent letters to meet you. My apology is one of the severest cold and coughs I have ever endured. It kept me housed more than a month, but is happily done with.

Lest any accident may have occurred to your letters, I will here state that your daughter was confined of a boy, in Nov. which lived only an hour. Mary was confined to her room for a good while, but is slowly recovering, and I doubt not, by this time, is out again. Our last letter is some weeks old, but I saw Ludlow [1] in Philadelphia in Dec. and he reported her down stairs, then, for the first time. All this and more, you have probably learned directly, but I thought it best to mention it.

My own family is well. Paul has commenced the water-cure, in this village, and the effects on him are wonderful. He is like a young colt, trotting off his eight and ten miles a day, on foot, and run[n]ing up and down the mountains like a goat. His mind keeps pace with his body, and he is getting to be Paul again.

I do not like the management of the war. There can be little doubt that our government has been disappointed in its expectations of compelling a peace by rapid conquests at first, and by intimidation. When I returned from Baltimore, on quitting your wife, Mr. Buchanan [2] travelled with me, as far as New York. I saw plainly that he expected Santa Ana [3] would bring peace. This was at the moment when our propositions were sent, and Santa Ana had just arrived. I dare [say] Senior Santa Ana would gladly make peace, unless he got a run of luck in the way of hostilities, but he will not risk his popularity in order to do so.

Now, we have gone too fast, for the purposes of economy, for the lives of our people, and for the great ends of the war. The volunteer system is breaking down. The men are excellent, fight like devils, remarkably well for the species of troops, but half are in the hospitals, or have been sent home invalided. The return soldiers, owing to these causes, almost equal the re-inforcements, and here in the eighth month of the war we have scarcely more men in position, than we had three months since. Six or eight thousand new troops are beginning to arrive, and will make some difference.

It would seem, however, that our conquests thus far, have been judiciously made as to nature and territory, though ill-timed. By raising regulars, as is now about to be done, giving a regular force of near 30,000 men, and waiting until the end of November, all that has been done could have been done at half the cost, in a fourth of the time, with a loss of life scarce worth mentioning (sickness is meant, not battle) and leaving us a force that would be available for any service. Now we have 18000 of these regulars, or even more to raise, and in March the vomito will be at work on the coast.

The conquests have been judiciously made, notwithstanding. With Tampico, Victoria, or New Santander (which is not yet ours, though it is thought it soon will be) Monter[r]ey, Saltillo and Parras in our possession, I understand the northern provinces are effectually cut off, and we can adjust a line for ourselves. The great difficulty is the slavery incubus, and the quarrels about it in the legislation of the country. Were this the long session, I should expect protracted and angry debates that might defeat every thing that is good. Time presses so much, however, that they seem sensible of the necessity of acting as well as talking.

We have had a bad year for naval disasters. The Truxtun, Boston, Somers and Shark are all gone.[4] The government is buying steamers wherever it can find them, and there will soon be six or eight in the gulf as cruisers. It is a thousand pities you have not a couple.

You have doubtless seen various paragraphs in the papers, assailing [David] Conner. I find that an opinion prevails among some in the service, that these articles are all calculated, in order to get Conner out of the way, to put [Matthew C.] Perry in his place. You know the two men, and can judge as well as I, which is the most fitted for the station. Conner behaved uncommonly well, in the attack on Alvarado, holding on to the last moment, and retiring only when remaining could be of no use. His conduct at Tampico, where he had Tatnall[5] to take the place of Sands,[6] has been excellent. Not a soul has been hurt, while every thing has been secured. On the other hand, why was Tobasco, which had not fired a gun, and which scarcely had a gun to fire, cannonaded, nay bombarded. It is said that forty or fifty women, children and unarmed persons were destroyed at Tobasco. It is such acts that inflame a country against its invaders. Towns should never be fired into, unless an important military object is to be gained. It is no excuse for bombarding a town, that a handful of men fire out of the streets. Fire back at these men, and knock down the part of the town where they are lodged, if you will, but Perry appears to have blazed away for a considerable time at an unresisting place. Indeed, one of his attacks would seem to have been to revenge Morris' death.[7] This is no excuse for such an extreme measure. Mr. Morris knew when he went to Tobasco that he ran the risk of being shot, but because he was shot in a skirmish with soldiers who were attacking a [town?], was no good reason for Perry's turning on the town. He did not assail the town to drive out these soldiers, but to punish Mexico for killing Morris. Had England done such a thing, to us, how should we have felt?

I see that the California expedition was at Rio in Nov. to sail direct for San Francisco on the 28th. It must be with you about the time you will recieve this – As for the war, many now begin to think it will last years. I do not believe it will end these two or three years. There is no way of compelling a peace. Taking the City of Mexico will not do it. There is a project now talked of to make the *people* of Mexico, as distinguished from the government, compel a peace. It is to let them establish state governments, to which it is said they are strongly attached, under our guarantee, and thus get them [on] [8] our side. But such a project can hardly succeed. It seems to be the opinion that the cabinet expects Santa Anna to be well enough disposed to come to terms, as soon as he can. There certainly was some reason for asking for the two million appropriation last session, and it may be connected with some promise on his part. My own opinion is, however, that Santa Ana has mystified Mr. Polk, and that he will act just as circumstances invite.

What a fate for the unfortunate Somers! [9] "Sarved her right" says Jack, and thousands believe it was a judgment on her. She had good beam, and was a vessel that one would not expect to turn turtle.

I see the return of Irvine [Shubrick], and have been hoping that he and his crew would be turned over to the Germantown, which is lying at Norfolk nearly ready for sea; as is the Plymouth at New York. By the way, I have seen Henry [Henry], who is savage enough. He is particularily fierce upon you, "Bill Shubrick" as he calls you, but there is a great deal of "vox pro terra" about Henry.

I met [Henry W.?] Ogden when down, early in December, looking better. He told me he was again an applicant for service. A journey had done him good. I should think a warm climate better for him than the one he is in. The project of shelving the old fellows, and idlers, has set every body in motion, in both services. No one wishes to be invalided. You are not to be surprised if you see old [James] Barron out in a schooner.

By the way, I hope you and [James] Biddle may get along well. I know you do not love each other, and I hope I have had some little agency in making you feel a little better disposed than might otherwise be the case. Biddle is a dangerous enemy for an inferior in rank, as he has talents enough to keep himself in the right, unless when urged on by passion. I rather think him inclined to be just and generous when left to his own impulses. My hope, however, is that you will not meet.

Letters are this moment recieved from Mary herself, who is well. You will hear this from herself, but I write it in case of accidents.

No promotions have yet been made. I suppose army and navy will come near the close of the session. There is no probability of [Charles] Stewarts going to the gulf, or of Conner's being superseded, unless at his own request.

I saw [John D.] Sloat, who gives a very sensible account of his proceedings. He says that he heard of the battles of the 8th and 9th May, and came to this conclusion – If we own to the Rio Grande, Mexico has invaded us, and it is my duty to act against her. If we do *not* own to the Rio Grande, we have invaded Mexico, and it is my business to follow the movements of my superiors, with or without signals. I call this pretty good logic for a Dutchman!

An awkward affair is just reported from Rio. It seems two of the Columbias were arrested for drunkenness in the streets. A Lieutenant, of the name of Davis,[10] demanded the men and got arrested too. Wise [11] then demanded the release of all hands. After a fruitless negotiation, [Lawrence] Rousseau is said to have cleared ship, and Wise sent word to the minister if the parties were not released in two hours, the paixhans would begin to talk. Mr. Davis was released, but the Brazilians held on to the men under some legal complaint — drunkenness, I believe. While a hot c[orr?]espondence was going on, the Preble, with her convoy, entered the harbor, which so frightened the Brazilians that they let the men go. Wise was now asked what 1000 (800) American soldiers were doing in the harbor, and it was some time before he could persuade the government that there was no murder intended. I give you the current story, just at this moment, lest you might not get the facts from any other quarter. It is said the Braz. G[ov.?] has demanded the recal[l] of both Wise and Rousseau. Both will be uncomfortable, if the half of what is reported be true, and an officer must be very right before he can menace a friendly town with bombardment. A month hence I may be able to send you more authentic particulars.

Talking of paix[h]ans, I met Bamford [12] the other day. He told me [he] had tried his big gun. It works to a miracle, throwing its shot *three measured miles and a half*. He said the earth trembled beneath it, at the report. One shell fell into a soft rock, three miles off, and made a hole twelve feet in diameter. A ship's standing such a visiter is out of the question. He seems to think that six planted in the harbour of New York will render the place too hot for any fleet. He can plant six in such positions that no vessel can get beyond the range of one or more of them.

[Lawrence] Kearny is furious at Perry's being offered the gulf squadron, as are most of his seniors I am told. Old Larry has got a son! James Lawrence Kearny, and when I saw him (Dec. 3d) was beating up for recruits to attend the christening. By the way, he spoke of Conner reverentially, as one ought to speak of a papa. You know, doubtless, that Nicolson is dead.[13]

The Ohio is reported ready for sea. It is said she is to go into the gulf, which I do not believe, but presume she is intended for you. Ned Myers told me that [Silas H.] Stringham had offered to take him along, and he meant to go. I do not know whether he is to go, or not, having heard nothing of, or from, him since, as I have expected to do. If he should appear out there, I wish you would have an eye to his interests.

I am writing this letter at odd moments, and have now got to the 22d Jan. I see by last nights papers that there are two accounts of the Rio affair. I have cut out of the Journal of Commerce conflicting accounts and send you both. I think it probable, however, that your Washington papers will give you something official on the subject. The papers of this evening are full of what they call Comm. Perrys plan to compel a peace. It seems he proposes to seize all the Mexican Ports, establish custom houses, and hold on until Don Montezuma comes to terms. Now I spoke of this plan six months since — I do not know but I mentioned it to you — and the Evening Post had an article to the same effect as far back as last Nov. Reflection satisfied me it would not do. In the first place such a scheme would cost more lives than an active campaign to begin with, since the ports must be held in summer by armed forces, and the vomito would do the fighting. Next, the scheme would not force the Mexicans to submit. They would retain their mines, and with them their dollars, and would ask nothing better. Then foreign nations might and would object to a system that would give us the control of the commerce of that country. It would be a certain means of making difficulties with France and England, the latter grumbling a good deal already at our using our conquests to flood Mexico with American manufactures. Vigilant blockades would answer all the purposes, at far less cost.

One of the great causes of embarrassment with which we have to contend is the disposition to make presidents by means of military renoun. Both sides manifest jealousy on this head, and Congress is influenced by the feeling.[14]

A great many vessels are bought by government as transports, supply vessels &c. Two or three ships have sailed quite lately for the gulf filled with barges that are described to be forty feet long, and capable of carrying a hundred men. Lenthall [15] is said to have drafted them, and there is said to be one hundred and fifty of them altogether; enough to transport 12 or 15000 men. What they are for I do not know. [Charles] Morris was very busy about them, or something else while I was down, though Ogden told me that the death of his son almost crazed him. Indeed he was out of his head for a few days. You know the young man was shot in Perry's attack on Tobasco. Some of the ships purchased are very fine, new ships, of 600 or 800 tons, and are given to lieutenants in the navy. The force in the Gulf is not increased, but diminished, though of better materials than it was. Conner took three fine schooner-gun boats that had been built at New York — sister craft to the Bonita, Petrel and Reefer [16] — though one of them has been wrecked since. One or two of Perry's prizes have been fitted out, too, so that Conner must have a dozen craft of a light draught of water, which he has much wanted.

There is a report that a passed midshipman, of the name of Fitzgerald,[17] has been pulling in an eight oar barge all round the Castle of San Juan d'Ulloa, and that he even entered one of the water batteries, examining it thoroughly. If this be true, I doubt if the winter go by without our hearing more of it. You have doubtless heard that a Lieut. Parker,[18] who I believe is a nephew of Lawrence's, accompanied by two or three midshipmen went in with a boat belonging to the Somers, and burned a schooner called the Creole that was actually moored to the castle. The fact is certain, though no official account of the affair has been published, as the whole thing was unauthorized by, and unknown to, the commander of the brig. I should send such heroes home.

I see that Biddle must have been on the coast some months before you. Whether he will take it into his head to remain there, or not, I am impatient to learn. He will visit the ports of California, I do not doubt, but he may not wish to remain, as his vessel's time must be nearly up. You had better hint to him that his ship may be wanted to batter San Juan.

I beg to be mentioned kindly to [Elie A. F.] Lavalette, whom I was sorry not to have seen when at Boston. Mention me also to Mr. [Benjamin] Page, and the other gentlemen whom I know on board the Independence. I met [Frederick A.?] Neville in Philadelphia, and he groaned greatly over his ill luck in missing the cruise.

Be careful about conquering any marshes after March, next. We shall lose ten men by the climate, where we lose one by shot. California is your country, where you can commence navy yards, or any other nautical wonder; dry docks for what I care. I think there is no manner of doubt that we shall hold that region, with a line nearly straight across the continent from the first great angle in the Rio Grande to some point near the head of the gulf. You may remember the allusion in your instructions Gu[a]ymas. There has been an article in the Union lately,[19] which has confirmed my opinion that is about the limit that the cabinet has carved out for its conquests.

Adieu — God Bless you. All my family join me in the best wishes.

As soon as I get any thing worth writing you shall hear from me again.

Com. Shubrick J. Fenimore Cooper

Did I tell you that your letter from Rio was just received?

MANUSCRIPT: Paul Fenimore Cooper, Cooperstown, New York.

1. Unidentified. The Shubricks were connected to the numerous Ludlow families through the marriage of John Templer Shubrick to Elizabeth Matilda Ludlow, daughter of Henry Ludlow, in 1814 and, evidently, through other intermarriages (S. L. C. Simmons, ed., "Notices of Ancestors . . . by the Rev. Paul Trapier," *Transactions of the Huguenot Society of South Carolina*, No. 58 [1953], 29–54.

2. Apparently James Buchanan, Secretary of State in President Polk's cabinet.

3. A circumflex above the "n" here and elsewhere may have been intended to double the letter.

4. The *Truxton*, a 331-ton, 10-gun ship built in 1842, was lost at Tuspan in 1846; the *Boston IV*, a 700-ton, 18-gun ship built in 1825, was lost at Eleuthera, West Indies, in 1846; the *Somers II*, a 259-ton, 10-gun ship built in 1842, sank off Vera Cruz in 1846; and the *Shark*, a 177-ton, 12-gun ship built in 1821, was lost at the Columbia River in 1846 (GNR).

5. Josiah Tattnall (1795–1871), appointed midshipman in 1812, lieutenant in 1818, commander in 1838, and captain in 1850 (GNR).

6. Probably Joshua R. Sands (d. 1883), appointed midshipman in 1812, lieutenant in 1818, commander in 1840, captain in 1854, and rear admiral on the retired list in 1866. Sands was awaiting orders in 1847. (GNR.)

7. Lieutenant Charles W. Morris, son of Commodore Charles Morris, died of wounds received in action on 1 November 1846 (GNR).

8. Cooper wrote "of."

9. Struck by a hurricane, the *Somers* sank within ten minutes.

10. Alonzo B. Davis (d. 1854), appointed midshipman in 1831, passed midshipman in 1837, and lieutenant in 1841 (GNR).

11. Henry A. Wise (d. 1869), appointed midshipman in 1834, passed midshipman in 1840, lieutenant in 1847, and captain in 1866 (GNR).

12. Unidentified.

13. Captain John B. Nicholson died on 9 November 1846 (GNR).

14. The following paragraph, unindented, begins on a new manuscript page.

15. John Lenthall (d. 1882), a naval constructer appointed in 1838 and placed in charge of the Bureau of Construction and Repair in 1863 (GNR).

16. All three vessels, the *Bonita*, the *Petrel*, and the *Reefer*, were 76-ton, 1-gun ships, purchased in 1846 and, except for the *Petrel*, sold in 1849. It was transferred to the coast survey. (GNR).

17. William B. Fitzgerald, appointed midshipman in 1838, passed midshipman in 1844, and lieutenant in 1852 (GNR).

18. According to William H. Parker, a group of spirited officers and sailors under the command of Lieutenant James L. Parker (d. 1847) of Pennsylvania "took a boat one afternoon and pulled in to visit the officers of an English man-of-war lying under Sacrificios island. It was quite usual to do this. After nightfall they

left the British ship and pulled directly for the schooner, which they boarded and carried. This, be it observed, was directly under the guns of the castle and the muskets of its garrison. The crew was secured, and finding the wind would not serve to take the vessel out it was resolved to burn her. Her captain made some resistance, and the sentinel on the walls called out to know what was the matter. Parker, who spoke Spanish remarkably well, replied that his men were drunk and he was putting them in irons. The party then set fire to the vessel and got safely away with their prisoners." (William Harwar Parker, *Recollections of a Naval Officers, 1841–1865* [New York: Charles Scribners' Sons, 1883], 59–60; GNR.)

19. Cooper may have alluded to an article entitled "The 'Rumor' from the Rio Grande" in *The Daily Union*, Washington, D.C., 13 January 1847; but his inference may have been based on one of the numerous other articles in the *Union* concerning troop movements and, directly and indirectly, the intentions of the Administration.

890. *To Francis Porteous Corbin*

Hall, Cooperstown, Jan 30th — 1847

My Dear Corbin,

I had the pleasure of recieving your missive a day or two since.[1] A line from you was gratifying, for I feel at all times a strong interest in what is going on in Europe, and especially among my friends.

I have seen your brothers Lygon and John, (that I believe is the name of the sailor) [2] occasionally at Heads where we all go, from time to time. Head is no longer head of the establishment, though he is head of the table. The house is the pleasantest in Philadelphia, though no longer in great request. Fifteen at table is a good number, and there are more frequently ten or twelve.

I saw Lewis Rogers when last down, on the point of sailing for France. He had just purchased 12000 barrels of flour at $5, he told me, on which he will not fail to make $20,000, if he has held it — a drop in the bucket of his speculations, however.

[William C.] Rives seems to be politically defunct — He over-reached himself, attaching rather more importance than it deserved, to his "associated wealth, the dynasty of modern nations." He, and the associated wealth are laid on the shelf together.

What has become of "his man, [Nathaniel] Niles," I know no farther than the fact that Mr. Rogers told me he was in New York — "The higher a monkey climbs the more we see his tail."

Do you remember Fowler and his pantaloons? In London, I mean, in 1833 — he who wanted Peabody to arrive, in order that he might buy a pair of pantaloon[s]. Well, I hear of him occasionally. He is poorer than ever inasmuch as he grows richer. The crisis of '36, they tell me, forced upon him a large amount of property as security, and this has so much increased in value, on his hands, that I believe he finds it necessary to go without pantaloons, altogether, Peabody or no Peabody. Who this Mr. Peabody is, or was, I never knew, but he must be a man singularily honoured to be selected to buy breeches for Joe Fowler!

You doubtless see what we are about here, as well as a man can see through the lying medium of the news-papers. The war is getting to be troublesome, and has not been well managed, I fear. There has been an ill-judged precipitation, an expectation and desire to pay off the note at Ninety days and the grace, which has urged the government into injudicious measures and expenditures. The idea of employing volunteers in a war of invasion, was a blunder. Had a law passed to increase the army to 50,000 men some 25,000, or 30,000 might now have been in Mexi[c]o, at less cost than half the number of volunteers, and been ready to move with all their [attiral?], like soldiers.

As for fighting, we are too much for any of the Spanish race, beyond a question. The militia of this country could overmatch the regulars of Mexico, if they had a chance, but the blackguards would waste more than they consumed, and march only when they were ready.

Then comes the question how is peace to be made? We have conquered already more territory than we want, and the Mexicans are like soft soap, an impression is easily made on them, but it leaves no mark. There is no body to treat with, nor any permanent government to put down. The Mexicans are like our frogs in the spring — "pronouncing" all over the pond; and when you hit one with a stone, "pee-weet" cries his cousin, half a mile off.

How, or when this business is to terminate, heaven knows. The worst of it is, that the short-sighted politicians fancy that renoun in arms is to make all their fortunes, and the quarrel is now who is to get the best chance. Gen. Butler [3] has been assailed, lest his wound might give him a claim. The administration seems really jealous of [Zachary] Taylor and his three victories, while Scott's "hasty plate of soup" has been pardoned, and he is sent to command. The attempt to make Benton a Lt. General, and the superior of all has seemingly failed,[4] as I make little doubt would his scheme of pacification had he been permitted to try it. His idea of living on the enemy, however, is the true one, as respects all those portions of the country we do not mean to hold. California we shall only yield when we can no longer keep it, let England and France bluster as much as they please.

I see your Paris journals will not believe that an American officer will ⟨not⟩ dare to emprison a French functionary. The facts, [John D.] Sloat tells me are these — The French consul at Monterey was troublesome, and the officer commanding on shore sent him word to be more prudent. This had no effect when Bob Stockton who had then succeeded Sloat, ordered him to keep his house, with an intimation that he should take up his quarters in the Calaboose if he meddled any more with what did not concern him. All depends on the provocation. This nation, however, is full of fight, and defies the devil.

Adieu, my dear Corbin. I enclose a line to Major Frye,[5] agreeably to your request, and which you will have the goodness to send to him. I remember him well, of course, having had an acquaintance with him that covered several years. He is a West Indian by birth, I believe, and is very much of a cosmopolite in feeling.

Truly Yours
J. Fenimore Cooper

How you all came to dub me "John" I do not know — my name, at your service, is James. There are no less than *Paul, Richard* and *James* Fenimore Cooper in this place, and James being nearest to John, I confiscated the letter. There is also an E. Fenimore Cooper, but not in Cooperstown.

ADDRESSED: Mr. Corbin | à Paris
MANUSCRIPT: Cooper Collection, Yale University Library.

Born at "The Reeds," Caroline County, Virginia, Corbin (1801–1876) was a cosmopolite, educated in England and France and widely traveled. His father Francis Corbin was a member of the Virginia Convention of 1788 which ratified the Constitution. Young Francis married at Philadelphia in 1825 Agnes Rebecca (1801–1893), the only daughter of James Hamilton of Philadelphia and St. Simonds, Georgia. (Return J. Meigs, *The Corbins of Virginia: A Genealogical Record of the the Descendants of Henry Corbin Who Settled in Virginia in 1654* [Westfield, New Jersey: mimeographed text, 1940], 14, 19.)

1. Corbin, who had known Cooper abroad and in Philadelphia in 1837–1838, wrote from Paris on 30 December 1846 to pay his respects and to explain that he was sending by a friend two recent books by a mutual friend Major William Edward Frye (1784–1853): a translation of the Danish A. G. Ohlenschläger's *The Gods of the North* (1845) and a translation into French verse *Trois Chants de l'Edda* (1844). Frye was an intimate of the Lafayette circle. (MSS: YCAL.)

2. Corbin had five brothers: Robert Beverley (d. 1868), William Lygon (1809–1884), John Sawbridge (d. 1883?), Washington Shirley (d. 1877), and Thomas Grosvenor (1820–1901). The sailor was not John, but Thomas who was appointed midshipman in 1838, past midshipman in 1844, lieutenant in 1852, captain in 1866. (Meigs, *The Corbins of Virginia*, 14–15; GNR.)

3. Major General William O. Butler (1791–1880), Democratic candidate for Vice-President of the United States in 1848 (*DAB*).

4. Thomas Hart Benton (1782–1858), United States senator from Missouri from 1821 to 1851 (*DAB*).

5. Cooper's letter to Frye is unlocated, but Frye's reply from Paris, dated 21 May 1847, gave the news of the Lafayette family and himself (MS: YCAL).

891. *To the Citizens of Otsego County*

March 8, 1847.

Fellow Citizens:

In urging you again to aid us in effecting this great and humane object, we believe very little argument will be necessary. As some persons, however, appear to think the accounts of suffering exaggerated, and that there is not a pressing necessity for our interference, we will answer that objection. The English government, necessarily in possession of all the facts, is now, and has been for many months, bestowing tens of thousands weekly for the support of the perishing poor of Ireland. — This certainly would not be done without sufficient evidence of its necessity. It is in proof that hundreds perish every week, in spite of this assistance. But money cannot relieve famine. *Food* is wanting, and that we possess in abundance. It is beyond cavil that the last potato crop was nearly a total failure in Ireland. Acquainted as we are with the habits of the people of that country, we *know* that intense want must follow.

We do not appeal to your pride, and your feelings of competition with those around you. What we ask, is solicited in the name of charity, and in obedience to the commands of God. A case has arisen when all who can, are bound to bestow of their superfluities, and we doubt not your readiness to do so, as soon as its necessities are presented to your minds. We refer you to the numerous well authenticated instances of suffering that are reported in the Journals, as proofs of the horrid want that afflicts portions of Europe, and we feel that no stronger appeals can be made to your sympathies.

J. Fenimore Cooper,
Henry Phinney,
Henry Scott,
G. A. Starkweather,
Seth Doubleday,
Geo. W. Stillman,
Lawrence McNamee } *Cen. Com.*

SOURCE: *The Otsego Democrat,* Cooperstown, New York, 11 March 1847.

On 4 March 1847 at a meeting of Otsego County citizens in Cooperstown, the novelist was designated chairman of a central committee with full power to collect, on behalf of the County, food, clothing, and money from the several towns for sufferers in the Irish famine. This letter, presumably written by Cooper as chairman of the committee, was published with a detailed description of the history and purpose of the committee.

892. *To Richard Bentley*

Otsego Hall, Cooperstown, March 27th 1847

Dear Sir,

By the steamer of the 4th April you will receive the May part of the Tale. The story has been finished some time, and, by a new arrangement with Mr. Graham it will make a full book. This will entitle me to the £350. I have drawn periodically, every two months, the bill for April 1st making £200 — I shall send one on the 1st June, and another 1st August. Then, according to your terms, I am to wait until the sheets go finally forward for the remaining £50. Now, Mr. Graham has been desirous of having seventeen numbers, instead of fifteen, which would make one of my ordinary tales, as to length. To this I have consented, cutting two of the last parts into four. In consequence of this arrangement the last number will be published March 1848, a good bit ahead. As for the manuscript, I shall get it copied with care, and confide to your discretion to deal fairly by Mr. Graham. It will be time enough, however, to send the whole sometime in the autumn, when I shall seek a private opportunity for so doing. I think the succeeding chapters of this story will have interest. Graham had three parts stolen in manuscript, and I have been obliged to rewrite them. This has impaired their interest, for one never writes as well, on such subjects, as at the first heat.

I have a new book about half done, which I now offer to you. It will be called "Mark's Reef, or the Crater; a Tale of the Pacific Ocean." It is a Robinson Crusoe story, but with features entirely original. What the peculiar feature is I can not state, unless you purchase, though I think it safe enough in my hands. No one else can deal with it, as it should be, without the same mixture of peculiar knowledge.

This book will be put to press about the time you get my letter, and will be ready to send forward by the 1st July. You can have it for £350, though I think £400 should be the price. I beg an answer by return of boat, as I must bargain early with some one else, should you decline my offer.

I wish also, you would give me authority to draw for the odd £50, two months after August 1st, or say Oct. 1st, or I may forget next year you will owe it to me.

We are contributing grain in all this country to feed the Irish. About 15000 barrels of meal have already been forwarded from New York, alone, and as many more will follow. We shall send about 1000 from this county, through a committee of which I am chairman. Widows give their sixpences and shillings, and I never knew a better spirit in the ascendant. The abundance of this country is in mysterious contrast to the want of Europe. Our crops were never better than last year, and while we sell, with one hand, for large profits to supply your necessities, I am glad to say we give freely with the other. I can raise better hops than you ever grow in England for the price your government has taken off the duty! [1]

Yours &c

Mr. Bentley — J. Fenimore Cooper

MANUSCRIPT: Cooper Collection, Yale University Library.

1. Bentley replied on 29 April:

"I beg to acknowledge receipt yesterday of your letter of the 27th Ult. Your account [or] statement of our Agreement for *'Capt Spike'* is quite correct; and I shall be ready to fulfil[l] my part of it. With regard to your drawing upon me for the balance, before the time agreed upon, I assure you the state of business here does not warrant us in anticipating payments — everything about us is discouraging to enterprize of any sort. In the midst of the gloom which pervades everything here it is certainly very gratifying to witness the generous sympathy evinced by your great country towards afflicted Ireland. May this kindly feeling be perpetually on the increase between both countries to their lasting benefit and honor!

"I beg to accept your new book on the terms you propose, namely £350. Now that I have purchased 'Mark's Reef' I should be glad to hear something of the nature of the story if you can find time to give me a notion of it. It may be useful to me in advertising it . . . I understand of course that Mark's Reef will extend to three volumes in the English edition like all your other stories." (MS: YCAL.)

893. *To Philander Benjamin Prindle*

Hall, Cooperstown, 30 M[ar]ch, '47.

Sir:

I can have no possible objection to answering your request [1] in the affirmative, which manifests a delicacy in reference to my private affiairs, to which my countrymen have very little familiarized me, other than the fact that it is a private affair, and I do not wish to appear in any way to be consenting to bringing my own before the world.

Hitherto, I have scrupulously abstained from so doing, unless in answer to public comment in newspapers, and do not wish to depart from the rule. Still, the document to which you refer is, to a certain extent, a public document, and every one has a right to use it whenever its use shall be proper. I shall not object, if I do not consent. In a word, you can do as your sense of propriety shall determine, though for myself, I question if the world will care enough about the fact to render any publication on the subject necessary.

If you have seen the petition and the law you will understand how true one of Webb's statements concerning me is; I mean that in which he asserted in his journal that I was in the habit of writing my name James F. Cooper previously to going to Europe, whereas I never used the F or the Fenimore [2] ever at all until just before I sailed. In this way has this audacious dealer with falsehoods circulated a hundred similar untruths of me and mine which contempt for him, and I may add of the public that tolerate such a creature, has prevented me from contradicting and exposing. There is a seeming contradiction between the petition and the act which, as you seem to feel an interest in the matter, I will explain: My mother had a small property in this county, which she had inherited by a transfer of lands in New Jersey from her father, and which she offered to give to me, if

I would take her family name in lieu of that of Cooper. My father opposed it. The latter died, leaving me an equal portion of his own estate. My mother survived him several years and repeated the offer from time to time. I would not accept the offer of the eight or ten farms she owned, but promised to make the change so far as to add her name to my father's, and to use both as a family name. My mother died several years before the law was passed, the delay arising from the circumstance that I was implicated in many lawsuits and change might produce confusion. In 1826 I got extricated from the law and was going abroad for health and variety. That was the time to redeem the pledge given my mother before her death. The application was, as I have said, to add Fenimore to the old family name, keeping both. The legislators, who always know more than their constituents, changed this application by authorizing me to take Fenimore as a middle name, a power I did not ask. As the law authorized me to use Fenimore, and my children were all so young as to render it a matter of indifference as respects them, I did no more in the way of legislation; though I have always used the name of Fenimore as part of my family name, except in discourse. My wife and children do the same, as will probably any descendants I may have hereafter in the male line. Thus the reason I write Fenimore in full, abbreviating the James for shortness.

Fenimore is derived from a manor in Oxfordshire that in Doomsday Book is called Finnimer and Finnimere. It is now called Finnimore. It is singular that while I was last in England proceedings were going on in Chancery to ascertain the rightful heir to the manor. I make no doubt the rightful male heir is in America, though the family is not uncommon. When the change in the spelling occurred I do not know, but I spell it as it was spelled by my mother before her marriage, and by my grandfather. My eldest brother was called Richard Fenimore Cooper, and his eldest grandson bears the same name. I had two cousins, Richard Fenimore Wilmeta and Richard Fenimore Heaton, and the name is extensively used in the connection as a Christian name, and has been for nearly seventy years. This is a country in which there is a community of property in everything, in name as well as in other things. One would think that as a name became illustrious, it would become more peculiarly the property of those who have a direct interest, but it is not thought so here. There are probably 10,000 Washingtons in America at this moment. Now, in a very small way, my name has been pirated too, though I think it is because our people fancy it is some new-fashioned Christian name that suits their fancy, rather than that it is the name of a race. I see the death of a Fenimore about once a year in the village newspaper. There seems to be a mortality among the children that use it, which may put a stop to the inroad. I endeavor to further that idea, for a greater set of little scamps than those who are called Fen in the streets of this village cannot well be found. As their parents probably read nothing, I am not at all flattered by the distinction. And now, sir, having answered a great deal more than you have asked, I leave you to do just as you please, washing my hands of any publication in the premises whatever.

Very respectfully yours,
J. Fenemor Cooper,
or
J. Fenimere Cooper,
or
J. Fenimore Cooper
which you like best.

SOURCE: *The* [New York] *Sun*, 6 October 1890, page 5.

An unmarried lawyer of Norwich, New York, Prindle (1807–1868) served for several years as clerk of the New York State Assembly (Franklin C. Prindle, *The Prindle Genealogy* . . . [New York: The Grafton Press, 1906], 88).

An introductory note, dated Syracuse, New York, 5 October 1890, explains that George M. Tillson, a Syracuse lawyer who had been a friend of Prindle, had found among his old papers a copy of Cooper's letter made before a fire in the Prindle homestead in Norwich, New York, destroyed the original. A memorandum by Prindle on the copy read: "In answer to a communication from me desiring his permission to take his petition from the files of 1826, relating to his change of name, and place it in my autograph collection, Mr. Cooper made the following reply."

1. Prindle wrote from Albany on 29 March: "There is on the files of the Assembly of the year 1826 your petition for the authorized insertion of 'Fenimore' as a middle name. I am making a collection of autographs of persons of prominence in the country. Will you give me permission to insert the above named petition in my book?" (MS: YCAL.)

Cooper's petition has disappeared. It was, presumably, removed from the files by Prindle and destroyed in the burning of the Prindle homestead or destroyed with some ninety per cent of the petitions in the State Library fire of 1911.

2. The copyist or compositor wrote "Fennimore" here and throughout the letter, clearly a careless misreading of Cooper's text.

894. *To James Knox Polk*

Hall, Cooperstown, April 29th 1847

Sir,

The late Dr. Lyman Foot, U. S. Army, who died last year, at Port Lavacca, Texas, while on duty in that country, was married to one of my nieces. Dr. Foot lost his life as much on service as if he had been killed in battle, leaving but little fortune, a widow and seven children; the youngest yet an infant. His character was excellent, and his rank that of the fifth surgeon in the army.

Under the foregoing circumstances, I have been applied to, to use any influence I might possess, to obtain a lieutenancy for Zephaniah Charles Foot, the second son of the late Dr. Foot.[1] I am not conscious of possessing any influence, but this it is not easy to impress on my connections, and I can not refuse to make the desired application, which I now ask leave respectfully to present to your consideration.

Mr. Zephaniah Charles Foot is about twenty. He was intended for the law, and is now on the last term of senior year in Geneva College, but finds it necessary to abandon his studies in consequence of the loss of support connected with the death of his father. He is the son of a Miss Platt of Plattsburgh in this State, (not being a child by my niece) and is very respectably connected. His character and principles are both better than common, and his intelligence quite equal to his education, the latter having been carefully attended to.

I am fully aware of the number of applications to which your high and responsible office must render you subject, and shall neither express nor feel disappointment, should my application fail; but, should it succeed, my own thanks shall be very sincerely added to those of the young man himself, and to those of his more immediate friends —[2]

Mr. Foot is now at Sackett's Harbour, in this State.

I am, Sir, | Very respectfully and sincerely | Your Ser.
J— Fenimore Cooper

James K. Polk | President of the United States.

ADDRESSED: To | James K. Polk Esquire | President U. S. A. | Washington. POSTMARKED: COOPERSTOWN N.Y. | [*illegible*] | [*illegible*] STAMPED: 10 ENDORSED: J. Fennimore Cooper | in behalf of young Fo[ot?] | eldest Son of Dr. Fo[ot?] Surgeon | U S Army who died at | [Lavacca?] Texas | May 3, 1847 | Referred to the | [Secretary?] of [Army?] | May [4?] 1847 | J. K. P.
MANUSCRIPT: Doheny Collection, St. John's Seminary, Camarillo, California.

1. For Cooper's earlier effort to assist Dr. Foot's sons, see Cooper to Lyman Foot, 14 July 1841.

2. Zephaniah Charles Foot found the resources to continue at Geneva College and graduate with his brother Isaac in the class of 1847. He subsequently became a lawyer and an insurance dealer at Syracuse, New York. (*Hobart College: General Catalogue*, 78.)

895. *To William Branford Shubrick*

Hall, Cooperstown, April 30th 1847

My dear Shubrick,

A letter came last evening from Mary,[1] advising me that a missive of mine might be in time for a special messenger, if sent immediately. I write, therefore, in a great hurry, and somewhat briefly.

Of your family, I shall merely say that all I hear speaks of Mrs. Shubrick's being a great deal more cheerful than you probably imagine. Her interest in Mary, who is now quite well I understand, has no doubt lessened her concern on your account. My family is well, with the exception of Mrs. Cooper, who is slowly recovering from the most severe illness I have ever known her to endure. Her recovery is slow, but she drives out, and improves. Paul is vastly better, being set up by the water-cure. All apprehensions on account of his lungs have ceased. The affection is nervous, coupled with an unequal circulation.

Well, you will have heard of our victories. [David] Conner was superseded by [Matthew C.] Perry just in time to allow the last to sign the capitulation of Vera Cruz. Glance your eyes at Perry's dispatches, and ask yourself what could have been the inducement for sending that which was written *within* the Castle of San Juan? [2]

It seems that Perry sent [Charles G.] Hunter, in a small steamer, down to Alvarado, with orders to lie off the port, but not to enter the river. Hunter began to try experiments with his big gun, and this brought off commissioners who offered to surrender the place, the troops having evacuated it. Finding that the

Mexicans were removing public property &c, Hunter ran in, got possession, and pushed his conquest[s?] some fifty miles up the river, and recieving the submissions of two or three towns — [Tlacotalpan] [3] for one, a place of 5 or 6000 souls. For this Perry has arrested him! What business had any man to prevent a wreath from entwining the brow of a Perry? I think this business will pretty nearly use the Commodore up.[4]

You have doubtless seen the death of your nephew.[5] All accounts agree that he behaved with great coolness and spirit, and he seems to be very generally regretted. His messmates write of him as "poor Tom Shubrick," and with great regard. He was killed instantaneously. Baldwin,[6] the lieutenant who was wounded, is an uncommonly clever fellow, and I have foreseen would do something, if he could get a chance. Our old ship-mate, [Isaac] Mayo,[7] and John Aulick commanded in the batteries, and Tat[t]nall [8] afloat — But all this, you will learn from the papers, which a Commander in Chief can not fail to recieve.

We have been led, here, to believe that [Robert F.] Stockton and [Stephen Watts] Kearny have had some trouble.[9] The impression made by the papers is in Kearny's favour, though one hardly knows when to believe them. Kearny is an old acquaintance, though I have not seen him for five and twenty years. He is, indeed, a connection of my wifes, Kearny's grandmother having been Mrs. Cooper's grandfather's sister. If an occasion offer, I wish you to tell him, with my regards, that we often mention him here, and wish him every success.

Your letter from Valparaiso [10] has not yet reached me, nor do I think the Levant [11] has arrived. Tha[t] from Monterey [12] came to hand a week since. I do not like the taste of calling the Californians "rebels," as Stockton terms them in his despatches, & as indeed does Col. Price [13] the New Mexicans, from Santa Fe. We have plenty of officers who can fight, but, as yet, Rough and Ready carries off all the glories of the pen. It is true that men may violate pledges, paroles and oaths, and thus become obnoxious to censure, but is it right to proffer oaths at all, to the inhabitants of a country overrun, rather than definitively conquered; or if given, are not those who have taken them released from the obligations whenever a re-conquest takes place. There is a spirit getting up, in reference to this war, which will bring all such questions into controversy, and it may be useful to you to give them your profound consideration. I believe the juris-consulti would decide the last of my points in the affirmative.

Where is [James] Biddle? Here, we have a rumour he is to go to Monterey. I suppose the missing letter will tell me all about him. I have a good opinion of Biddle, and hope you may get along smoothly with him.[14] I think him honorable, and manly, though a little irritable. If he comes home, I take it he will bring Stockton with him. The Ohio,[15] Mary tells us, is to sail soon to join you. With [Elie A. F.] Lavalette, [Silas H.] Stringham and Dupont [16] you will be sustained — I do not know the rest of your captains, though I have favourable opinions of Montgomery.[17]

Does not your Monterey News paper fib a little? It is a failing of news papers in general, and I am curious to know how early the disease is taken, as it might be in the natural way.

You will have seen that the four oldest commanders are promoted. So the report of the commission goes for nothing. I never liked that commission, I must say, and think Bancroft was wrong in ordering it.[18] I could communicate much more naval gossip had I been in town, this spring, but Mrs. Cooper's indisposition has kept me at home. I shall go in a few days, and shall write by the Ohio.

I confess I am agreeably disappointed in the circumstance of there being no Mexican privateers out. It really seems incredible, that, with a trade like ours, not a single craft under the flag has been taken at sea. As for this project of collecting the revenue of Mexico, and turning it to our own use, the Mexicans appear to have devised a plan to overreach us. They insist that all duties for goods sent into the gulf, must be paid at the Havanna, and certificates taken, else would they be siezed in the country. This might do, if there were no such things as smugglers, and our armies were not likely to cover so much of the interior as to open up wide markets where the Mexican lance or lasso never penetrated.

We are all anxious to learn that Scott has got into the mountains. There is a report that 2000 of his men are down with the fever, but the Vera Cruz papers tell a different story.[19] One never knows. The time for fever (April 9th) was at hand, and when it does come, I am told it comes suddenly.

Worth [20] is breveted a Major General. I think [John Ellis] Wool will be so. I also think Totten and Bankhead [21] will get brevets, as chiefs of the e[n]gineers and artillery. The siege was certainly very creditable to our arms, being managed not only with success, but with skill and method. It is much the most military movement ever achieved under the flag. Conner put the army ashore, beautifully, and has obtained great credit for the manner in which it was done. It would seem that not a man was hurt, or a knapsack lost in the disembarcation.

You ought to have a [couple?] of steamers in your squadron. They should be built in the Pacific. One of your first measures will be, I suppose, to establish a yard, as far as your powers will permit, and that yard should be a building yard. There seems to be no expectation here that California will ever be given up, nor ought it ever to be yielded. Mexico can never keep it, and we must occupy it to prevent the French, or English from attempting to do so.

England has her hands more than full with the famine. She is paying war contributions to keep the Irish and Scotch poor from starving, and her politicians calculate that 2,000,000 will die, notwithstanding all her efforts! These efforts are noble, and do her infinite credit, in the way of liberality, though they would seem to be somewhat too hardy. This country will contribute near half a million in charity.

Our spring is cold and dry, with a tremendous fall of snow. Sunday the 16th, the thermometer here, fell to about 10° above zero, and earlier in the month, we had the snow three feet deep. Late in March there was an awful tempest; one of the severest gales I have ever seen inland. For days we had no mail.

I shall endeavour to write by the Ohio, with more small talk. But this must go at once, with the best wishes of every body here, myself among the foremost

As ever yours

Commodore Shubrick — J. Fenimore Cooper

P — S — My regard[s?] to Lavallette.

MANUSCRIPT: Paul Fenimore Cooper, Cooperstown, New York.

1. Unlocated.

2. Perry relieved Conner as commander of the Home Squadron before Vera Cruz on 21 March 1847, and the city capitulated on 24 March. To the texts of the articles of capitulation and the official dispatch, dated from his flagship, describing the occupation of Vera Cruz and the castle of San Juan de Ulúa, Perry added the superfluous postcript: "1 P.M., March 29, | Within the Castle of S. Juan de Ulúa, | I write this within the castle. The batteries in the city are now saluting. The American flags are already hoisted on two forts of the city. The American colors will be next displayed on the castle. | M. C. Perry," (Edward M. Barrows, *The Great Commodore: The Exploits of Matthew Calbraith Perry* [Indianapolis and New York: The Bobbs-Merrill Co., 1935], 189–91; *The New York Herald*, 13 April 1847.)

3. Cooper apparently wrote "Fra Co Talpan."

4. According to Perry's biographer, Hunter's disobedience spoiled a diversionary action intended to permit a detachment approaching from the rear to capture much-needed reserve horses from the Mexicans. Perry's course in court-martialing, reprimanding, and dismissing Hunter from the squadron was decidedly unpopular, however; and "Alvarado" Hunter (1813–1873), as the culprit was soon called, became something of a hero. (Barrows, *The Great Commodore*, 195; William Harwar Parker, *Recollections of a Naval Officer, 1841–1865* [New York: Charles Scribner's Sons, 1883], 103–05; *NCAB*, IX, 186.)

5. Thomas Branford Shubrick (1825–1847), the son of Irvine Shubrick, was killed on 23 March in the act of pointing a gun during the bombardment of Vera Cruz (*ACAB*).

6. Augustus S. Baldwin (d. 1876), appointed midshipman in 1829, passed midshipman in 1836, lieutenant in 1841, and captain on the retired list in 1867 (GNR).

7. See Cooper to Mayo, 25–28? February 1850.

8. Josiah Tattnall exhibited daring as commander of the Mosquito division in the storming of Vera Cruz (*ACAB*).

9. Stockton's orders from the Navy Department were to assume chief command after the surrender of California, and Kearny's orders from the War Department were identical. Neither man would yield; and John Charles Frémont, appointed civil governor by Stockton, refused to obey Kearney, though Kearny's authority was finally sustained.

10. Dated *Independence*, Bay of Valparaiso, Chile, 5 December 1846 (MS: YCAL).

11. An 18-gun, 792-ton vessel, built in 1837 (GNR).

12. Shubrick's letter dated Monterey, Upper California, 23 January 1847, continued a letter dated North Pacific Ocean, Latitude 1° 19′ N, Longitude 111° 25′ W, 31 December 1846 (MS: YCAL).

13. Colonel Sterling Price (d. 1867) of the second Missouri infantry (*Historical Register and Dictionary of the United States Army*).

14. Shubrick, en route to California, and Biddle, returning from China, exchanged signals off Valparaiso on 2 December 1846. Shubrick reported in his letter of 5 December 1846 that his subsequent relations with Biddle had been quite harmonious and that Biddle had proceeded to Callao and Lima to obtain his orders. (MS: YCAL.)

15. A 2700-ton ship launched in 1820 (GNR).

16. Samuel Francis Du Pont (1803–1865), appointed midshipman in 1815, lieutenant in 1826, commander in 1842, captain in 1855, and rear admiral in 1862 (*DAB*, GNR).

17. John Berrien Montgomery (1794–1873), appointed midshipman in 1812, lieutenant in 1818, commander in 1839, captain in 1853, and rear admiral on the retired list in 1866 (*DAB*, GNR).

18. Cooper instanced the failure of Bancroft's policy of promoting according

to merit and not according to seniority. Charles Gauntt, William Ramsay, Henry Henry, and Samuel W. Downing were promoted to captain in February 1847. Henry W. Ogden, whom they outranked in seniority, but who outranked them in ability, was promoted a year later. (Navy *Register* for 1847 and 1848.)

19. Scott's army, suffering from disease and exposure to heavy rains, was encamped near the city of Japala, about sixty-five miles from Vera Cruz (H. Judge Moore, *Scott's Campaign in Mexico . . .* [Charleston, South Carolina: J. B. Nixon, 1849], 69).

20. William Jenkins Worth (d. 1849), breveted for gallantry and meritorious conduct at Monterey on 23 September 1846 (*Historical Register and Dictionary of the United States Army*).

21. Joseph Gilbert Totten (d. 1864) and James Bankhead were breveted brigadier general on 29 March 1847 for gallantry and meritorious conduct at the siege of Vera Cruz (*Historical Register and Dictionary of the United States Army*).

896. *To Mrs. William Branford Shubrick*

Hall, Cooperstown, May 2d 1847

Dear Mrs. Shubrick,

I was, honestly speaking, on the point of writing to you, when I got a letter from Shubrick concluding with a pardon of all my sins of omission as regards himself, if I would only endeavour to cheer you up with an occasional letter.[1] I, who know how gay and merry you are, have answered him properly, keeping your secret, and now pursue my original intention, just as if he had said nothing about you.

I saw poor Tom's death,[2] and wished among things that his parents should hear how much we all felt for them. I remember him as a child, and only as a child, but I hear the best accounts of him. I may write to Irvine [Shubrick], myself, but should any letters pass among you, I wish it might be said to them that I mentioned our sympathy in letters to you.

I got a letter from the Commodore last night. It was written at Valparaiso; and must have come ⟨from⟩ by the Levant. I have also heard over land.[3]

I am glad to find that [James] Biddle treats him with so much kindness. The Columbus, I make no doubt, is now on her way home. I suppose you know all about it, but, lest your careless husband should have forgotten to tell you, I may just put in, that Biddle went to Callao for his orders; that Shubrick advised him to go down on the enemy's coast just to show his ship, and frighten them, and then to come home. Biddle did not want to go, but rather yielded to the persuasion. [Robert F.] Stockton, of course, will come home as soon as he can. He is rather a rum author. Old [John D.] Sloat can beat him at a proclamation, and give him ten. Well, we shall now see what Commodore Shubrick can do in that way. I wish they had all been sent to school to Rough & Ready, who really writes like a book. I do not believe a word about that Major Bliss' writing his letters.[4] I'll engage Bliss has learned more from Taylor, than Taylor has learned from Bliss.

By the way, what a figure Matthew Perry cuts! He sends an officer down to Alvarado, with orders I suppose not to enter until he got there, and because that officer *accepted* an offer of surrender, and takes possession of the whole country, he arrests him! This is beautiful. Hunter says that he got possession of Alvarado on the 31st March, and Perry says he took possession on the 2d April. Did the Mexicans re-conquer the place in the interval? All this is very much like relieving Conner just in time to sign the capitulation. Then the despatch written *in* the Castle! What a wreath of glory was that, for the country. It was equal to firing a salute, on a fourth of July, in no latitude and no longitude, and reporting it in a despatch. The country will open its eyes, after a while. The Tobasco cannonading was bad enough, but this last affair is worse.[5]

Paul is better; so much so, as to remove all apprehensions about his lungs. He has resumed his studies. My regards to Dr. Clymer, and tell him I believe in water cure — for all nervous affections, unequal circulation, and dispepsia. Every thing indeed, but bone-setting and active maladies, and for some of them. I desire to thank him for the registers, which I ascribed to the right person. Has his brother Tom ever come back to see that bouncing Miss Harris?[6] The happiness of the Clymers will never be perfected until that lady is secured — I ought to have said is lassoed.

I have half a mind to come on and see you, and certainly should if I had time. But this spring is so backward, and my work is so backward, that I am afraid I shall not get further than Philadelphia, for which place I start next Tuesday.

I see that both Trapiers have resigned; St. Paul his church, and St T'other his commission.[7] I question whether the last do not regret what he has done. Every body that is in the Navy, wishes he was out, and every body that is out wishes he was in. I trust the Doctor is convinced that it is easier to cure a sailor than a landsman.

Do you not mean to come and see us this summer? I will come for you whenever you shall say the word, but can not Clymer and Mary come along? All the people at the yard will be in the Mexican hospitals by August, and the Doctor will have nothing to do. We will reflect on this plan.

The Commodore writes me that his passage from Rio to Valparaiso was glorious. Yes, glorious is the word; but, I can tell him, glory is not easily obtained in these Vera Cruzan Buena Vistan times. No man is glorious that has not scalped and eaten a Mexican, or been run through with half a dozen of their lances. Nevertheless. it was doing pretty well to make that passage in thirty three days. Shubrick says the Portsmouth is the only ship that ever beat it, and she made it in twenty nine days. Let him tickle himself with that notion awhile, but I'll take very good care to undecieve him. A namesake of mine once told me he went from Buenos Ayres to Valparaiso in thirty days, which *was* travelling! But *he* was a Cooper. Thirty three and a half were pretty well for a Shubrick. My namesake, moreover, was in a merchant vessel, and those fellows always lie one day about the time of sailing, and another about the time of arriving. The Independence must be a pretty good goer, after all. Shubrick says that she stands up well, though she is over sparred, but I don't believe him, and expect to hear she has rolled quite over, one of these days. What a proclamation we should get from Stockton, if he could get rid of his senior in that fashion — his senior, though he wears his own hair, which is more than Stockton does, or has done this many a day.

What a figure our friend on the other side of the continent would cut marching a hundred and fifty miles, on foot, and then at pulling a cannon up a hill! He will not do much of either. He is no so'ger, to use his legs. I'll warrant you the City of the Angels never sees *him*. No, no; he will stick by the ship, until palanquins are introduced from the East Indies.

I suppose Charlotte has let you know how ill my wife has been. I think she has been more reduced, and is getting along more slowly than I have ever known her to do. She does get better, however, and is no[w] so much recovered that I can venture to leave her, a thing I have not dared to do before this spring. On the 15th March I had my trunk packed to go down, and I am yet. Tuesday Deo Volente I shall get under way.

Mrs. Cooper sends you lots of love, and begs you to come and see her this summer. Poor Mrs. Laight, since the death of her husband, will not come near us.[8] I fear we shall never get [her] here, again. As yet, I have not even seen her. You must come and supply her place.

The girls and Paul, all hands in short, unite in love.

Yours most truly

Mrs. W. B. Shubrick. J. Fenimore Cooper

P. S. You can not imagine what a nice little correspondent I have got.[9] She describes herself as ten years old, and almost professes to be in love with me. I dare say she thinks I am some sentimental looking youth, with a waist that she can clasp with her slender fingers, fine frenzy-like eyes, and dark curls. How she will be disappointed when we meet! I believe I shall turn her over to the Commodore, who is just the sort of love-sick swain she would like; but I'll engage no young lady volunteers to write *him* letters.

MANUSCRIPT: Paul Fenimore Cooper, Cooperstown, New York.

1. Shubrick's letter of 23 January 1847 concluded with the postscript: "You owe me many letters — — I will forgive you some of them if you will write to my poor wife and cheer her up a little" (MS: YCAL).

2. See the preceding letter.

3. The first letter was dated *Independence*, Bay of Valparaiso, Chile, 5 December 1846; two other letters were dated: North Pacific Ocean, Latitude 1° 19′ N, Longitude 111° 28′ W, 31 December 1846; and Monterey, Upper California, 23 January 1847 (MSS: YCAL).

4. Chief of staff to General Taylor during the Mexican War, William Wallace Smith Bliss (1815–1853, West Point 1833) became President Taylor's private secretary. He married Taylor's youngest daughter. (*ACAB*.)

5. See the preceding letter.

6. Cooper evidently referred to Dr. George Clymer's brother Thomas Willing Clymer (1802–1872, College of New Jersey [Princeton] 1822), a lawyer who died unmarried (James Rieman Macfarlane, *George Clymer . . . His Family and Descendants* [Sewickley, Pennsylvania: Sewickley Printing-shop, 1927], 15–16). The "bouncing Miss Harris" is unidentified.

7. Richard S. Trapier, appointed midshipman in 1831, passed midshipman in

1837, and lieutenant in 1841, resigned his commission on 30 December 1846 (GNR). His brother Paul Trapier (see Cooper to Shubrick, 25–30? January – 5 February 1824) resigned as rector of St. Michael's Church, Charleston, South Carolina, on 25 November 1846, after announcing that he would administer the Lord's Supper only to persons who had been confirmed or were ready and desirous to be confirmed (George W. Williams, ed., *Incidents in My Life: The Autobiography of the Rev. Paul Trapier, S.T.D. . . . ,* Publications of the Dalcho Historical Society of the Diocese of South Carolina, No. 7 [Charleston, South Carolina, 1954], 25, 52–55).

8. Henry Laight died on 6 November 1846 (*The* [New York] *Evening Post,* 7 November 1846).

9. See Cooper to Mary A. Doolittle, 25 December 1847.

897. *To Horatio Greenough*

Globe Hotel, New York, May 6th 1847.

Dear Greenough,

This letter will be handed to you by my friend Mr. W. W. Campbell late an M. C, from the City of New York.[1] Mr. Campbell is an Otsego County man by birth, where his family is resident for a century, and that is as long a period in America as a thousand years in Italy.

You gave a letter for me to some of my towns-folk, while at Graeffe[n]berg, as I *hear,* but the letter was put in a trunk which was lost, and I have never seen it. Last evening I met Morse on the battery, not having seen him before in three years. The man is astride of streaks of lightening half his time, and one can never *fix* him. We had a long talk, and I am happy to find he is beginning to realize. I should think $10,000 will hardly cover his receipts the coming year.

Do what you can to render Florence agreeable to Mr. Campbell, my dear Greenough. Keep him out of the hands of the Philistines, and keep him in your own.

Is not the Capt Burgwin who is just killed, (1st U. S. dragoons) a brother of your connection? [2]

Write to me, you rogue, and mail the letter according to rule, and trust no more widows with your missives.

I am gray, weigh 205 llbs, and in excellent health. Can you beat that. My wife has been ill this spring, and is thin, but is now convalescent – The rest all well and happy – My table is covered with dresses bought for the girls, and excellent girls they are.

Paul has been out of health, but he has been in Mr. [Nerf's?] establishment, since his return, and it has done wonders for him.

You are to be envied — a man who has an ample excuse for quitting America to pass his days in Italy! Adieu — it makes me melancholy to think of it — Take care of Campbell —

Yours as ever,

H. Greenough E[s?] quire. J— Fenimore Cooper

ADDRESSED: Horatio Greenough Esquire | Florence

MANUSCRIPT: Clifton Waller Barrett Collection of American Literature, University of Virginia.

1. See the following letter.

2. Greenough's cousin Anna Greenough (b. 1817) married in 1838 Henry King Burgwyn (1813–1877), a cousin of Captain John Henry King Burgwin (West Point 1830), who died on 7 February 1847 of wounds received three days earlier in an assault on Pueblo de Taos, New Mexico (John H. Sheppard, "Genealogy of the Greenough Family" *The New England Historical and Genealogical Register*, XVII (April 1863), 169; Walter Burgwyn Jones, *John Burgwin, Carolinian; John Jones, Virginian; Their Ancestors and Descendants* [Montgomery, Alabama?: privately published, 1913], 29, 39–41; *Historical Register and Dictionary of the United States Army*).

898. *To William W. Campbell*

Hall, Cooperstown, May. 22d 1847

My Dear Sir,

I have written you letters to a few persons who I think may be useful to you, while absent in Europe. I do not know how many of the acquaintances I made when abroad still remember me, for I have kept up very little communication with the old world since my return home. Should you, however, fall in with any who knew me, and who, you may be inclined to think, might feel disposed to give any weight to an introduction from me, I beg you will show them this letter, which will answer the purpose of such an [opening] [1] for acquaintance. If accident should throw you in the way of any of my friends, I hope they may be disposed to recieve you as my friend and neighbor, for my sake, and I shall not fail to appreciate such kindness as favors conferred on myself.

I wish you a pleasant and instructive journey. Your trip can hardly fail of being both, and the American who passes a year, or two, on the other side of the water, will have occasion to remember them with satisfaction for the rest of his days. If you go to Russia, ask Mr. Ivanhoff, at Paris, to give you a letter or two to St. Petersbourg.

Adieu — | Yours truly
J. Fenimore Cooper

W—W—Campbell Esquire | Late Member of Congress From New York.

MANUSCRIPT: A. Pennington Whitehead, New York City and Cherry Valley, New York.

As a native of Cherry Valley, Otsego County, Campbell (1806–1881, Union 1827) had long known and been known by the Cooper family. A letter from Campbell to Cooper, dated 6 May 1847 (MS: YCAL) shows that Campbell had written about his forthcoming trip abroad and that Cooper replied in a note of 2 May 1847 (unlocated). Cooper's general letter of introduction apparently resulted from their subsequent meeting for which Campbell requested the novelist to set a time.

A lawyer, jurist, and historian, Campbell was a congressman from 1845 to 1847; but he gave his most distinguished service as justice of the New York State Supreme Court from 1857 to 1865. His publications, the best known of which is *Annals of Tryon County* (1831), reveal his antiquarian bent. (Hurd, *History of Otsego County*, 138–40; *DAB*.)

1. Cooper seems to have written "openining."

899. *To Richard Bentley*

Hall, Cooperstown, May 28th 1847

Dear Sir,

Your letter, accepting my offer of the new book, at ⟨$⟩350£s has been recieved.[1] I have changed the name, but you can keep "Mark's Reef," if you prefer it. I shall call it here, "The Crater, or Vulcan's Peak, A Tale of the Pacific."

As I shall shortly send you the sheets of Vol. 1, and within 60 days the whole work, any summary will be unnecessary — The work differs, however, from other works of this character in the great leading circumstance that the vessel gets embayed among volcanic reefs, where there are the elements of soil, but no soil in activity, and consequently no vegetation. All this was to be created, and is. Then eruptions induce changes, and a colony is gradually formed. The ship is not lost, but is saved, though carried into a place whence she can not be got out. All her crew but two are drowned, and one of these two, after a few months is swept away by hurricane. Every thing comes round, in time, and a charming little colony is formed and flourishes.

The semi-monthly departures of the steamers will allow me

to send you Rose Budd earlier than before. The July number went on the 15th, and a duplicate goes next week. The same course will be pursued with the others.

We shall publish the "Crater" here in all July.

Yours truly

Mr. Bentley | London J. Fenimore Cooper

MANUSCRIPT: Cooper Collection, Yale University Library.

1. See Cooper to Bentley, 27 March 1847.

900. *To Henry and Elihu Phinney*

[1846–1847?]

Gentlemen,

The new edition,[1] will like all new editions, be corrected, both as to style and matter. It will be a little enlarged, and some important notes will be added. As for portraits, Paul Jones [2],[2] [Edward] Preble [1], [Isaac] Hull [5], [Oliver Hazard] Perry [6], [Thomas] McDonough [4] and [Stephen] Decatur [3], are the six most prominent. I number them as I concieve them most distinguished. [James] Lawrence, [William] Bainbridge, [Nicholas] Biddle and the rest will suggest themselves to your minds.

If you choose diagrams, I can obtain some for you; or make them for you, myself. A few of the engravings of the battles, now known, and sufficiently accurate, such as Wasp & Frolick, Macedonian & U. States, Constitution & Guerriere – They are to be seen every where, and if shown to me I could point out the accurate. Many are detestable.

There have been many portraits of Naval Men, in Port Folio, Analectic Magazine &c &c, but in general they are very indifferent – My own, as now possessed by Mr. Evans, is only so so, I think.

Yours &c

Messrs Phinney. J– Fenimore Cooper

MANUSCRIPT: Paul Fenimore Cooper, Cooperstown, New York.

1. This letter contains Cooper's instructions concerning the third edition of his *History of the Navy of the United States of America,* issued in two volumes, with corrections and additions, by Henry and Elihu Phinney at Cooperstown and by Lea and Blanchard at Philadelphia.

2. The numerals were inserted over the names. Some of the numbers are crossed out and underlined as if they had been used in the preparation of the volumes.

Part Twenty

MICHIGAN LANDS

1847–1848

1848. CENTRAL RAIL ROAD LINE. 1848.

THE NEW AND SPLENDID UPPER CABIN STEAMER CANADA,

H. VAN ALLEN, MASTER,

WILL RUN BETWEEN BUFFALO AND DETROIT, DURING THE SEASON, AS FOLLOWS:

Leaves Buffalo, Wednesdays and Saturdays, at 9 o'clock, A. M.

Leaves Detroit, Mondays and Thursdays, at 6 o'clock, P. M.

Canada, off Buffalo. Friday, June 30th 1848

Dearest,

Five days trial, and no verdict, again. We have gained ground, however. Got all the law settled on our side, and all our way clear. I am well. Went to Kalamazoo last Saturday, and left Detroit yesterday. I shall pass Sunday at Geneva, and be home on Tuesday.

Ogden's testimony is improving, though he would thrust in opinions with his facts, and it was these opinions that did the mischief.

I am in good spirits, and shall go to work as usual.

Yours tenderly

J. Fenimore Cooper

Cooper to Mrs. Cooper, June 30, 1848

MICHIGAN LANDS

1847–1848

When *The Oak Openings* appeared in August 1848, Michigan readers could congratulate themselves on Cooper's compliment to their state. In the preface and final chapter, written during his journey to Michigan in June 1848 or immediately after his return, the novelist intruded his enthusiasm directly. The revolution in transportation had brought a revelation. The trip by rail from Fort Plain to Utica and on to Buffalo, a distance requiring more than a week a few years earlier, blended innumerable rich and beautiful scenes in a mere twenty-four hours. At Buffalo, after an interval of thirty-eight years, Cooper revisited the "surpassing loveliness of Niagara" and boarded the British steamer *Canada* for the agreeable passage down Lake Erie to Detroit, which, seen from a nearby island, "resembled a miniature picture of Constantinople." Thence he proceeded by rail through the first prairie he had ever seen to Kalamazoo, "an unusually pretty village" of about 2000 persons, and on by buggy to Schoolcraft through the remarkable Prairie Round, where he saw a demonstration of the ingenious Moore-Hascall harvesting machine. The charm of the unspoiled, rolling countryside wooded with "burr-oaks"; the wide stretches of wheat fields suggesting "how America could feed the world"; and the unmistakable aura of prosperity, respectability, and health impressed Cooper so deeply that he wished to write about them. But he had not visited Michigan as a sightseer, primarily, or even as a novelist gathering materials for a book.

The complications that were to bring Cooper to Michigan on at least five occasions between 1847 and 1850 began in the mid-1830's when he returned to the United States with money to invest and when the Michigan land fever was at its height. With a modest initial investment, Judge William Cooper had made a substantial fortune speculating in New York lands; and Horace H. Comstock, a young speculator in Illinois and Michigan lands who married the Judge's granddaughter Sabina Cooper, found it easy to tempt the Judge's son. Boasting that he could more than double any investment in a year, Comstock obtained Cooper's letter of credit for $6,000, a sum he invested at his own discretion in a joint purchase of Chicago lands. Fretting from losses in his cotton speculations, however, Cooper was becoming a nervous investor. Within six months, or by October 1835, he was asking for the return of his money. Reluctantly, Comstock agreed to pay $8,650 ($2,500 as profit and $150 as interest) in four equal notes with interest at six, twelve, eighteen, and twenty-four months, respectively. After some delay, the first two notes were paid, apparently in August 1836. When the last two notes were presented at the Commercial Bank in Albany in May 1837, they were protested. Comstock's bubble had burst in the onrush of the depression, and the would-be financier admitted his "necessities."

Meanwhile, Cooper had discounted both notes, the third with his friend James De Peyster Ogden, who had given half its value, and the fourth with Robert McDermutt. The novelist reclaimed the fourth note immediately, chiefly by exchanging Carey's notes for it, and repaid Ogden with interest in 1844. As a gesture of good faith, Comstock at first deposited with his brother-in-law Morris Cooper, the novelist's nephew, a "valuable" bond and mortgage as security for the two protested notes. By January 1839, Cooper's pressure on Comstock brought a promissory note for $2,250, dated 1 January 1839, at six months with interest, signed by Sidney Ketchum and endorsed by J. Wright Gordon, George C. Gibbs, and James S. Sandford. In better times, Ketchum had been a prosperous real estate magnate in Marshall, Michigan; and Gordon, Sandford, and evidently Comstock had been his business associates. At Cooper's request, Ogden seems to have taken half of this note as security for his half-interest in Comstock's third note and discounted the other half. When Ogden presented Ketchum's note for payment on 1 July 1839, it too was protested.

Liable at this point to prosecution from several directions, Ketchum began what looks suspiciously like a shell game. On or about 4 September 1839, Isaac Schuyler, a New York associate of Ketchum, accepted Ketchum's draft for $2,350, drawn to his own order, with interest, for sixty days. Ketchum left this draft with Ogden without written understanding as to whether it was security for his protested note or a substitute for it. When the draft came due in November, Ketchum and Schuyler together visited Ogden with a story of Ketchum's disappointment in not receiving funds from Boston. Since Ogden did not object to a renewal for thirty days, Ketchum gave Ogden a new note or draft for $2,350, drawn to his own order, accepted by Schuyler, and made payable in thirty days. Ketchum gave Ogden some money, possibly interest. This draft was also protested. In the ensuing litigation, still in progress at the time of Cooper's death, the endorsers of Ketchum's original note sought to show that Ogden took the draft accepted by Schuyler as a substitute for the note and that the renewal was, in effect, an agreement to give time. If allowed, this construction would legally exonerate the three endorsers. Schuyler's function, as their witness, was to testify fiercely that he could have paid if his acceptance had been called in 1839. He would not be in funds, of course, when the case was tried.

Ketchum's scheme may have been more or less deliberate than this summary suggests, and Comstock may or may not have been a party to the deception. Cooper was inclined to judge both men leniently. Ketchum he found an engaging, enterprising rogue, if rogue he was; and Comstock he considered more ineffectual and gullible than dishonest. Probably because he hoped Ketchum would eventually pay, he moved slowly with the prosecution, permitting Comstock to sue Ketchum in Michigan before he obtained a judgment in his own name for $3,339.46 on 17 November 1845. But any prospect of recovery from Ketchum was a delusion, as Cooper subsequently discovered.

The endorsers of Ketchum's original note were the better hope; and, spurred by the statute of limitation, Cooper began proceedings early in 1845 against J. Wright Gordon and George C. Gibbs in the United States Circuit Court in Michigan and against James S. Sandford, then a resident of New York State, in New York. The action against Sandford was lost and a counteraction for costs was adjudicated in 1849. The case against Gordon and Gibbs received full-dress trials at Detroit in mid-October 1847, late June 1848, and late October 1848; but each jury found itself divided. Cooper was repeatedly disappointed at Ogden's bumbling manner in testifying; but he was surprised and delighted that Schuyler, the defendants' star witness, testified under oath that Ketchum obtained his (Schuyler's) acceptance by fraud. Even this incontestable evidence of Ketchum's trickery was insufficient; and Cooper wrote to his wife in the midst of the hotly contested final trial: "I expect nothing from Michigan, and heartily wish I had never heard of the state." Had he been able to attend the trial scheduled for October 1851, the month after his death, he would probably still have lost the avails of Comstock's third note.

With the fourth note, repurchased from Robert McDermutt, Cooper was more fortunate. Though the records are incomplete, Comstock appears to have secured this note with two notes of Ketchum for $1,125 each, payable on 1 January 1841 and secured by bond and mortgage. When, inevitably, these notes were protested, Comstock deeded to Cooper eighteen lots, valued at $2,500, in the village of Kalamazoo. (Twelve of the lots form the block now bounded by Kalamazoo Avenue and Burdick, Edwards, and Willard streets. The other six are on the south side of Kalamazoo Avenue between Burdick and Edwards streets.) In sum, Comstock's two unpaid notes yielded Cooper in partial return a novel and eighteen town lots, most of which he left to his wife and children. He was more fortunate than many of the victims of the cunning Michigan magicians who, according to Mrs. Caroline M. S. Kirkland's *A New Home — Who'll Follow?* (1839), turned "burr-oaks . . . into marble tables, tall tamaracks into draperied bedsteads, lakes into looking-glasses, and huge expanses of wet marsh into velvet couches and carpets from the looms of Agra and of Ind."

901. *To George E. Hand*

New-York — June 9th [1847]

Dear Sir,

I am sorry to say that Mr. [James De Peyster] Ogden, on his return from Albany, says he can not possibly be at Detroit, this month, having an engagement at Washington. I suppose his future fortune is materially connected with this movement.

[Isaac] Schuyler could come, but, under the peculiar circumstances, and taking into consideration the fact that defendants got delay last autumn on account of [Sidney] Ketchum, who has not the least thought of going this summer, I trust the court will grant delay, under stipulations to try next summer.

I have seen a good deal of Ketchum, who has let me into his speculations &c (showing me his contracts and the property with which he is connected) and I rather think he will pay the judgment, himself, shortly after the autumn sales of land re-commence. He has written to Mr. Gibbs [1] on the subject, and possibly the defendants will consent to delay on his suggestion.

Should the court refuse to lay the cause over, it would be well to ask for a postponement, and by writing me immediately, through the telegraph viâ Utica, I might be on the ground with Schuyler, in season to prevent a verdict. Ketchum will not be there, and with Schuyler, alone, I should not be much afraid of them. He would tear Ketchum all to pieces, and is as ferocious as a bull dog. In four or five days after notice we could be in Detroit. Nevertheless it would be every way better to get the cause laid over. Ogden is very, very material, and I have strong expectations of Ketchum's paying me, which will be the best mode of disposing of the matter.

Please to let me hear from you, in any event, as soon as possible, and direct to Cooperstown, where I go to-morrow.

I may see you in Detroit next month, in any case —

Is any land of mine, in Kalamazoo advertised for taxes — Ask Goodwin [2] that question, and let me know if you please. Ask him to pay the taxes, if such should be the case — The sum can not be more than a dollar or two, and I will repay it at once.

Success attend you.

Geo— E— Hand Esqu J— Fenimore Cooper

In my opinion Ketchum is about to make a fortune.

MANUSCRIPT: Cooper Collection, Yale University Library.

A Connecticut man by birth and death, Hand (1809–1889, Yale 1829) spent his entire professional life in Michigan, where he studied and practiced law, served as county probate judge, United States district attorney, state representative, and accumulated a fortune by buying and selling lands (*Michigan Biographies* . . . [Lansing, Michigan: The Michigan Historical Commission, 1924], I, 369).

1. Lawyer, court reporter, and state representative, George C. Gibbs lived in Marshall, Calhoun County, and later in Barry County (Washington Gardner, *His-*

tory of Calhoun County, Michigan . . . [Chicago and New York: The Lewis Publishing Company, 1913], I, 239).

2. A law partner of George E. Hand, Daniel Goodwin (1799–1887, Union 1819) was federal district attorney in Michigan under Presidents Jackson and Van Buren and a justice of the Michigan Supreme Court from 1843 to 1846 (James Junius Goodwin, *The Goodwins of Hartford, Connecticut* . . . [Hartford, Connecticut: Brown and Gross, 1891], 454–61).

902. *To Mrs. Cooper*

New York, June 16th 1847

Dearest,

Here I am, and here I shall remain until to-morrow (Thursday) evening. Ogden can not be stirred. It is well I came, however, as Hand was altogether on a false scent. I have now got Ogden's testimony straight. The effect will be, I think, that the cause will not be tried. This is excessively provoking, but I can not help it. I think the defendants will move for delay. Ogden might very well go, but will not budge.

I saw Jim yesterday. He and his wife [1] will be up early in July. I have bought the candlesticks, and may send them across by the stage-driver on Friday. If they come give the driver a quarter of a dollar. Mrs. Laight, who has not yet seen me, but who may see me to-day, has sent the articles you will find with the candlesticks.

I hope to find a letter at Detroit, or at Buffaloe, on my return. Perhaps the last will be best. The molasses and rice are ordered, and the rose-water will be in the rice.

Miss Cruger told me yesterday (old Ditto's daughter) [2] that Mrs. James [Hamilton?] is a showy woman, but that her sister [3] was the better woman of the two. Mrs. James loved show &c, and would like to figure. Her great recommendation was walking particularily well. Harry Munro [4] is completely used up, and Mrs. Bayley [5] with him. Jim seems to be very well understood. He is looking unusually well.

Cortlandt Parker [6] is about to be married — to whom I did not learn.

Ogden's company is completely ruined — lost every thing, and is about to close. They blow on Ogden, whose day is gone in his own set. He keeps up his spirits, however, and will take care of himself. His decline will not be happy, I am afraid. Now, a wife and children would be a relief to him.

I am quite well, and ready for a start

Ever your[s?],

J. F. C.

MANUSCRIPT: Cooper Collection, Yale University Library. PUBLISHED, IN PART: *Correspondence*, II, 570–71.

1. Thomas James De Lancey, Jr., married Frances Augusta, daughter of Dr. Edward N. Bibby of Yonkers, New York, on 3 February 1847 (*The* [New York] *Evening Post*, 4 February 1847).

2. "Old Ditto" and his daughter are unidentified.

3. Mrs. James Hamilton had three half sisters: Emma (1805–1867), Catherine (1806–1870), and Anna Carolina (1808–1889). The last died unmarried. (E. F. De Lancey, "Original Family Records, *Cruger*," *The New York Genealogical and Biographical Record*, VI [April 1875], 79; Cruger Family Chart.)

4. Henry Munro (1802–1862) of Mamaroneck, New York, son of Peter Jay Munro and his wife Margaret (White), was the brother of Mrs. William Heathcote De Lancey (Robert Bolton, *The History of the Several Towns, Manors, and Patents of the County of Westchester* . . . [New York: Charles F. Roper, 1881], I, 502–03; *Jay Cemetery, Rye, New York*, facing page 11).

5. Cooper apparently referred to Mrs. Richard Bayley (1786–1878), who was Catharine, daughter of Henry and Anne (Van Cortlandt) White. Her daughter Anna Margaret married Henry Munro in 1840. (Charles Barney Whittelsey, *The Roosevelt Genealogy, 1649–1902* [Hartford, Connecticut: J. B. Burr, 1902], 43–45, 57.)

6. A lawyer who was to be a popular Republican orator, Cortlandt Parker (1818–1907, Rutgers 1836) married Elizabeth Wolcott, daughter of Richard Wayne Stites of Morristown, New Jersey, on 15 September 1847 (*NCAB*, XXXVI, 282–83).

903. *To Mrs. Cooper*

American Hotel, Buffaloe, June 20th 1847

Dearest,

I left town Thursday evening, sans Ogden, but with his testimony straight, full and direct. My presence in town was all important.

I sent you the candlesticks, some things from Mrs. Laight, and a dozen pines, from Fort Plain. I found Mr. [Alfred B.] Beach, *on a pilgrimage*, in the cars. Jack was also in the cars, going home, and later in the day, John C. Jay, his wife and two sisters,[1] joined us. I did intend passing the night at Geneva; but it rained and Mr. Beach induced me to go on to Rochester, where we arrived at 4. A. M. I went to bed, and slept until eleven, rose and breakfasted. I then went to the City Bank to beat up Tom Rochester. He was at Canandaigua, but his father[2] took me in charge, covered me with civility, and pressed me to stay some time. I went with him in a carriage, even to the landing, saw the outside of every thing, and found Rochester a far pleasanter, as well as larger place than I expected to see. The country is very fine, and this town the base of a really noble place. Some say it has 30,000 and some pretend as many as 40,000 inhabitants.

I have just come from church. A Mr. Schuyler [3] preached, and very well. He reads far better than common. Grosvenor Clark [4] knew me, and gave me a seat. The church was greatly crowded, having but one parson for three congregations —

I shall proceed to-morrow morning in the London. This will bring me to Detroit a little late, but I presume the cause will not be tried until I arrive. The papers, however, went ahead of me. I shall be home at the close of the week, and, if I gain my cause, you and I, and Fan and Caroline must have a look at the falls yet, this summer.

Beach did not seem very sanguine of success, but I think he may get the call. It is about $1200 a year, and no house. As yet, the water has no effect on me, though I drink plenty, and have not touched any other fluid, coffee excepted. Best love to all.

Yours most tenderly,

J. F. C.

ADDRESSED: Mrs. Fenimore Cooper | Cooperstown | New York POSTMARKED: BUFFALO N.Y. | JUN 20

MANUSCRIPT: Cooper Collection, Yale University Library. PUBLISHED, IN PART: *Correspondence,* II, 571.

1. See Cooper to John C. Jay, 27 February 1843.
2. Thomas Hart Rochester (1797–1864), son of the founder of the city of Rochester and father of Paul Cooper's friend Thomas F. Rochester (Edward R. Foreman, ed., *Centennial History of Rochester, New York* [Rochester: Rochester Public Library, 1931], I, 187).
3. Montgomery Schuyler (1814–1896, Union 1834) was rector of St. John's Church in Buffalo, New York, from 1845 to 1854 (*ACAB*).
4. Grosvenor Clark was a dry-goods merchant at 46 Main Street in Buffalo (*The Commercial Advertiser Directory for the City of Buffalo, 1847–1848 . . .* [Buffalo: Jewett, Thomas & Co. and T. S. Cutting, 1847]).

904. *To Rufus G. Beardslee*

Hall, Cooperstown, July [6th] [1] 1847

Sir,

I dare not engage to give the lecture you desire.[2] My engagements forbid it, and it is better to say "no," at once, than to say "yes" and disappoint you.

I have an ancient regard for Albany, having known the place from childhood, and having once been a school-boy in it. I know no town in which I would sooner go out of my way to oblige, if I saw my way clear, but I do not and must ask leave to decline.

Your hand writing is very good, but owing to an accident your name is so written that I can not make it out. Under the circumstances — I have just found that what I took for the name is merely your official station, and the name is plain enough among the words that I mistook for the usual conclusion of a letter.

Your Obed. Ser.

R. G. Beardslee Esquire — J. Fenimore Cooper

SOURCE: Facsimile reproduction in *The Month at Goodspeed's*, March 1933, page 211.

Beardslee (1822–1902) was a young lawyer temporarily in Albany. He practiced in New York City from about 1856 to 1902 and served in several educational posts. (Isaac H. Beardsley, *Genealogical History of the Beardsley-lee Family in America* [Denver, Colorado: John Dove, 1902], 335; *Hoffman's Albany Directory . . . for . . . 1847 '48* [Albany: L. G. Hoffman, 1847].)

1. Possibly "8th."

2. Corresponding secretary and chairman of the Lecture Committee of the Young Men's Association of Albany, Beardslee wrote on 28 June 1847 inviting Cooper to deliver one or two addresses before the association between 1 December and 1 March of the following season (MS: YCAL).

905. *To Richard Bentley*

Hall, Cooperstown, August 4th 1847

Dear Sir,

Your letter of July 6th has just reached me.[1] The *dates* of the drafts are of no consequence, my arrangements having been closely made to prevent their going forward except at the stipulated periods. I have drawn six drafts as against Spike, but the last one is not to go forward until August 1st. I shall not draw the seventh until the close of the book is sent.

As respects the Crater, I have as yet drawn no bill at all. I did think of drawing for £150, or £200, when I sent the first few sheets, but understanding the pressure in England, and not wanting money, I decided to wait. It is very well as it is, for, though I fully expected the book would have been finished in June, it is only just written now. About half has been stereotyped, and the other half is still in my hands in manuscript. Hitherto, we have stereotyped through the mail, but I usually wind up a book by visiting Philadelphia in person. I go there immediately and shall have the last of the sheets ready, I trust, by the 20th. As for publication, you need be under no concern. To help you along however, I shall send by steamer of 16th as much as is done, and the rest as soon as done. Of course you will publish as early as you can.

I shall probably draw for £200, as I go through New York, and for the balance of £150, when the last sheets go.

I like the book myself, and think it will have a good deal of success.

Our crops are excellent, and abundance may be said to reign in this country. For the last four years, the potatoes in my kitchen garden have rotted a great deal, usually commencing about the last of July. On my farm, where I raise them by the acre[s?], I have not suffered much, though the potatoes have rotted a good deal in the winter. This year, as yet, I can hear of no decay in the potatoe, any where near me. The vines look well and some potatoes that I imported from Lancashire expressly to change the seed, which for the last two years have been sickly, this year look as flourishing as I ever saw potatoes.

I ought to have explained that the delay in Crater is owing to my having been compelled to go to Michigan to prosecute a considerable claim I have there, in Circuit Court of United States.

Yours truly

Mr. Bentley. J. Fenimore Cooper

MANUSCRIPT: Cooper Collection, Yale University Library.

1. Bentley had written on 6 July:

"This morning your draft on me dated Cooperstown 2nd Feby. was presented here, being the fifth for Capt Spike. This no doubt is the bill you allude to as to be issued by you on the 1st June. I have already accepted one draft dated Feb 1.

"On referring to your last letter, I find that you propose 'shortly to send the sheets of Vol I. of The Crater, and within 60 days the Whole Work.' Your letter is dated May 28. At the end you add, that you will *publish in U. S in all July*.

"We have now arrived at the 6th, and I have not a single sheet; and if I do not receive the Work till the 28th July, of course I cannot publish so as to secure any copyright, and thus my purchase will be of no value to me.

"But this I trust was an oversight on your part, and that as on previous occasions you will protect my copyright here by at least a fortnight's precedence.

"This letter will arrive in time I trust to prevent any possibility of mistake.

"We are looking here a little more cheerily. Hitherto the potato has escaped

V. Portrait of William Heathcote De Lancey (1845), Bishop of Western New York, by W. Boyle.

VI. Portrait of Samuel Nelson (1864), Associate Justice of the United States Supreme Court, by Carl Ludwig Brandt.

VII. Portrait of James De Peyster Ogden (1855) by Charles Loring Elliott.

VIII. Portrait of General Winfield Scott (1851) by Miner K. Kellogg.

the disease, and the grain harvest promises to be abundant. I trust we have turned an ugly corner, and with the blessing of Providence upon us the careful faces may be changed into smiling ones." (MS: YCAL.)

906. *To Mrs. Cooper*

United States Hotel. Wednesday 11th 1847 | August.

Dearest,

Here I am, hard at work. They promise me 40 pages a day, at which rate I shall be home by the 20th. My health is better, though the affection continued until to-day. Yesterday I eat four peaches, all sourish, and last night I ate a supper, but one glass of brandy and water corrected every thing.

[Joseph R.] Ingersoll is not here. Ogden looked a little ashamed, but pleaded his engagement. I gave him a bill for £200 which pays him to about $400. The $400 I shall pay on my return, and that important affair will be settled. Including interest I have now paid to exceed $5000.

It is very warm, and I shall keep out of the streets in the day time. One learns how to prize Cooperstown and the Hall, here.

In the cars I found the Danas and Louis[a?].[1] They had been to Niagara, where they passed a day. Mrs. Dana and her daughter remained in Albany, intending for home next day and the youth and Louis[a?] came down with me. He took good care of her, and she seemed a very good traveller.

Stephen Rensselaer was on board.[2] He told me he was getting on well enough with his tenants, selling to raise money to pay his debts. His brother has mortgaged and left Beverwy[c]k,[3] the popular notion being that he is ruined. Of course this can not be so. I was sorry to find that Stephen spoke coldly of him, as if he had few communications with him. ⟨Bailey⟩ Abraham Ogden told me that Phill Schuyler [Van Rensselaer]'s friends thought Stephen had been hard with *him*, but when I told him that Stephen's furniture had been sold to pay Phill's debts he got a new idea.

I have nothing more to say, unless it be to tell you how much I love you. Eat chickens and all other nice things in my absence, but leave enough for Mr. [George E.] Hand.

Adieu dearest —

[*Cooper omitted his signature.*]

I left the spoons with Tenny,[4] but he thought it questionable if he could make them. He was to see. He has spoons a little larger, and a good deal like, though not as gentille, I think, for $15 —

ADDRESSED: Mrs. Fenimore Cooper | Cooperstown | New York POSTMARKED: PHIL[A] Pa. | AUG | 11 | 5 cts

MANUSCRIPT: Cooper Collection, Yale University Library. PUBLISHED, IN PART: *Correspondence*, II, 571–72.

1. Evidently Cooper did not refer to either of the Richard H. Dana families. New York State had many Danas.

2. Cooper referred in this paragraph to three sons and heirs of General Stephen Van Rensselaer: Stephen IV, William Paterson, and Philip Schuyler. See Cooper to Mrs. Cooper, 19 December 1839.

3. Beverwyck, designed by the English architect Frederic Diaper and built by William Paterson Van Rensselaer between 1839 and 1843 at Rensselaer, New York, was one of the most magnificent American residences of the period.

4. William I. Tenney, jeweler, 251 Broadway (*Doggett's New-York City Directory, for 1845 & 1846* [New York: John Doggett, Jr., 1845]).

907. *To Mrs. Cooper*

United States Hotel. Thursday, Aug. 12th 1847

Dearest,

I wrote you yesterday, and resume to-day, journal wise. I forgot to say in my last that I met [William C.] Maitland in the street. He told me that he was not going to Europe, and would bring his wife up himself. How serious he was, I can not say. He asked how we liked the niece.[1] I told him very much. He seemed to demur, and then complained that she was captain. On asking an explanation, he seemed to think that she was extravagant. But allowances must be made for a bride, and I dare say the *trustee* was a little in the affair. Sometimes such persons like to hold on to the cash. They can not have spent much this summer.

Here, every one appears to be in the country. Yesterday was furiously hot, though it is not so much so to-day. I miss Heads intensely, and shall not pay long visits, here, in future. There is not, now, a gentlemanlike tavern in the place. I have not seen [Joseph] Head, and fear he can not get a new establishment. I have seen about five and twenty pages, and have the promise of some twenty more to-night. Six chapters remain to be read, and five to be mottoed. Home I shall be, deo volente, next week. Fagan arrived from Cape May last evening, and was here this morning. He says that in six days, I shall have my discharge.

I gave Englebert [2] your slippers last night. The rest are done.

Sunday afternoon — August 15th. Last night I saw 114th page of vol IId leaving about four more day's work to be done. As it is safest to finish while about it, I shall do so. I expect to leave here Thursday afternoon, and to be home Saturday the 21st. Should Mr. Hand appear, with or without his brother, ask him to stay with you. I expect, however to meet him at Fort Plain, on Saturday. Perhaps I may get home on Friday.

Joe Ingersoll has gone to Athens, in Georgia, to deliver an oration! Hot times for that. Miss Leslie [3] is staying in the house. She gives me a terrible account of [Rufus W.] Griswold's propensity to misstate the truth. I have not seen him, and do not much desire to, after what I have heard. Charles Ingersoll and wife are here, and I have seen them. Also the Henrys. [James] Biddle is expected home in October — I think he must here sooner.

I do not think I shall write again, for the letter would scarcely reach you. I shall expect to find one from you at the Globe. Henry Carey has lost his wife.[4] She was a sister of Miss Leslie's you know. The latter told me her cookery book had made her between four and five thousand dollars. I told her we had not succeed[ed] with cream cheeses, and she said she got her reciept from a woman in the market who was celebrated for them. But, she added, that she had found that persons who lived by making any thing often suppressed some ingredient, or particular in giving her their reciepts. This she had found out. She has published a new volume, which I shall bring up. The cookery-book has reached its 28th edition. She has been aided much, I should think, by having had Carey for a brother in Law.

I like my new book [*The Crater*] exceedingly, and the part which I was afraid was ill done, is the best done; I mean the close. Altogether, it is a remarkable book, and ought to make a noise. If any one else had written it, it would be the next six month's talk. As it is, it will probably not be much read in this country. Well, there is not much love lost between us. It is a contemptible public opinion, at the best.

No news from General Scott, though important tidings are hourly expected. Of his success when he does move, there can be but little doubt. [David] Conner is in Maryland, and I have not seen him. [Foxhall A.] Parker was here a day or two since, and he tells me that some imputations are endeavoured to be brought against [John H.] Aulich's courage. He is accused of refusing to give a seat behind a good cover, to a wounded officer. The facts are, that, while waiting for ammunition, every body was ordered to keep covered. Aulich and two or three more, got a good place, and sat there for some time. At last Aulich got up, and went to some other part of the battery. While gone Mr. [Augustus S.] Baldwin was wounded – no blood being showing – and was put into Aulich's berth. When the latter came back he said, laughingly, "Why you have got my place," whereupon Baldwin offered to relinquish it, but Aulich refused to take it. But Aulich is thought to be a tartar, and every thing he say[s], or does, is judged harshly.

One of the best things going is an apologue on [Matthew C.] Perry and [Charles G.] Hunter. A party went out to kill a wolf. They drove the animal into a hole, and set one of their number to watch him, while they went for hoes and dogs. The wolf stuck his head out, and got it caught in the hole, when the sentinel killed it with a club. Presently the rest came back, with loud demonstrations of what they meant to do. Great was their rage at finding the wolf killed. "Why did you do this?" they demanded; "you had no hoe at all, and not so much as one dog, and here we have a dozen hoes and a whole pack, and yet you presumed to kill this wolf. Go home – we are going to kill a possum this evening, but you shan't go along – you spoil every thing."

Parker told me that Perry was much out of favour at the Department. His movement against Alvarado is said to have cost the country an enormous sum of money, by cutting off Quitman [5] from his supplies, already agreed for, and retarding Scott's march many days. Conner is said to have given up the squadron in a pet, on recieving unexpected orders to let Perry have command. He ought not to have done it, and I believe now thinks so himself. Parker laugh'd heartily at Perry's reporting [Alexander S.] McKenzie wounded at Tu[x?]pan, because he got hurt, accidentally, the day after the fight! All the navy men have seen this folly and laughed at it.

It has been terrifically hot here. To-day it is much cooler. I have now slept five nights within six feet of an open window, and most of the time without even a sheet on me. I keep quiet, and thus keep cool. I eat light meals, and little fruit, drink three glasses of wine at dinner, and am as well as I ever was in my life.

Yesterday I met Joe Miller, fanning away. He was going to Bordentown for lodgings, the town being too hot for him. Mrs. Miller was at her daughters. Joe greeted me with a hearty laugh, but fanned away.

Adieu. By the time you get this I shall be about packing up. My stay in New York will not exceed one night, if it be even that.

Yours tenderly

J. F C–

ADDRESSED: Mrs. Fenimore Cooper | Cooperstown | New York POSTMARKED: PHILADA. Pa. | AUG | 15 STAMPED: M. POPE MITCHELL | UNITED STATES | HOTEL. | PHILADELPHIA.

MANUSCRIPT: Cooper Collection, Yale University Library. PUBLISHED, IN PART: *Correspondence*, II, 572–76.

1. Mrs. Thomas James De Lancey, Jr., the former Frances Augusta Bibby.

2. *McElroy's Philadelphia Directory for 1847* lists two ladies' shoemakers of this name: J. Englebert, 74 South Fourth Street, and Cornelius Englebert, 87 South Eighth Street.

3. Sister of Charles Robert Leslie the painter, Eliza Leslie (1787–1858) was a prodigiously successful author of books on domestic economy, the first of which was *Seventy-five Receipts for Pastry, Cakes, and Sweetmeats* (1837). Though she also wrote juvenile fiction and magazine stories, her great success was *The Domestic Cookery Book* (1837), which went through thirty-eight editions by 1851. (*DAB*.)

4. Henry Charles Carey married Martha Leslie in 1819 (Arnold W. Green, *Henry Charles Carey: Nineteenth-Century Sociologist* [Philadelphia: University of Pennsylvania Press, 1951], 17–18).

5. Subsequently elected to the governorship of Mississippi and to Congress, John Anthony Quitman (1798–1858) distinguished himself as a general in the main engagements of the Mexican War (John F. H. Claiborne, *Life and Correspondence of John Anthony Quitman* [New York: Harper & Brothers, 1860]).

908. *To James De Peyster Ogden*

Hall, Cooperstown, Sept. 1st 1847

Dear Ogden

It is true that you discounted my own note, at 90 days, for $1000, in the spring of 1839, which note I paid at maturity by a draft on Bentley, for £250, you paying me the balance. This is the note that you took up yourself, and which has been mislaid. But it has nothing to do with this transaction.[1]

I paid you and [Gorham A.] Worth, $2200 each, *in cash,* for your equitable interests in the Chicago lots, and sold out myself to Comstock, without your having any connection with the affair. Comstock's notes were discounted by you, like any other notes, either in our cotton transactions, or to accomodate me. Two were paid; the third protested. This note was dated Jan. 1st 1836, and was for $2160 on interest. My settlement with you was made Oct 16th 1844. Now, let us calculate.

Note — Jan 1st 1836. for	$2160	
	7	
	151.20	
	8	8 years 9.½ m[onth's] interest
	1209.60	
	120	9½ months
	1329.60	
add note	2160	
	$3489 60	Amount of Comstock's
	1559.	note Oct 16th 1844
	$5048.	the Amount of two notes.
Ketchum'[s] note dated Jan 1,	1839, for $2250	
one half —	$1125.	
	7	
	78.75	
	5	Five years 9½ months Int.
	393.75	
	61.07	9½ months.
	434.82	
add note	1125—	
	1559.82	

Now I gave you three notes for my debt — Two at $1668, and one for $1723.73.

1668
$1668
1723.73
$5059.73

The difference of two or three dollars arises no doubt from my calculation not being close enough, and charges of protest &c.

That is I gave you my notes Oct. 16th 1844 for $5059.73. For what did I give these notes? Why to meet my endorsement on Comstock's protested note, and my indebtedness for the *half* of Comstock's note, which you deposited to my credit in the New York Bank in Feb or March 1839, as you will find by asking at the bank. $1125 are not $1000, and you will find both sums deposited there in the spring of 1839. My letters will also show these facts, as would yours to me, if I could lay my hands on them, but the letters recieved at Philadelphia have been mislaid, and I do not know where to find them. I am certain of the transactions. The amount of the two sums demonstrate the truth of the circumstances — (turn over)

As the debts are paid, and you have your money with interest, it is of no moment except as relates to your testimony. I sent you Ketchum's note from Philadelphia, as soon as I recieved it, telling you that I considered one half should go to you, on account of Comstock's note, and the other half I would keep for my own use, and desired you to discount my half. Now, you gave me that money, whatever you may think about it now. Neither of us anticipated any difficulty then, and had the note been paid at maturity, Comstock's and my indebtedness to you, would have been less than $2000; or about $1700. It was not paid, and I have been obliged to repay you the money, as was right.

I earnestly beg you will ready to go to Detroit in October. Of course I will pay your expenses, and will go with you. By timing our arrival properly, the whole excursion need not consume much more than a week, and some $5000 depend on it, including costs. They intend to set up *payment*, must do it, indeed, according to Ketchum's testimony, and from that testimony he can not depart. Your presence and testimony will set all right, and I shall get a verdict.[2]

If you would say you will go, it might save us some further expense. Let me hear from you, again.

Yours truly

J. D. P. Ogden Esquire. J. Fenimore Cooper

MANUSCRIPT: The Library of Congress.

1. Replying from New York on 30 August 1847 to Cooper's letter of 28 August (unlocated), Ogden confused two separate business transactions with Cooper in 1839; in one, the novelist obtained $1,000 from Ogden for a discounted note; in the other, he obtained $1,125 as an advance against one of two notes of Sidney Ketchum left with Ogden as collateral security for Horace H. Comstock's unpaid note of $2,160 (see Cooper to Ogden, 11 November 1839). Ogden admitted this confusion in his letter of 6 September 1847. (MSS: YCAL.)

2. "As regards going to Detroit in Oct.," Ogden answered from New York on 6 September, "I will go if I can, indeed unless something occurs absolutely to prevent me — I merely suggested to Judge Hand that he had better have every thing prepared in the shape of question and answer, lest something should prevent" (MS: YCAL).

909. *To William Branford Shubrick*

Hall, Cooperstown, Sept. 25th 1847

My Dear Shubrick,

So many reports of your speedy return have reached me that, until quite lately, I have supposed it useless to write. Now, I learn you will not return in several months, and that a letter sent at once, may reach you in ninety days.

First, as to health. We are all well, and your wife I hear, marvellously so. Paul is much better, and at work with the law, again. My wife has been seriously ill of a fever; more so than I have ever known her, but she has recovered entirely, and is now quite well. I still weigh 200 llbs.

Secondly, as to the war. You know its outlines. The march of Scott on Mexico has been one of the boldest, as well as the most successful military movements of modern times. To march so great a distance, through so strong and populous a country, with so small a force, overturning, capturing and storming every thing in his way, raises Scott, in a military point of view, far above any soldier this country has yet produced. What adds to his glory is the fact that he had to change his army, in one sense, by the discharge of the twelve month's men, in the midst of the enemy's country. In my opinion Scott, unless he meet with reverses, will yet be *the* "hero of the war." "The hasty plate of soup" is already forgotten.[1] San Juan d'Ulloa obliterated that; Cerro Gordo made it [wit?], and Churubusco will be likely to raise it to wisdom.

The navy is not in as much favour. [Matthew C.] Perry has been sending his smal[l] craft up the rivers, until the yellow fever is desolating the squadron. I was told the other day, that much dissatisfaction prevailed at Washington. Then [Charles G] Hunter's affair has set his old friends, the news papers, on him — That business he botched vilely. Hunter has a new command.[2] [Alexander S.] McKenzie, who Perry reports as wounded the day *after* the affair at [Tuxpan],[3] gets nothing but newspaper puffs.

You will hear that we are waiting in suspense to learn whether peace is, or is not to be the result of Scott's late successes. In any case, I think a large force must be maintained in the country. If California be ceded, appropriations will probably be made for permanent establishments in the ⟨Medit?⟩ Pacific.

We have a troublesome, but a very silly question to settle relative to slavery in the conquered country. The silliness of the question arises from the entire unconstitutionality of any provisions at all, in the matter. Each state can decide that point for itself, and if Congress can controul the domestic institutions of a state, under its power to admit new states, then can it controul it in other matters, and make constitutions, by this indirect process, whenever states are admitted. Does any one suppose that Missouri can not abolish slavery if it choose, or Ohio establish it? If they can what becomes of your compromises and ordinances? They are each and all arrogating power to Congress that does not belong to it. It appears to me that each territory should be left to controul its own policy in this behalf, as it certainly can and will do as a state.

I do not know whether you were acquainted with Mr. Peter G. Stuyvesant. He was a lineal descendant of the last Dutch Governor in New York, and a man of large hereditary estate, as well as a gentleman. We classed him among our friends, though he properly belonged to a generation in advance of us. He was childless, and in the habit of travelling in the summer, with his wife. This summer they went to Niagara. Here poor Stuyvesant went into a bath in the river, fainted, fell into the water and two hours later was found dead.

Mr. Stu[y]vesant was twice married; his first wife was a Miss Barclay, a relation of my wifes — a sister of Tom Barclay of the B[ritish] Navy, whom you know, and his second a Miss Rutherfurd, a daughter of the late John Rutherfurd of New Jersey.[4] By neither wife has he left children. Hamilton Fish's mother was Mr. S's sister, and he recieves by his uncle's will something more than half a million of dollars. He gives to two nephews, and to a great-great nephew of his own, who is a great nephew also of his wife, a boy of some four years, rather more than half of an estate that will reach three millions. The rest of the property he divides in shares of about $60 or 70,000 each to a dozen nephews and nieces. To some he leaves nothing.

Talking of nephews I have just got a letter from one of mine, your old acquaintance Bill Cooper. He has left the ocean for the innermost parts of the earth, and is half way to California. He is at Fort Des Moines in Iowa, which is as far west as the Lake of the Woods. He is married, has a farm, and has every thing man can wish but money. A dollar is a phenomenon, though he talks of his horses, and guns, and dogs, and bees, and corn, as if these were without end. He tells me that for two years he has not even heard from one of us, or of us. He says you are abused a little in the western papers, for having opposed Col. Fremont, but adds that he takes your part! [5]

As for this abuse, I have seen none of it; nor do the papers here seem to have any very determined notions of the Californian questions. Kearny and Fremont are both at Washington, the last under arrest. Kearny will have Benton's interest to oppose, but I do not see how Fremont's course can be justified, if we have any correct statement of his data. There is a good deal of the bull-dog in Kearny, who is a very resolute man, besides being pitched on a pretty high key. The whole question, as I understand it, must turn on the character in which Fremont was acting. As a soldier, it is not easy to see how he could have been right; as a civilian, the case presents another aspect.[6]

We are about to have a great battle in the church. The convention of this dio[c]ese sits next week, and that of the U. S. the week after — A strong effort is to be made to restore the two suspended bishops. That of Bishop Henry [U. Onderdonk] may succeed, as he has acted with great prudence, and they say he is a sincere penitent — and one may judge of a reformation in a drunkard, though it is not easy to see how matters are on the other point — but Bishop Benjamin [T. Onderdonk] can not be restored in this diocese without rending it in twain. Paul and myself go to New York, next week, as delegates.

I have been at Niagara this summer, and found it exceeding my expectations. I was not as much struck with the grandeur of the cataract as with its surpassing beauty. The place has few of the terrific features I had supposed, and more of the winning. I am obliged to go to Detroit this autumn, and shall probably take another look at the wonders.

By the way, your admirer Miss Christine [Kean], and her mother,[7] are now in this house, being on their way from Butternuts to New York. My sister in law, Mrs. Isaac Cooper, who is Mrs. Baker's sister, has just returned from the west, where she has been passing three years with different children. Cooperstown is far enough west for her, she tells me, no reflection on California being intended. Two of her daughters were married to officers in the army. One (Dr. [Lyman] Foot) was the fourth surgeon on the list. He died last Oct. at Port Lavacca, of fever contracted in service. The other ([Henry W.] Wessel[l]s) is a captain in the 2d Infantry, and was wounded at this last battle, in front of Mexico. Seven officers of his regiment were killed and wounded in that affair, neither Col, nor Lt. Colonel serving with it — or its Lt Col. (Riley) acting as a brigadier, being a brevet Colonel.[8] I think not more than five and twenty officers could have been serving with the regiment, and the loss must have been equal to one fourth. It lost a captain at Vera Cruz, and another lost a hand at Cerro Gordo. Capt. Wessel[l]s' wound is slight, a hit in the hand, and he is already at duty, again.

You have doubtless the news of poor Charles Chauncey's death, from yellow fever. Many others will follow him.

A dead set has been made at [John H.] Aulick, by some inimical to him on account of his unyielding disposition, I fancy. They accuse him of cowardice, a weakness he would be very little likely to betray, in my opinion. One of the miserable letter writers seems to be at the bottom of the affair, no responsible officer, so far as I can learn, coming forward to back the charge. The whole affair seems to be blowing over.

We have all been astonished at Bancroft's conduct.[9] I saw your orders, which as clearly made you commander in chief as any orders could, and I do not see how the duplicity can be explained away. He appeared to be your friend, always spoke of you in the highest terms, and as if desirous of giving you a chance, and here is perfect deception as relates to a man ten thousand miles from home! The department is well rid of him.

Taylor has got the Ohio! [10] By all I can learn the Relief would be too important a trust for him. Perry's influence is apparent in this. He would make a Rhode Island gunner a Commodore if he could. Most of her officers have been changed. I have not heard how the ship behaved while [Silas H.] Stringham had her, further than a report that she sailed well.

[Lawrence] Kearny has a son! I expect you will perform wonders too, when you get back. If [George C.] Read can do the same, the Navy will begin to look up in the next generation. Samuel L. Breese has given up the Albany, and is ashore. Bolton has just gone to sea in the James Town, for the coast of Africa. Your old ship, the Macedonian, is now out under George De Kay, having been to carry food to Ireland.[11]

The season here has been glorious. The crops never were finer, and the country is full of good things. I believe in a revolution in the seasons, owing to some unknow[n] cause, which produces a succession of warm summers once in about half a century. We are now getting into the tropics, once more. Wine is so plenty in France, that vessels can not be had to hold it all. England too, has had excellent crops.

I think Europe is on the verge of very serious troubles. Every thing indicates that much, and the impetus seems to be owing to a cause no one could have anticipated, a liberal pope. Pius IX has come out a reformer, and he appears to be as firm as a rock. One battle in Italy, will set Europe in a flame. Louis Phillipe is on the despotic side, and he may yet live long enough to be dethroned.

Every body sends their kindest regards. Adieu

Commodore Shubrick. J. Fenimore Cooper

MANUSCRIPT: Paul Fenimore Cooper, Cooperstown, New York.

1. Scott had used this phrase innocently but irrelevantly in a letter of 25 May 1846 to Secretary of War Marcy: "Your letter of this date, received at about 6 p.m., as I sat down to take a hasty plate of soup, demands a prompt reply." By using the phrase out of context, the General's political enemies promptly made it a synonym for any peccadillo or broken engagement. (Elliott, *Winfield Scott*, 429.)

2. According to the Navy *Register* for 1848, Hunter had been assigned to command the schooner *Taney*.

3. Cooper wrote "T[eu?]pan."

4. Peter Gerard Stuyvesant died on 16 August 1847. He married in 1803 Susan Barclay (d. 1805), daughter of Thomas Barclay, British consul general for the eastern states; he married second in 1809 Helena Sarah Rutherfurd (d. 1873), daughter of John Rutherfurd. Susan Barclay's brother was Thomas Edmund Barclay (1783–1838), post captain in the Royal Navy. (*ACAB*; R. Burnham Moffat, *The Barclays of New York* [New York: Robert Grier Cooke, 1904], 114–15.)

5. William Cooper's letter is dated Fort Desmoines, Polk County, Iowa, 1 September 1847 (MS: YCAL).

6. See Cooper to Shubrick, 1 February 1848.

7. Christine A. W. Kean (1826–1915), daughter of Peter P. J. and Sarah Sabina (Morris) Kean. The mother was Mrs. Lööe Baker in 1847. (Stuyvesant Fish, *Ancestors of Hamilton Fish and Julia Ursin Niemcewicz Kean, His Wife* [New York: privately published, 1929?], 77.)

8. An experienced soldier and Indian fighter, Bennet Riley (1787–1853) gained fame for his daring assault on the rear of the Mexican position at Contreras on 20 August 1847 (*DAB*).

9. Bancroft also issued orders to Commodore James Biddle which seemed to place him in command.

10. William Vigneron Taylor (1780–1858), who served under Perry at the Battle of Lake Erie, commanded the *Ohio* from 1847 until 1848 (*DAB*).

11. See Cooper to Mrs. Cooper, 21 February 1849.

910. *To John Young Mason*

Cooperstown, Sept 28th 1847

Sir,

I have been requested to assist the friends of young Mr. Charles Ogden Hammond, of this state, in an application for a warrant.[1] This young gentleman has claims, derived from his ancestors that would, I should think, tell more in his favour than any recommendation of mine. I have known his family all my life, and can testify that his connections are of the best sort. I understand that he has been educated with a view to this application, and make no doubt that he would prove an acquisition to the service.

This young gentleman has a merit that is rather uncommon. He is not to be placed in the navy to be provided for, or to be got out of the way. He is in no need of a support, and is an only son. I understand indeed, he is the only male descendant, in his generation, of his worthy old grandfather, who was an officer of the revolution, and was well known to every body in this part of the country.

I am not conscious of possessing either interest or claims at

Washington, but confess I should like to see a son and grandson of two old friends succeed in this application.

I remain, Sir, | Very Respectfully | Yours
J— Fenimore Cooper

John Y. Mason Esquire | Sec. Navy.

MANUSCRIPT: Knox College Library.

Secretary of the Navy during the administrations of Tyler and Polk for two periods, Mason (1799–1859, University of North Carolina 1816) was also a congressman from North Carolina (1831–1837), a federal judge (1837–1844), attorney general under Polk (1845–1846), and minister to France (1853–1859) (*DAB*).

1. Charles L. Ogden Hammond, the son of Mary Cochran B. Edwards and Abraham Ogden Hammond and grandson of Catharine L. Ogden and Abijah Hammond, was appointed midshipman in the United States Navy on 8 November 1847. He resigned on 23 March 1854. (Wheeler, *The Ogden Family*, 188, 299; GNR.)

911. *To Mrs. Cooper*

Detroit, *Wednesday*, Oct. 20th 1847 | Morning

My Dearest Sue,

Here I am yet, this making the *tenth* day I have been in Detroit. The cause commenced on Friday, and the testimony closed last Saturday. On Monday Judge [George E.] Hand spoke all day. Their counsel are now about drawing, and Mr. [Daniel] Goodwin will close for me in the course of the day, to-morrow.

Our case does not look as well as I could wish. Tell Paul that they have produced a recent Pennsylvania case, which is strictly analogous to ours, which lays down the law that taking security, with a definite period to run, as an acceptance at sixty days is an agreement to give time, and that the plaintiff must show that the rights of the endorsers must be reserved, by express agreement. This decision is opposed to old decisions, but alleges that it is in conformity with recent English decisions. If the judge should charge that this is law, we shall undoubtedly be beaten, though we have the chance of the Supreme Court's taking a different view of the matter. There is a very recent decision of the Supreme Court, which makes a good deal in our favour though it is not quite as explicit as we could wish. The difficulty apprehended, is with the Judge. He is a Pennsylvanian, and is said to defer profoundly to Pennsylvania authorities. Still he can not but respect those of the court above him. It is a sickening business altogether, and I am heartily tired of it. I am called on to pay every cent, even to the last, and my debtors evade payment by every possible expedient. I fear the worst, at this circuit.

Ogden left here last night. I shall probably get off for Kalamazoo, where I do not anticipate any sales, the day after to morrow. How long I shall be detained, is more than I know. In the Big Bible is the manuscript of Rose Budd [*Jack Tier*]. Let Paul take the part which comes next, about eight pages, and enclose [1] it in one of the *large* envelopes, and direct it to —

George Graham Esquire
Graham's Magazine
Philadelphia.

He will know which part to take by its number, he taking the lowest number of course. The paging will also be a guide for him. I can not now say when I shall be back. If you want money, use the gold and silver — the last first. I am so anxious to realize something from this debt that I may stay a week at Kalamazoo — All will depend on the prospect of sales. One witness swears that the lots are worth, in his judgment $3000 — If they are worth $2500, it is a good deal. There is also some hope that [Sidney] Ketchum, as well as [Isaac] Schuyler can pay. Then we have San[d]ford,[2] so that, after all, if beaten here, I may lose nothing but time and trouble. The *time* is very expensive to me, however.

We dined with Mrs. Morell last Sunday and a capital game dinner she gave us, or Mrs. Chester, rather.[3] The quails run about the streets, here — literally, for we have met them twice. They are often in the gardens, and are very cheap.

[Horace H.] Comstock has not appeared, and will not. I rather think he has not the means to come, and it is better, on the whole, that he should stay away, as he might do mischief.

I am quite well, but anxious to get away. Now Ogden is gone, I have no company, and write this letter to relieve your anxiety and to employ myself.

I think we should have beaten, without this Pennsylvania case, as our position looked well, until it was produced. Now, I have no great hopes at this circuit, though both Hand and Goodwin regard the matter less gloomily than they did last evening. Hand was in just this minute, and appeared in good spirits. I am writing in his office.

If Mary [Mrs. Isaac Cooper] should want Money before I return give her $50 of the gold, or let Paul get [Henry] Scott to take it especially, until I get back. I shall not be back until the last of the month, or near it, I should think.

The taxes appear to be paid on the lots, *here*. How it is at Kalamazoo I must enquire.

Give my tenderest love to the children,

Yours as ever,

J. F. C.

Tell Dick to look out at Rochester.

MANUSCRIPT: Cooper Collection, Yale University Library.

1. The manuscript has a superfluous "in" at this point.

2. James S. Sandford (1815–1885), one of the endorsers of Ketchum's note, was a lawyer, formerly of Marshall, Michigan, of New York City in 1847 (Josephine Sandford Ware, *Robert Sandford and His Wife Ann Adams Sandford* [Rutland, Vermont: The Tuttle Company, 1930], 31–32).

3. Mrs. Morrell was Maria, daughter of General Samuel B. Webb and widow of George Morrell (1786–1845, Williams 1807), former chief justice of the Michigan Supreme Court. Mrs. Chester was her daughter Catharine M., who married John (1813–1852), son of Stephen and Elizabeth (Mitchell) Chester of Hartford County, Connecticut. (Calvin Durfee, *Williams Biographical Annals* [Boston and New York: Lee, Shephard and Dillingham, 1871], 282–83; Edward Strong, *Descendants of Leonard Chester, of Blaby, Eng., and Wethersfield, Conn.* [Boston: David Clapp & Co., 1868], 8.]

912. *To Mrs. Cooper*

Detroit, Thursday afternoon, Oct 21st 1847

Dearest Sue,

The cause has been tried. The Judge charged as we feared, Pennsylvania law, and as strong for the defendants as words could make it. I had no doubt that he would carry the jury with him, and left the court under the impression they would give a verdict for the defendants in ten minutes. At the end of two hours they came in, and said they could not agree. The judge charged them anew; they staid out another hour, and came back with the same story. The court then discharged them. So the case must be tried over again before Judge McLean,[1] in the spring.

I hear that the jury stood eight for me to four for them; in other words, two to one. This gives us some advantage for the future. Our opponents are sorely disappointed.

I go to Kalamazoo to-morrow, and shall return here on Monday. Go down in the Canada Monday night, and sleep at Rochester Tuesday night, if in time. This will bring me home somewhere about Thursday, or Friday. Detention, however, may occur at Kalamazoo, if I make any sales. I am anxious to get home, and shall hurry all I can.

With best love I am ever yours
J— F. C.

The result is almost as much as I hoped for, under a favourable charge. The judge charged up and down, that the taking an acceptance that had sixty days to run, was giving time in law. This was the effect of the Pennsylvania decision, out and out.

MANUSCRIPT: Cooper Collection, Yale University Library.

1. Appointed to the United States Supreme Court in 1829 by President Jackson after distinguishing himself as congressman, Postmaster General, and jurist, John McLean (1785–1861) presided over the United States Circuit Court which included Ohio, Indiana, Illinois, and Michigan from 1836 to 1861 (*DAB*).

913. *To Richard Bentley*

Hall, Cooperstown, Nov. 6th 1847

Dear Sir,

Enclosed you have the last of Capt. Spike. I send it in advance, according to your request, relying on your not anticipating the publications in Graham, which will not end until March. I shall send printed sheets to meet accidents, as they appear.

I have a new work in hand, scene Michigan, time the commencement of the war of 1812, incidents those of the wilderness but in a somewhat new form. I shall call it either "The Oak Openings," or "The Bee Hunter." A Beehunter is the hero, mingled with Indians, Lake sailors and a little touch of war. I offer it on the terms of the "Crater."

Please to let me hear of the reciept of this manuscript. As my task is done, and I am entitled to the last 50£s, I shall draw for the same when I go to town.[1]

Yours &c
Mr. Bentley J. Fenimore Cooper

MANUSCRIPT: Cooper Collection, Yale University Library.

1. Bentley replied on 4 December, acknowledging receipt of the conclusion of

Captain Spike [*Jack Tier*], reporting acceptance of Cooper's bill for £50, agreeing to Cooper's stipulation about the publication of *Captain Spike*, and accepting the terms proposed for *The Oak Openings* (MS: YCAL).

914. *To Richard Bentley*

New-York, Nov. 11th 1847

Dear Sir

I wrote you from Cooperstown that the two last chapters of Manuscript of Spike were ready to be sent. I now write to advise you that they will go by the Washington, and that I have drawn on you, in favour of J. De Peyster Ogden Esq for the last Fifty pounds, according to our agreement.

Yours truly
J. Fenimore Cooper

Mr. Richard Bentley | Publisher | London

MANUSCRIPT: Cooper Collection, Yale University Library.

915. *To Mrs. Cooper*

Globe, Sunday Nov. 14th 1847

Dearest,

I hoped to have arranged with the publishers by this time, but they wish to get the next book for the price of the last, which would be a loss to me of $150. Some arrangement will probably be made, as they are very desirous of getting the next book, this having done so well. In the mean time I am endeavouring to sell the cherubs.

The sheets have come from Philadelphia, and that is all right. I shall probably be absent my forthnight, but I hope no longer.

I have not yet seen Mrs. Laight, nor any one but my neighbors the Crugers, and Mrs. Banyer and Miss Jay. No one is satisfied with the condition in which Gen[eral] Con[vention] has left the diocese. It amounts to just nothing.

With Cruger I dined yesterday several ladies being of the party. He says Mrs. Cruger writes most amicably to her sister,[1] but proposes nothing definite, and until she does he can and will do nothing. I suspect the poor woman finds herself alone and homeless and begins to see some of her folly. They are all at

Graffenburg, and in the baths, even to the nurses. It is a general wash.

Bishop [Horatio] Potter has this diocese for three months, the standing committee having taken the responsibility of not convening the convention. As [Benjamin T.] Onderdonk has his salary until the meeting of the diocesan convention next after the session of Gen[eral] Con[vention], this makes him comfortable until next autumn.

Adieu — I am as well as can be, and head nearly well.

Love to all —

J— F— C.

The enclosed is written by a son of Col. Gibb's.[2]

ADDRESSED: Mrs. Fenimore Cooper | Cooperstown | N. Y. POSTMARKED: N[EW-YORK] | 14 | NOV | 5 cts

MANUSCRIPT: Cooper Collection, Yale University Library. PUBLISHED, IN PART: *Correspondence,* II, 576.

1. Mrs. Cruger's sister Elizabeth Mary (1799–1852) married James Monroe (1799–1870, West Point 1815), nephew of the President and Whig representative from New York to the Twenty-sixth Congress. Mrs. Cruger's neurotic refusal or inability to settle her personal and financial relations with her husband had led to protracted litigation and had cost her, at times, the sympathy of the Monroes. (Angus Davidson, *Miss Douglas of New York: A Biography* [New York: The Viking Press, 1953], 207–24; *BDAC.*)

2. Cooper's late friend Colonel George Gibbs (1776–1833) had four sons: George (1815–1873, Harvard 1838), an ethnologist; Oliver Wolcott (1822–1908, Columbia 1841), a chemist; Alfred (1823–1868, West Point 1846), an army officer, and Francis Sarason (1831–1882), a merchant. The "enclosed" is unidentified. (George Gibbs, *The Gibbs Family of Rhode Island and Some Related Families* [New York: privately published, 1933], 168–69 and *passim.*)

916. *To Mrs. Cooper*

Globe. Nov. 17th 1847

Dearest,

Here I am still, and here I shall probably remain for the rest of the week. I am afraid I shall do nothing with the cherubs, or picture, but have just made a bargain with Burgess,[1] which will enable me to come home as soon as I please. I do not like to give up the statue, and shall make one more effort.

I am glad to see that [Henry W.] Wessel[l]s is honorably mentioned, as having distinguished himself at Contreras.[2] I have not seen the report of Col. [Bennet] Riley, but from the manner in which his name is introduced by [Winfield] Scott, I think he must have been conspicuously engaged in the great charge of Riley's brigade, when they stormed the Mexican camp.

I have not seen Mrs. Laight, but shall call to-morrow, or next day.

Jim [De Lancey] and his wife, with young Van Cortlandt,[3] I found in lodgings in Houston Street; two rooms with folding doors, gas lights, and a game dinner at six. Every thing was handsome and at, I should think, at least $50 per week. Perhaps his income will stand it. She looks well, and without symptoms.

I have not a line from home, beyond the proof sheets which got here after I had recieved them from Philadelphia.

Tell Mary [Mrs. Isaac Cooper] I paid for the piano ($195) yesterday. I shall keep the reciept until I come home.

Ned [Myers] has been to see me. He is well, and grumbling as usual. He has some hopes, however, of getting his back pension, which will be quite a little fortune for him. Lucy, he says, is as fat as butter, and as sweet, By the way, butter is about 18 cents in Otsego. This makes farming more profitable.

I believe I shall come home soon, for I am getting tired here. My absence will not go beyond the forthnight. Adieu.

Phil Kearny has lost his left arm above the elbow, He suffered intolerably until the arm was taken away, which was about, three hours, after he was hit —[4] I saw his father to-day — *I think* Wm. Dawson is courting Miss Maitland.[5]

[*unsigned*]

ADDRESSED: Mrs. Fenimore Cooper | Cooperstown | New York POSTMARKED: NEW-YORK | NO [V] | 18 | 5 cts

MANUSCRIPT: Cooper Collection, Yale University Library. PUBLISHED, IN PART: *Correspondence*, II, 576–77.

1. Wesley F. Burgess was a partner in the bookselling firm of Burgess, Stringer & Co., 222 Broadway, from about 1844 to about 1848. He continued by himself from about 1849 to about 1854. (*Doggett's New-York City Directory, for 1847 & 1848*; directories for other years.)

2. Wessells was breveted major on 20 August 1847 for gallant and meritorious conduct in the battles of Contreras and Churubusco, Mexico (*Historical Register and Dictionary of the United States Army*). See Cooper to L. W. Wessells, 29 December 1849.

3. Possibly Augustus Van Courtlandt (1826–1884) (*Jay Cemetery, Rye, New York*).

4. The bones of Kearny's left arm were irremediably shattered on a charge well in advance of his main forces, and he rode back in excruciating pain. Franklin Pierce held his head while the arm was amputated.

5. William Dawson (1798–1852), a New York merchant, was the widower of Sarah (1811–1846), daughter of Peter A. Jay. He never remarried. (*Jay Cemetery, Rye, New York.*)

917. *To George Palmer Putnam?*

Hall, Cooperstown, Dec. 10th 1847

Sir,

The late Commodore Elliott caused a medal of me to be struck at the mint, shortly after the decision in my favour by the arbitrators who decided the points referred to them in connection with the controversy about the Battle of Lake Erie.[1] This medal was made not only without my concurrence, but contrary to my wishes, as it seemed likely to bring me into a species of ridicule, as having a medal struck in honour of so trifling an affair. I did remonstrate with Commodore Elliott on the subject, though my opposition was not as earnest as it might otherwise have been, as the feeling of gratitude it manifested in Commodore Elliott was respectable in him. I had no agency whatever in causing this medal to be struck or presented to any one.

I believe Mr. Adams was requested to present one of these medals to some body in Rhode Island, and that the body in question refused to recieve it on the ground that I had not done justice to their hero, Commodore Perry, in my account of the Battle.[2] I am not very certain about these facts, however, my own investigations having satisfied me that the Historical Society of Rhode Island, and its Legislature I believe, in one instance, have manifested that they acted in a partisan spirit in this matter, rather than with any wish to obtain, or to promulgate, truth. I can not pretend, therefore, to give you very exact information on this branch of the subject, as, to be frank, I cared very little about opinions formed under such an influence.

I am, Sir, | Respectfully Yours

J. Fenimore Cooper

MANUSCRIPT: Clifton Waller Barrett Collection of American Literature, University of Virginia.

The holograph bears the notation "George P Putnam, Esq" in an unidentified script, but no other suggestion as to the identity of the recipient.

1. See Plate I.
2. At Jesse Duncan Elliott's request and in his name, John Quincy Adams

transmitted with a letter of 17 March 1845 to John Howland, president of the Rhode Island Historical Society, the medal honoring Cooper "for the historical justice which he has awarded to the character and conduct of Commodore Elliott in his published writings." The matter was referred on 9 April 1845 to a committee which drafted resolutions thanking Adams, but refusing the medal because the society could "neither adopt nor sanction" Cooper's opinions on the Battle of Lake Erie. After striking out the resolution thanking Adams, the society voted unanimously at its meeting on 10 September 1845 to return the medal to Adams with the request that he return it to Elliott with a copy of the society's resolution attesting its regard for Oliver Hazard Perry. This office Adams icily refused in a letter dated Quincy, Massachusetts, 29 September 1845. (MSS: Rhode Island Historical Society.)

918. *To Mary Abigail Doolittle*

Otsego Hall, Cooperstown, Dec. 25th 1847

Chère Petite,

In the first place, I wish you, and your parents, a very Merry Christmas. I have just come from church myself, and have met a great many happy faces, this morning, particularily among my great nephews and nieces — my own nephews and nieces being now so old that Santa Claus (good old St Nicholas de Flué)[1] will no longer call on them in his annual journeys. Watches, Dragoons, Tu[r?]ks, Dolls, Tops, &c &c are very numerous in the family, just now, to say nothing of cornucopiæ filled with sweets.

I am very grateful at being honoured with one of your first efforts with the pen, — I do not know but it may have been the very first — and hope you will recollect what I told you of my being a bad correspondent, in explanation of the delay in answering it.

It is very true that I was at Rochester, under the circumstances you mention. For the first time in my life I passed through your place this summer, and what is a little remarkable, I have been four times in Rochester already. On the first occasion, I passed half a day there, and was the whole time with Mr. Rochester,[2] who had the civility to take me to all the points worth seeing. I thought of you, and inquired of Mr. Rochester concerning you and your family. He did not know your father, but was aware of his being in the town, but I could not quit him with propriety to make the visit I intended. On the second occasion young Mr. [Thomas F.] Rochester took me to see the falls, and my time was fully occupied. On the two other occasions I merely made the stops of the cars, and did not go any distance from them.

Next June I shall again be in Rochester, *Deo Volente,* (ask your father what that means) when I hope to make your acquaintance. Remember, you are not to expect a smart, handsome young fellow, with a poetical look, but a heavy, elderly gentleman, with gray hairs, and who has begun to go downward in the vale of years. I was fifty eight, on the 15th of last September — a very safe age, I trust mama will think, for our correspondence.

And, now you have begun to write for yourself, let me take an old man's privilege, and give you a piece of advice. Write what comes uppermost, naturally and without any more effort than you would use in conversing with one you respected. In this way, you will soon come to make a very nice little correspondent. With my respects to your parents, I remain

Chère petite, votre affectionné

Mademoiselle Doolittle. J. Fenimore Cooper

MANUSCRIPT: Paul Fenimore Cooper, Cooperstown, New York. PUBLISHED: *Correspondence,* II, 577–78.

Mary Doolittle (b. 1836) was the young daughter of Isaac (1784–1852) and Filisfectu Higgins (d. 1896) Doolittle. Her father, an inventor, had been a prisoner of war in France during part of the war between England and France and, reportedly, had published a book on steam navigation in French before 1821. In 1847 he owned and operated at Rochester, New York, a patented stave machine which could cut 1000 barrel staves an hour from round, knot-free timber. Mary is said to have become an effective teacher, especially of biblical literature. (William F. Doolittle, *The Doolittle Family in America* [Cleveland, Ohio: privately published, 1903–1904], III, 303–04; V, 504; *Daily American Directory of the City of Rochester, for 1847–8 . . .* [Rochester: Jerome & Brother, 1847].)

1. Nicholas Lowenbrügger (1417–1487), a revered hermit of Sachseln, Switzerland, was known as Nicholas von der Flüe or "Bruder Klaus."

2. See Cooper to Mrs. Cooper, 20 June 1847.

JOURNAL XXVI

1 JANUARY to 2 JANUARY 1848

Saturday, 1 January.

Read St. John. No church. Weather very mild though snow fell in the night. Walking very bad and I paid no visits out of my immediate connections. Had Dick Cooper, Alice,[1] Georgeanne

Woolson, Platt & Charley Foot at dinner. A very merry evening with the young people. Played chess with my wife — Wrote a little to-day in "Oak Openings," to begin the year well.

1. Richard Fenimore Cooper (1832–1875) and Alice Cooper (b. 1832) were children of Richard Cooper by his first wife Mary Storrs (W. W. Cooper, "Cooper Genealogy," *Proceedings of the New York State Historical Association*, XVI [1917], 210).

Sunday, 2 January.

Went to church in the sleigh, but the streets were all mud — Weather quite mild — All the ice disappeared. Dick dined here with his two eldest sons.[1] After dinner he went to Hyde, taking Alice and Georgeanne with him, who return to school — Dick and Gold staid with us. Grew cooler towards evening. Read in St. John in the morning.

1. Richard Cooper's two oldest sons by his first wife Mary Storrs were Richard Fenimore and Goldsborough (1836–1862) (W. W. Cooper, "Cooper Genealogy," 210).

MANUSCRIPT: Cooper Collection, Yale University Library. PUBLISHED: *Correspondence*, II, 727.

919. *To Mrs. Charles Jarvis Woolson (Hannah Cooper Pomeroy)*

Hall, Cooperstown, Jan. 3d 1848

My Dear Hannah,

Your daughter [Georgianna] left us yesterday afternoon, along with Alice Cooper, both attended by the latters father. They went to Hyde [Hall] to pass the night, and were to go, and doubtless did go, to Albany to-day. Owing to a little legerdemain the holidays covered two complete weeks, and a little more, as Georgeanne was with *us* just fifteen days; long enough to make us all love her. You have every reason to be satisfied with your daughter, my dear. She is a great favourite here, I can assure you, and will be most welcome when she repeats the visit, as she has promised to do, if *she can* — a very proper salvo, for a young lady of her time of life. To me she appears to be ingennuous, very warm-hearted, sincere, and quite clever. She strikes your aunt in the same way, and Paul says she is one of the cleverest girls of his acquaintance. Paul being a miracle himself, you are to be highly flattered by this opinion. We are all obliged to you for letting your daughter come, and trust you will hear her story and let her come again.

Was there ever such a winter, in these mountains. There was something like one week of *cold* weather in December, the remainder of the month was almost warm — many of the days like April, as we have April. There is no ice in the lake; not even a bay for the boys to skate in.

You know that your Aunt Mary [Mrs. Isaac Cooper] and three of her children, are here, Mrs. [Lyman] Foot has the rectory, and Mrs. [Henry W.] Wessel[l]s and her two children live with her. Dr. Foot left some ten or twelve thousand dollars, and we hope to get her half-pay, which will add $360 per an. to her means. If she get the pension, she will be quite comfortable.

Wessel[l]s turns up a trump, after all. He was at Vera Cruz, Cerro Gordo, where he charged up the hill under [Bennet] Riley, and at Contreras. At Contreras, he was detached the first day, and covered a flank against cavalry, behaving well. In the charge he distinguished himself, and actually was present with a small party that compelled 200 horse to surrender — In this last affair he was wounded in the [ankle].[1] But mounting the horse of one of the prisoners, he continued on with his regiment, and was even warmly engaged at Churubusco — Nor did he go into hospital, until after the 2d his regiment entered Mexico, where it had quite a sharp street fight. There he laid up, and was about to return to duty, when his wife last heard from him. He is mentioned with marked credit in the dispatches, and will doubtless get a brevet, if he get nothing else. Two years since he was half way down the list of 1st lieutenants in his regiment — now he is the ninth captain. His wife evidently expects to go to the Halls of the Montezumas, nor do I think her expectation at all unreasonable. If the Whigs make their alliance with Mexico a little more active, the war may yet last five years — If *they* will be neuter, six months will bring it to a close.

All here unite with me in affectionate remembrances — we wish also to be remembered to your husband and to Mrs. [Robert] Campbell. Georgeanne said the other day, that Mrs. Campbell was making some enquiries about Wm. [M.?] of that Ilk. I got a letter from a friend in Florence, a day or two since, which was written to acknowledge the reciept of a letter of Introduction I had given W. W. Campbell.[2] The latter had sent the letter from

Geneva, not going to Florence, in consequence of having been suddenly recalled to London — I am afraid that the house on which he had his credits may have stopped, or that some thing in that way may have stopped him on his road to Italy. This is purely conjecture, however, though it is conjecture sustained by a report that he is expected home in a few days, and by a knowledge of the state of the London money market.[3]

Adieu, my dear — | Your affectionate Uncle
J. Fenimore Cooper

Mrs. C. J. Woolson | Cleveland, | Ohio —

MANUSCRIPT: Mrs. R. H. Bishop, Jr., Novelty, Ohio. PUBLISHED: *Correspondence*, II, 580–82.

1. Cooper seems to have written "ancle."

2. See Cooper to Horatio Greenough, 6 May 1847. Greenough's letter to Cooper is unlocated.

3. Mrs. Woolson affectionately acknowledged Cooper's letter, writing from Cleveland, Ohio, on 11 January 1848, and expressed her gratitude for the Coopers' kindness to her daughter. Her own invalidism, she explained, had thrust the responsibilities of nurse and housekeeper prematurely on her daughter Georgianna. (MS: YCAL.)

JOURNAL XXVII

3 JANUARY TO 14 JANUARY 1848

Monday, 3 January.

Weather a little cooler, though still very pleasant. Wrote in Openings, and drove wife to the Chalet, but sleighing execrable. On my return read in St. John — Worked on the Openings, as usual. Evening, played chess with wife, who beat me, though she was not very well. Young Dick and Gold [Cooper] still here.

Tuesday, 4 January.

St. John. Paid Harvey Clark [1] and Fish & Payne.[2] Worked on openings. No snow and weather quite mild, though it grew colder towards night. Dick & Gold left us. Paul told me he was going to Utica. Wrote to Capt— [Henry W.] Wessel[l]s and sent him an Army list. Chess in the evening with wife. Read the papers to her. Frank and Morris Foot [3] dined here, but were so noisy that I sent them home immediately after dinner.

1. See Cooper to Richard Cooper, 16 June 1835.

2. Fish & Paine, Cooperstown blacksmiths (Livermore, *A Condensed History of Cooperstown*, 92).

3. Francis Waite Foot (1842–1878) and Morris Cooper Foot (1843–1905) were younger sons of Dr. Lyman Foot. Morris Foot retired from the Army a brigadier general in 1803. (Abram W. Foote, *Foote Family* . . . [Rutland, Vermont: The Tuttle Company, 1907], I, 324, 454.)

Wednesday, 5 January.

Paul went early. St. John — two of the doctrinal chapters. Weather pleasant but cooler. Began to read Siborne's Waterloo,[1] again. Find in it less impartiality than I at first supposed. Chess with wife. Worked on "Openings," which gets on slowly — It tries to snow, and ice begins to make a little in the lake, but on the whole the weather pleasant.

1. William Siborne, *History of the War in France and Belgium, in 1815* (London: T. and W. Boone, 1844). A third and revised edition was published in 1848.

Thursday, 6 January.

Weather still pleasant. Ice about a mile up the lake. Went to-day to the farm, but found the sleighing execrable — St — John in the morning — Chess with wife in the evening — Still pleasant, with occasional spitting of snow. Dick came down from Hyde, after having taken Alice [Cooper] & Georgie [Woolson] to Albany.

Friday, 7 January.

Weather much the same, but moderating and growing cooler, by turns — Towards evening getting quite cool. St. John. Work on Openings — Dick got back from Albany on Wednesday, and reappeared here at dinner yesterday. To day he took Jenny [1] back to Hyde, and did not dine with us. Began to snow in the evening. Chess with wife, as usual. Grows colder.

1. Jane (b. 1843), daughter of Richard and Mary (Storrs) Cooper (Storrs, *The Storrs Family*, 458).

Saturday, 8 January.

Some little snow had fallen. St. John — Work on Openings — Took wife to Chalet, but found the sleighing very poor — better, however, than the last time — Went through the woods w[h]ere we did pretty well. Lippet had taken away the big cow, for which he is to pay me $40. Chess in the evening — Weather moderating and more like snow.

Sunday, 9 January.

Snowed in the night. Finished St. John. Went to church in the sleigh. About six inches of snow, but so light that the runners still cut through. Getting packed, however, and hope sleighing will be pretty good to-morrow. Parson preached in behalf of foreign missions, but postponed the collection till next Sunday. Snowing at times throughout the day.

Monday, 10 January.

Began the Acts. Last night was severely cold, as has been to-day. Thermometer in cold places below zero all day. Went with wife to Chalet, but were nearly frozen. Caught a turkey and killed it myself, and bought a keg of oysters on my way back. Sleighing tolerable, but not as good as we are accustomed to at this season. Paul returned — Chess with wife, she beating outrageously. No more ice.

Tuesday, 11 January.

Last night a tickler. Acts. An oyster breakfast, with thermometer at 40 in the hall. Lake frozen as far as we can see. As the wind has changed, I think it will moderate. I find the thermometers stood before sunrise, at 25°, 26°, & 27, below zero. This is within four or five degrees of our coldest weather — Moderates [sensibly],[1] some thermometers ranging as high as 15° above 0.

1. Cooper wrote "sensible."

Wednesday, 12 January.

John Morris [1] arrived last evening. He reports his uncle John [Cox Morris] as failing daily — Acts. The weather much milder. Worked at "Openings," and drove wife to Chalet, and afterwards around Great Lazy Man. Marmaduke [2] came back to school this morning. Dick [Cooper] dined here. Chess with wife — she beat, handsomely. Weather much milder; hardly down to freezing at 3. P. M.

1. Cooper's friend John Cox Morris had two nephews who were namesakes,

one (1839–1884), son of Jacob Walton and Serena (Burgess) Morris, the other (1822–1882), son of Lewis Lee and Elizabeth Ann (Gilbert) Morris (Lefferts, *Descendants of Lewis Morris*, Chart E, II).

2. Marmaduke (1840–1862), son of Richard and Mary (Storrs) Cooper (Storrs, *The Storrs Family*, 458).

Thursday, 13 January.

Weather still mild, but clouded. Acts — worked at "Openings." This book is more than a fourth done. Dick brought Willy[1] and Jenny down from Hyde, this morning. This afternoon a tea-party, and a dance in the hall after the piano. Jane Morris,[2] Mrs. Henry Van Rensselear,[3] John Morris, Cally Foot,[4] Mary Farmer, Platt and Charley [Foot], Kate Prentiss,[5] &c & — No chess this evening. My big cow weighed 834 llbs dead —

1. William Storrs (b. 1845), youngest son of Richard and Mary (Storrs) Cooper (Storrs, *The Storrs Family*, 458).

2. Probably Jane Elizabeth Morris (1828–1875), daughter of Jacob Walton and Serena (Burgess) Morris (Lefferts, *Descendants of Lewis Morris*, Chart E, II).

3. Probably Joanna Franchot (1817–1895) of Butternuts who married Henry Van Rensselaer (1817–1888), son of Captain Robert Hendrick Van Rensselaer, on 4 October 1843 (Florence Van Rensselaer, *The Van Rensselaers in Holland and America* [New York: privately published, 1856], 44, 64).

4. Caroline Adriance Foot (b. 1830) married George Pomeroy Keese in 1849 (Abram Foote, *Foote Family* . . . [Rutland, Vermont: The Tuttle Company, 1907], I, 323).

5. Catherine Lucretia, daughter of Colonel John Holmes and Catherine Cox (Morris) Prentiss. She married John C. Dodge in 1848. (Hurd, *History of Otsego County*, 285; Cooperstown *Freeman's Journal*, 30 December 1848.)

Friday, 14 January.

Thawing. Acts; martyrdom of Stephen — Lent John [Clayton?] the sleigh, and did not go to Chalet. Work at Openings. Took a walk, but walking bad. The wind has got round to the westward, but still very mild. John Morris left us to-day. Dick dined here. In the evening all the children went out, leaving me alone with my wife. Chess, at which I beat three games.

MANUSCRIPT: Cooper Collection, Yale University Library. PUBLISHED: *Correspondence*, II, 727–30.

920. *To John Fagan*

Hall, Cooperstown Jan. 15th 1848

Dear Fagan,

Herewith I send you the last sheet of Jack Tier; that for February being out about the time you will get this. I wish you to finish the plates as soon as you can, and to send them on to Burgess & Stringer so that they can get them early in February. I send a short preface, of which you need not send me a proof.[1]

I wish you to acknowledge the reciept of this, and to let me know the day my next note will be due, and the precise amount — I have mislaid the memorandum.[2] Our English drawee has faced the storm well. I had nine bills on him this season, most of which fell due in the height of the tempest. Eight are *paid* — and the ninth, only for £50, was accepted the 4th Dec, and will be due 5th February. Yours are *all* paid. I sold one bill for £200 to the Bank of State of New York, which sent it to Reid, Irving & Co. The house stopped, and the proceeds of my bill, which was paid at maturity, were lost to the bank, but not to me.

I have a new book that is already sold both in this country and in England. Its title will be

The
Oak Openings
or
The Bee Hunter.

I shall send you a volume soon, to be stereotyped forthwith. Early in March, I shall see you.

Adieu

Mr. John Fagan. J. Fenimore Cooper

MANUSCRIPT: Simon Gratz Collection, The Historical Society of Pennsylvania.

1. "I enclose a proof of the 3 pages of Preface," replied Fagan on 24 January, "and will await its return before casting. I had nearly all the work cast close up, so I have only a dozen pages to set up in order to finish. Vol. I. made 244 pages, and the IId may not quite reach that number. I can send the plates to B. & S. on the 4th of February, unless you think that too soon. In the absence of anything to the contrary from you, I will send them forward on that day." (MS: YCAL.)

2. "The exact amount of your note is $389.65, and it falls due on the 21st February" (MS: Fagan to Cooper, 24 January 1848, YCAL).

JOURNAL XXVIII

15 JANUARY TO 23 JANUARY

Saturday, 15 January.

Rained in the night, and continues mild. Snow going fast. Acts. Wrote letters to-day. Dick did not come down from Hyde — rained most of the day. Chess in evening — wife beat grievously, and neatly — two check mates, with half the pieces on the board. The third time I beat, but a mere hammering game.

Sunday, 16 January.

A little cooler in the night, and sun rose clear. A lovely day. Acts — Was unwell, and did not go to church. Dick brought Jenny down, about noon. Reports roads good, and thawing in the sun. No change in the weather all this day. No one at dinner. Nothing new in the papers, Congress quarrelling about the war, one side endeavoring to make capital out of it, and the other the reverse.

Monday, 17 January.

Beautiful day. Begin to think the predicted comet may influence the weather. Acts. Openings. Took a long walk on the planks, where wife joined me. Dick down to take leave before going below. Paid girls $10 each, of allowance. Company in the evening. Chess — I beating, all hollow. Fine weather continues.

Tuesday, 18 January.

Acts — Had a bad night, from eating Boston buiscuits. Nothing Yankee agrees with me. Better in the morning. Flurries of snow, but not enough to cover the bare spots. Took a long walk on the plank. Openings — finished 10th Chapt. Chess with wife in the evening — I beat. Wife nervous. She grows fatter, but wants air & exercise. Out of Carter potatoes to my regret —

Wednesday, 19 January.

Grew much colder in the night, but no snow. Wheeling good, but not a bit of sleighing. Acts. Revising Openings. Thaws in warm places, but a fair winter day — House very comfortable. Franklin in our room has not been lighted this winter. Took a long walk, wife with me part of the time. She wants air very much, and we miss our sleighing. Chess, both beat. I lost queen early, and at end had a castle and two pawns against a queen. Beat handsomely.

Thursday, 20 January.

Still pleasant, though cool. Acts. Took a very long walk — weather charming, though freezing a very little in the shade. Wind S. W. and mild — No sign of snow, and wheeling capital. Chess in the evening. I beat altogether. Began to revise Openings to-day, of which ten chapters are done. Congress making a fool of itself by betraying its [utter] [1] ignorance of the Constitution.

1. Cooper wrote "utterance."

Friday, 21 January.

Weather still more moderate, and an April day. Acts. After breakfast drove wife to farm, on wheels — roads capital. Did no work to-day. Congress does not seem to be aware it can not order the Constitutional Commander in Chief to send a regiment any where — Chess — wife gave me two out and out check mates.

Saturday, 22 January.

Acts — Another fine day, but cooler than yesterday. Drove wife to farm on wheels — Cattle doing well on this weather. Steer improved, and store cattle in good heart. Feeding out the English potatoes, which turn out indifferent. The Carters are decidedly our best [passus?].[1] Got no New York mail this evening. Chess, wife beat me two games ignominiously — Check-mated both times with nearly all the pieces on the boar[d].

1. Cooper probably intended to write "potatoes."

Sunday, 23 January.

Acts. Another charming day — cool, but clear and pleasant. Mr. Hull [1] preached. Brewer was married in church,[2] just before the sermon, and Dolphin the brewer [3] was buried in our Church yard, though the service was at the Methodist building. Dick and Gold [Cooper], who came up from school on Friday, went back this afternoon.

1. Andrew Hull (1811–1896, Hamilton 1836, General Theological Seminary 1839), rector of St. Andrew's Church, New Berlin, Chenango County (*Hobart College: General Catalogue*, 93; *Journal of the Proceedings of the Eleventh Annual Convention of the Protestant Episcopal Church in the Diocese of Western New-York* [Utica, New York: published for the Convention, 1848], 5).

2. John Brewer married Eunice Temple in Christ Church, Cooperstown, on 23 January 1848 (Cooperstown *Freeman's Journal*, 12 February 1848).

3. Unidentified.

MANUSCRIPT: Cooper Collection, Yale University Library. PUBLISHED: *Correspondence*, II, 730–32.

921. *To an Unidentified Autograph Collector*

Otsego Hall, Cooperstown | Jan. 23d 1848

I have long been of opinion that there is some yet undiscovered cause for a succession of cold and a succession of warm seasons. About thirty years ago we had several cold summers in succession; now, it appears to me that we are getting as many warm summers. Fifty years ago my father raised very good grapes within the grounds of this house, *not wall-fruit*, and *now*, I can not get grapes to ripen well, as wall-fruit. Are we approaching the warm summers? I think so — This winter has been milder, on the whole (a few snapping days excepted) than either of the two winters I passed in Italy. In 1828–9 we skated at Florence, and in 1829–30, not only Soracte, but the entire Campagna was often covered with snow. As yet, we have had no sleighing in this Count[r?]y — not sleighing worth mentioning.

J. Fenimore Cooper

SOURCE: Photostat, Houghton Library, Harvard University.

JOURNAL XXIX

24 JANUARY TO 27 JANUARY 1848

Monday, 24 January.

Finished Acts. Another glorious day. Openings. Drove wife to farm. This afternoon walked on the planks until after sunset. The evening a very little cool, but delightful. Chess — wife beat me two games nefariously — fairly *walloped* me. I got the third game. Wife plays much better than she did. Practice makes perfect.

Tuesday, 25 January.

Began Romans. Another mild day, but not so pleasant as yesterday. Openings. Drove wife as far as Myrtle Grove, by the new road, which is a very pretty drive, and a great addition to our outlets. But the Grove is spoiled. This place is a monument of the "people's" honesty, and appreciation of liberty! I know them and would as soon as confide in convicts. Chess.

Wednesday, 26 January.

Romans. Weather still mild, but not pleasant enough to ride out. Rained a little, indeed. Openings — In evening, chess. Wife gave me another of her quick check-mates — terrible defeats these — I beat her two games, afterwards, however. The Whigs at Washington seem about to cut their own throats again, on the question of war. Does Mr. Clay understand the Constitution, or is it ignorance?

Thursday, 27 January.

Romans — Rained in the night, and all the forenoon — Wind North East. Sent 10 Chapters of Openings to Fagan, by Express.[1] Got a letter from him in the afternoon — All right as to Jack Tier. Chess — wife beat one of her slapping games, again, but I beat her two afterwards. One of these beats puts her in good spirits for a whole evening, and I delight to see it.

1. See the following letter.

MANUSCRIPT: Cooper Collection, Yale University Library. PUBLISHED: *Correspondence*, II, 732–33.

922. *To John Fagan*

Hall, Cooperstown Jan 28th 1848

Dear Fagan,

It is lucky I enquired about the note, as I had got the idea it fell due about the middle of March.[1] Enclosed is a bill for a hundred pounds to be used in the following manner.

If you can do no better, and want your money, keep it in your own hands until its date — Feb — 21st 1848, then sell, and take up my note, and remit me the balance.

But I would prefer this arrangement. Send me the $200 which I want to make out my cash until March — keep the balance for the note — take up the note yourself, and hold it until I come down, say 15th March. And keep the bill until you can send the ten chapters of "Openings" to Bentley, which ought to be in a month, or six weeks at latest. As for interest and commission I will settle that to your satisfaction when we meet.

Now, I do not exact this last arrangement, but it would be a convenience to me, and enable me to keep at work here until the Hudson opens, without borrowing of the Bank. It is my business to pay my note, and unless quite convenient to you to take the other course, there is the bill to do it with; I leave you to decide for yourself.[2]

In either case the sheets finished must be sent to Bentley a little before the bill goes forward. I would prefer to send the whole ten chapters already forwarded to you *by express*, but five will do; or as many as may happen to be done. By making a push I think we might get off ten or twelve forms in three weeks. The sheets must go in duplicate, one package by New York Steamer, and the other by Boston, and an account kept of the number of pages.[3]

Let me know at once your determination. If you remit money, get a draft on New York from one of your banks and enclose it to me.

I also wish two titles of "Jack Tier," which book you can send to B & S, as soon as you are ready.[4]

Yours truly

Mr. Fagan J. Fenimore Cooper

You will find the motto of the *book* in Graham, prefixed to the numbers.

MANUSCRIPT: Simon Gratz Collection, The Historical Society of Pennsylvania.

1. See Cooper to Fagan, 15 January 1848.

2. "I enclose a draft on the National Bank of New York for $200. I will attend to the Note due on the 21st, with great pleasure; and will observe your directions respecting the £100 Exchange which you sent me . . . The pecuniary arrangement will occasion me no inconvenience, though, if it were otherwise, I owe it to you on many accounts." (MS: Fagan to Cooper, 2 February 1848, YCAL.)

3. Fagan replied on 2 February that he would at once begin stereotyping the 80 pages of manuscript of *The Oak Openings* received that afternoon and that he expected to be able to forward as many as 160 pages in print to England in three

weeks. To this end, he requested Cooper to return each proof sheet as soon as possible. (MS: YCAL.)

4. "I send also the two copies of title page of '*Jack Tier.*' In a day or two, I will forward to B. & S. the plates of that book." (MS: Fagan to Cooper, 2 February 1848, YCAL.)

JOURNAL XXX

28 JANUARY TO 31 JANUARY 1848

Friday, 28 January.

More ⟨fine⟩ mild weather, with a little rain. Romans. A little, but very little snow fell in the night. Dick got back — demurrer not reached. Chess — I beat this evening, altogether. Wrote to Fagan and enclosed a bill on Bent[l]ey for £100 Sterling. With this bill he is to meet my note to him for Crater, and remit to me the balance.

Saturday, 29 January.

Romans. Weather still mild, and a very little more snow. The thaw has cut up the mud in the road, which prevents the sleigh from running. Openings, again — I have been reading D'Israeli's Curiosities of Literature,[1] a curious work, but of less interest than I had supposed. Chess — Wife check mated in her slapping way, but I beat her atrociously in a second game.

1. Isaac Disraeli's *Curiosities of Literature* (1793) was frequently revised and reprinted during the nineteenth century.

Sunday, 30 January.

Romans. Still fine weather, though a little cooler. No sleighing. Thaws freely in the sun. Was not well enough to quit the house. This evening recieved a letter from Commodore Shubrick, dated Monterey, Oct. 2d '47. He was about to sail on an expedition to capture Guaymas, [Mazatlán] [1] and Acapulco. The two first our advices, overland, tell us have been taken.

1. Cooper wrote "Matzalan."

Monday, 31 January.

Romans. Another beautiful day. Such a winter as this, thus far, has scarce been ever seen in this region. It is as mild as a

Philadelphia winter, certainly; and in some respects, milder. Went to farm in wagon — met a team that ran against us and broke both my shafts. Horse began to plunge and I told wife to jump. She did so, without injury. The horse plunged for a short distance, when I turned him into the upper ditch, where he stopped. It was a marvellous escape. Wife had to walk a mile in the mud.

This month, generally, has been one of the pleasantest ever known in these mountains. On two occasions it has been cold, but only for short periods, and most of the time the weather has been quite mild and clear. I have remarked that the sun has had more power than is usual in January, many days having been hot —

Congress has been out-doing its own out-doings this month — Talk, talk, talk — The President asked for ten new regiments to carry on the war, and Congress has been talking on the subject, until some of the patriots have come out with a declaration it is now too late to raise the men, as the sickly season would overtake them!

MANUSCRIPT: Cooper Collection, Yale University Library. PUBLISHED: *Correspondence*, II, 733–34.

923. *To William Branford Shubrick*

Hall, Cooperstown, Feb. 1st 1848

My Dear Shubrick,

I recieved your letter of Oct. 2d night before last. Yesterday I wrote to Mr. [John Y.] Mason.[1] I told him that you greatly regretted the asking for a recall, and are now desirous of remaining out under almost any arrangement. I did not suggest the two squadrons, for I did not think it would be quite just to [Thomas Ap Catesby] Jones, who has gone out expecting to command in the Pacific; but I did suggest this, which will virtually amount to the same thing, viz — I asked the Secretary to send out permission for you to remain on the station, should Jones and yourself think it expedient. It would certainly have been better to have remained Commander in Chief, but, as that is now out of the question, I saw no project better than the one I proposed. This permission, if granted and I think it will be, will put it in your power to be governed by circumstances. We hear you have taken [Guaymas] [2] and Mazatlan – if to these places you should add San Blas and Acapulco, there will be scarcely any thing left for the squadron to do. Now, there is some hope of peace. But for the factious proceedings of Congress, I think peace would be sure, and that quite soon – In the event of peace, you would have come home in course this season, and would no doubt be glad to come home, now. Should circumstances induce you to remain, Jones would no doubt employ you as [James] Biddle seems to have done, and any unfavourable impression produced by asking for the recall would be effaced.

Here, it appears to be understood that you asked a recall in consequence of finding yourself second in command, when you expected to be first. This of itself, is a justification with most persons, though I regretted it, for I think an officer always safest when he does even more than duty absolutely requires. I have found, however, whenever I have mentioned that you sailed expecting to be Commander in Chief, and were superseded by Biddle under positive orders, and without any very obvious necessity for his services, that your conduct has appeared natural and dignified. You say nothing of this reason for your course, but the letters to your family leave no doubt on my mind that it had great influence. Notwithstanding your change of views, *if such has been the fact,* I am not certain that your wisest course would not have been to rest there, and return when your relief arrive. Should you take all the important ports before Jones meets you, it will leave your position well enough. Every body can understand why an officer should be hurt by a disappointment like that you were obliged to recieve, and, as there will be little other duty than simple blockading, and not much of that even after the ports are taken, I do not see that you could be much better off, under all the circumstances; especially if you succeed in taking all the important ports. A victory, no doubt, carries with it a certain amount of éclat, but if the enemy will not, or can not, fight, you can not help it.

I write in great haste, in order to make sure of getting my letter off in time to reach you. I should have written many times since my last, but have supposed that you would be on your way home before my letter could get out. We are now told that Jones will go to Valparaiso to meet the Ohio, which will give you plenty of time to work out your projects in the Gulf and on the coast. The Ohio was still at Rio, early in December, and Capt. [William V.] Taylor may never get her round the Cape, though I presume Capt. Long[3] can do it for him.

But you will know all this before my letter reaches you. We are all well — Paul much better, and have one of the mildest winters ever known in these mountains. God bless you, and be of good cheer — I almost hope that the Mexicans will resist at Acapulco, though it were more humane to desire a bloodless conquest. A little glory, in these glory-seeking times, however, goes a great way. Your two nephews have done well — one laid down his life, while the other has reaped laurels as a soldier. If you can gain a victory, you may set all detractors at defiance — though I do not know that any thing has been even hinted to your prejudice — The Biddle matter was a prodigious provocation, though Biddle, himself, appears to have behaved perfectly well.

Has not [Winfield] Scott achieved marvels! Yet his accursed General Order has almost obliterated the recollection of his victories.[4] As a soldier, Wellington is the only man living whose fame can now eclipse his, and Wellington succeeded with vastly greater advantages than those possessed by Scott, after allowing for the difference between Frenchmen and Mexicans.

We hear occasionally from your family, and always good news. My own opinion is that peace will be made so early as to greatly simplify your position, and suffer you to return this summer, even though permitted to remain out.

I can tell you nothing of Fremont. He has been tried, but the sentence is not known. [Thomas Hart] Benton will probably have influence enough to save him, let what may come. It is a bad sign for his case that he alleges the witness (Gen. [Stephen W.] Kearny) has testified falsely. Such a thing may have been, but it is not very likely.[5]

All here send best regards — | Yours as Ever

Comm. Shubrick J— Fenimore Cooper

MANUSCRIPT: Paul Fenimore Cooper, Cooperstown, New York.

1. Neither Shubrick's nor Cooper's letter is located, though their contents can be, in part, inferred.

2. Cooper wrote "Guyamus."

3. Commander Andrew K. Long (d. 1866), who entered the service in 1818 and retired in 1864, was Taylor's second-in-command (GNR).

4. Scott's General Order No. 349, 12 November 1847, rebuked two officers harshly and somewhat unjustly for complicity in newspaper accounts attributing his accomplishments to themselves. The resulting squabble led to Scott's being superseded as commander in chief of the Army in Mexico. (Elliott, *Winfield Scott*, 565–75.)

5. In this famous court-martial (2 November 1847 to 31 January 1848), Frémont (1813–1890, Charleston College n.g.) was charged with mutiny for accepting the governorship of California from Captain Stockton, whose authority was subsequently discredited; with disobedience of his superior General Kearny; and with conduct prejudicial to good order. President Polk concurred in the sentence of guilty but remitted the sentence. Senator Benton (1782–1858, University of North Carolina n.g.), Frémont's father-in-law, used his influence maladroitly and probably injured Frémont's cause. (Allan Nevins, *Frémont: Pathmarker of the West* [New York: D. Appleton-Century Company, 1939], 327–42.)

Part Twenty-one

THE MYSTERIOUS DEATH OF GENERAL WOODHULL

1848

THE MYSTERIOUS DEATH OF GENERAL WOODHULL

1848

From 21 to 27 February 1849, New York's Broadway Theatre featured an historical melodrama by Charles Edwards Lester called *Kate Woodhull, or, The Price of Liberty.* It commemorated, in heroic extravaganza, the supposed martyrdom of General Nathaniel Woodhull, president of the New York Provincial Congress and brigadier general of the militia of Suffolk and Queens counties, Long Island, who died of gangrene within British lines at New Utrecht on 20 September 1776. According to Lorenzo Sabine's *American Loyalists* (1847), Woodhull surrendered to Captain Oliver De Lancey after receiving a promise of protection; whereupon, the Captain struck Woodhull "and permitted his men to cut and hack him at pleasure." Despite the patriotic gore and, perhaps, the patronage of Caleb Smith Woodhull, a relative of the General and mayor of New York City from 1849 to 1851, the play won more ridicule than praise. It was a mere incident in the curious history of Woodhull's legend, transmitted in ballad, elegy, chronicle, panegyric of every description, and painting (though no reliable likeness of the General survived). The Woodhull Monument Association in 1848 set about collecting $50,000 as the first installment toward the erection of a monument to Woodhull which should be 300 feet high, 40 feet square, and contain six rooms each 50 feet high. This sudden flowering of the legend in 1848 and 1849 resulted, in large part, from an epistolary controversy Cooper unintentionally provoked in *The Home Journal.*

Some years before his entrance to authorship, Cooper had begun ambitiously to compile a genealogy of the De Lancey family. Though he never completed the task, he continued to investigate sources; and he regarded himself (and was regarded) as something of an authority on his wife's family. The Woodhull story was especially fascinating to the Coopers; for, in its crudest version, one of Mrs. Cooper's second cousins commits atrocities on the person of the husband of one of her third cousins. Encountering Sabine's reference to the incident and other presumed misstatements in *The American Loyalists,* Cooper followed his usual instinct to set the record straight by writing a letter for publication, this time to the editors of *The Home Journal.* Nathaniel P. Willis and George P. Morris were delighted to receive copy from Cooper and even more delighted to receive rejoinders to which Cooper was obliged to reply. The exchanges, which continued from February into July 1848, consisted of thirteen letters: five by Cooper; one by Henry Cruger Van Schaack, a lawyer and local historian of Manlius, New York; two by Sabine; three by Henry Onderdonk, Jr., a teacher and student of Revolutionary and Queens County history; and two by anonymous contributors, one of whom styled himself Vindex.[1]

The disputation was outwardly polite. Sabine acknowledged Cooper's corrections gracefully and deferred to his personal knowledge, though he became impatient as the correspondence dragged on and Cooper's own information proved less than encyclopedic. A conscientious compiler, he was perfectly willing to admit that his book was not definitive; but he winced publicly at having his pioneering contribution employed as a whipping boy. Henry Onderdonk, Jr., was less complaisant. A stubborn, rather literal-minded person bent on ferreting out the truth, he obviously found Cooper's virtuoso manner inappropriate to the high seriousness of antiquarian research. He took inordinate delight in debunking the reputation of a De Lancey or a Cooper. Allowing that the novelist's knowledge "might do very well for fire-side conversation," he pinned his hopes to an affidavit of Robert Troup, attested in 1776 and published in his own *Documents and Letters Intended to Illustrate the Revolutionary Incidents of Queens County* (1846), and to his success in casting doubt on Cooper's sources: Benjamin F. Thompson's *History of Long Island* (1843), Silas Wood's *Sketch of the First Settlement of the Several Towns*

1. The dates of the pertinent issues of *The Home Journal,* with the names of the respective contributors are: 12 February 1848, Cooper; 11 March 1848, Van Schaack; 18 March 1848, Sabine; 25 March 1848, Cooper; 1 April 1848, Cooper; 8 April 1848, anonymous; 15 April 1848, Sabine; 6 May 1848, Cooper; 20 May 1848, Onderdonk; 27 May 1848, Onderdonk; 3 June 1848, Cooper; 3 June 1848, Vindex; 8 July 1848, Onderdonk.

on Long-Island (1828), and the then-unpublished manuscript of Thomas Jones's *History of New York during the Revolutionary War* (1879). Though the victory was uncertain, "Vindex" awarded the palm to Cooper: "That the patriotic general [Woodhull] was somewhere, and by somebody, most barbarously mutilated, is most certain; but that Oliver De Lancey was not the officer by whom, or by whose assent or connivance it was done, is, I think, incontestably proven by the evidence Mr. Cooper has adduced." A month after the publication of Cooper's final letter, Onderdonk tried unsuccessfully to lure him into further combat.

W. H. W. Sabine's *Suppressed History of General Nathaniel Woodhull* (1954), a twentieth-century postscript to the controversy, suggests that the contest was all in vain. Acting on Cooper's recommendation that the "death of General Woodhull . . . deserves to be thoroughly investigated," this modern Sabine has demonstrated that Woodhull, despite his prominence as patriot, renewed his loyalty to the King near the time of his capture, and that the celebrated wounds, probably slight, might well have been inflicted to lend credibility to the account of his capture. An order from General William Howe, transmitted by Major General Oliver De Lancey (the Captain's father) and dated Jamaica, Long Island, 1 September 1776, stated that Nathaniel Woodhull and Samuel Phillips had signified that the residents of Suffolk County were "desirous of laying down their Arms and again becoming loyal and obedient Subjects, [and] that for the Peace and Ease and Security of the Inhabitants he is willing to accept of their Submission, and promise them Protection." This order, obtained from the British by a provincial agent and published unabridged in the *Connecticut Gazette* on 27 September 1776, explains why General Washington made only nominal efforts to liberate Woodhull and why the New York Convention and Woodhull's own family accepted his death in unexplained silence. As W. H. W. Sabine has shown, Woodhull's submission in his complex and compelling circumstances need not be harshly judged. Sabine exceeded his evidence altogether, however, in insinuating that Cooper, acting for the De Lanceys of his generation, knowingly or unknowingly suppressed facts to protect the reputation of Captain De Lancey. If Cooper *had* possessed the information exhumed by Sabine, he would have used it cheerfully, both because it tends to clear Captain De Lancey's name and because it affords a new perspective on the mystery of General Woodhull's death.

924. *To George Pope Morris and Nathaniel Parker Willis, for* The Home Journal

[1 – 7 February? 1848] [1]

Messrs. Editors: –

At page 254 of Sabine's "American Loyalists," is the following paragraph: "His treatment of General Nathaniel Woodhull, an estimable Whig of New York, who became his prisoner in 1776, should never be forgotten. *There seems no room to doubt,*[2] that, when that unfortunate gentleman surrendered his sword to De Lancey, he stipulated for, and was promised, protection; but that his Loyalist countryman basely struck him, and permitted his men to cut and hack him at pleasure."

The De Lancey alluded to here, was Oliver, the son of Oliver [*1718–1785*],[3] who was the second [*third and youngest surviving*] son of Stephen [*1663–1741*], the Huguenot. This Oliver De Lancey [*1749–1822*] was educated in Europe; put early in the 17th Light Dragoons; was a captain at the commencement of the Revolution; became a Major in 1776; a Lt. Colonel a year or two later, and succeeded André as Adjutant General of the British Army in America. On his return to Europe, he was made Deputy Adjutant General of England; as a Maj. General he got the Colonelcy of the 17th Light Dragoons; was subsequently made Barrack Master General of the British Empire; rose through the grade of Lt. General to that of General, and died, some six or eight-and-twenty years since, nearly at the head of the English Army List.

The imputation of Mr. Sabine ought not to rest on a man who ran such a career, unless merited. I have no means of learning this writer's authority, but I much question if it be any better than that I shall now quote in contradiction of his statement.

Mr. Thompson, the historian of Long Island, was related to Gen. Woodhull, lives among the connections of his family, and near the scene of the event itself. At page 411, vol. ii, of Thompson's Long Island,[4] is the following paragraph, article "Woodhull," viz: —

"The General [*Woodhull*] immediately, on being discovered, gave up his sword in token of surrender. The ruffian who first approached him, (said to be a Major Baird, of the 71st,) as reported, ordered him to say, *God save the King*; the General replied, 'God save us all'; on which he most cowardly and cruelly assailed the defenceless General with his broad sword, and would have killed him upon the spot, if he had not been prevented by the interference of an officer of more honor and humanity, (said to be Major Delancey of the dragoons,) who arrested his savage violence."

It furnishes some reason for distrusting Mr. Sabine's sources of information, that he has certainly fallen into numberless errors throughout his work. Among the De Lanceys introduced, there is great confusion. The James De Lancey mentioned at page 246, is confounded throughout the article with his cousin of the same name. He wishes to describe James [*1732–1800*], the son of the James [*b. 1703*] who died at the head of the government of the colony in 1760, by Anne, daughter of Col. Heathcote; but, in a large portion of his article does, in fact, describe James [*1747–1804*], the son of Peter [*1705–1770*], of Westchester, by Elizabeth, daughter of Lt. Gov. Cadwallader Colden.[5] James, the son of James, the person intended to be described, held no station in the army during the war of '76; neither lived nor died in Nova Scotia, and had a wife whose name was Margaret, and not Martha. This James De Lancey went to England early in the struggle, and lived and died at Bath.

The same confusion exists in Mr. Sabine's account of his two Olivers De Lancey. They were father and son, and both general officers. Mr. Sabine says that the father went to England, got a seat in parliament, and died in [1785].[6] He is of opinion that Mr. Van Schaack alludes to this gentleman, where he speaks of an old friend who had declared that Beverley should "hold his bones." Now, Gen. De Lancey, the father, died in command on

Long Island, about the middle of the war, and was buried in the family vault, in Trinity Church.[7] The person who was desirous of leaving his bones at Beverley, in Yorkshire, has, most probably, been some descendant of the ancient family of Beverley, which migrated to Virginia nearly two centuries since, and has diffused its blood, as well as its name, over so many southern families. The Beverley Robinsons,[8] of New-York, were of this connection; and one of that family may have wished to die at Beverley.

It is a fact worth mentioning, that the venerable seat of the Beverleys, at Beverley, in Yorkshire, after an alienation of more than a century, has returned to the old stock, one of the Virginia Beverleys having purchased it, and dwelling there, at this hour. But, between the De Lanceys and the Beverleys, there was no connection, and there was no motive why General De Lancey should wish to "leave his bones there." Gen. De Lancey, the father, was not in parliament, as stated by Mr. Sabine, though the son was; nor could the father be "considered as belonging to the council" in 1782, having then been dead several years.

Mr. Sabine [*page 252*] makes a daughter of Lt. Gov. Jas. De Lancey marry Sir William Draper [*1721–1787*], so well known for his controversy with Junius. Sir William Draper married Susan [*d. 1778*], daughter of Oliver De Lancey, senior, and the sister of the person whom he supposes to have permitted the outrages on Gen. Woodhull.

Oliver De Lancey belonged to the middle, or Bloomingdale, branch of his family, which is now extinct in the male line; its last man having been killed at Waterloo, in the person of Sir Wm. H. De Lancey [*1778–1815*], the Quarter-master General of Wellington's army. There is no very near relative, in this country, to defend the memory of the accused; though a daughter is living in England. Still, justice should be done, and, in the interest of truth, I have written this communication. I complain not of the temper of Mr. Sabine's book, which is sufficiently liberal and well-intentioned. Its fault, in my opinion, is in attempting that which, in the nature of things, it would almost exceed the means of any man to do with entire accuracy. Nevertheless, Mr. Sabine has collected much curious information that is true, and the great difficulty in his case, will be, as I apprehend is usual with historians, to winnow the kernel from the chaff.

Yours truly,

J. Fenimore Cooper.

SOURCE: *The Home Journal*, 12 February 1848.

"General" Morris (1802–1864), the doughty, sentimental Knickerbocker best known for "Woodman, Spare that Tree," and Willis (1806–1867), the foppish dilettante of letters who excelled at light verse and travel reporting, were old collaborators and old acquaintances of Cooper when they founded the New York weekly miscellany *The Home Journal* in 1846. Prospering under their combined talents, the *Journal* afforded them a comfortable celebrity until shortly before Morris' death. (Henry A. Beers, *Nathaniel Parker Willis* [Boston: Houghton Mifflin and Company, 1885]; *DAB*.)

1. A letter from "Morris & Willis," dated New York, 9 February 1848, thanked Cooper for his contribution and enclosed the issue of *The Home Journal* containing it (MS: YCAL).

2. Italics Cooper's. Like other passages quoted by Cooper in these letters for *The Home Journal*, this excerpt from Lorenzo Sabine's *The American Loyalists, or Biographical Sketches of Adherents to the British Crown in the War of the Revolution . . .* (Boston: Charles C. Little and James Brown, 1847) is edited slightly to conform to its source.

3. The italicized information in square brackets, provided for clarification in Cooper's letters for *The Home Journal* and sometimes duplicated in other parts of this edition, derives mainly from Story, *The deLanceys*, the *DNB*, and the *DAB*.

4. Benjamin F. Thompson, *The History of Long Island; from Its Discovery and Settlement, to the Present Time* (New York: Gould, Banks & Co., 1843).

5. See Story, *The deLanceys*, 17–19, 50–53.

6. The source has "1788," Sabine (page 254) "1785."

7. In a courteous letter in *The Home Journal* of 11 March 1848, Henry C. Van Schaack indicated errors in this paragraph. The letter of 24 December 1785 quoted by Sabine (page 254) from page 411 of Henry C. Van Schaack's *The Life of Peter Van Schaack, LL.D. . . .* (New York: D. Appleton and Co., 1842) was not written, as Sabine and Cooper assumed, by Peter Van Schaack, but by John Watts to Peter Van Schaack. And H. C. Van Schaack provided evidence to show that the elder Oliver De Lancey did not die prior to 1782. Presumably his information was insufficient to corroborate Sabine's assertions that the older Oliver went to England in 1782 and died at Beverley in 1785.

Meanwhile, in a letter dated Eastport, Maine, 19 February 1848, and published in *The Home Journal* of 18 March 1848, Sabine modestly deferred to Cooper, explaining the difficulties of his research and citing his authorities for statements to which the novelist objected. On the older Oliver De Lancey at least, Sabine's information appears to have been more accurate than Cooper's.

8. Beverley Robinson (1723–1792), the wealthy New York Loyalist banished by New York State in 1779, was the son of John Robinson, at one time president of the Virginia Council and acting governor of Virginia at the time of his death in 1749. Beverley Robinson married the New York heiress Susanna, daughter of Frederick Philipse and sister of Mary the wife of Roger Morris. (*DAB*.)

JOURNAL XXXI

1 FEBRUARY TO 9 FEBRUARY 1848

Tuesday, 1 February.

Finished Romans. It snowed in the night but the foundation for sleighing is not good. Could not persuade wife to venture out. Grew mild as the day advanced, and the road soon got bad. Chess. Wife beating terribly at times. Commenced on new part of Openings, and work moderately, but not con amore. This book is not a labour of love, but a labour.

Wednesday, 2 February.

⟨Romans.⟩ Corinthians. A little colder, in the night, nay a cold night, but a charming day. Drove out Cally Foot in the cutter, wife being still too skitish to venture. Road very indifferent. Chess, both beating, I most however. There were some young folk this evening, and a good deal of laughing, and chatting as is usual with them.

Thursday, 3 February.

⟨Romans.⟩ Corinthians. Another cold night. Wife went with me to farm to-day. Did pretty well by keeping on the side of the road. Fortunately Pumpkin was not at all frightened the other day, and behaves as well as ever, which is not particularily well. Chess; both beat. Wife certainly plays this game much better than she did thirty years ago. Paul's birth-day.

Friday, 4 February.

⟨Roman⟩ Corinthians. It was a very mild night and to-day it thaws freely. Went on the plank walk, and shovelled off the snow myself. Afterwards walked there more than an hour. Half sold my hop-poles while there. Chess, as usual, both beating. I have been astounded by a published letter of Judge [John] McLean. He affirms the right in Congress to controul the movements of the army, among other monstrosities.

Saturday, 5 February.

Corinthians — It snowed in the night, leaving about seven inches on the grounds. The roads were not in the best condition for it, but, on the whole, the sleighing is good. Went to farm with Sue, who is getting over her alarm. Wm. is drawing wood, and we are likely to get through the winter comfortably. Chess — five games — Wife beat two slappingly, and I beat three. A little side-talk lost me one. ⟨Dick came down⟩ Fen and Gold [1] came up this afternoon.

1. Richard Fenimore and Goldsborough Cooper, Richard's sons.

Sunday, 6 February.

Corinthians. Snowed a little, but always mild — almost thawing, and quite so whenever the sun appears — A good deal of snow fell in the course of the day, and the weather is somew[h]at colder — No more thaw — Dick, his two eldest sons and Jenny [Cooper], with us, to-day. Went to the rectory, which is a hospital. The old lady very well, but all the rest with colds. Looks like more snow.

Monday, 7 February.

Corinthians. Not cold at all, but a feathery snow falling, throughout much of the day. Drove wife out, but did not go to farm. Plenty of snow, a foot or more, and sleighing will be good as soon as the roads are [beaten].[1] Chess. Wife beat *awfully* first game, but I retaliated the next. Children in high glee around the fire when I went to bed.

1. Cooper wrote "beateen."

Tuesday, 8 February.

Finished 1st Corinthians. Grew cold in the night. Joe Tom brought in a report that Union Factory was burned down in the night. Drove to the *chalet,* sleighing good. The cattle look well, and are evidently improving. The young oxen grow and are getting heavier. Got the first proof sheet of Openings, this evening. Chess, wife beating two games smashingly. She certainly improves.

Wednesday, 9 February.

2d Corinthians. A cold clear morning. Worked as usual, and

drove wife to Chalet. Pleasanter than yesterday, and sleighing royal — Carried some meat up to the poultry. Butcher told me it was a piece of [Hobley?]! Chess — four games; wife beating three and I one. All these games were played rapidly, and my beat, and her first beat, did not take half an hour for the two.

MANUSCRIPT: Cooper Collection, Yale University Library. PUBLISHED: *Correspondence*, II, 734–36.

925. *To Richard Bentley*

Otsego Hall, Cooperstown, Feb. 10th 1848

Dear Sir,

All of Spike has gone forward, regularily, in duplicate, and no vessel has been lost in which any part of it was sent.[1] Doubtless you have it all long before this.

As for "Oak Openings" it can not be kept back as long as you wish — at least I think not — but Burgess and Stringer may consent — but it can be kept back until July, or August.[2] Nevertheless, I must get it off my hands earlier. Volume 1st will reach you about the middle of March, by which time the Stereotyper has promised to have it ready — So long as a work is in his hands I am kept tied to one spot in order to read proofs, of which not enough is done as it is.

Burgess & Stringer have the same reasons for wishing to keep back "The Oak Openings" as you, they publishing Spike early in March; but I do not think that a book which has gone through a magazine can greatly interfere with an entirely new work. I have proposed to B & S to keep back "Openings" and they have expressed a wish to do so. As to sheets, give yourself no concern; your rights will be fully protected by my care in the case of this book, as in those which have gone before. We call the book "The Oak Openings; or the Bee Hunter," If you would like "The Bee Hunter, or the Oak Openings" better, you can just transfer the names. I prefer "Openings."

I have sent to John Fagan a bill for £100 drawn against this book, in order to pay for stereotyping. The bill will go forward with vol. I, probably by the steamer of March 1st, or soon after. It will fall due, in that case, about the middle of May. I shall draw for another £100 against vol IId, and the remainder when the last of the work is sent. Vol. IId will be sent about the beginning of April — after that I shall be regulated by the time of publication, as it is always wisest to hold the sheets in my own hands, though I think you and B & S. might perfectly depend on each other, if a day were agreed on; you publishing a day or two the soonest, if that should make any difference —[3]

Yours truly

Mr. Bentley — J— Fenimore Cooper

MANUSCRIPT: Cooper Collection, Yale University Library.

1. Bentley had opened his letter of 4 December 1847 to report in a postscript that certain sheets of *Captain Spike* or *Jack Tier*, supposedly sent, could not be located. He acknowledged his error in his letter of 11 March 1848, noting his publication of the book on this day. (MSS: YCAL.)

2. According to Bentley, the publication of *Captain Spike* in March 1848 made desirable the postponement of the appearance of *The Oak Openings* until autumn 1848 (MS: Bentley to Cooper, 4 December 1847, YCAL).

3. "If Messrs. Burgess & Stringer gave me a week's start in the publication of Oak Openings," wrote Bentley on 11 March 1848, "it would not matter to them, and would be better for me. *July* would be better than *August* for the publication of this Work this last month being generally deplorably dull with us. With y[ou]r permission I should prefer to call the new Work 'The Beehunter or The Oak Openings.' I note what you say about the bills, the first of which for £100. I am to expect shortly. With regard to the other two I must beg you to draw when you do so at *90* days instead of *60*. The present state of business, and the anxious look-out of every-body just now makes this necessary; and indeed I shall thus make the payment pretty well *l'argent comptant*." (MS: YCAL.)

JOURNAL XXXII

10 FEBRUARY TO 11 FEBRUARY 1848

Thursday, 10 February.

Corinthians. Much more moderate, and looks like snow — Began to snow in the forenoon and two or three inches were added to our supply. Did not drive out on account of weather. Chess. Beat and Beat. More news from Shubrick, who is very down-hearted in consequence of having asked his recall. We hear, however, that he has taken [Guaymas] [1] and Mazatlan.

1. Cooper wrote "Guyamas."

Friday, 11 February.

Corinthians — A very fine day and sleighing glib. Getting ice to-day and yesterday. It is better than I expected to see. Pack away this year forty loads, which I think must hold out. I have got rectory ice-house as well as my own. Chess — Wife rather on stilts. The weather is more mild, but still cold — Thermometer has been at zero several times this week.

MANUSCRIPT: Cooper Collection, Yale University Library. PUBLISHED: *Correspondence*, II, 736–37.

926. *To Alice Trumbull Worthington*

Otsego Hall, Cooperstown, Feb. 12, 1848.

My dear Miss Alice Worthington,

I have received your letter with the most profound sentiments of gratitude. The compliments from the newspapers did not make half the impression that was made by your letter; but the attentions of a young lady of your tender years, to an old man, who is old enough to be her grandfather, are not so easily overlooked. Nor must you mistake the value I attach to the passage cut from the paper, for, even that coming through your little hands is far sweeter than would have been two candy-horns filled with sugar-plums.[1]

I hope that you and I and John [2] will have an opportunity of visiting the blackberry bushes next summer. I now invite you to select your party — of as many little girls, and boys, too, if you can find those you like, to go to my farm. It shall be your party, and the invitations must go out in your name. You can have your school if you like. I shall ask only one guest myself, and that will be John,[3] who knows the road.

With highest consideration,

Your most obliged and humble servant,
J. Fenimore Cooper.

SOURCE: Mary E. Phillips, *James Fenimore Cooper* (New York: John Lane Company, 1913), 304.

The ten-year-old daughter of John Richard and Mary Alice (Dorrance) Worthington of Cooperstown, Alice was an especial friend of Cooper, who in 1844 gave her a primer picture book "written on large paper, with a large seal." With the book came a note (unlocated), dated Hall, Cooperstown, 22 April 1844, written after the novelist had seen Alice and her cousin parading with fur muffs on the warm April day. The note read, in part: "Mr. Fenimore Cooper begs Miss Alice Worthington will do him the favor to accept the accompanying book (which was written expressly for Princess Alice of Great Britain). Mr. Cooper felt quite distressed for Miss Worthington's muff during the late hot weather, and begs to offer her the use of his new ice-house should the muff complain."

Miss Worthington (1838–1913) married the Reverend Stephen Henry Synnott in 1863. Her brother John (1840–1909), who became United States consul at Malta, married in 1862 as his first wife Jennie Cooper, daughter of Richard and Mary (Storrs) Cooper and the novelist's step-grandchild. (George Worthington, *The Genealogy of the Worthington Family* [Cleveland, Ohio: privately published, 1894], 215, 313–14, 382; Mary E. Phillips, *James Fenimore Cooper* [New York and London: John Lane, 1913], 302–03.)

1. Miss Worthington's letter and its complimentary enclosure clipped from a newspaper are unlocated.
2. Probably John Worthington, Alice's brother.
3. Probably John Clayton, Cooper's hired man.

JOURNAL XXXIII

12 FEBRUARY TO 29 FEBRUARY 1848

Saturday, 12 February.

Corinthians — Still milder — Went to Chalet, capital sleighing. Hens begin to lay, though a little snubbed by the cold weather. We have had about a hundred eggs since January, which is much better than last winter. A little party in the evening, including a Miss Dering from Utica — Nicoll's daughter [1] — No chess.

1. Nicoll H. Dering (1794–1867), brother of Charles T. Dering (see Cooper to Andrew T. Goodrich, 19–20? October 1820), had six daughters (Jacob E. Mallmann, *Historical Papers on Shelter Island and Its Presbyterian Church . . .* [New York: privately printed, 1899], 177–78).

Sunday, 13 February.

Finished Corinthians. Milder — Church in forenoon. Congregation about 100, which is now our usual number. All the parsons in Cooperstown, Campbell [1] excepted want to depart, I hear. Nay, two have gone *faute de viande.* Dick got back two or three days since, and was down to-day, but would not dine. Congress acting like intrinsic knaves, which a good many are.

1. Alfred E. Campbell (d. 1874, Union 1820), brother of William W. Campbell of Cherry Valley, New York, was pastor of the combined First and Second Presbyterian Churches in Cooperstown from 1834 to about 1848 (Hurd, *History of Otsego County*, 272; *Union College: Centennial Catalog*, 19).

Monday, 14 February.

Galatians. Much milder. Until to-day I have found the hall

at 38°, every morning for a week, notwithstanding the fires have been kept up. To day it was at 42, and soon rose to temperate. Went to Chalet, and killed a turkey. Got but one more on the eating list, and not many poulets. Chess. Wife beat two, right off the reel. Then I beat two — all quick games.

Tuesday, 15 February.

Galatians. Much more moderate. Thermometer at 50° in the hall when I came out. Drove to chalet, and found sleighing tolerable. Chess in the evening — one game, I beating rather magnificently. Miss Beebe [1] passed the evening with us, to take leave of us — At 8 o'clock this evening Mrs. Crippen was brought to bed of a girl.[2] Doing well. Letter from Morris Cooper announcing his marriage.[3]

1. Miss Beebe may have been Emma F. Wright Beebe whom Rensselaer R. Nelson, son of Judge Samuel Nelson, married on 3 November 1858 (*DAB*).

2. Julia Fish Crippen, daughter of Mrs. Schuyler Crippen (Anna Pomeroy Cooper) was born on 15 February 1848 (Lefferts, *Descendants of Lewis Morris,* Chart E, II).

3. Jacob Morris Cooper (1814–1853), son of Isaac and Mary Ann (Morris) Cooper, married Josephine Mary Robins on 27 January 1848 (Lefferts, *Descendants of Lewis Morris,* Chart E, II).

Wednesday, 16 February.

Finished Galatians. 5th a noble chapter. Another fine day, and mild. Took a good long walk, and was about a good deal in the air this morning. No one seemed disposed to drive out — It is cooler than I had thought, though clear and a bright day. Thaws in the sun, but no where else. Chess. I beat once — wife beat awfully, and I beat again. One game was pretty long.

Thursday, 17 February.

Ephesians. Weather colder; so much so as to cover the windows with frost. Most of the ice-houses are now filled — I work at Openings steadily. Sold my hop poles this morning. Went to Chalet — weather quite mild, but sleighing going as a matter of course. A great "ride" this afternoon — Paul goes, but no one else from the hall. Chess — both beating. Miss M. Bowers [1] and Mrs. [William A.] Collins sat an hour with us.

1. Martha Stewart Bowers (d. 1881), daughter of John M. and Margaretta

M. S. (Wilson) Bowers and sister of Mrs. Collins (*A Family History: Johnston, Stewart, Wilson, Bowers* [Cooperstown: privately published, 1886], 18).

Friday, 18 February.

Ephesians. Still another bright day. Drove wife to châlet across the lake. Went on at foot of West Street and off at two Mile Point. Found Dick [Cooper]'s track, who has now been up and down three times. Some one followed us, and the road is made. Chess — wife made a tremendous hit — quite ashamed of myself — I beat next game. Young Dick and Gold [Cooper] came up from Hartwick.

Saturday, 19 February.

Finished Ephesians. Of all these epistles I like those to the Corinthians the least. A part of Ephesians is wonderfully comprehensive and fine. Weather clear and a little cold, but not enough to prevent thawing in the sun. For six weeks, unless when it has snowed we have had clear bright weather. This is the best February I have ever known at this place. Chess. Wife gave a slashing beat, but I got my revenge.

Sunday, 20 February.

Philippians. It thawed in the night and snow seems to be going. Unless it change the road will break up. Read service to wife and Sue at home, we three not liking to encounter the bad weather. Dick and Gold [Cooper] went back to school shortly after dinner. Mr. Amos Beach preached, our parson relieving guard. In the evening looked over Eusebius, which strikes me as a singular book. Must read it altogether, and closely.

Monday, 21 February.

Finished Philippians. Still very mild but no rain. Wind got up, and got round to the west, but continued mild. Took ⟨a⟩ long walks on the planks, forenoon and afternoon, and found it delightful. Five of the ladies joined me in the afternoon. Chess — Wife not well, and I beat one game somewhat easily. She played no more and I read Eusebius — an author not much to my taste.

Tuesday, 22 February.

All of Colossians. Still mild. Stiffened a little in the night, but scarcely froze. There were beautiful rose coloured northern lights last evening, which I forgot to mention. Very fine, though I have seen finer — It tried to snow to-day, with wind easterly, but could not succeed. The little fell melted immediately. Chess — wife gave one terrible beat. I retaliated, then came the conqueror, which got to be king and castle on each side. I beat finally by an oversight of Sue's.

Wednesday, 23 February.

First of Thessalonians. Still mild. A very little snow in the night, but scarcely enough to whiten the roofs. It has been a very beautiful day, and I have had two long walks on the planks. About two it was as warm as April. I have no recollection of so mild a winter in this climate, and particularily of so much sunshine — Chess. Wife beat twice; both times slappingly, but I got the third game almost as triumphantly. One of my beats was shameful.

Thursday, 24 February.

2d Thessalonians. Weather not bright, but still mild. Tries to snow, but there does not seem to be any humidity in the atmosphere to congeal. Had northern lights, last evening. News from Mexico very pacific — The projet of a treaty, indeed, is said to be in Washington. Old Quincy Adams dead.[1] He died in harness, falling in a fit in his place, in Congress. Chess was terrible — Two beats slap bang.

1. Adams suffered a paralytic stroke in his seat at the Capitol on 21 February 1848 and died on 23 February.

Friday, 25 February.

1st Timothy. Grew colder in the night. Paul came in from a supper at Roselawn, having driven down the lake, at midnight. To-day clear and cold. We hear that Quincy Adams is still living, but unable to be removed from the capitol. I got a good walk on the planks to-day, and [a] good thrashing at Chess, in the evening; two ignominious beats. A third game I beat, though nothing brilliant.

Saturday, 26 February.

2d Timothy — Clear but chilling weather. The sun has great power. I paid John Clayton $100 to-day, the first cent he has asked for though he and his wife have now lived with us nearly ten months, at $160 per annum. Small pox in town — some say varioloid. No chess, having a nervous attack. The mail brought the news of Mr. Adams' decease. He literally died in the capitol, never having been removed from the speaker's room.

Sunday, 27 February.

Titus — Philemon. Much milder, and looks like snow — Not well enough to go to church in the forenoon. Wife went, however. The peace news increases in intensity. I have thought these six months that peace must follow our successes if the whigs will allow it to come. Tries, but can not snow. News from Washington not quite so pacific this evening. Some doubts about the treaty's being accepted.

Monday, 28 February.

Hebrews — Much colder to-day. A cold night, in fact. Hannah [Wessells] came over with several letters from Wessel[l]s. He writes in pretty good spirits. Wound quite healed, and he amusing himself with looking at the different fields of battle. His wife read us the reports in which her husband is commended. Capt. [Carey?], in particular, speaks of Wessel[l]s in very favourable terms. Chess. Two ignominious defeats, and one rather clever victory.

Tuesday, 29 February.

Hebrews — This book is much superior to most of the writings attributed to St. Paul, though passages in the other books are very admirable. A little snow in the night, and cold to-day. I think a sleigh might run tolerably well. Small pox, or varioloid increases. Calvin Graves has it, now, though no bad case, except one of Adsit,[1] — a blacksmith, is very serious. There must be six or eight cases in the village.

This month has been unusually fine. The brightness of the days has been its most remarkable feature. I finished vol. 1 of Oak Openings to-day. And in the evening got a long letter from

Mrs. Pomeroy — Chess. Two infernal beats again, slap-bang, and one victory. Well, this delights my wife, and so I care not. I *can* beat, if I try.

1. Possibly Smith Adsit (1815–1889), listed in the Adsit genealogy as a Cooperstown shoemaker, though there were other Adsits in the locality (Newman Ward Adsit, *Descendants of John Adsit of Lyme, Connecticut* [n.p.: privately published, 1959?], 61).

MANUSCRIPT: Cooper Collection, Yale University Library. PUBLISHED: *Correspondence*, II, 737–41.

927. *To Mrs. George Pomeroy*

Hall, Cooperstown, March 1st 1848

My Dear Nancy,

Your letter[1] reached me last evening, and I enclose the draft for $35 — the interest due about the middle of this month. I have been to see Messrs. Ernst[2] and [Henry] Phinney. The former remitted $119.96 on the 7th ult, and the last sent $100 a week or two since. These two sums, with the money I now send will make a total of $254.96, which I suppose from your letter will be all you will want. I hesitated about adding a hundred to my remittance, but came to the opinion that you would draw should you be pressed for the money, and that you might prefer to keep the sum in my hands unbroken if you could. Should you want any more funds, do not hesitate about drawing, giving a few days sight, according to the amount of the draft. For less than $100 six or ten days will suffice.

We are all well, though the small pox is in the village — not badly, but enough so to make a great noise. The court is sitting, nevertheless, and I suppose that no very serious danger exists. The doctors have been round vaccinating, and I hear find that nearly half the people have not been vaccinated.

There has been a good deal of gaiety lately, though Susan and I stay at home. I have not been in a house in the village, out of my own connections, this winter. We play chess every night, and my wife has got to be so skilled as to give me ignominious defeats almost every night.

Ann has a girl, and I have just paid my first visit. It is a nice child, and is named after Julia Fish. I saw Dick Morris[3] to-day — out on a law-suit, but he does not go near his relations.

From what Harry Phinney tells me (who by the way is President of the Bank) the difficulty with [Samuel Wootton] Beall is arranged. I think you had better keep on good terms with that family, quarrels among connections being bad things. A little forbearance usually brings matters round, and there is no saying more true than that "blood is thicker than water." Perhaps Beall had some reason for what he did, as regards Phinney, and did not like to broach the matter to you. Indeed had he spoken of the tax sale before the time for redemption was passed, it might have defeated his purpose altogether.

We were all much pleased with your grand daughter [Georgianna Pomeroy Woolson]. She is quite clever, and far from unpleasing to the eye. In person she will be rather striking, and her face, if not positively handsome, will be agreeable. We all liked her, and there is a spice of sincerity among us that goes even farther than good breeding, and I presume that she soon felt she was a favourite, and that was the chief cause of her finding the visit so agreeable. As Caroline wishes to write to you,[4] I must conclude, with regards to Pomeroy.

Yours very affectionately
J. Fenimore Cooper

Mrs. F— says there is a little strut about your neighbour the ex-g——r.

MANUSCRIPT: Woolson House, Rollins College. PUBLISHED, IN PART: Clare Benedict, ed., *Voices Out of the Past: Five Generations (1785–1923)* . . . (London: Ellis, 1929), 43–44.

Constance Fenimore Woolson later required this letter from Cooper to her grandmother as an autograph.

1. Unlocated.
2. Probably George W. Ernst (1813?–1898), a prominent businessman and civic leader in Cooperstown (Hurd, *History of Otsego County*, 260).
3. See Cooper to Mrs. Cooper, 26 June 1834.
4. Susan Fenimore Cooper, not Caroline, wrote to her aunt on the available space of the same manuscript. Only a part of her letter remains.

JOURNAL XXXIV

1 MARCH to 9 MARCH 1848

Wednesday, 1 March.

Hebrews — This book is so much superior to the rest of Paul's epistles that I must think some one wrote it for him. The allusion to Melchisidec is most extraordinary and I scarce know what to make of it. Calvin Graves is now said not to have the small pox. Weather windy but not cold. Snow[s?] at times. Chess. A most degrading defeat. I grow quite ashamed of myself and must be getting old. Ætatis suæ 59th.

Thursday, 2 March.

Finished Hebrews and all of James. I like this last apostle. In my childhood he appeared to be a sort of relation, on account of his name. Day clear, but pretty cold. Chess as usual. Wife beat me again with a *dig*! I can only say that I play somewhat carelessly, for I dislike plodding over the board. Then Susy is so inwardly delighted to beat, while I care nothing about a defeat. "So [besser?]."

Friday, 3 March.

First of Peter. Easterly weather and snow. March is likely to turn out a sleighing month. Old Adams is buried, and a good deal of old Adam with him, notwithstanding all their eulogies. He was a learned man, but his mind wanted a balance wheel. His father was much the abler man of the two. Chess, and I beat twice. Rather rappingly.

Saturday, 4 March.

Second of Peter. A good plain book. Weather clear and coldish, though not very cold — No frost on the windows. The wind blew fiercely in the night. The day has not been cold and the sleighing is good. The treaty is said to encounter difficulties in the Senate. I think we are now sure of Mexico's coming in, as deputies are said to be at Washington, to urge an admission into the Union, for three of the northern provinces. If so, the central government must come to.

Sunday, 5 March.

The three epistles of St. John, and that of St. Jude. The celebrated passage touching the divinity of Christ, is so embedded in similar doctrine that it strikes me the whole chapter must go if those two verses go. But is not the entire new testament full of this doctrine? The pride of man makes him cavil at that which he can not comprehend, while every thing he sees has a mystery in it! Church to-day in the forenoon.

Monday, 6 March.

Revelations. Milder, and snowing at intervals. The snow did not amount to much, but the weather is unpleasant. Chess. I beat twice rappingly, wife once, and one drawn game. Of course we played very fast, at which sport I usually get the best of it. One more bad case of small pox, Susan Brimmer the mantua-maker, a granddaughter of my father's old gardener.

Tuesday, 7 March.

Revelations. Day clear and reasonably cold. Grew milder, and drove wife to châlet. Pumpkin quite lame. The wind has got to the south, and promises a thaw. Town meeting to-day. It is a sad commentary on human wisdom that men quarrel just as much about these town offices as for those of the state, *giving the same reasons for it*! Chess and I beat.

Wednesday, 8 March.

Revelations. Ash Wednesday. Went to church. Uncommonly soft, spring-like weather. The snow goes very fast. Sleighing indeed gone. Looks like rain. No New York mail to-night – probably on account of the ice's moving at Albany. Recieved a copy of the report of Commissioners to revise practice of the Courts. Many things in it that are good, and some that will never, never do!

Thursday, 9 March.

Revelations – Snowed in the night. Snowing more or less all

day. Susan Brimmer — is dead of the small-pox — a most malignant case, the pustules filling with blood. She was vaccinated a few days before she was taken ill, and the pustule actually formed well, but it also filled with blood. Chess — mama beat.

MANUSCRIPT: Cooper Collection, Yale University Library. PUBLISHED: *Correspondence*, II, 742–44.

928. *To Edward Floyd De Lancey*

Hall, Cooperstown, March 10th 1848

Dear Ned,

As soon as you send me a line to say that the boats will run in a day, or two, I shall come down, as I wait only for the ice to move. It is probable that I shall stay twenty four hours in Albany.

Mr. Sabine is to answer me this week, when I shall answer him. The whole story will be told in my next letter. As to your queries —[1]

1st Peter De Lancey [*1705–1770*][2] of West-Chester was a country gentleman, owning a considerable estate, with mills &c, at and around West Farms. I can not tell you *when* he died. He represented the borough, and played a considerable part in local politics. In character, he was a gentlemanly rowdy, racing horses, fighting cocks &c, but always maintaining his social position, and being remarkable for impressing the black guards of the cock-pit and race course with his manners.

2. John [De Lancey V (*1741–1820*)], Mrs. [Joseph Christopher] Yates' father,[3] was a chip of the old block. His second marriage threw him out of the circle of his natural friends.

3. Mrs. Yates' mother was a Miss [Dorothy] Wickhan.

4. I know nothing of the Rowley's except from aunt Cally, but have understood *her* that Lady Rowley was a grand-daughter of Lady Draper. I can tell you nothing of the issue of Mrs. Payne-Galway, for the latter was the name by which she was known.[4]

5. Your grand fathers eldest brother James [De Lancey V (*1732—1800*)], served as a young man, and was an aid of [Abercrombie][5] at the defeat of Ty. His father [James De Lancey IV (*1703–1760*)] died intestate (of apoplexy) and he succeeded to the whole real estate. He ⟨married⟩ was educated at Cambridge, Eng. and married Margaret daughter of Chief Justice [William] Allen

[*1704–1780*], Penn. He was the head of the court, or church party, and represented New York. In the revolution, he went quite early to England, leaving his family behind. Your grandfather accompanied the last, when it went to join him. In England he lived at Bath, in considerable affluence, having saved a good deal of his personals, and recieving at one time, £26000 indemnity. This sum, I think, was subsequently increased to £40,000. Even this last amount was less than what the Bowery estate sold for under the hammer, which was $202,000, specie, or specie value. His losses were probably double the indemnity. He was an indolent man and loved his ease, the reason for quitting America, as he did. In this country, he lived in the highest style known to the colonies, and was deemed a principal personage in New York.

6. Oliver [III *1749–1820*], Peter's son, was in the Navy. It was said he refused to serve against this country, and resigned. It is certain he left the navy, and lived and died at West Farms. He married beneath him as to family, and above him as to morals. He was a very elegant man in appearance when dressed, and also as to manners when he chose.

7. The commander of the Cow Boys was Lt. Col. *James* de Lancey [VI *1747–1804*], Peter's son, the Lt. Col. James De Lancey mentioned by Sabine, and whom he confounds with your uncle James [Thomas James De Lancey (*1789–1822*)]. He had been sheriff of West-Chester, and his corps was kept in that county, to keep open communications and to cover the arrival of supplies — Hence the sobriquet of Cow-Boys, as probably when the beeves would not come of themselves, they made them come. This James did not marry the mother of his children [Martha Tippett (*1754?–1827*)], who were numerous, until all, or nearly all were born. He said it made a woman proud to marry her. This was doubt⟨ful⟩ less Mr. Sabine's "Martha." Who she was, I never heard, but of common extraction, no doubt.

8. Warren [De Lancey II (*1761–c. 1847*)] entered the 17th Lt. Dra. as a cornet, late in the war, and remained in it, a few years in Europe. He first married a Miss [Ann] Taylor, a woman of great respectability, and a sister of the late Mr. Francis Bayard Winthrop of New York.[6] She divorced him. He then married a Miss [Mary] Lawrence [*d. 1788*] a relation of the Morris, and a

grand-daughter of old Lewis of Morrisania. Not content with this he intrigued with her niece [Rebecca Lawrence], and when his wife died, he married the niece, who is now his widow. One or two of his children was born out of wedlock. There are now about as many De Lancey's of the illegitimate as of the legitimate stock. The Guernsey De L's, all of James' (West-chester) descendants, and a good many of Warren's belong to the illegitimates.

9. I do not know who the James De L[ancey] is that Mr. Sabine says was a collector at N[ew] P[rovidence]. It is probable, however, a son of either James or Stephen, of the West-Chester Branch.[7]

10. I know little of Stephen [De Lancey], of West-Chester, beyond this. He filled some office at Albany, before the war, as clerk of some court, and was a considerable man there. He had a large family, and they all removed to Nova Scotia.[8]

No 11, is too long an answer to be given now.

12. *Ancienne noblesse* means nobles of so many ages — four centuries I believe was the period. They had the privilege of riding in the King's coach &c &c —

The *Major* [Robert William] Leake, afterwards General I believe, who married Miss [Margaret] Watts was a brother of the Mr. [John G.] Leake who left the funds of the Leake & Watts charity.[9]

Lt. Col. Stephen [De Lancey VI (*1748–1798*)] (Bloomingdale Branch) married Cornelia Barclay.

Adieu —

E. F. De Lancey Esquire. J. Fenimore Cooper

Aunty says she thinks Warren [De Lancey]'s first wife was a Miss [Mary] Lawrence, Miss [Ann] Taylor the second, and Miss [Rebecca] Lawrence the niece the third.[10]

Dont forget to give me an early hint about the river.

ENDORSED: J. Fenimore Cooper | March 13th 1848. | Seriatim replies | to 12 questions of | mine about mem | bers of the de Lancey | family —

MANUSCRIPT: Paul Fenimore Cooper, Cooperstown, New York. PUBLISHED, IN PART: *Correspondence*, II, 582–85.

Historian, world traveler, and lawyer in Albany and New York City, Edward Floyd De Lancey (1821–1905, Geneva College [Hobart] 1843) was the eldest son of Bishop De Lancey. His publications, the most important of which was his edition of Thomas Jones's *History of New York during the Revolutionary War* (1879), included editions, biographies, local histories, and lectures and addresses on historical subjects. He was a prominent member of the New York Genealogical and Biographical Society, the Westchester County Historical Society, the St. Nicholas Society, and the New-York Historical Society. (Story, *The deLanceys*, 38–39; *ACAB*.)

1. In a letter dated Albany, 7 March 1848, E. F. De Lancey applauded Cooper's course in replying to Sabine and corrected Cooper's error about Oliver De Lancey's having died at Beverley, England, describing his and his father's visit to the grave at Beverley. He asked the novelist the following questions:

"1 What was the character, occupation, life, & career of *Peter* the son of the Huguenot?

"2 What those of his son *John*[,] Mrs. Yates Father?

"3 Was Mrs. Yates's *Mother* Alida Ludlum or Fanny Wickham?

"4 From which of Oliver 1st[']s daughters is *Admiral Rowley's wife* descended? *Aunt Cally says* from Mrs. Payne Galloway?

"5 What was the history &c, of James de L.[,] *Grandfathers eldest brother*?

"6 What was the history &c of Oliver, the father of Mrs. Coster?

"7 Who was the *John* de L who Commanded the *Cow-Boys* and what became of him?

"8 What is the history of *Warren* de Lancey, & what are the *facts* about his wives & children, *how* are the latter illegitimate?

"9 Who can the James De L be, on Sabine's 252d page, a Collector at New Providence?

"10 Do you know any thing of *Stephen* one of the sons of Peter & Miss Colden?

"11 Will you give me an account of your visit to *Caen & Valerie*, & what you found out there, & also the result of your investigations into the family at the *Bibliothèque du Roi.*

"12 Please explain the *technical* meaning of 'ancienne *noblesse*,' or tell me *where* to look for it.

"13 Do you know the first name of Col L[e]ake who married Margaret Watts[,] grand[d]aughter of Stephen the Huguenot; and the first name of the Barclay whom *Stephen* the son of the 'old Brig' married?" (MS: YCAL.)

2. The dates, additions, and corrections supplied in square brackets in this letter derive from Story, *The deLanceys* and the *DNB*.

3. Comma supplied.

4. The connection between the Draper and Rowley families, if it existed, is obscure. Lieutenant General Sir William Draper (1721–1787) married in 1770 as his second wife Susannah, daughter of Brigadier General Oliver and Phila (Frank) De Lancey. Their daughter (1773–1793) married John Gore in 1790, but she is not known to have left descendants. Lady Elizabeth Rowley, to whom Cooper presumably referred, was the wife of Admiral Sir Charles Rowley and the youngest daughter of Admiral Sir Richard King. Susannah De Lancey's sister Phila married in 1774 Stephen P. Gallway, governor of Antigua, whose baronetcy passed to the Paynes, as Payne-Gallway, by the marriage of his sister Margaret to Ralph Payne, third baronet. (Story, *The deLanceys*, 73–74, 90–91; *DNB*.)

5. Cooper wrote "Ambrecombie's."

6. Francis Bayard Winthrop (1754–1817), son of John Still and Jane (Borland) Winthrop, married as his second wife Phebe, daughter of John Taylor of New York (Josephine C. Frost, *Ancestors of Henry Rogers Winthrop and His Wife Alice Woodward Babcock* [Privately published, 1927], 13–14).

7. Sabine referred to James De Lancey VII (1767–1808), son of James V, son of James IV, who was the eldest surviving son of Stephen and Anne (Van Cortlandt) De Lancey. In 1805, after his retirement as ensign in the 18th Royal Irish and after his failure as a sugar planter in the Bahama Islands, he obtained an appointment as collector of customs at South Crooked Island, one of the Bahama group. (Story, *The deLanceys*, 17–21, 31–32.)

8. A lawyer, Stephen De Lancey V (1738–1809) was the eldest son of Peter I,

son of Stephen and Anne (Van Cortlandt) De Lancey. He served as clerk of the city and county of Albany, as recorder of the city, and as a member of the New York Committee of Safety in 1775. A Loyalist, he was under arrest during much of the Revolution; and he moved to Nova Scotia when peace was declared. (Story, *The deLanceys,* 16, 46–48.)

9. By an inadvertency, funds with which John G. Leake had intended to found an orphans' home were inherited by Robert Watts and, as a result of Robert Watts's premature and almost immediate death, by his father John Watts. John Watts used the benefaction to establish the well-known Leake and Watts Orphan House, incorporated in 1831 and dedicated in 1843. Before 1891, when it was moved to Yonkers, it occupied a part of the site of the Cathedral of St. John the Divine.

10. The order of wives suggested here appears to be correct (Story, *The deLanceys,* 66).

JOURNAL XXXV

10 MARCH TO 11 MARCH 1848

Friday, 10 March.

Finished Revelations, a most extraordinary book. It is genuine beyond a question, from internal evidence, if from no other. Snowed a good deal to-day, and grew a little colder towards night. One or two more cases of small pox, but none very bad, now. Adsit, who has been at death's door, is recovering. Chess — I beat out and out. I think success depends on the humour.

Saturday, 11 March.

Genesis 5 chapters. A strange account! Yet much profound understanding of the subject in it. The weather is milder, and looks like a thaw. Went to the Chalet — Not an egg. Stock doing so so, except Wm's own cow, which is sick — Four rapping games of chess. Two beat, two got beat. All played quickly — Wife is plucking up spirit, and often beats me when I little expect it.

MANUSCRIPT: Cooper Collection, Yale University Library. PUBLISHED: *Correspondence,* II, 744.

929. *To Henry Onderdonk, Jr.*

Hall, Cooperstown, March 11th | 1848

Dear Sir,

Yours recieved.[1] On the subject of O[liver] De Lancey's death, I am now convinced I have been misled; *how* you will see stated in the Home Journal. It is odd that my wife, one of the very best authorities now living in family lore, should have fallen into the same mistake, though not at all conscious of having got her impressions from the same source as myself. In collecting materials for a family history, I distinctly asked her father, O[liver] De Lancey's nephew, fellow soldier, and who was in England himself in 1785, where the "*old Brig.*" as he was called in the family died, and he gave the answers I have stated. Thus I wrote it down, and thus have I stated in writing to various persons, in the last thirty years. Of course it has been a *misapprehension*, my father in laws mind dwelling on some other person when I supposed him to be talking of his uncle. He even gave the year of his death 1778. But it will all be explained in the H. J.

When Bishop De Lancey of the Western Diocese of N. York was in Eng. in 36, he visited his great uncle's grave at Beverley, as I now learn,[2] several of the grand children and great-grand children living there at this moment. I knew of the existence of these persons, and had seen one or two of them, but have no recollection of having heard that they had any thing to do with Beverley.

The body is buried in the choir of the Minster — one of the finest in England — and a mural monument, with a long description stands just under the transept. This removes all doubt.[3]

As for O[liver] De Lancey's participation in the outrage on Gen. Woodhull I have great doubts — There are strong points in the account, in favour of the fact, and strong points against it.[4]

Thompson tells us, himself, that his grand mother was a Woodhull.[5] We are almost as nearly connected with Gen. Woodhull, as we were with Gen. De Lancey. The last was a father's cousin, the first a grandfather's. I will give you a sketch of the De Lancey's, in a few word[s].

[*At this point in the manuscript, Cooper inserted the genealogical chart transcribed on pages 298–299.*]

Peter [*b. 1744*], of [the] West-Chester Branch was killed in a duel, unmarried.

John [*1741–1820*] married Miss [Dorothy] Wick[h]am, and left a daughter [Ann Elizabeth], now widow of Gov. [Joseph C.] Yates.

Stephen [De Lancey, *1663–1741*], The Hug[u]enot

James, Lt. G[ov.] — Anne Heathcote.
[*1703–1760*]

Susan[nah] — Sir P[eter] Warren
[*1707–1791*] [*1703–1752*]
[*In the holograph and in the present transcription, Cooper's description of Sir Peter Warren's descendants follows this chart.*]

James [*1732–1800*]	Margaret Allen.	Two sons and three daughters. All single but one, Margaret [*1773–1804*] who married Sir J[uckes-Granville Juckes-] Clifton Bart [*1769–1852*], and is dead without issue.
Stephen [*1734–1775*]	H[annah] Saskett, no issue.	
John Peter [*1753–1828*]	E[lizabeth] Floyd. [*1758–1820*]	Thomas James [*1789–1822*], Rt Rev. Wm. H[eathcote,* *1797–1865*], E[dward] Floyd, [*1795–1820*]. Mrs. [John Loudon] McAdam [Anne Charlotte, *1786–1852*,] Mrs. Cooper [Susan Augusta, *1792–1852*],† and two unmarried daughters.
Anne [*1745–1817*]	Thom[as] Jones—no issue [*1731–1792*]	
Mary [*d. 1796*]	Wm. Walton [*1731–1796*] —	[James] De L[ancey] Walton, Rear Admiral [Jacob] Walton, Mrs. [Daniel] Crommeline Verplanck [Anne Walton], and Miss Mary Walton. All dead, the admiral and Mrs. Verplanck leaving issue

Of this branch — Thom[as] James [De Lancey, *1822–1859*], son of Thom[as] James, lately married to Frances Bibby, the Bishop of [Western] N. Y. and his four sons, and Lt Col. James De Lancey [*1785–1857*], late of 1st Drag. Guards, England, the only surviving son of James and Margaret Allen, are all the males now living. Through females, there are the descendants of Mrs. Verplanck, my children, and Admiral Walton's children. This uses up the oldest, or New York Branch.

There is an illegitimate branch, called the Guernsey. It is descended from Maj. John. De Lancey [*1765–1809*; see Story, *The deLanceys*, 21–24], of the island of Guernsey, a natural son of James, son of James, son of Stephen. Of this branch was the Col. Oliver De Lancey [*1801–1837*] who was killed in Spain as adj. gen. to Sir De Lacy Evans' army. It is a highly respectable branch, in all respects, but the unfortunate bar in the arms.

* Henry Onderdonk, Jr., wrote "owe" after the letter "H," noting, erroneously, "after Gen. Sir Wm. Howe, 1776."

† "wife of J. Fenimore Cooper | H.O. Jr."

chart]

— Anne Van Cortlandt

Oliver B.G. [*1718–1785*] — Phila Frank, of Philadelphia [*d. 1811*]

Oliver [*1749–1822*]. Lt. Gen. unmarried but ⟨left⟩ had a son and a daughter. Son dead.

Stephen [*1748–1798*] — Cornelia Barclay [*d. 1817*] — Sir Wm. Howe De Lancey [*1778–1815*], and several daughters [see Story, *The deLanceys*, 80] one of whom [Susannah, *1780–1832*] married Sir Hudson Lowe [*1769–1844*], of St Helena memory.

Susan [*d. 1778*] — Sir Wm. Draper [*1721–1787*] — a Mrs. Gower [Mrs. John Gore, *d. 1793*], an only child

Anne [*1744–1822*] — Lt. Col. [John Harris] Cruger [*1738–1807*] — no issue

Phila — Stephen Payne-Gal[l]way — Issue — Lady Rowley, wife of Sir ——— Rowley an Admiral, is a grand daughter. [*Cooper was apparently in error about Lady Rowley. See Story,* The deLanceys, *91, and Cooper to Onderdonk, 2 December 1844.*]

Charlotte [*1761–1840*] — Field Marshall, Sir David Dundas [*1735–1820*] — no issue

Branch extinct in male line

[Anne —] John Watt[, Sr.] [*Here and in the holograph, the descendants of Anne De Lancey are enumerated and described in the text following this chart.*]

Peter, — E[lizabeth] Colden of West [Farms] [*1705–1770*]

Peter.

John —

James

Stephen

Oliver

Warren.

Mrs. Col. Barclay

Mrs. John Watts

Mr[s?]. Cox

Mrs. Izard

[*The descriptive information concerning descendants of Peter De Lancey follows this chart here and in the manuscript.*]

[*Cooper evidently intended to conclude the chart proper at this point, but he continued his genealogical description on the same page beneath the chart to the words "(turn over)" in the text following.*]

James [*1747–1804*] was Lt. Col. James,[6] commander of the Cow Boys. *He* went to Nova Scotia, where his issue are to be found.

Stephen [*1738–1809*] — the same, but in civil life.

Oliver [*1749–1820*] was *old Noll* of Westchester. Left the navy at the commencement of the war, and is father of Mrs. Dan Coster [Julia] &c.

Warren [*1761–1847?*][7] died *zanie,* near me, a year or two since. Was in the 17th Lt. Dragoons a short time. He left issue.

Mrs. [Thomas] Barclay [Susannah, *1754–1837*] was the wife of the Col. Mrs. [John] Watts [Jane, *1756–1809*] married her cousin-german the late John Watts [Jr., *1749–1836*] of N. York. Mrs. [John] Cox [Anne, *1743–1818*] left no issue. Mrs. [Ralph] Izard [Alice, *1746–1832*] was the mother of the late Gen. [George] Izard [*1776–1828*] &c.

Of the descendants of this branch, there are a good many — indeed all the remaining De Lancey's are of this branch, though a good many of them were born out of wedlock.

(turn over)

Lady Warren [Susannah, *1707–1791*] left three daughters, viz The Countess of Abingdon [Charlotte, *d. 1794*], mother of the present Earl [Montague Bertie, fifth Earl of Abingdon, *1784–1854*].

Lady Southampton [Anne, *d. 1807*], grand-mother of the present Lord [Charles, third Baron Southampton, *1804–1872*].

Mrs. ⟨Stephen⟩ Skinner [Susannah], wife of Maj. General [William] Skinner, of the New-Jersey family, and brother of the Brig. General [Cortlandt] Skinner [*1728–1799*] of the revolution. Her only child [Susannah Maria, *d. 1821*] married Henry [Hall], 3d Viscount Gage [*1761–1808*], and was mother of the present viscount [Henry, *1791–1877*]. Gen. Skinner was a cousin german of Lady Warren, their mothers having been two of the daughters of Stephen Van Cortlandt.[8]

Mrs. [John] Watts [Anne, *1723–1775*] left ⟨two⟩ three sons, and ⟨three⟩ four daughters.

Robert married Lady Mary Alexander, daug. of Lord Sterling,[9] and left issue — great grand children now in existence —

John [*1749–1836*] — married Jane De Lancey [*1756–1809*],

West-Chester. By his own cousin, numerous issue, but nearly run out. One daughter [Mrs. Henry Laight] only remains of all the children, and three grand children [John Watts De Peyster, Philip Kearny, and Susan (Kearny) Macomb], with their children. The Watts line, however, extinct in this branch.

Stephen [*b. 1754*] British Army — issue plenty, all in England, army and navy.

One daughter, Susan[nah, *1747?–1823*] I think, married P[hilip] Kearny [*d. 1798*] of New Jersey. Brig. Gen. [Stephen Watts] Kearny [*1794–1848*], is one of her sons. Numerous issue.

Another, Mary [Watts, *1753–1815*] married Sir John Johnson Bart. [*1742–1830*] and was grandmother of the present Sir William Johnson. Numerous issue.

Another [Anne, *1744–1793*] married Archibald Kennedy [*d. 1794*], afterwards [*1792*] Earl of Cassil[l?]is. Their eldest son [Archibald Kennedy, *1770–1846*] is the present [*late*] Marquis of Ailsa.

Another [Margaret] married Gen. [*Major* Robert William] Leake, British army.[10] This General Leake, or Col. Leake was a brother of the person [John G. Leake] who left the large estate to an orphan asylum, but Rob[ert] Watts got it under a former will, died just as he got it, when his father old John [Watts, Jr.] nobly gave it, some $200,000, to those for whom it was destined by Mr. Leake.

The blood of old Stephen, the Huguenot is now to be found in some thirty or forty English families of mark, the intermarriages carrying it far and near. The first wife of the present Duke of Beaufort, was his great-great grand daughter, &c & — *Her* mother was a sister of Wellington's.[11]

J. Fenimore Cooper

MANUSCRIPT: The Long Island Historical Society.

1. In a letter dated Jamaica, Long Island, February 1848, Onderdonk corrected Cooper's erroneous statement in *The Home Journal* as to the place of Brigadier General Oliver De Lancey's death by referring to De Lancey's obituary in his own (Onderdonk's) *Documents and Letters Intended to Illustrate the Revolutionary Incidents of Queens County* (1846), 244. Onderdonk noted also that a passage in this book, page 106, was Sabine's unacknowledged source for the allegations concerning Oliver De Lancey's part in the mutilation of General Woodhull. (MS: YCAL.) An annotation on the manuscript of Cooper's letter at this point

states: "*I sent him the evidence of O. D. striking Woodhull; & 2d. the obituary notice of Brig. Gen. Delancey. H. O. Jr.*" Other annotations by Onderdonk follow.

2. "*Mr. Cooper must have written to Bishop Delancey after he recd. my letter, & recd. the following in reply which bears me out. H. O. Jr.*" Actually, Cooper had been informed of his error by E. F. De Lancey's unsolicited letter of 7 March 1848. See the preceding letter.

3. "*Did not my obituary notice from the Gent. Mag. of 1785 remove all doubt? H. O. Jr.*" Story in *The deLanceys*, 71, stated that General De Lancey "was buried in one of the choir aisles of the magnificent Cathedral of Beverley, a slab in the pavement marking his grave."

4. "*The points against it are Mr*[*s?*]. *Cooper's disbelief of it. He forget*[*s*] *that* [*in?*] *civil war brother hates brother. H. O. Jr.*"

5. Benjamin Thompson's grandmother was Mary, Mrs. Jonathan (Woodhull) Thompson (1711–1801), a cousin of General Nathaniel Woodhull (Mary G. Woodhull and Francis B. Stevens, *Woodhull Genealogy* . . . [Philadelphia: Henry T. Coates & Co., 1904], 62–63, 68–69).

6. "A Lt. Col. James m. Miss [French?] in Jamaica L I. Could it be this one?" – Onderdonk's note.

7. Story's *The deLanceys*, 45, gives 1855 as the year of Warren De Lancey's death, but on pages 65–66 questions the accuracy of this date, citing Cooper's statement in this letter as evidence.

8. General Skinner's mother was Elizabeth, wife of the Reverend William Skinner of Perth Amboy, New Jersey. Lady Warren's mother was Anne, wife of Stephen De Lancey, the Huguenot. (De Lancey, "Original Family Records," 71–72.)

9. William Alexander (1726–1783), in later life major general of the Continental Army, assumed the title Earl of Sterling (or Stirling) about 1759, twenty years after it became dormant, and so styled himself until his death. His claim was referred to the House of Lords by petition in 1760, but his right to the title was never confirmed. (*Complete Peerage,* XII, Part I, Appendices, 14–15.)

10. The apparently meaningless phrase "dead unmarried" has been deleted from the text at this point.

11. Georgiana Frederica (1792–1821), first wife of Henry, seventh Duke of Beaufort (1792–1853), was the daughter of Henry Fitzroy, son of Charles, first Lord Southampton, by Anne, sister of the celebrated Duke of Wellington and daughter of Garrett, first Earl of Mornington. Baron Southampton married in 1758 Anne, daughter of Sir Peter Warren and Susannah, daughter of Stephen De Lancey, the Huguenot. (*Complete Peerage,* II, 56; XII, Part I, 135–36.)

JOURNAL XXXVI

12 MARCH TO 14 MARCH 1848

Sunday, 12 March.

Genesis. A cold night. No church to-day, and read service at home. It grew milder towards noon, and began to rain in the evening. The accounts by to-day's mail say that the Senate has approved of the Trist [1] treaty, with certain exceptions. Begins to rain, and threatens a thaw, and a break up. Mr. Van Schaa[c]k's letter came in Home Journal.[2]

1. The Treaty of Guadalupe Hidalgo, which set the terms of the peace with Mexico and which was negotiated by Nicholas P. Trist, chief clerk of the State Department, was signed on 8 January and ratified by the Senate on 10 March 1848.
2. See Cooper's letter for *The Home Journal,* 15–23? March 1848.

Monday, 13 March.

Genesis. Grew colder in the night, and has been all day a most unpleasant, chilling day, snowing a little. This month is very reluctant and cold, without being very cold. It is better for us, however, than warmer weather. No papers to-night. Chess — beat and beat. A long talk in the evening with Paul about Junius. He reasons well, and laughs at the notion of Horace Walpole's having been Junius.

Tuesday, 14 March.

Genesis — A cold, disagreeably wintry day. The weather has now been good January weather for nearly the whole month. Went to the chalet but got only three eggs. Found all *my* cattle eating *straw,* and my man's shut up, well supplied with the best of my hay! So the world wags. Chess — wify rather walloped me. She enjoys success so much, I like to see her beat.

MANUSCRIPT: Cooper Collection, Yale University Library. PUBLISHED: *Correspondence,* II, 744–45.

930. *To Benjamin Franklin Thompson*

Hall, Cooperstown, March 15th 1848

Dear Sir,

I was your classmate! [1] [Jacob] Sutherland entered my class, and left it at the end of a year. Bissel[l][2] Doughty,[3] Norton,[4] Wilkinson,[5] Waterman,[6] Lowndes Brown,[7] Lucius Smith,[8] Olcott,[9] Canfield,[10] two Huntington cousins,[11] Bliss,[12] Mosel[e]y,[13] Goodwin [14] &c &c — I remember you, but did not recollect your class. I also lost sight of you, which is explained by your letter.

My family is from New Jersey, having been at the same place, opposite to Philadelphia, where it still owns a handsome estate, ever since 1687. We came from Buckinghamshire in 1679, went to Burlington, and my great-grand-father crossed the river into Bucks, Pennsylvania, about the year 1700. My grandfather and father were born in Bucks — My father came to this place in 1786, and we have been here ever since. My descent in this country runs thus, William (emigrant), James; William; James; William,[15] James Fenimore Cooper. My father was the first First Judge of this county (Otsego), and was first elected to Congress in 1794. In 1801 he resigned all his public situations, and died in 1809. We have given many members to Congress. John Cooper,[16] who was elected to the Congress of 1776, but did not attend, being much engaged in the Provincial Congress at Trenton, where the battle was really fought, was a cousin of my grandfather. Richard Matlack Cooper,[17] Wm. R. Cooper,[18] all of New Jersey, M. C— and Thomas[19] (I think) of Delaware M. C— as well as William Cooper[20] late Governor of the State, James of Pennsylvania,[21] M. C. are all of our race.

If I told you that John De Lancey, son of Peter & Elisabeth Colden, married a Ludlum, I was wrong. He married [Dorothy] Wickham.[22]

I could give most of the dates,[23] but not without a long search among old papers, and I am just now on the wing for town. At one time I thought of printing for private use, an account of the connections of my own family, and made large collections, but abandoned the idea, and have put my papers away where it would take Sam Jones himself to find them. Look at the Home Journal of this week and the next.

Yours truly

B. F. Thompson Esquire J. Fenimore Cooper

MANUSCRIPT: Lee Kohns Memorial Collection, The New York Public Library.

Cooper's classmate at Yale from 1803 to about 1804, Thompson (1784–1849, Yale n.g.) became a physician (1808?–1818), then a lawyer (1821–1849), serving as district attorney in Queens County, New York, from 1826 to 1836. With revisions in 1843 and 1918, his *History of Long Island* has been a standard work since its publication in 1839. (Charles J. Werner, "Biography of Benjamin F. Thompson," in Thompson's *History of Long Island from Its Discovery and Settlement to the Present Time*, 3rd ed. [New York: Robert H. Dodd, 1918], I, xxv–1.)

1. Not suspecting his old acquaintance with Cooper, Thompson read Cooper's letters in *The Home Journal* and, in a letter dated Hempstead, Long Island, 20 February 1848, asked the novelist for genealogical information on the De Lancey family for the third edition of his *History*. In a letter of 8 March (unlocated), Cooper evidently queried Thompson about his attendance at Yale; for Thompson replied on 13 March: "I was of the class in Yale College which graduated in 1806, but did not graduate myself, having only remained at New Haven about two years. The late Judge Southerland [*sic*] was of my class, but in consequence of ill health, he was absent a year, & finally joined the class that graduated in 1807. The present

Gov. of Connecticut Clark Bissell was a class mate, & we have kept up our acquaintance ever since — Isaac M. Ely and Chas. J. Doughty who were of the same class have been dead about two years." (MSS: YCAL.)

2. Clark Bissell (1782–1857, Yale 1806), lawyer and jurist, was elected governor of Connecticut in 1847 and 1848. He later taught law at Yale. (Dexter, *Graduates of Yale College*, VI, 6–8.)

3. Charles John Doughty (1784–1844, Yale 1806), lawyer, served successively as pastor of two Swedenborgian churches in New York City (Dexter, *Graduates of Yale College*, VI, 25).

4. Heman Norton (1785–1847, Yale 1806), who began life as a farmer, became a merchant in New York State at Canandaigua, Rochester, and New York (Dexter, *Graduates of Yale College*, VI, 48–49).

5. Robert Wilkinson (1786–1849, Yale 1806) was a lawyer in Glens Falls and Poughkeepsie, New York (Dexter, *Graduates of Yale College*, VI, 80–81).

6. See Cooper to J. A. Collier, 14 December 1832.

7. Rawlins Lowndes Brown (d. 1845?, Yale 1806) served in the United States infantry from 1812 to 1819 (Dexter, *Graduates of Yale College*, VI, 10–11).

8. See Cooper to W. H. De Lancey, 5 October 1838.

9. George Olcott (1785–1864, Yale 1805) was a lawyer and banker in Charlestown, New Hampshire (Dexter, *Graduates of Yale College*, V, 786–88).

10. Henry Judson Canfield (1789–1856, Yale 1806), lawyer, managed his father's extensive properties at Canfield, Ohio (Dexter, *Graduates of Yale College*, VI, 12).

11. Jabez Williams Huntington (1788–1847, Yale 1806), lawyer and jurist, served as United States senator from 1840 to his death. His cousin Nathaniel Gilbert Huntington (1785–1848, Yale 1806) was a Congregational minister at Woodbridge, Connecticut, until he retired in 1823 because of ill health to supervise a small farm. (Dexter, *Graduates of Yale College*, VI, 38–42.)

12. Edmund Bliss (1786–1821, Yale 1806) became a lawyer in Springfield, Massachusetts (Dexter, *Graduates of Yale College*, VI, 9).

13. Charles Moseley (1786?–1815, Yale 1806) studied law and began to practice in Hartford, Connecticut, before his early death (Dexter, *Graduates of Yale College*, VI, 46).

14. George Goodwin (1786–1878, Yale 1806) entered a grocer's business but became a bookseller, printer, and publisher in Hartford and East Hartford, Connecticut (Dexter, *Graduates of Yale College*, VI, 31–32).

15. Comma supplied.

16. See Cooper to Paul Fenimore Cooper, 17 February 1841.

17. See Cooper to Richard Cooper, 25 May 1831.

18. William Raworth Cooper (1793–1856), a farmer of Gloucester County, New Jersey, served from 1839 to 1841 as a Democrat in the Twenty-sixth Congress (*BDAC*).

19. Thomas Cooper (1764–1829), a lawyer of Sussex County, Delaware, was a Federalist representative in Congress from 1813 to 1817 (*BDAC*).

20. William B. Cooper (1770?–1848), lawyer and jurist of Laurel in Sussex County, served as governor of Delaware from 1841 to 1845 (Henry C. Conrad, *History of the State of Delaware* [Wilmington, Delaware: privately published, 1908], III, 838).

21. James Cooper (1810–1863, Washington [Washington and Jefferson College] 1832), lawyer and general, served as a Whig congressman from 1839 to 1843 and as a United States senator from 1849 to 1855 (*BDAC*).

22. Cooper wrote "Frances." See Cooper to E. F. De Lancey, 10 March 1848.

23. Referring to Cooper's letter of 8 March answering queries about the De Lancey family, Thompson had written on 13 March: "I should have been gratified had you given the dates of births, marriages & deaths, but this was probably out of your power — It is curious that we should have all been so much mistaken in

the date of Gov. De Lancey's death — You fix his death in July 1760, but do not name the day." (MS: YCAL.)

931. *To George Pope Morris and Nathaniel Parker Willis, for* The Home Journal

[15–23? March 1848]

Messrs. Editors: —

Several private letters have been written to me, in addition to the published communication of Mr. Van Schaack.[1] They leave no doubt that I was mistaken in saying that Brig. Gen. De Lancey died in the war. He unquestionably did die at Beverley, in 1785, and his body is interred in the choir of the Minster, while a monument, standing near the transept, records his services. By an extract from a manuscript history of the Revolution, written by the late Judge Thomas Jones, of Fort Neck, and which manuscript is now in the possession of the De Lancey family, I also learn that Oliver, sen., left New-York at the evacuation, in 1783, went to England, and died at Beverley.[2]

My own mistake has arisen from some strange misapprehension of the meaning of one whom I was questioning on such subjects, with a view to print a little family history for private use. My informant's mind has probably reverted to some other person, when I supposed he was talking of Oliver De Lancey. My error has been one of more than thirty years standing, and, in that time, I may have misstated the facts in writing to some twenty persons.

Whether Gen. De Lancey was in parliament, or not, does not appear by my letters. I said he was *not,* because I believed him *dead*; but now, that he is so unexpectedly revived, I profess to have no knowledge on the subject.[3] I can see no reason why he should choose Beverley for a residence; still, if he went to England, he must live somewhere, and he might select that town, as well as any other. If really a member *from* Beverley, it would at once explain his wish to die there. Oliver De Lancey, sen., so far as I can discover, had not a drop of English blood in his veins. His father was a Frenchman, and of purely French extraction, for centuries. His mother was a Van Cortlandt; *her* mother a Schuyler; and *her* mother, a lady from Holland,[4] whose name I can neither spell nor pronounce; though Judge Benson,[5] my authority for this latter fact, tried hard to teach me how to do both.

I think it probable, moreover, that of the three conjectures concerning the allusions in the memoirs of Mr. Van Schaack, that of Mr. Sabine's is the true one, while Mr. H. C. Van Schaack and myself are mistaken. Mr. Van Schaack thinks that Mr. Watts referred to the elder Beverley Robinson.[6] He is probably ignorant that Mr. Watts and General De Lancey were brothers-in-law, a circumstance that, taken in connection with the facts that Oliver, sen., did certainly die at Beverley, as well as the date of his (Mr. Watt's) letter, renders it highly probable that Mr. Sabine's conjecture, after all, is the true one.

In all other respects, I believe, my statements are accurate, and Mr. Sabine has been misled. I do not now allude to the outrage on Gen. Woodhull, about which I never professed to know anything beyond the authority quoted. I learn that Mr. Sabine has some imposing authority on this point, to which, however, he made no reference in his book; but, as I see you promise us a letter from that gentleman on the subject, I shall reserve my remarks until it appears.[7]

Mr. Van Schaack is quite right in supposing I did not question Mr. Sabine's *intentions*. I think as much was distinctly said in my former letter; still, he has not consulted good authorities, in very many instances, in reference to persons and families of the middle states. Take one instance in proof of what I say. At page 687, Mr. Sabine gives the issue of Harry White [*1732–1786*] and Eve Van Cortlandt [*1736–1836*]. One son he gives as *Lieutenant*-General [Henry] White [*1763–1822*]. I do not know that this gentleman is now living, but I think he must have been made a *general*, years since — I saw him a Lieutenant-General, nearly thirty years ago. The difference is of little moment as a fact in history, but in personal accounts, like those of Mr. Sabine, it becomes a mistake. The same error exists as to the rank of John White, whom Mr. Sabine calls *Rear*-Admiral White. This gentleman died as Sir John Chambers White [*d. 1845*], *Vice*-Admiral of the White, two or three years before Mr. Sabine's book appeared. Here he is two steps in naval rank out of the way, in addition to overlooking the Order of the Bath. Peter Jay *Monroe* [*1767–1833*] should be

Munro; and this gentleman, instead of marrying the Dowager Lady Hayes (Anne White) did in fact marry her sister, Margaret White [*1771–1837*]. All these errors are to be found in four consecutive lines of the book. They are, unquestionably, the fruits of difficulties inherent in the subject. I agree with Mr. Van Schaack in thinking the omissions of the most moment. I will point out a few. Mr. Sabine tells us that one of the daughters of Brig. Gen. [Cortlandt] Skinner [*1728–1799*], of New Jersey, married Sir Wm. Robinson, the late Commissary General; but he does not tell us that her sister [Maria] married the present Field Marshal Sir George Nugent, Bart. [*1757–1849*], at this hour the oldest officer, in the way of service, in the English army. He tells us that one son was Capt. John Skinner, of the royal packet service, between Dublin and Holyhead; but he does not tell us that another was Lieut. Gen. Philip [Kearny] Skinner, of the British Army. He does not tell us that Gens. De Lancey and Skinner were sons of two of the daughters of Stephen Van Cortlandt,[8] a fact of some interest, as connected with their common career in the Revolution.

On page 677, Mr. Sabine gives the name of John Watts, of whom he disposes in just four lines and one word. All that he says is accurate, but observe how much he omits. John Watts, the gentleman mentioned by Mr. Van Schaack, married Anne De Lancey [*1723–1775*], a daughter of the Huguenot. Of children, that grew up and married, there were three sons, Robert, John, and Stephen, and four daughters. Robert [*b. 1743*] married Lady Mary Alexander, a daughter of Lord Sterling's,[9] and has left a numerous issue. John [*1749–1836*], the person whom Mr. Sabine calls "the late venerable John Watts," and who made the munificent donation to the Orphan Asylum, married his cousin-german, Jane De Lancey [*1756–1809*], and left descendants, one of whom is the Captain Philip Kearny [*1814–1862*], 1st dragoons, who lost an arm lately, in charging up to the gates of Mexico. This last fact, however, was too recent to be mentioned by Mr. Sabine. Of the daughters, the only one named by Mr. Sabine, was Mary [*1753–1815*], who married Sir John Johnson [*1742–1830*]. This is accurate: Lady Johnson having been the mother of the late Sir Gordon Johnson, and the grandmother of the present Sir William. This is the only daughter Mr. Sabine mentions. Susan [*1747?–*

1823] married Philip Kearny [*d. 1798*], of New Jersey, and, among other children, was the mother of Stephen Watts Kearny [*1794–1848*], Brig. Gen. U. S. Army, whose services in New Mexico and California, and march across the continent, now form a part of the history of the country. Anne, (I think it was) was unquestionably the female mentioned in this brief allusion of Mr. Sabine's, at page 409, viz: – "*A* Captain Kennedy and *wife*, of New-York, went to England, and were there in 1785." I think Mr. Sabine, himself, will smile when he reads what follows.

Archibald Kennedy [*d. 1894*], the person named, was the descendant of a Scottish family of rank, a branch of which came to America early in the eighteenth century. He was put in the navy, where he served with reputation, and became the Commodore Kennedy, of whom all the old ante-revolutionists so often spoke. Mr. Sabine will find him mentioned in Franklin's Autobiography, as having saved the vessel in which both were going to Europe, from shipwreck.[10] Commodore Kennedy resided in the house at the corner of Broadway and the Battery; that has now been in possession of the Prime family, for the last thirty or forty years. He built that house, I believe. He was twice married; firstly, to a Macomb, an aunt of the late Major General Macomb's, I *think*, who died without issue.[11] His second wife was the Anne Watts [*1744–1793*], who was the mother of all his children, and who accompanied him to England. In 1792, the elder branch of the Kennedys failed, and Commodore Kennedy succeeded to the titles and large estates of his family, as Earl of Cassilis, (pronounced Cass-ils) in the kingdom of Scotland. Both Lord and Lady Cassilis died previously to 1795, when their oldest son [Archibald Kennedy, *1770–1846*], also born in America, succeeded [*1794*] as the twelfth earl. This Lord Cassilis was made a peer of the United Kingdom in 1806. He married an heiress [Margaret, *1772?–1848*] of the Erskines, whose estate was settled on the second son. This second son was subsequently known as the Hon. Mr. [John] Kennedy Erskine [*1802–1831*], and married one of the daughters [Lady Augusta Fitz-Clarence] of William IVth, by Mrs. Jordan. This lady was the Lady Kennedy Erskine, who was so often mentioned in the English journals, during the reign of her father. In consequence of the connection between their children, as I have always supposed, early in the reign of William IVth, Lord Cassilis was elevated in the peerage, and became Marquis of Ailsa, his present rank, if living. I advise Mr. Sabine to shake the Skinner family tree well; it will yield him excellent nuts to crack. I have been amused with the quotation Mr. Van Schaack has given us, in connection with the burning of the Bloomingdale House. It is as much as if the council of safety had said, "We meant to confiscate that house, and it was like burning our own property." [12] As respects the treatment of the females on that occasion, it was not very gentle certainly, but was probably a mere consequence of the wish that they might not escape and give the alarm. Besides servants, the only persons in the house were Mrs. De Lancey, (Phila Franks, of Philadelphia,) her daughter, Charlotte [*1761–1840*], afterwards the wife of Field Marshal Sir David Dundas [*1735–1820*], at one time Commander-in-chief of the British Army, and Elizabeth [*1758–1820*], a daughter of the Richard Floyd [*1731–1791*] mentioned by Mr. Sabine, at page 289. The last was subsequently the mother of my wife, and I have often heard her relate the particulars. Poor old Mrs. De Lancey, who was as deaf as an adder, hid herself in a dog-kennel, and came near being burned there; while her daughter and her friend, two of the loveliest young women America ever produced, wandered about in a wood, for hours, *barefooted*, in their night clothes, and in the month of November! Towards evening of the succeeding day, they stole into the seat of the Abthorpes, one of the adjoining houses.

I must conclude. It has been stated to me by letter, that Mr. Sabine is not alone in saying that Sir Wm. Draper married a daughter of *James* DeLancey. I have never supposed that Mr. Sabine has stated anything for which he did not *believe* he had authority. But he, and all others who have fancied this, are wrong, as I will now show by the highest proof of which the case admits. Your female readers, in particular, may pardon a good deal of dry explanation, for the sake of learning how marriages were managed in the olden time:

BY THE HONORABLE
CADWALLADER COLDEN, ESQUIRE,

His Majesty's Lieutenant Governor, and Commander-in-

Chief of the PROVINCE of NEW-YORK, and the Territories depending thereon in AMERICA.

TO ANY PROTESTANT MINISTER OF THE GOSPEL.

Whereas, There is a mutual purpose of marriage between Sir William Draper, Knight of the Bath, of the one party, and Miss Susanna De Lancey, daughter of the Honorable Oliver De Lancey, Esquire, of the other party, for which they have desired my License, and have given Bond, upon condition, that neither of them have any lawful Let, Impediment of Pre-Contract, Affinity, or Consanguinity, to hinder their being joined in the Holy Bands of Matrimony: – These are therefore to authorize and empower you, to join the said Sir William Draper and Susanna De Lancey in the Holy Bands of Matrimony, and them to pronounce man and wife.

Given under my Hand, and the Prerogative Seal of the Province of New-York, at Fort George, in the City of New-York, the Tenth day of October, in the Tenth Year of the Reign of our Sovereign Lord, GEORGE *the Third, by the Grace of* GOD, *of Great Britain, France, and Ireland,* KING, *Defender of the Faith, &c.,* Annoq: Domini, 1770.

CADWALLADER COLDEN.

By his Honor's Command,
GO. BANYAR, D. Sec'ry.

On the back of this license, which is *printed* with blanks for names and dates, and at one corner, is written, in a fair, round hand,

> "*The within named couple were married by me, Octo. the 13th,* 1770. SAM'L AUCHMUTY."

The original of this document has been lying among my papers five-and-thirty years, having descended to my wife from a maiden aunt, along with divers other curious relics.

Yours, &c.,
J. Fenimore Cooper.

SOURCE: *The Home Journal,* 25 March 1848.

1. Henry C. Van Schaack's letter in *The Home Journal* of 11 March 1848. See Cooper's letter of 1–7? February 1848 for *The Home Journal.*

2. See Edward Floyd De Lancey's edition of the *History of New York during the Revolutionary War . . . by Thomas Jones* (New York: The New-York Historical Society, 1879), I, 157.

3. Brigadier General Oliver De Lancey (1718–1785) did not serve in Parliament. His son General Oliver De Lancey (1749–1822) was M.P. for Maidstone from 1796 to 1802. (*DNB.*)

4. Brigadier General Oliver De Lancey's mother was Anne (Van Cortlandt) De Lancey, daughter of Gertrude (Schuyler) Van Cortlandt, daughter of Margareta (Van Slichtenhorst) Schuyler, daughter of Brant Arentse Van Slichtenhorst who

came to Beverwyck in 1648 as resident-director of the colony of Rensselaerwyck (George W. Schuyler, *Colonial New York: Philip Schuyler and His Family* [New York: Charles Scribner's Sons, 1885], I, 171, 185, 187; De Lancey, "Original Family Records," 71).

5. Lawyer, legislator, jurist, and author, Egbert Benson (1746–1833, King's College [Columbia] 1765) wrote a posthumously published monograph *Memoir on Dutch Names of Places* (1835) (*ACAB*).

6. Sabine quoted (*The American Loyalists,* 254) a letter dated London, 24 December 1785, from John Watts to Peter Van Schaack (Henry C. Van Schaack, *The Life of Peter Van Schaack,* 411) identifying as Brigadier General Oliver De Lancey the person alluded to in the following sentence: "Our old friend has at last taken his departure from Beverley, which he said should hold his bones." In his letter of 1–7? February 1848 for *The Home Journal,* Cooper suggested that the person referred to was a member of the Beverley Robinson family. Henry C. Van Schaack's conjecture that the person was the elder Beverley Robinson was contained in his letter in *The Home Journal* of 11 March 1848.

7. See Cooper's letter of 24 March 1848 for *The Home Journal.*

8. Brigadier General Oliver De Lancey's mother was Anne; Brigadier General Cortlandt Skinner's mother was Elizabeth (De Lancey, "Original Family Records," 71–72).

9. See Cooper to Henry Onderdonk, Jr., 11 March 1848.

10. See Max Farrand, ed., *The Autobiography of Benjamin Franklin* (Berkeley and Los Angeles: University of California Press, 1949), 204–05.

11. Cooper was in error here. Archibald Kennedy's first wife was Katherine (*d. 1768*), daughter of Peter Schuyler of New Jersey (*Complete Peerage,* III, 80).

12. Cooper referred to a letter from the Council of Safety to Governor Clinton concerning the burning of Brigadier General Oliver De Lancey's house: "We think this a most unequal method of waging war with the enemy, because neither we nor they can possibly destroy any but what are properly our own houses; and we fear that so conspicuous an example as the destruction of Mr. Delancey's mansion-house, will be most industriously followed by the enemy, to the ruin of many of the good subjects of this state. For those reasons, sir, we must earnestly entreat your utmost exertions to put a stop to practices, on our part, which may be attended with the most destructive retaliations by the enemy." (*The Home Journal,* 11 March 1848.)

JOURNAL XXXVII

15 MARCH TO 21 MARCH 1848

Wednesday, 15 March.

Genesis — A cold, cold night. The thermometer must have been down to something like ten above. Making ready to go to town. How wonderful is the sacrifice of Isaac by Abraham. Wife says the *place* is thought to be Calvary. Thermometer was *below* zero, this morning! Chess, both beating. Cold enough this evening.

Thursday, 16 March.

Genesis. What an extraordinary history! It is impossible for us to appreciate conduct, when a power like that of God is directly brought to bear on it — Obedience to him is our first law — Thermometer only 16° below zero this morning. Weather grows milder, however, this has been the coldest March I have ever known — Chess. Wifey gave an awful check-mate. Then a drawn-game, then I wore the laurel.

Friday, 17 March.

Genesis — Extraordinary! Extraordinary! Night not quite so cold as the last, but very wintry. Day clear, and sun has power. Thaws fast in the sun. I have postponed going below to next week. [Samuel] Nelson has got home, full of Washington news. 8° below zero this morning! Went to châlet on the ice — cool ride.

Saturday, 18 March.

Genesis. The more I read of this book the more I feel convinced that sin is "transgression against the Law," and nothing else. Much milder. Thermometer at 20° *above*, at day-light, and thawing, though cloudy, all day. Wind still at east. Chess, one game. I beat, when Judge Nelson came in, and sat until near ten — He is full of Washington news.

Sunday, 19 March.

Genesis — The history of Joseph — A colder night than the last, though not very cold. Day clear and bright. Not a robin has yet made its appearance. The astounding news of a revolution in France has just reached us. I have always thought that Louis Philippe would have to decamp, and I expect yet to see the Duc de Bordeaux on the Throne. [The] [1] rumour is that a republic is set up.

1. Cooper wrote "They."

Monday, 20 March.

Finished Genesis. Much milder to day, but drove wife to Châlet viâ the lake. Sleighing good on the lake, bad on the land. Preparing to go to town. Gave my orders on the farm and returned home to get ready for my journey. The papers continue to give us more tidings from France, all showing that the revolution is thorough. Chess, as usual, both beating.

Tuesday, 21 March.

This morning rose early, breakfasted and left home for town. Went in open wagon, with four horses. Roads not very bad, but covered with a light mud that spattered us all famously — Saved the cars by two hours. Reached Albany in good season and went to Delavan House. The ice not started, but a steam-boat only five miles from Albany. Saw the [Hamilton] Fishes.

MANUSCRIPT: Cooper Collection, Yale University Library. PUBLISHED: *Correspondence*, II, 745–46.

932. *To Mrs. Cooper*

Ned's Office. Tuesday 22d Mar. 1848

Dearest,

Got down well enough, no rain worth mentioning, unless it might be mud. Saw the girls,[1] Jemmy [2] and the [Hamilton] Fishes last evening. To day have been busy examining papers, &c &c. Intend to see the girls, again — *Heard* Madame & Blanche,[3] and am sorry to say neither is in very good taste.

The ice went off this morning, and a boat is getting ready to go down to-morrow, so that I hit the nail on the head. Gil Verplanck is here, as are various other folk. The Fishes have a house to themselves, in effect, and live very well, a little aristocratically perhaps.

Ned [Edward F. De Lancey] has two suits, he tells me, one of which is aunty's — He is a Commissioner for Ack — of Deeds, and has taken two acknowledgements to-day — 37½ cents. He is full of De Lancey documents, and is for carrying the war into the enemy's country. I am more moderate, and shall temper his ardour.

I expect to remain in town but one day, and push for P[hiladelphia]. *There* my business can not detain me long, and then back again.

The girls are crazy to come up with me, but this I do not know. I shall be back, I think, by the 10th, which will be eleven days before their vacation, and almost too much time to lose. Consider all this, consult with Dick, and let me know.

I hear no news. The Fishes will go down in a forth night, and glad enough to get back. Julia [Mrs. Hamilton Fish] looked well — a little thin, but quite well.

Adieu — with tenderest love to all — Do you miss the chess?

Yours

J. F. C.

MANUSCRIPT: Cooper Collection, Yale University Library.

1. Cooper's grandnieces Alice, daughter of Richard and Mary (Storrs) Cooper, and Georgianna, daughter of Charles J. and Hannah (Pomeroy) Woolson, were in school in Albany, probably at the Albany Female Academy.

2. James Stevenson.

3. Unidentified.

933. *To Edwin Croswell, for the* Albany Argus

[22–23? March 1848]

Whatever may be the termination of this recent antic in European politics, the world is now likely to learn the truth in reference to the real character of the dethroned monarch. Hitherto, flattery, the influence of his high position, and the selfishness of those in surrounding States, who preferred even *him*, to a republic, has kept back from the world facts that ought long since to have been as familiar as household terms. — The writer of this communication knew the late sovereign of France personally; had a hundred opportunities of forming an estimate of him, both as a man and as a Prince, that were wanting to those on this side of the water; and has never held but one opinion of the individual, or the sovereign, as is well known to many around him. The event that has just occurred, has been delayed longer than he supposed possible, for nothing but the early death of the king could possibly prevent it.

Louis Philippe d'Orleans is neither the man of talents, nor the man of probity (as a politician, at least,) for which he has had an unmerited reputation. His talents consist in cunning, and in little else. He was an arch dissimulator, and his position enabled him to practice this power to an extent that places all the exploits of Napoleon (one of rare qualifications as a political mystifier,) in the same way, altogether in the shade. The following brief catalogue of his exploits, as a deceiver, are proof of what I say.

Louis Philippe sent the duc de Mortemart [1] to stay the advance of Nicholas, in 1830, on the plea that he only meant to hold the throne for *the elder branch, until France was quieted.* — After remaining a few weeks at St. Petersburg, that highly respectable nobleman found that he had been duped, and returned to Paris in disgust. The fact substantially rests on his own statements. Marshall Maison, ambassador to Vienna,[2] and La Fitte, prime minister,[3] the last as honest a man as France possesses, both resigned in indignation, because each found that the king *was carrying on private communications that contradicted his public despatches.*

La Fayette told the writer of this article, that he and Louis Philippe had virtually given each other "*the lie,*" as respects the celebrated programme of the Hotel de Ville. The good old General regarded the king as the prince of dissimulators.

My limits admit of but one other instance of Louis Philippe's deep duplicity, though a hundred might be given.

In 1832, when the French were collecting that army on the northern frontier, which shortly after beseiged the citadel of Antwerp, a Peer of England reproached the ministers for suffering Belgium to be thus menaced. Another Peer, a whig, answered him by reminding the complainant that the tories, in 1831, had actually suffered the French to march to Brussels. Hereupon, Wellington — the premier of the preceding year — arose and said that the ministry of which he had been the head, allowed the French to enter Belgium because he held the "*pledges of the present head of the French Government, that he intended to carry out the provisions of the treaty of 1815.*" Lord Grey corroborated the truth of this statement. Here, then, were whigs and tories affirming that Louis Philippe had given *them* the same sort of pledges that he had given the duc de Mortemart!

There is no question that Louis Philippe was indifferent to the passage of our own indemnity law, in 1834. After having signed a treaty to pay us the money, I had it from La Fayette at the time, that he had said among his courtiers, that "he would cut us down to fifteen millions."

Louis Philippe owes his elevation to the throne to *circumstances*; his downfall to *himself*. Twenty times would he have been dethroned, had there been an alternative between him and the republic. The only available French Prince, he became a sort of *"roi inevitable,"* and he owed all his success to accidents. The monied interests sustained him as the friend of peace; hence all his power, all his seeming talent. — The intense selfishness of his character began to develop itself in time, and flattery, fraud, and cunning could no longer keep him on the throne.

I have never doubted as to the place that Louis Philippe was to fill in history. There he will appear as he ought to be represented, as a sovereign remarkable only for the boldness and extent of his duplicity, and as a signal instance of that high truth in morals which teaches us how apt "is cunning to overreach itself."

A Traveller.

SOURCE: *Albany Argus*, 24 March 1848.

The style and content of this piece betray Cooper's authorship. Of it Croswell wrote editorially: "The article, in another column, which sketches in outline some of the prominent traits in the character of Louis Philippe, is from a source distinguished in the reading world. The writer is perhaps as familiar with his subject as any one in this country. Although the opinion now expressed by him, is, as we know, the result of no sudden or new impression, but of convictions derived from observation and reflection; yet there are those whose opinions of public men undergo change with events. Such, if we recollect aright, has been the tone of the London Times. In the possession of the throne, and wielding the power of a great empire, Louis Philippe was ranked amongst the ablest of the monarchs of the age. Now, in his downfall and abdication — a fugitive perhaps from his government and country — he is only a creature of faults and weaknesses."

1. Victor Louis Victurnien de Mortemart (1783–1834) (*GE*).

2. Nicolas Joseph, Marquis de Maison (1771–1840), became ambassador to Vienna in 1831. He later served Louis Philippe as ambassador to St. Petersburg and as minister of war. (*GE*.)

3. Jacques Laffitte (1767–1844), the prominent financier and politician (*GE*).

JOURNAL XXXVIII

22 MARCH TO 24 MARCH 1848

Wednesday, 22 March.

Went to the capitol this morning, and examined documents in the library. Paid visits to my neices, Alice [Cooper] and Georgiann [Woolson], promising to take them home with me on my return. Met Maj. Douglass,[1] and had a long talk with him. It is a pity so able a man should not have a permanent situation.

Passed the evening with [James] Stevenson, Mrs. [Daniel D.] Barnard and the [Hamilton] Fishes, with lots of children, being there. The ice moved off this morning, quietly and without damage.

1. Major Douglass ("Major" was apparently employed as a Christian name) is listed as a boarder at Delavan House in *Hoffman's Albany Directory, and City Register, for the Years 1848 '49* (Albany: L. G. Hoffman, 1848).

Thursday, 23 March.

Went to see Barnard this morning. Said that he had seen J— Q. Adams last spring at Washington. He then said our union would last about 8 years. "I shall not see it, but you may." On Barnard's telling him how well he looked, he answered, "yes, I am pretty well, now; but I shall die in about a year." He did die in about a year! Left Albany this afternoon in the steam boat.

Friday, 24 March.

Reached town in good season, and went to the Globe — Town dirty, dirty, dirty. Globe nearly empty — Distributed my papers &c, and set about my affairs — Saw [Rufus W.] Griswold in the street, who came home with me. Jack Tier is doing well; better than common. I went to see no one, where my business did not call me — In the afternoon left for Philadelphia, arriving at nine.

MANUSCRIPT: Cooper Collection, Yale University Library. PUBLISHED: *Correspondence*, II, 746–47.

934. *To George Pope Morris and Nathaniel Parker Willis, for* The Home Journal.

Globe Hotel, New-York, March 24th, 1848.

Messrs. Editors: —

I have read the letter of Mr. Sabine with interest and attention. The affidavit he produces is formidable evidence, so far as the character of the witness is concerned, but defective I think in several respects.[1] The truth also compels me to say that I cannot think the statement of Colonel Troup fully sustains that of the American loyalists, even accepting the former as uncontrovertible. I believe that the candor of Mr. Sabine will induce him to admit this himself, when the matter is closely looked into. I am now on my way south, to return home in a few days. When once at my own working-table again, and among my papers, I shall ask the favor of inserting in your columns one other communication on this subject.

I will take this occasion to set Mr. Sabine right as to my understanding of another point. I have never supposed that the James De Lancey arrested and sent to Hartford, and to whom Mr. Jay's letter is addressed, was James, of New-York. I have very little doubt that he was right in thinking *this* individual and the James subsequently of Nova Scotia, to be the same person.[2] James [*1732–1800*], of New-York, was the elder brother of my wife's father, and such an event as his arrest, &c., could hardly have happened and we not know something about it. None of my family ever heard of such an occurrence, while I have often heard that James, of West Chester [*1747–1804*], *was* taken prisoner in the war, and sent somewhere to the eastward. John Jay was related, though not very nearly, to all of the name of De Lancey, his mother having been a grand-daughter (I think) of James Van Cortlandt, while Stephen De Lancey [*1663–1741*], the Huguenot, married a daughter [Anne] of Stephen Van Cortlandt, the brother of that James. This would make John Jay and Brigadier General [Oliver] De Lancey [*1718–1785*] second cousins, and John Jay and the two Jameses second-and-third cousins, which I believe was the precise degree of affinity between them.[3] But John Jay was much more intimate in the West Chester branch of the De Lanceys, than in either of the others; and this, I take it, explains the interest he took in the fate of James of that branch. James, of New-York, was one of the richest men in America, and would scarcely have stood in need of Mr. Jay's handsome offer of money. His immediate family would have taken care that he was early supplied with that great necessary, had he been arrested.

I did not include *this*, among the other supposed mistakes of Mr. Sabine, in my first letter, because, my testimony being wholly negative, that of never having heard of the arrest of James, of New-York, there was a *possibility* that Mr. Sabine might be right; yet, with all this caution, I fell into the great mistake of saying that Oliver De Lancey was dead, when in truth he was alive! A brief explanation as respects these two Jameses may assist Mr. Sabine hereafter.

James De Lancey [*1703–1760*], of New-York, Lieut. Governor, &c., was the eldest [*surviving*] son of the Huguenot, while Peter [*1705–1770*], of West Chester, was his youngest [*second surviving son*]. James [*1732–1800*] was the eldest son of James, Lieutenant Governor, and James [*1747–1804*] was the second, or third [*the fourth*], son of Peter, of West Chester.

James, of New-York, was educated at Corpus Christi College, Cambridge, England, in which college his father had been educated before him. On quitting college, he entered the army, rising to the rank of captain. In the unfortunate campaign against Ticonderoga, he was an aid of Abercrombie's. When his father died, or shortly after, Captain De Lancey sold out, inheriting the principal estates of his family. He married [*in 1771*] Margaret, a daughter of Chief Justice [William] Allen [*1704–1780*], of Pennsylvania, whose other daughter [Ann] married Richard (I think it was, though it may have been *John*, for I am writing with "*une plume d'auberge*,") Penn,[4] a proprietor and governor of that colony. The person called *Captain* De Lancey in the assembly journals of New-York, between 1769 and 1775, is *this* James; while his cousin, for a part of the time, figures in the same journals, as *Mr.* De Lancey.

Early in the Revolution, James, of New-York, went to England, whither he was followed, some time after, by his wife and children. Eventually he established himself at Bath. *He* was the vice president of the board of loyalists, &c., mentioned by Mr. Sabine. Five of the children of James De Lancey and Margaret Allen grew up, viz., two sons and three daughters. Charles [*1772–1840*], the eldest son, was in the navy, and died a bachelor. James [*1785–1857*], late Lieutenant Colonel 1st Dragoon Guards, is living, also a bachelor. Two of the daughters Anne [*1776?–1851*] and Susan [*1783–1866*], are single, and still living; while Margaret [*1773–1804*] married the present Sir Juckes [Granville-]Clifton, baronet, and died early, childless.

James, of West Chester, was a son of Peter De Lancey [*1705–1770*] and Elizabeth Colden. He was, for a considerable period, the sheriff of West Chester, an office in that day of credit and importance. He took a battalion in the brigade of his uncle, Oliver De Lancey, and was the only *Lieutenant Colonel James* De Lancey, who lived in that day.

In consequence of his familiarity with the county, Lieutenant Colonel James De Lancey was stationed much of his time in West Chester, to keep open the means of procuring supplies. His corps made free with the cattle of that part of the country, and got the *soubriquet* of "Cow Boys," in revenge for their knowledge in the article of beef. I do not know the name of his wife, nor those of his children.[5] Two, or three of the last, I have understood were put in the British army; and one, if not two of his sons, I believe, were killed in Canada, during the war of 1812.

I hold myself at the disposal of Mr. Sabine to communicate any facts, in my possession, that he may wish to learn on this subject, or that of his book generally. I could choose, however, to do so by letter, in preference to inflicting on the public traditions in which it probably takes very little interest.

Respectfully yours,
J. Fenimore Cooper.

SOURCE: *The Home Journal*, 1 April 1848.

1. In a letter dated Eastport, Maine, 19 February 1848, in *The Home Journal* of 18 March 1848, Sabine cited as his chief source on General Woodhull's death an affidavit by Woodhull's fellow prisoner Robert Troup, sworn to on 17 January 1777 and published by Henry Onderdonk, Jr., in *Documents and Letters Intended to Illustrate the Revolutionary Incidents of Queens County* . . . (New York: Leavitt, Trow and Company, 1846), 106.

2. The account of James De Lancey "of New York" in Sabine's *American Loyalists* (245–46) quoted a letter dated Poughkeepsie, New York, 2 January 1778, from John Jay to James De Lancey, a Tory friend then imprisoned in Hartford, Connecticut. Cooper's initial letter for *The Home Journal* stated that the James De Lancey mentioned here had been "confounded throughout the article with his cousin of the same name." In his reply of 19 February 1848, Sabine good-naturedly accepted Cooper's authority, maintaining only that he had used his sources with due care.

3. Cooper's account of the genealogical relationships appears to be correct. See William Jay, *The Life of John Jay* (New York: J. and J. Harper, 1833), I, 10, and De Lancey, "Original Family Records," 71.

4. Chief Justice Allen's daughter Ann (d. 1830) married John Penn (1729–1795) lieutenant governor of Pennsylvania, in 1766 (*DAB*).

5. According to D. A. Story, James De Lancey married Martha Tippett (1754?–1827) and had six sons, at least two of whom were in the British Army, and four daughters. See Story, *The deLanceys*, 50–56.

JOURNAL XXXIX
25 MARCH TO 27 MARCH 1848

Saturday, 25 March.

Saw [John] Fagan who promised to let me off early in the week. Got all ready for operations — In the evening went to Charles Ingersolls. Made a few other calls but found no one at home. Old Mrs. Cadwalader is dead, as is one of the Miss McCall's her sister.[1] I do not think the country is much in advance of New-York, or New York as much as usual in advance of Otsego. Sold bills to Fagan.

1. Harriet McCall (1777–1847), daughter of Archibald and Gertrude (Bayard) McCall, and her sister Mrs. Mary Cadwalader (1764–1848), widow of Lambert Cadwalader, a veteran of the First United States Congress (Gregory B. Keen, "The Descendants of Jöran Kyn, the Founder of Upland," *The Pennsylvania Magazine of History and Biography*, VI [1882], 209–16).

Sunday, 26 March.

I did not go to church to-day, but read in my room. Took a long walk before dinner, as far as Schuylkill, and meeting Mr. Timberlake,[1] returned as far as the Delaware, thus crossing the peninsula twice, making near five miles altogether. Went to see Dr. [Robert] Hare in the evening. His children have all flitted and left him and his wife alone. They were in good spirits — Prime [2] is at Naples.

1. Unidentified.
2. Frederick Prime (see Cooper to P. A. Jay, 14 September 1835) married as his second wife in 1838 Lydia (1818?–1883), daughter of Dr. Robert Hare (*Some Account of the Family of Prime of Rowley, Mass. . . .* [New York: 1887], 12).

Monday, 27 March.

Getting on rapidly with the volume, and shall be off tomorrow. Passed the day at home working, and the evening with [Dr. Thomas D.] Mutter. Met Mrs. McEwen [1] for the first time, and her son. Passed a very pleasant evening. Mutter is well, and his wife grows into a very fine woman. Clever she always was, and will be. We had much amusing chat.

1. Unidentified.

MANUSCRIPT: Cooper Collection, Yale University Library. PUBLISHED: *Correspondence*, II, 747–48.

935. *To Mrs. Cooper*

Washington House, Phil. March. 27th 1848

Dearest,

I came over on Saturday, but Fagan had sent me so many proofs through the mail, to New York, that I have very little to do here. He tells me I can get away to-morrow, in which case I shall be home the present week.

The season is very backward here, and, as yet, I have not seen a single spring bird. The spring is commencing, however, and the grass begins to show itself in favourable spots. I passed last evening with Dr. and Mrs. [Robert] Hare, and Mr. and Mrs. Charles Ingersoll. The former are quite alone, all their children having left them. The Primes [1] are in Italy, and intend remaining there some little time. *His* [Prime's] eldest daughter is seventeen. The son who had an *appartement* in the rear of the Dr's. dwelling is in Maryland on a farm.[2] The Dr. grows old, and Hare-Powell,[3] I am told, is very much broken, a decrepit old man, though five years his brother's junior. Mr. and Mrs. Clark Hare [4] were there, and *discussatory*, as usual. Joshua Fisher [5] was also there.

The Ingersolls, as is [their?] [6] wont, had much to tell me. Mrs. [Thomas] Willing is reviving a little. Her sister quite unwell — water-curish. Uncle Joe [Ingersoll] well and gay, the [Harry] McCalls in deep mourning on various accounts. A child [Alice De Lancey McCall]; a cousin, Peter's brother, down at the south,[7] and two aunts, Mrs. Cadwalader, and the oldest Miss [Harriet] McCall, all of whom have gone off this winter — Mrs. Erving with her husband, at Cincinnati. Miss Mary Wilcocks — still Miss Mary; staying with her sister.

I saw [Robert F.] Stockton in the streets, but could not get near enough to hail him. [James] Biddle looks uncommonly well, I hear, and is rejuvinated. Have not seen him. David Colden dined next to me to-day, on his way to Washington. Says Mrs. Wilkes is well, active and with all her faculties at eighty six.[8] The race was tough, about a hundred years since. Lady Cochrane is living and well. Her son, Sir Thomas, has been commanding in the China seas.[9]

Globe. Thursday Morning.

I got here yesterday, and did [not] intend to leave town for home until to-morrow, but Dick's letter has just reached me. I shall see John Jay, on the subject, and make an affidavit myself. The note is attached, I *believe* to [witness?] the notary's examination, in order to swear to the protest. Let Dick either send his papers to John Jay, or tell his lawyer to ask him for my affidavit. The whole thing is too palpable a trick to admit of a question.

I have paid the money as directed, and have got every thing from Mrs. Maitland in my possession. The shawl is very pretty and rich, and Charlotte says it is nearly twice as large as one that she paid $30 for, a few years since. It is such a shawl as $28 were paid for a few weeks since, even.

The desk and bible are bought. The [Theodore] Keeses are packing up and very busy.

I have not one line from you! I am almost ready to say, *as usual.*

I do not know whether it will be worth my while to remain here until Monday, though it can be done. Perhaps I may, though it will not be agreeable to me. After reading Dick again I see that I shall be obliged to remain.

I will write again on Saturday, unless something from home should induce me to quit town sooner. Quite well, with love to all —

J. F. C.

MANUSCRIPT: Cooper Collection, Yale University Library. PUBLISHED IN PART: *Correspondence,* II, 586–87.

1. Frederick and Lydia (Hare) Prime.

2. Probably Robert Harford Hare, fourth child of Dr. Robert and Harriet (Clark) Hare (Jordan, *Colonial Families of Philadelphia,* II, 977).

3. John Powel Hare (1786–1856), brother of Dr. Robert Hare, changed his name to John Hare-Powel on his adoption by a maternal aunt. He served as a colonel in the Army during the War of 1812 and later served as secretary of legation at the Court of St. James. (Jordan, *Colonial Families of Philadelphia,* II, 975.)

4. Lawyer, jurist, teacher, and scholar, John Innes Clark Hare (1817–1907, University of Pennsylvania 1834), son of Dr. Robert and Harriet (Clark) Hare, married Esther C., daughter of Horace and Elizabeth (Coxe) Binney (Jordan, *Colonial Families of Philadelphia,* II, 976–77).

5. Though he was never a particularly close friend of Cooper, Joshua Francis Fisher (1807–1873, Harvard 1825) was connected by family and friendship with the Ingersolls, the Willings, the Powels, the Middletons, and other families in Cooper's circle. Fisher was a historian, philanthropist, and political thinker, prominent in Philadelphia society. (*DAB.*)

6. Cooper wrote "there."

7. John Gibson McCall (d. 1848, College of New Jersey [Princeton] 1823), United States consul in Mexico (John H. Martin, *Martin's Bench and Bar of Philadelphia* [Philadelphia: Rees Welsh & Co., 1883], 239).

8. Son of Cadwallader D. Colden, David Cadwallader Colden (1797–1850, Union 1817), a New York lawyer noted for his unselfish devotion to his friends and to civic enterprises, married in 1819 Frances (1796–1877), daughter of Cooper's old friend Charles (1764–1833) and Janet (1762–1851) Wilkes (Edwin R. Purple, "Notes . . . of the Colden Family . . . ," *The New York Genealogical and Biographical Record*, IV [October 1873], 180–81; Ray C. Sawyer, *Gravestone Inscriptions of Trinity Cemetery, New York City* [1931, manuscript copy at the American Antiquarian Society], II, 25).

9. Rear Admiral Sir Thomas John Cochrane (1789–1872), commander of the Royal Navy in China seas from 1845 to 1847, was the son of Admiral Sir Alexander Forrester Inglis Cochrane (see Cooper to John Rodgers, 19 February 1827) and Maria, widow of Captain Sir Jacob Waite before she married Cochrane in 1788 (*DNB*). The Coldens and Cochranes were related.

JOURNAL XL

28 MARCH TO 29 MARCH 1848

Tuesday, 28 March.

Finished off to-day, and ⟨at 5 p. m. returned to New York, reaching the⟩ got ready for a departure in the morning. I have made mistakes [in] these entries, visiting [Joseph R.] Ingersoll, Sunday, [Dr. Robert] Hare Monday, and [Dr. Thomas D.] Mutter to-night. They all asked me to dine, but I excused myself on the plea of going away. No one seems to have much confidence in the immortality of the French republick. Clark Hare visited me this morning.

Wednesday, 29 March.

Breakfasted, and was off at nine. Reached New York at one. Found letters &c, and made my arrangements for leaving town to-morrow so as to get home on Friday, or Saturday if the girls go up — This kept me busy making purchases and transacting business. It has been a working day with me, and I have got through with a great deal —

MANUSCRIPT: Cooper Collection, Yale University Library. PUBLISHED: *Correspondence*, II, 748.

936. *To Richard Bentley*

New-York, March 30th 1848

Dear Sir,

By the Caledonia I send the remainder of Vol. Ist Oak Openings, and by the American Steamer a duplicate of the entire volume.

I have drawn for a second hundred pounds, against these sheets, which complete half the work.

I shall order the first 100 p.p. of vol. IId to be sent as soon as ready, in order that you may print at your convenience, but shall keep back the last of the book until the close of June. As for publication that must be matter of arrangement between us, and I should like to hear from you on the subject.

I shall not draw for the balance on this book (£150) until the last sheets go forward, or the end of June — my arrangements are made to that effect. The work might be got ready earlier, but I understand you not to wish to push the book. Luckily Burgess & Stringer are behind hand with Capt. Spike, which is just published, and are in no hurry.

I fear the world will be in trouble, by the end of a twelvemonth.[1] Your government is not likely to repeat the folly of 1792, but a war once commenced, no one can tell where it will end. As for a *democratic*-republick in France, it is an absurdity. An aristocratick — or narrow republick may exist quite as well as a monarchy if the upper classes will stand firm. In this sense England is a republick without encountering the dangers of electing an executive periodically. I sincerely hope your ministers will have the good sense to keep the peace —

I am about to publish a work on American Democracy. It will be a bold book, taking the bull by the horn, and showing the mistakes of popular opinion on that subject, as it exists here. I shall write you again shortly, touching this work, which, while it will be republican will also be conservative in a high degree —

Yours truly

Mr. R. Bentley. J. Fenimore Cooper

MANUSCRIPT: Cooper Collection, Yale University Library.

1. "What think you of the new French Revolution?" Bentley had asked in his

letter of 11 March. "In this country there is no desire on the part either of the Government or of the people to do any thing which may interfere with the friendly feeling existing between the two nations; and I trust *they* will endeavour to improve their new institutions without disturbing others. *Nous verrons.*" (MS: YCAL.)

JOURNAL XLI

30 MARCH TO 31 MARCH 1848

Thursday, 30 March.

This morning recieved letters which will compel me to remain here until Monday evening. Tiresome enough, but no help for it. Went to see Mrs. Ellet.[1] Found her in, and a nice little woman. Talked a great deal of her book. Then finished my purchases, and put my papers into John Jay's hands for preparation. He is to resist a motion in court for me.

1. A student of literature and history, foreign and domestic, Mrs. Elizabeth Fries (Lummis) Ellet (1818–1877) was in 1848 preparing her *Women of the American Revolution* (1848), which she said in a letter to Cooper dated New York, 11 March, was to present "biographical sketches of women of that day, distinguished for eminent position or influence, heroic conduct, & patriotic sacrifices." In answer to his letter (unlocated) indicating a willingness to assist, Mrs. Ellis wrote on 21 March thanking Cooper and inviting him to call at 96 Liberty Street at his convenience. (MSS: YCAL; *DAB*.)

Friday, 31 March.

Loafing about. Met Capt. [Samuel L.] Breese and went to look at some new steamers with him — the United States and the Southerner.[1] Both fine vessels; particularily the first. Had another but a very short interview with Mrs. [Elizabeth] Ellet. Dined with [Henry D.] Cruger nearly every day I have been here. His brother, Lewis, and sister, Caroline[2] are with him. Went to see Christie's minstrels this evening, with Cruger, and his two cousins.

1. The *United States,* built in 1847 as a New York-New Orleans steam packet, was the first steam vessel to cross the Atlantic relying entirely on steam. The *Southerner,* built in 1848 as a New York-Charleston packet, did briefly serve her original purpose. Operation of both ships was expensive, however; and the *United States* was sold to the Prussian government after only a few voyages. (William Armstrong Fairburn, *Merchant Sail* [Center Lovell, Maine: Fairburn Marine Educational Foundation, Inc., 1945–1955], 1330–32.)

2. A lawyer like his brother Henry and a hypochondriac, Lewis Trezevant Cruger (1803–1879) married Louise E. Williamson in 1855. Their unmarried sister

Anna Carolina Cruger (1808–1889) lived with Henry in New York and later at Saugerties, New York. (Cruger Family Chart.)

MANUSCRIPT: Cooper Collection, Yale University Library. PUBLISHED: *Correspondence*, II, 748–49.

937. *To John Fagan*

Globe. Friday morning [31 March 1848] [1]

Dear Fagan,

A couple of pretty dunderheads! Dunderhead you, and dunderhead I! Well, here they are *signed*. Write a line to say they are safe, and send it to Cooperstown; or you can say it when you remit, by the way.[2]

Thank you for the letter.[3] It related to a motion in court, and notified me of an important movement in good season.

Yours truly

Mr. John Fagan. J. Fenimore Cooper

MANUSCRIPT: Ferdinand Dreer Collection, The Historical Society of Pennsylvania. PUBLISHED: *A Catalogue of the Collection of Autographs Formed by Ferdinand Julius Dreer* (Philadelphia: privately printed, 1890), I, 137.

1. The date 31 March 1848, supplied in the *Catalogue* of the Dreer Collection, is confirmed by the date of Fagan's letter, 30 March 1848, to which Cooper here replied.

2. Fagan had written Cooper on 30 March enclosing two bills of exchange on Bentley which the novelist had forgotten to sign. Fagan acknowledged receipt of the signed documents on 5 April 1848. (MSS: YCAL.)

3. "I sent you by mail yesterday a packet which arrived here [in Philadelphia] from Cooperstown" (MS: Fagan to Cooper, 30 March 1848, YCAL).

938. *To Mrs. Cooper*

Globe, ⟨March.⟩ April 1st 1848

Dearest,

But for Dick's missive I should now have been between Albany and Schenectady. All *my* business is done, and I am impatient to be off. As usual Dick has forgotten something. He has not told me to whom he sends his papers, and I have been obliged to employ John Jay, thus getting two lawyers to do that which one might have performed.

I sent to Mr. [James S.] Sandford to know whether he would consent to delay, and John [Jay] brought me back for answer that he (Sandford) was willing to furnish us with all the necessary copies of the note &c — I immediately called on him and offered to try the cause as soon as my lawyer and papers could be got here, if he would admit the note and notice &c. But the shoe pinched. He intended no such thing, and is on another trick. I shall stay and fight him out, and make such an affidavit as will cause him to wince. I wish, however, Dick would think a little more, when he has any thing to do. Here I am waiting his movements, among one thousand lawyers without knowing to whom I am to apply.

A letter from Dick has just arrived. Tell him Sandford will consent to no delay. I can see what he is after. I rather think I shall leave the matter in John Jay's hands. He is quite as clever as [Daniel] Lord, understands himself, and has now some idea of what is to be done. No decent Judge can ever order us to try the cause until after June circuit at Detroit, and, after that circuit, I would rather try it than not. As for a non-suit that is out of the question.

I could not see Mrs. Laight. She has been ill, and does not quit her room, though better. Mrs. Bany[e?]r is better and John tells me will get well. She begins to sit up. The Maitlands are all well, and the children actually exceedingly pretty. Martha is a curious little thing and is rather the prettiest. They are painting, and the house is very uncomfo[r]table.

Last evening I went to see Christie's minstrels with [Henry D.] Cruger, Miss Caroline Cruger, Miss Matilda Oakley. It was amusing, but I got enough. That I am pretty well you will see in the fact that I walked from Mechanic's Hall to 23d street, at ten P. M. and thence down to the Globe, a distance altogether of near five miles — a large four certainly. Cruger was with me. We stopped at a fashionable confectioners, ½ past ten, and took some Roman Punch by way of keeping up our courage. Several parties came in from the Opera, in full dress, à la Naples — but, it was *gros* de Naples, rum folk, rum fashionables, and rum punch. New York always reminds me of the silk purse and the sow's ear.

I saw Mrs. [Elizabeth] Ellett yesterday. She is so so. Ardent and hard working, but with a husband and no children, which lessens one's interest in her labours. She told me that she was coming to see old Mrs. Wilson, in whose father's house *her* grandfather, a Gen. Maxwell,[1] had died.

I have made every purchase but the *garden* seeds. What does Sue want of *garden* seed? Flower seed I can understand, and I suppose that is what she means. I shall bring up a bundle.

By the way, I hear that Jack Tier takes unusually well. [Rufus W.] Griswold told me, yesterday, that it was thought one of the very best of my books. I do not so regard it, certainly, but condensed I dare say it reads off smoothly enough. The Crater is worth two of it. It is selling well. I have bought Now and Then,[2] but Griswold says that people are disappointed in it. Something Eyre[3] is much talked of, but he puts the Bachelor of the Albany[4] among the very best books of the season. Or as he politely expressed it, after Jack Tier, The Bachelor comes next. I should think there is nothing in common between them.

To day J. J. Astor goes to the tomb. It is said that he sent checks of $100,000 each to several grand children a few days before he died, in order to place them at their ease from the start. [Washington] Irving is an executor, and report says with a legacy of $50,000.[5] What an instinct that man has for gold! He is to be Astor's biographer! Columbus and John Jacob Astor. I dare say Irving will make the last the greatest man.

I met Bore[e]l[6] in the street the day his grand-papa breathed his last. He had letters from Paris. De Remusat[7] was in the palace in the morning of the 24th when the maitre d'hotel announced breakfast. De Remusat's feelings then broke out, just as the king said to him — "Allons — dejeunez avec nous Mons de Remusat — la reine sera charmée de vous voir &c — " "Sire, ab[i?]diquez — abdiquez en faveur du Comte de Paris — peutetre il y a encore du temps — abdiquez, Sire, je vous en prie." The king laughed, told him he was "un peu" disordered in mind. In less than half an hour after that conversation, the king and queen were wading through the mob in the place de la Concorde, to get into a cittadine, and were driven off at a gallop! You have doubtless seen all the details of his escape. I shall bring up some foreign papers — pos[s]ibly some French.

The changes produced by this last revolution will be very great. I shall not be surprised if Austria is compelled to concede, though I am persuaded France will be torn to pieces by factions.

[Herman] Thorn has just lost a suit with Mr. Jauncey. I believe he thought of setting up the defence that the children were not his sons, but was persuaded not to do it. Mrs. Thorn, however, talked very strongly against her daughter-in-law, who has now got $3500 per annum, for herself and children. The other son-in-law de Ferussac, has also prevailed against his papa, and the whole family is broken up. Thorn himself is eyed jealously, and has more suits depending with Jauncey's heirs.[8]

Young Rives is to marry Miss Barclay in May.[9] Several other engagements are spoken of, but I do not know the parties. The affair of Eliza Jay seems to be forgotten.

I shall get away from this place as soon as I can, but this motion may detain me unless Dick's papers arrive. Should they arrive, I shall probably leave town Monday evening, and be home next day. The [Theodore] Keeses may come with me.

Yours very tenderly
J. Fenimore Cooper

MANUSCRIPT: Paul Fenimore Cooper, Cooperstown, New York. PUBLISHED, IN PART: Cooper, *The Yale Review*, n.s. V, 826–27; *Correspondence*, II, 587–89.

1. Known as "Scotch Willie," General William Maxwell (c. 1733–1796) was a reliable and valuable soldier during critical Revolutionary campaigns in New Jersey and Pennsylvania. He was a member of the Provincial Congress at Trenton in 1775 and of the New Jersey Assembly in 1783. (*DAB*.)

2. Samuel Warren, *Now and Then* (Edinburgh and London: W. Blackwood and Sons, c. 1847).

3. *Jane Eyre. An Autobiography*, Currer Bell (Charlotte Brontë), ed. (New York: Harper & Brothers, 1848).

4. *The Bachelor of the Albany*. By the author [Marmion W. Savage] of *The Falcon Family* (New York: Harper & Brothers, 1848).

5. Astor died on 29 March 1848, and Irving received $10,592.66 as executor (Stanley T. Williams, *The Life of Washington Irving* [New York: Oxford University Press, 1935], II, 210, 392).

6. Cooper probably meant Robert Boreel of Holland who married Sarah, granddaughter of John Jacob Astor and daughter of Dorothea (Astor) and Walter Langdon of the New Hampshire Langdons (Richard H. Greene, *The Todd Genealogy, or Register of the Descendants of Adam Todd . . .* [New York: Wilbur & Hastings, 1867], 43, 45, 47).

7. Philosopher, author, and statesman, Charles François Marie, Comte de Rémusat (1797–1875), served in the French Chamber of Deputies from 1830 to 1847 and, from time to time, in cabinet posts (*GE*).

8. The Thorn-Jauncey dispute concerned money inherited by the Thorn family from Mrs. Thorn's father, the enormously wealthy William Jauncey. By officially changing their surnames from Thorn to Jauncey, the two elder sons of Herman Thorn — William and James — qualified in 1829 for large inherited estates from their grandfather. William died, intestate and single, in 1830 from a fall from his horse; and James died in the mid-1840's, leaving a widow and three children. Other, somewhat less generous provision was made for the other children.

The division of the money caused much dissention. Amadée, Comte de Ferussac, was married to Alice Thorn. (Joseph Outerbridge Brown, *The Jaunceys of New York* [New York: privately published, 1876], 20–24.)

9. Francis Robert Rives, son of William Cabell Rives, married Matilda Antonia Barclay on 16 May 1848 (Alexander Brown, *The Cabells and Their Kin . . .* [Boston and New York: Houghton Mifflin and Company, 1895], 414–15).

JOURNAL XLII

1 APRIL TO 4 APRIL

Saturday, 1 April.

Still loafing. This town is getting to be large. Last night I walked to twenty third street, with Miss [Caroline?] Cruger and Miss [Matilda] Oakley, a distance of near three miles from the Globe — What is more we walked back again. This afternoon did almost as much more, with Cruger. We supported nature by ices and Roman punch, by the way. Every where I see signs of rapid growth, and of an improving taste.

Sunday, 2 April.

Went to Trinity this morning, and heard Dr. Haight.[1] Sat in the Cruger pew. Mrs. Heyward was there — Dined with [Henry D.] Cruger. Peter Cruger, his sister Mrs. Heyward,[2] Lewis Cruger, and myself were the guests. As usual, a good dinner, and a good glass of wine. Staid until nine, went home, and went to bed. Cruger and I took a long walk this forenoon, or afternoon; between 4 and 5.

1. Benjamin I. Haight (1809–1879, Columbia 1828), rector first of St. Peter's and then of All Saints' in New York City, taught pastoral theology in the General Theological Seminary from 1837 to 1855 (*ACAB*).

2. Bertram Peter Cruger (1774–1854), usually referred to as Peter Cruger, and his half sister Mrs. Sarah Heyward (1787–1868), children of Nicholas Cruger by his first wife Anna de Nully and by his second wife Anna Markoe, respectively (Cruger Family Chart).

Monday, 3 April.

To-day gave myself up to the business in court. It detained me until one. Then I got ready and packed up. Ran over to say good bye to the Crugers, and left the Globe at 5. Went on board Isaac Newton. Bought three noble shad. Found Roy Keese on board who goes up before his parents, in order to get Edgewater in readiness.

Tuesday, 4 April.

Reached Albany early in the morning. Roy [Keese] took charge of the shad and went on, while I repaired to the Delavan [House]. Passed the day with Ned [Edward F. De Lancey], and Major Douglass, paying a visit to the girls to let them know when to be ready. [James] Stevenson has gone to Charleston, and when he is absent I find little to do in Albany. Saw Mrs. [Hamilton] Fish and Mrs. [John A.] Collier [1] in the former's carriage.

1. Mrs. Fish and Mrs. Collier were cousins.

MANUSCRIPT: Cooper Collection, Yale University Library. PUBLISHED: *Correspondence*, II, 749–50.

939. *To Edwin Croswell, for the* Albany Argus

[4? April 1848]

Mr. Editor —

All eyes are turned towards France. Can the French maintain a Republic, and what is to be the end of all this? — are questions which all ask and few seem ready to answer. The result is at the disposal of a wise Providence, which directs every thing for good, though by means that to us often seem contradictory and inexplicable. Our powers extend little beyond calculations, founded on the knowledge we have been able to glean, and the results are constantly disappointing the best founded of our hopes. Still, we may speculate on the future, and array the reasons and facts that lead us to our conclusions, defective as the last usually are.

France has made an immense progress in the art of self-government, during the last half century. In this respect, the country is no longer the same. As *theorists*, the French are the ablest politicians living; their weakness is in *practice*, where our own strength exists. The boldest violations of the Constitution are daily proposed by politicians in this country, but they do not produce the fruits which might be expected, because the nation is so accustomed to work in the harness it has placed on itself, that nothing seems seriously to arrest the movement of the great national car. As respects politics, the great difference between France and America is this: Among that class of the French who alone are entitled to be estimated at all in such a comparison, opinion is in advance of facts; in America, facts are, in nearly all things, in advance of opinion. This is not the popular notion, I am well aware; but I feel as certain of its justice as of any moral truth on which I have ever been required to reflect.

That country is safest, in which political opinion is behind its facts. When the last lead, they usually conduct the body politic at a safe pace and in a useful direction. Opinion being founded on speculation is apt to take the character of its parent, and run wide of the track of practical usefulness. Nevertheless, France is not to be misunderstood, by what appears on the surface. One of the ordinances of the Provisional Government, for instance, strikes most men here as childishly absurd. It is that which declares that the palaces are to be sold, and the avails distributed among the sufferers by the recent events. Who is to purchase a palace? is the idea that first presents itself to the mind. Palaces cost millions, and are nearly useless as respects the ordinary interests of life. The amount of the purchase money would probably be the value of the materials, less the cost of demolishing, and the risks of counter-revolutions. Why then has this ordinance been proclaimed? Unquestionably to stay the hands of the populace, who were destroying the palaces. In this manner, then, are we to judge of many of the primary measures of the new government.

If war occur, as may or may not be the case, I think the outward pressure will bind the nation together so compactly as to enable the republic to go on for years; possibly for an indefinite period. If the monarchs abstain from war, the danger to the internal peace of France will be greatly increased. The neighboring states have made one great acquisition in political knowledge, in the course of the changes of the present century. They can operate in Paris, by means of paid agents, almost as effectually as by armies in the field, and at infinitely less risk and cost. The extent to which such agencies are used in Europe, is incredible. Even the last government had recourse to it, in principle, in order to secure its power. It was proved in court early in the reign of Louis Philippe, that the agents of the government were active in getting up riots, the object being to harrass the National Guard and to render them hostile to the republicans, who had to bear all the blame. I have heard the shop-keepers of Paris, muttering their anathemas against "Messieurs les Republicains," as they closed their shutters at the sound of the "*rappel*," although I felt convinced that Vidoc[q] [1] and his corps were at work producing the disturbance, *by command*. Such is the character of one of the dangers with which the new government will have to contend.

To the idea that *all* classes in France now unite in believing that there is an end to the French monarchy, I do not subscribe. That all classes may *seem* thus to unite, for the moment, is probable enough; the object being to preserve order, stay the torrent, and prevent national bankruptcy. The last would be a calamity that would touch all classes of the rich — carlist as well as banker; republican as well as monarchist. But who that knows France, or the men, can believe that Mons. Berryer,[2] or Mons. de la Rochejaquel[e]in [3] is at heart a republican? As for Odilon Barrot, he presented an important feature in his political creed in the last words of a conversation held with him in 1830, when he said to me, "*Enfin, Monsieur, la France a besoin de se sentir gouvernée.*" [4] "In a word, sir, France has need to *feel* that she is *governed*." A more sagacious political axiom, in my judgment, was never uttered, in reference to France, than that which was contained in these few words. France must constantly *feel* that she is ruled, or she will not be ruled. Her habits require this.

I make no doubt that the Carlists have now strong hopes of seeing Henri V. on the throne of his ancestors; nor is the hope by any means as illusory as most may think. A vast proportion of France have a deep veneration for their ancient monarchs, notwithstanding all the bluster to the contrary. This is less true of the towns, than of the villages; of the north and east, than of the south and west. In the south and west, I make little doubt that, in a perfectly fair strife of voices, Henri V. would beat, even at this hour, the Republic itself. But Paris counts for so much in all the movements of France, that the minority literally has sway there. Let, however, a war occur, an invasion follow, and the white flag be again hoisted, and the partisans of the descendants of St. Louis would be found in thousands. The Duc de Bordeaux has made two blunders, each of which will lessen his chances of success. He has married an Austrian, and has grown fat. The latter circumstance will tell against him to a degree of which we have little notion here.

On quitting France some years after the accession of Louis Philippe, I brought to this country two opinions that I found no one here to coincide in — one related to the real character and abilities of Louis Philippe; the other to the position of the Duc de Bordeaux. My friends were all surprised to hear the sentiments then uttered, and the events predicted. They were these: that the reigning monarch would be dethroned, if he lived ten years, and would pass into history as an object of detestation, and a practiser of the vilest political frauds; and that Henri V. would one day ascend the throne of his family. The first of these predictions has come as near to its fulfilment as any human event could come; and I think the second is on the precise course that is most likely to produce the result I look for, and for eighteen years have not ceased to foretell. Still, I do not conceive myself to be a prophet, and am ready to admit that many events may occur to keep the head of the Bourbons to the hour of his death, in his present comparative obscurity. As for a Republic, that is to go on harmoniously, and with any thing like tolerable quiet, law and order, I hold it to be just as impracticable as it would be to set up a Doge of Venice and a Council of Ten in the State of New-York. One thing must be borne in mind, in relation to this subject. We hear only the voices of the revolutionists — the rest of the nation being temporarily mute. The day will come, however, when the last will speak.

A Traveller.

SOURCE: *Albany Argus*, 5 April 1848.

1. A thief, soldier, gambler, and convict before he became a celebrated detective, François Eugène Vidocq (1775?–1857) was employed by the French government for political purposes in the early 1830's (*GE*).

2. Antoine Pierre Berryer (1790–1868), a well-known lawyer and political orator, was a legitimist and champion of divine right (*GE*).

3. A legitimist who tried to reconcile monarchial principles and popular rights, Henri Auguste Georges Duverger, Marquis de La Rochejacquelein (1805–1867), was frequently at odds with his fellow legitimists (*GE*).

4. Camille Hyacinthe Odilon Barrot (1791–1873), in 1830 prefect of the

Seine at Paris and an active member of Lafayette's National Guards, served Louis Philippe and, later, Louis Napoleon in the hope of liberalizing their regimes, only to be cast off when his usefulness ended (*GE*). The Yale Cooper Collection contains a note of November 1830 from the Barrots inviting Cooper to dine on 18 November 1830 and another, dated 24 January 1831, inviting him to dine on 27 January 1831.

JOURNAL XLIII

5 APRIL TO 14 APRIL 1848

Wednesday, 5 April.

Left Albany with Alice [Cooper] and Georgianne [Woolson] at ½ past 7. Reached Fort Plain by 11, but could not get off until near 12. Went off in hired wagons, but met the stage on the hill — Changed passengers, and came wallowing on for nine mortal hours, to get through twenty two miles. I never knew the roads much worse. Reached Cooperstown at ½ past 9. P. M.

Thursday, 6 April.

Tired enough to-day. Scarcely left the house. Distributed presents, however, and settled the quarter with my children.[1] The spring is fairly opening. Find I have two calves, and all looking well. This evening the Keeses arrived, getting in about the same hour we did. Paul talks of venturing down.

1. Cooper employed later pages in the *Diary* to record allowances paid to his children. His daughters evidently received $25 a quarter and Paul, though not uniformly, $50.

Friday, 7 April.

Pleasant weather, and roads drying fast. To every body's astonishment mail came in at seven this evening. The improvement in the roads almost miraculous. I am preparing hot-beds &c, and have set [William] Coll[a?]r fairly at work to make garden, certainly three weeks earlier than we were last year, hot beds excepted — Chess, as usual, both beating.

Saturday, 8 April.

This morning Paul was off. No doubt he got down in good season as the mail was in before dark last night. At work in the garden. William [Collar] was down yesterday and to-day to haul manure for the hot-beds. Got most of them ready, and intend to get in many seeds next week. Chess, not much difference in the play.

Sunday, 9 April.

Exodus — Went to church this morning. One of the loveliest days of the season. Ice nearly gone, floating about in large cakes but of no consistency. No snow worth mentioning any where to be seen, and every sign of an early spring. Mail in by four o'clock this afternoon. A change of five hours in four days!

Monday, 10 April.

Exodus. Another lovely day, even milder than that of yesterday. The ice has altogether disappeared, and we have the lake clear again. John [Collar?] at work with his hot-beds. Got in melons and various other seeds. Went to Chalet with wife, where the farm is getting a spring look. Joe Tom [Husbands] bought and took away the boar. Chess, each beat, and that ignominously.

Tuesday, 11 April.

Another charming spring day. Exodus. Bill Coll[a?]r came to work to-day, and we are making great progress with the garden. More news of revolutions in Europe. Austria is among the constitutional countries. All this is well, as the people must gain by publicity, and by having a voice in taxing. Chess. Both beat. We play very rapidly, and not very well.

Wednesday, 12 April.

Exodus. Another delightful day, though it rained towards ten at night. The grass on the lawn is starting, and a week will make it green. Still at the garden. Got asparagus beds spaded and cleaned, and put in divers early seeds. It may be too soon for their own good. Chess, both beat as usual.

Thursday, 13 April.

Exodus. Weather cooler, and a good deal of snow fell. At one time it looked like leaving a coat of white, but it soon disappeared. Salted my asparagus beds, but no one worked in garden. It has not been a working day to day, in any form. Papers still full of the late news. The King of Prussia seems to be playing a great game. A German nation is a great and useful idea! Chess.

Friday, 14 April.

Exodus — More snow, but does not whiten the ground — The earth must have been too warm for that. [John] Collar and his son repairing fences. I had brine put on two of the asparagus beds this morning.

MANUSCRIPT: Cooper Collection, Yale University Librray. PUBLISHED: *Correspondence,* II, 750–52.

940. *To George Pope Morris and Nathaniel Parker Willis, for* The Home Journal

[15 April — 5 May? 1848]

Messrs. Editors: —

Mr. Sabine, in the *American Loyalists,* [*page 254,*] says, in connection with the question before us, and alluding to the late General De Lancey: —

> "His treatment of General Nathaniel Woodhull, an estimable Whig of New York, who became his prisoner in 1776, should never be forgotten. There seems no room to doubt, that, when that unfortunate gentleman surrendered his sword to De Lancey, he stipulated for, and was promised, protection; but that his Loyalist countryman basely struck him, and permitted his men to cut and hack him at pleasure."

As authority for this statement, Mr. Sabine now refers to the following deposition of the late Colonel Troup, which is to be found at page 106 of the Revolutionary Incidents of Queens County, edited by Mr. Henry Onderdonk, jun., who got *his* extract from a document published by the Provincial Congress of New-York, with a view to lay before the public the treatment extended to the American prisoners: — [1]

Robert Troup says,

> "that while he was confined on board a transport, Brigadier General Woodhull was also brought on board in a shocking mangled condition; that he asked the General the particulars of his capture, and *was told* [2] that he had been taken by a party of light-horse under command of Capt. Oliver Delancey; that he was asked by said Captain if he would surrender; that he answered in the affirmative, provided he would treat him like a gentleman, which Capt. Delancey assured him he would; whereupon the General delivered his sword, and that im-

mediately after the said Oliver Delancey, Jr., struck him; and others of his party, imitating his example, did cruelly cut and hack him in the manner he then was; that although he was in such a mangled and horrid situation, he had nevertheless been obliged to sleep on the filthy deck or bare floor of said transport, had not a lieutenant lent him a mattress; that Gen. Woodhull was afterwards carried to the hospital in the church of New Utrecht, where he perished, as the deponent was on good authority informed, through want of care and other necessaries."

The last words of this very deposition contradict, by necessary implication, I think, one of the statements connected with this subject — that one which says the account of General Woodhull was given in *articulo mortis. If he perished from neglect* some days after making his statement, it leaves a sufficiently fair inference that he did not believe himself to be dying at the time it was made. I do not attach much importance to the fact myself, though it comes quite fairly within the scope of a critical examination of the case.

Nor is this all: Colonel Troup does not say that General Woodhull told him anything. He says, "He asked the general the particulars," &c., "and *was told,*" &c. Now this of itself is a remarkable mode of testifying. Every word might be true, and General Woodhull have said nothing at all. The expression is so singular as to excite distrust; for why should not a witness on oath state a thing clearly, and in the usual mode, if that thing ever happened? According to this statement, a question may have been put to the general, and an attendant have given the reply.

Let any man see, in the first place, what the reader is required to believe, according to this alleged deposition — I say *alleged* deposition, for I do not find that the document itself is given, but simply this extract from it. He is to believe that a troop of horse, with hearts filled with vengeance, would pause to enter into terms of capitulation with a single man, and having got his sword, fell upon the victim, and cut and hacked at will upon him. He is to believe that one born and educated a gentleman, of established spirit and courage, a soldier by profession, and not one taking up arms in the heat of a civil war, was guilty, firstly, of the treachery imputed; secondly, of the cowardice; and lastly, of the barbarity; — and all without any other provocation than that which existed previously to the prisoner's giving up his sword, or his general offences against the king! And this he is to believe on *hearsay*, taking the very best view of the testimony, as an *ex parte* deposition, without any cross interrogatories, and all so [loosely][3] expressed, that the deposition might be true in its *term*, (not in its just spirit, I allow), and yet mislead the public. He is to believe all this, on account of a statement made in the dark moments of a revolution, when every human motive existed for urging men to espouse the cause of the insurgents, in a document that, on its face, was presented in order to produce a political effect. This very summer will probably produce fifty — nay, five hundred — similar depositions — all drawn with art, and circulated to affect an election.

Next come the contrary rumors that prevail near the scene of the event. Messrs. Wood and Thompson, annalists of Long Island, make Oliver De Lancey the preserver of General Woodhull, instead of his murderer,[4] which he would be if the story of the deposition is to be believed. It is true, that they impute the death of General Woodhull to a Major, or a Captain, Baird, of the [71st][5]; and why should not an officer of the name of De Lancey commit this act, as well as an officer of the name of Baird? For my own part, I have never supposed that any officer at all assailed General Woodhull, until inquiry brought the new and important testimony I shall presently lay before the reader. I did suppose it possible that some person of the name of Baird might have assailed the prisoner during the existence of some excitement, in consequence of General Woodhull's evading the demand to cry, "God save the king!" and that Oliver De Lancey interposed his authority to put an end to the injuries — rumor so confounding the name, as to accuse *Major* Baird. In the Scottish regiments, it will be remembered, half-a-dozen names will sometimes serve a whole company.

That a party of the [71st] was present at the capture of General Woodhull, I believe to be true. There are several statements that go to render this probable. There are also no less than four accounts of this event, given by Mr. Onderdonk himself — each of which conflicts with this of the deposition. Mr. Onderdonk says, as the substance of his own information, (p. 104): —

"As the General came out of the house, took his horse from under the shed, and laid his hands on the reins, the light-horse . . . galloped up, their swords gleaming in the lightning's red glare. The first salutation was, 'Surrender, you d——d rebel.' The General delivered his sword. 'Say God save the King,' they cried. His only reply was, 'God save all honest men.' 'God save the King,' they again shouted, and showered their sabre blows on his devoted head, and arm as it was uplifted to ward off the strokes."

This statement does not agree with that of Colonel Troup, in several essentials. It contains the account of the command to cry, "God save the King!" and General Woodhull's mode of evading compliance — which the deposition does not. Such an occurrence would, of itself, change the whole character of the affair, and take it out of the category of the deposition altogether.

At page 106, Mr. [Onderdonk][6] has another account, viz: —

"The Hartford Courant, September 9, '76, says: 'Woodhull refused to give up his sidearms, and was wounded on his head, *and had a bayonet thrust through his arm.*' "[7]

This last fact accords with the idea of a party of the [71st] being present. There is still another account given by Mr. Onderdonk, whose book is not a history, but a collection of materials for history, with occasional remarks by the editor. I shall reserve this fourth account until I produce some evidence of my own, for the reason that it strikes me that this particular view of the affair goes to corroborate the statements I have elsewhere discovered. With these hasty explanations made, I will now come more directly to the point.

When I first saw the statement in the *American Loyalists,* I believed it to be entirely new to me. Reflection, however, has satisfied me that I once before heard of this charge against Oliver De Lancey, though it was under circumstances not to produce much impression on my mind.

My wife was a daughter of the late John Peter De Lancey, of Mamaroneck, West Chester, and Elizabeth, daughter of Richard Floyd, of Mastick, Long Island. In consequence of this connection, both General De Lancey and General Woodhull were related to the De Lanceys of Mamaroneck. Oliver and John Peter De Lancey were not only brother's sons, but they were brother soldiers. Both had been educated in Europe, and placed in the army young. Oliver was the oldest, and had the highest rank; but John Peter was a field officer, in service in this country as early as in 1777, and was quite in a way to hear and know all the rumors of the camp. On the other hand, the Floyds and Woodhulls were related by blood — how near, I cannot stop to ascertain — but General Woodhull himself married Ruth Floyd [*1732–1822*], a cousin-german of Richard Floyd [*1731–1791*], of Mastick.[8]

I now distinctly remember a conversation, at Mamaroneck, which commenced by inquiries made by myself concerning General Woodhull, the affinity with him, &c. After conversing for some time, Mr. [John Peter] De Lancey, the Major De Lancey of 1777, it will be remembered, suddenly said: — "They endeavored to put the death of General Woodhull on my cousin, General De Lancey. Colonel Troup made an affidavit, which Gouverneur Morris published. Troup and Morris are (both were then living) respectable men, certainly — *but Oliver always indignantly denied it!*"

My recollections of this conversation are now so distinct, that I do not believe I have changed half-a-dozen words in the foregoing quotation. It was something gained to be assured, on the testimony of one who must have known the fact, that the accused strenuously denied the truth of the charge. It showed there were two sides to the question, at least.

It next occurred to me that the manuscript history, by Thomas Jones, of [Fort Neck],[9] to which I alluded in my [third][10] letter, *ought* certainly to make some allusion to this event. In order that the reader may appreciate his testimony, it may be well to show who this historian was. Thomas Jones was a Judge of the Supreme Court of New-York, under the crown, as indeed had been his father before him. He was the head of the very respectable family of Jones, of Queens County, having succeeded to its largest and oldest estate, that of [Fort Neck], which lies some fifteen or twenty miles from the spot where General Woodhull was captured. The Jones family has now furnished legislators and jurists to the colony and state more than a century. Judge David Jones [*1699–1775*], the father of Judge Thomas Jones, is better known to the provincial history by his title of "Mr. Speaker," having filled that office —

then one of distinction — many years. A sister of Judge Thomas Jones was married to Richard Floyd, of Mastick, and he was then connected with General Woodhull. Whether any other affinity existed between them or not, I cannot say, though I think it probable some distant connection must — as nearly all of the respectable old families of Long Island, particularly those of Queens and Suffolk, were more or less related. On the other hand, Judge Jones married Anne [*1745?–1817*], a daughter of James De Lancey, and a cousin-german of Oliver, the party accused. It will be seen that, from connection, *residence*, and social position, the historian was every way fitted for his task. It was next to impossible that he should not have heard the story and its contradiction, and that, undertaking to leave behind him a written account of the occurrences, he should not have used the means he possessed to learn the truth.

Of the authenticity of the manuscript, and of the accuracy of the quotations I am about to make, there can be no question. The history was written in England, after the war, as I understand it, and was left by Judge Jones, at his death, to his own great-niece, (who was his wife's niece, and the adopted daughter of both)[11] Anne, the widow of John Loudon McAdam, so well known for his improvements in the English roads; and by her it was bestowed on her brother, Dr. De Lancey, the Bishop of Western New-York, in whose possession it now is. The extract has been made by one of the family, at my request. I now quote from it, as it has been sent to me:

"General Nathaniel Woodhull," says Judge Jones, "was a native of Suffolk County, in the province of New York . . . When the war, which commenced in 1755, broke out, he entered the provincial service, and served the whole war in the different characters of Captain, Major, Lieutenant-Colonel, and Colonel. He behaved well as an officer, was bold and resolute. He was a rigid Presbyterian, of course a flaming republican. In 1769, he was elected a member to serve in General Assembly for the County of Suffolk. He continued in the House until the commotions in America commenced. In 1775, a Provincial Convention was elected for the Province of New York. Of this Convention he was a member, and was appointed their President, or Chairman. When Congress ordered an Army raised, and the Militia embodied, Woodhull was appointed Brigadier-General, and Commander-in-Chief of all the

Militia upon Long Island. When the British Army landed, he was upon his march down the Island to join the rebel army at Brookland. Before he reached Jamaica the battle of Brookland was decided. No possibility remained now of his joining Washington. He took up his quarters at an inn about two miles east of Jamaica. His Militia, panic struck, left him, and returned home, about forty excepted. A party of Light Horse were sent to Jamaica the evening after the battle, as an escort to some prisoners taken in the action. Receiving information where Woodhull was, they surrounded the house and made him and his party all prisoners. Not the least opposition was made, not a gun fired. They asked for quarter, and it was generously granted. It may, from this state of the case, be naturally asked, how the General came to be so desperately wounded as to die of those wounds a few days afterwards? The fact is shortly this. The General, after his surrender, favoured by the darkness of the night, attempted to make his escape, but being discovered by the sentries while attempting to get over a board fence, he received several strokes from their broad swords, particularly one upon the arm. He was carried on board a Man-of-War and treated with hospitality. The Surgeons advised amputation. To this he would not consent. The wound mortified, and he died in a few days. He bore the character of an honest man, an affectionate husband, a good master, and a kind parent; and I really believe he died in what he thought a good and righteous cause." [12]

Here is an entirely new version of the affair! Let us examine how far it is corroborated. At page 105, Mr. Onderdonk says: —

"Wm. Warne, who left Long Island, September 5, reports to Congress that a light-horse told him he had taken Gen. Woodhull in a barn in the dark, and before he would answer, when spoken to, the General had received a cut on the head and both arms."

Might not this have happened when General Woodhull was endeavoring to escape? Might not the demands to say, "God save the King!" [have] [13] then occurred, and the interposition of Oliver De Lancey, of which we hear so much, have been between these sentries and the party attempting to escape? Allowing for the minor errors that attend all accounts of this nature, the leading facts of Judge Jones are perfectly reconcilable with those of Wood and Thompson, (always excepting the *Major* Baird,) while they are perfectly irreconcilable with that of the legislative document.

The more I examine this legislative document, the less it commands my respect. It was so easy, so much in rule, and so *necessary* to state that General Woodhull "told" Lieutenant Troup, that the omission to do so obtains great significance. *Care had to be taken to avoid stating this.* The straightforward way would have been to say, "He asked the general the particulars of his capture, and *he* told him," &c., &c.; or "and was told by him"; or "by said general." Now, Mr. Troup, *a young lieutenant,* shocked at seeing a general officer so mangled, may well have put his questions; but it is even more probable that the answer came from some one *with* General Woodhull, than that a man of his rank, "in a shocking mangled condition," should disturb himself to go into all these details with a young subaltern.

The whole deposition has this character of looseness, or of art. It says, "He, (General Woodhull) notwithstanding his mangled condition, had, nevertheless, been obliged to sleep on the filthy deck, or bare floor of said transport — had *not a lieutenant lent him a mattress.*" [14] This is like saying he would have been compelled to do a thing, had he been so compelled. It is nonsense, and is evidently intended to make out a case, as indeed was the undeniable object of the whole legislative document. It was desirable to connect a De Lancey with any act of this sort, for the influence of the family was great in New-York, and the father of this very Captain De Lancey was just then raising a brigade for the crown. Hearsay is so much used in the affidavits, that the deponent is made to tell what he had *heard* concerning the death of General Woodhull, after they were separated! The whole document was to exhibit British cruelty — this particular affidavit forming only a small part of it.

It may be questioned whether Colonel Troup would acquiesce in such an equivocal affidavit. The true answer to this would be, to ask why he had not directly stated, in his affidavit, *who* told him these things. But Colonel Troup was then a young man, an ardent partisan, and probably did not draw up his own deposition. He stated nothing that was not true in terms, and that is as much as could be expected from most young men, with legislative machinery at work around them. Besides, if he and the party who drew up the affidavit *believed* the account given, no very great moral wrong was done. It was *all* hearsay, and the offence amounted to no more than confounding informants. Unpracticed men, with the best intentions, often make these mistakes. It is less than two years since I had occasion to correct, myself, two formal misstatements in connection with anti-rentism, that appeared in a report to the Senate of this State, made by a committee of its own body, and all on very pretty looking testimony, too. It was evidently the wish of the committee of 1776, to make as much of the witness as it could – else why ask him to testify to what he had *heard* as occurring at General Woodhull's death, when evidence of a direct character could not have been wanting? Those who told Colonel Troup might have also told the committee.

There is another point entitled to much consideration. Had Oliver De Lancey treated General Woodhull as stated in this affidavit, the fact must have been known to the British army. There was no possibility of concealing it. Now, whatever political paragraphists may say, an English army contains as many high-minded and humane gentlemen as any army in the world. In my opinion, Sir Henry Clinton would not have ventured to make a man who lay under the obloquy of such a charge, and involving cruelty, cowardice, treachery, and murder, his adjutant-general.

Mr. Sabine says that Oliver De Lancey "permitted" his men to "cut and hack" General Woodhull *"at pleasure."* I ask that gentleman to look again at the deposition. It does not even say that Oliver De Lancey *permitted* his men to touch the prisoner. Its statement is that he, himself, first *struck* him, (not with a sword, it is fair to presume, or the fact would have been so presented,) and that the men, "imitating his example," struck him in their turn. Now, all this, or the interference of the men, might have been against their officer's wish, instead of with his permission. Such things pass in a moment of time, and four or five sabres would have inflicted as many wounds, simultaneously. One thing is certain: had the men been "permitted to cut and hack at pleasure," the victim would, in all probability, have been cut to pieces. I think that even the deposition, defective and contradicted as it is, does not sustain the account of the *American Loyalists*. The difference between them might cover more than the difference between manslaughter and murder.

Respectfully yours,
J. Fenimore Cooper.

SOURCE: *The Home Journal,* 6 May 1848.

1. Sabine cited Troup's affidavit as a source in two letters: the first, dated Eastport, Maine, 19 February 1848, published in *The Home Journal* of 18 March 1848; and the second, dated Eastport, Maine, 31 March 1848, published in *The Home Journal* of 15 April 1848. Although Cooper was obviously puzzled by the text of Troup's affidavit, neither he nor Sabine knew at this point that it was inaccurately quoted in their source, Onderdonk's *Documents and Letters Intended to Illustrate the Revolutionary Incidents of Queens County.* See Cooper's letter of 20–27? May 1848 for *The Home Journal.*

2. Italics Cooper's. Onderdonk's omission here, without indication, of the phrase "by the said General" aroused Cooper's concern about the ambiguity of the passage.

3. A substitution, "loosely" for "loudly," indicated in Cooper's letter of 20–27? May 1848 for *The Home Journal.*

4. See Silas Wood, *A Sketch of the First Settlement of the Several Towns on Long-Island . . .* [Brooklyn: Alden Spooner, 1828], 128–30; and Benjamin F. Thompson, *The History of Long Island; from Its Discovery and Settlement, to the Present Time . . .* [New York: Gould, Banks & Co., 1843], II, 410–11.

5. The source, here and elsewhere, has "70th," corrected in Cooper's letter of 20–27? May 1848 for *The Home Journal.*

6. "Woodhull" in the source.

7. Italics Cooper's.

8. Mrs. Woodhull and Mrs. Cooper's mother were first cousins (John H. Jones, *The Jones Family of Long Island . . .* [New York: Tobias A. Wright, 1907], 194–95).

9. "Fertneck" in the source.

10. The source has "second."

11. Parentheses editorially supplied.

12. The quoted text has been brought into conformity with the text in Edward Floyd De Lancey's edition of the *History of New York during the Revolutionary War . . . by Thomas Jones* (New York: The New-York Historical Society, 1879), II, 331–32.

13. The word "have" is editorially supplied.

14. The passage, as quoted in Onderdonk's *Documents and Letters Intended to Illustrate the Revolutionary Incidents of Queens County,* page 106, reads: ". . . although he was in such a mangled and horrid situation, he had nevertheless been obliged to sleep on the filthy deck or bare floor of said transport, had not a lieutenant lent him a mattress."

941. *To Richard Bentley*

Hall, Cooperstown, N. Y. April 25th 1848

Dear Sir,

I know nothing of any Mr. Heuby [*Newby*], nor have I sold sheets or copy to any part of the world but to yourself, and my regular American publisher.[1] No one has any authority to dispose of this work, on my account.

Nothing will be easier than to give Mr. Heuby [*Newby*] a black eye. I shall take care to send you a fairly written manuscript of the few last chapters, which are snug enough yet in my cranium.

Only half the book has as yet gone into the stereotypers hands. If Mr. Newby, for I see that is his name, is an ordinarily honest man he will give up his scheme, for the sheets he possesses must be *stolen*. You are at perfect liberty to state this from me, in any way you please, to him.

As to the book give yourself no concern. We ordinarily finish the books in a few days that I give my personal attention to it, and you shall have *time* and manuscript. As for an assignment I annex one to this letter. Your publishers must be worse than ours, for no respectable house here would re-print under such circumstances.

Whatever may be your law, I apprehend Mr. Newby would hardly run the risk of publishing in the face of your edition, once out and in the market. Perhaps it may be well for me to write a paragraph especially for publication, should it be deemed necessary. This I will do hereafter. But give yourself no concern. You shall have several of the closing chapters in manuscript, and that in sufficient time to cover the publication, before the book *all* goes to press here. I shall keep the control in my hands.

I think this trick can be stopped in the office — Fagan, my stereotyper can manage to get a chapter so stereotyped, as to prevent copies getting abroad, and by locking up the plates mak[e] all secure in that way. I shall write to him on the subject. Let Mr. Newby throw away his money if he see fit — he will lose both cash and credit by the operation.

Yours in haste

Rich. Bentley Esquir[e] J. Fenimore Cooper

A pretty mess they are in in France!

P. S. A good deal of Openings *written*, several chapters, that is lying in my family bible, where I always keep my manuscript. Thieves never touch a bible.

It has just occurred to me that I can stereotype a chapter or two in this village. I have done this already, with three books, old editions, and Mr. Newby's agent would as soon think [of] going to the moon as sending here for his sheets. By keeping silent, this will leave a gap he can not jump over. Add to this the precautions of Fagan, of manuscript and of time, and you can have nothing to apprehend. Mr. Newby has cut his own throat by advertising — You will remember that Cooperstown is three hundred miles from Philadelphia.

MANUSCRIPT: Cooper Collection, Yale University Library.

1. As Cooper learned from Bentley's letter of 5 April 1848, Thomas Cantly Newby (the novelist at first misread the name), a London publisher at 72 Mortimer Street, Cavendish Square, had announced *The Oak Openings*. On sending a friend S. Morgan to interrogate Newby, Bentley discovered that the interloper had obtained as much of the text of the novel as himself and that Newby intended to publish, in spite of Morgan's warning, if his suppliers "fulfilled their promises." Bentley urged Cooper to investigate the fraud and to institute "summary proceedings"; he also requested "forthwith" a predated assignment of copyright and the remainder of the manuscript to enable him to anticipate the American appearance of *The Oak Openings* by a full month. Bentley's letter with a copy of Morgan's account of his interview with Newby, dated 5 April 1848 (MS: YCAL), is published in Spiller and Blackburn, *Bibliography*, 241–43.

JOURNAL XLIV

13 MAY TO 14 MAY 1848

Saturday, 13 May.

Numbers. Weather cool, and more rain towards evening — My planting gets on but slowly. Drove wife to Chalet, however, and went up to the new corn-field, and so down the cliff, across the new meadow. The grafts all look unusually well. Towards evening it rained smartly, with a promise of its continuing all night — Chess. Only one game which I got. No news this evening. Mexican treaty still in doubt.

Sunday, 14 May.

Numbers. Raining and cool. Most of us went to church, notwithstanding. About seventy persons attended. The Judge [Samuel Nelson] was there, having got home last evening. In the afternoon I read the service for my wife, who did not like to risk the weather. About five the wind went down, and it cleared — It seems as if all the clouds that passed in the last easterly storm, have been driven back by this from the west.

MANUSCRIPT: Cooper Collection, Yale University Library. PUBLISHED: *Correspondence*, II, 752.

942. *To George Pope Morris and Nathaniel Parker Willis, for* The Home Journal

[20–27? May 1848] [1]

Messrs. Editors: –

I confess that the reasoning of Mr. Onderdonk does not strike me as at all conclusive against the credit that is due to the history of Judge Jones. No one of his objections is unanswerable, and most of them manifest a bias to regard only one side of the question.

That Judge Jones was mistaken in supposing that General Woodhull was stopped on his march to join Washington by the battle of the 26th, I was aware at the time I copied the statement. To believe, however, that his mistake in this respect, contributes to show that his manuscript is "utterly worthless as an historical document," involves the necessity of believing that "Marshall's Life of Washington" is also "utterly worthless," for something very like the same reason.[2] These sweeping charges seldom convince. Judge Jones, in this particular, gave what appears to have been the prevailing opinion of the time; and he gave it temperately, without any imputation on General Woodhull's conduct. Now, Marshall, the highest American authority, has pretty much the same idea, with the addition of supposing that General Woodhull remained at or near Jamaica, contrary to his orders. All this has been explained since, but it was not until 1834, that even Judge Marshall was made aware of the nature of the particular duty on which General Woodhull was employed. The mistake of Judge Marshall, and its correction, is given at length, [*Volume II,*] p. 413 [*–18*], in "Thompson's History of Long Island." [3]

This is the only circumstance adduced by Mr. Onderdonk that appears to me to require a serious answer. The historical fact involved, is of no great general importance, and is of none whatever as connected with the particular inquiry before us. Judge Jones was mistaken on a very immaterial fact, so far as the main history of events was concerned, in common with Judge Marshall. He is in respectable company, and I question if "Marshall's Life of Washington" will lose its high character on account of the mistake into which its author fell.

Mr. Onderdonk tells us that, in quoting Judge Jones, he italicizes the mistakes of the writer. I will follow him, *seriatim*.[4] After pointing out the errors connected with what was certainly a mistake in supposing that General Woodhull wished to join Washington, he italicizes the word "quarters," though I do not see that he makes any comments on its use. If Judge Jones miscalled a halt "quarters," it is not a very grave offence in an unprinted work.

The next objection that Mr. Onderdonk raises, is to the statement of Judge Jones, that the dragoons were sent to escort prisoners from Jamaica to Brooklyn, "the evening after the battle." Mr. Onderdonk thinks there *were* no prisoners, and says, correctly enough, that the dragoons did not arrive until the evening of *the day* after the battle.

As respects the first objection, there might have been prisoners of whom Mr. Onderdonk knows nothing. Then a party might have been sent, under a misapprehension of the fact where the prisoners actually made were. Such things as useless marches and countermarches are of constant occurrence in war. What should we think of the historian who denied that General Taylor countermarched from near Victoria all the way to Monterey, in order to aid in repelling an attack on Saltillo, on the ground that Saltillo was not attacked!

Judge Jones evidently was aware of the charges against the English, in connection with the death of Gen. Woodhull, and it seems to me that he has given his statement expressly in reference to these charges. Now, the historian and the officer commanding these dragoons, were pretty nearly connected. They saw each other constantly, and, under the circumstances, I take it for granted that Judge Jones got many of his facts from Oliver De Lancey himself, and this among others. It was of no moment, in any sense, except to the truth, whether the dragoons were sent to escort prisoners, or to seize General Woodhull; and *why* should Judge Jones state the fact unless he had authority for it? Mr. Onderdonk gives no authority for *his* assertion that the dragoons went out to take General Woodhull.

As for the "evening after the battle," admitting it to be a mistake, it is merely a mistake of a day in a date, and a matter of very little moment. I confess, however, that I understood the writer to mean the evening of the next day. The omission of the words "of the day" being just such an error as an unprinted work would be apt to contain.

An uncorrected work should always be received with large allowances. Very few unpractised writers avoid such errors — errors of mere oversight. The expression was colloquial, and as many persons would probably understand it in one sense as in the other.

The use of the words "generously granted," in reference to the "quarter" given to the party with General Woodhull, convinces me that Judge Jones wrote with the charges distinctly in his mind. Mr. Onderdonk italicizes the words, and answers them by showing how the 71st (Highlanders) had bayoneted the Americans the previous day, on the field! Men in the heat of battle do many things they would not dream of doing in their cooler moments. After showing how these Highlanders *slaughtered* the Americans, Mr. Onderdonk, not very logically — to say nothing of any other quality — adds, that the facts "show that the British army regarded the Americans with much the same feeling as Mr. Cooper does the anti-renters." I quote the passage to give its writer the full benefit of his mode of illustrating.

"The manuscript speaks of Woodhull's having *one* wound on the arm," says Mr. Onderdonk. "There are persons now living, who have heard an eye-witness, and who watched at his bed-side that night, say his arm was hacked as a butcher would hack a shin of beef. There were seven gashes on the arm, but there may have been *one* deeper than the rest."

Here, I think, Mr. Onderdonk meets his own objection. Judge Jones obviously means to say that, the "particularly *one* (wound) on the arm" was the serious wound. We are told, elsewhere, that one cut was on the elbow, a hurt that produced the mortification, which terminated in death; and the allusion is so very apparent to this fact, that it strikes me the italics might have been spared in this instance, without at all weakening the criticism. To have made his own statement perfectly fair, moreover, Mr. Onderdonk ought to have added that Judge Jones says General Woodhull "received several strokes from their broadswords, particularly *one* on the arm."

"The manuscript says," continues Mr. Onderdonk, "Woodhull

was carried on board a *man-of-war*. There, considering his high rank, he ought to have been carried, but was not. Robert Troup, Esquire, was, with seventy or eighty officers, put on board a vessel used for conveying livestock from England, and while there, Woodhull was also brought on board. Troup's affidavit shows what *hospitality* Woodhull received."

As respects the preference between a *man-of-war* and a transport, for a wounded man, and as a rule, I think Mr. Onderdonk is evidently in an error. Certainly, if going off to a fleet containing empty transports and cruisers, a wounded man and among strangers, I should choose the transport in preference to the cruiser. A cruiser has all her room occupied. The captain alone has more room than he absolutely wants, and entering *his* cabin is like intruding into a private dwelling. On the other hand, empty transports usually are comfortable, and can be treated more like inns. It is a delicate thing to intrude into a vessel of war, and often leads to the most unpleasant collisions. I think any prudent commanding officer, who had empty transports at his disposal, would, *as an indulgence to his prisoners*, send them on board such vessels, instead of taking them into his cruisers.

Judge Jones was mistaken in calling the vessel a "man-of-war." This may have arisen from having been told that the prisoners had been sent aboard the "fleet." Very few landsmen understand the term "man-of-war," as it is used by seamen. Half the papers at the south speak daily of this "United States steamer," and that "United States ship," meaning transports or store-ships, that are owned by the government. A man-of-war's-man would call these craft "transports," or "store-ships," or, at most, "government vessels." Judge Jones may have been misinformed as to the character of the vessel in which the prisoners were kept, or he may have deceived himself in his terms. I think it pretty evident that Mr. Onderdonk is under the popular notion that a "man-of-war" is a ship of the line. This is a mistake; the *smallest* cruiser in that fleet having been just as much a "man-of-war" as the largest. A brig, or a schooner, is a "man-of-war," as well as a three-decker. A transport for beeves, is usually a large vessel, and, if thoroughly cleaned, and free from smell, would make a good hospital-ship, on account of its size. Mr. Onderdonk thinks General Woodhull's rank entitled him to especial attention. I think so, too; though I should not have selected a man-of-war to receive him, did a comfortable transport offer. Humanity is always policy. Notwithstanding Mr. Onderdonk's notions of British cruelty, it has been said, "Had Sir Guy Carleton [5] commanded, he would have conquered America by his kindness." Still, we are not to forget that the English recognized no rank in General Woodhull. In this they were perfectly consistent, and perhaps wise. He had no legal authority, according to their notions, and they had as much right to these notions as we had to ours. It was a struggle that was to get its character from the result. As respects this cattle-ship, I will add, that the English fleet was near, or quite three months in making its passage; and that there was consequently time to get rid of the oxen, and to air the ship. Such a vessel cleaned, is like any other vessel.

Mr. Onderdonk's last stricture is on Judge Jones' statement that General Woodhull refused to have his arm amputated, whereas he insists that the arm *was* amputated. Did Judge Jones and Mr. Onderdonk refer to the same moment of time, or to the same incident, the objection would have more weight. Judge Jones clearly refers to what passed on board ship, with the intention of showing that General Woodhull was not neglected, as well as of showing *why* he died, where, as he says, "The Surgeons advised amputation. To this he would not consent. The wound mortified, and he died in a few days." Now, all this is not only perfectly reconcilable with the fact, that after the prisoner was sent on shore he changed his mind, but it is perfectly *natural.* The reluctance of men to lose their limbs is well known, and what is here stated often happens. I have quite as much difficulty in believing that the English surgeons neglected their duty, in a case of this sort, as in believing that any officer behaved to General Woodhull as has been stated. Judge Jones means that General Woodhull died in consequence of refusing to submit to an amputation when first offered. This is true, if the offer were ever made. It is nowhere proved that such an offer was not made.

As for Colonel Troup's statement of the treatment offered to the prisoner, so far as it appears in the affidavit as published, I have already shown its value. He says that the general would have been obliged to lie on the naked deck, *had he not been supplied with a mattress by a lieutenant!* In the English service, a transport, almost uniformly, has a second-lieutenant in her, as the "agent." He controls everything. So that this statement, taking it the other end foremost, amounts to just this: — "The officer in command furnished the prisoner with a mattress, thereby *preventing* his lying on the naked deck." How differently a thing reads by looking at it on its two sides! As for the *deck,* this may, or may not have been a disadvantage. At anchor, in smooth water, it was probably the best place for a man in General Woodhull's situation. [Oliver Hazard] Perry died on his cabin-floor, and [Thomas] Claxton lay on the sand floor about the same time, I believe. [Horatio] Nelson died on a mattress in the Victory's cockpit, I think, though my memory may deceive me. I believe [James] Lawrence, also, died in some such situation.[6] It is an every-day occurrence on board ship, whether I am right or not in the instances last quoted.

The charge against Oliver De Lancey is of the most improbable nature, and ought to be sustained by the clearest proof. Instead of that, it seems to rest entirely on one of the flimsiest affidavits I ever read. Ex parte, got up for political effect, on its face — hearsay at the very best, with all the chances of misconception of meaning, and then so vague in its terms that the deponent does not distinctly say *who* told him a single thing to which he swears! The language usual to such documents is evaded, in order to produce the statement that is published. The circumstance that Mr. Troup *asked* General Woodhull how he got hurt, is set forth distinctly, though of no moment at all, *unless to assist in mystifying,* while the all important fact that Mr. Troup was told the story he repeats by the wounded man, is so slurred over as to tell nothing clearly. No man has a right to say, from that affidavit, that Mr. Troup swears that General Woodhull told him anything. On the contrary, the departure from the closeness and distinctness usual to fair-dealing affidavits, leaves a fair presumption that he did not. The very same number of words as those actually used, might have made the matter perfectly clear. "He asked the general the particulars of his capture, *who told him that*" — would have put this all important point beyond dispute.

"And he told him," would sound better, perhaps, or "was told by him." There was no want of skill in drawing up the affidavit, which is *otherwise* quite artistically done, and when the deponent says that he "was informed" that General Woodhull perished subsequently for want of care, the necessity of adding "on good authority," is felt.[7] No court in Christendom would accept this affidavit as establishing the fact that General Woodhull "told" Colonel Troup the account of his own capture.

Mr. Onderdonk attributes Judge Jones' mistakes to the fact that he was not at Fort Neck when the battle of Long Island was fought. Now, this reasoning happens to apply very well to the facts in which Judge Jones is clearly wrong, while it does not apply at all to the parts of his account that have any connection with the matter at issue. If Judge Jones had been at Fort Neck when General Woodhull marched down the island, he might not have made the mistake of supposing he did not reach Jamaica; but what could his absence have to do with the knowledge he subsequently obtained of the attempt to escape? He was at home when the affidavit appeared — was in the way of hearing all that was said about *that,* and learning the manner in which it was met. Oliver De Lancey was his wife's cousin; they saw each other constantly; and what is more, Judge Jones must have been in the constant habit of seeing *others* who were probably of the party at Jamaica. In a word, he was so situated as unavoidably to hear both sides of the question. Now, such a man, sitting down to leave a record of facts behind him — not to *publish to produce a political effect,* but to remain in manuscript as matter of record for his friends — would be very apt to state what he had ascertained on proper inquiry. He was often in Jamaica, and possessed all the necessary means to ascertain the truth touching a fact that had become matter of public interest. It is not reasonable to suppose he neglected to use these means. This is a very different matter from taking up a false impression as to General Woodhull's having got a few miles further, or a few miles less on his march.

Now, look at the probabilities. Mr. Woodhull was a political man, as well as a soldier. By English law, he was a rebel; liable to be hanged. He was the first man of that character, who had been taken with arms in his hands; or taken at all, I believe. The result must have troubled him. Then he is described as a bold, resolute man. It was night, and there was a thunder-storm. Judge Jones says that he attempted to escape. Mr. Onderdonk himself tells us that "the General came out of the house, *took his horse from under the shed, and laid his hands on the reins,*" when the dragoons came up. William Warne says, a dragoon told him he took General Woodhull *in a barn, in the dark,* and *refusing to answer,* the general received his hurts, etc.[8]

All this looks very much as if General Woodhull was endeavoring to profit by the darkness and the storm, and to get off. Mr. Onderdonk's particularity about his just getting the *reins of his horse,* is significant. He has doubtless heard this somewhere, and it sounds very much as if the general was about to mount, to be off. It is nowhere stated that he knew the dragoons were coming; and would he be likely to start in the height of the "lightning's red glare," unless with a design to escape?

It is admitted all round, that much ambiguity and doubt exists as to the case of General Woodhull. Mr. Onderdonk himself allows this, by the conflicting accounts he gives. Now this business of escaping is an affair that obtains its character from the result, as much as anything else in the world. When a man of dignified station is *caught* in an attempt to escape, no matter how elevated the motive, he suffers in public estimation, in a certain way. Any allusion to the event must be painful to such a man. This fact may have produced much of the confusion that exists in the accounts. When I ascertained that General Woodhull was said to have been wounded in attempting to escape, it at once occurred to me that a reluctance to dwell on the circumstances may have induced him to give such a mutilated and disjointed account to Colonel Troup as to have misled that witness; and this without any deliberate design to deceive, in either party. Such *may* have been the fact; but when the affidavit was closely examined, and the significant omission was properly noted, I came to the conclusion that some other person has been thus misled, which other person "told" Colonel Troup.

From the character of General Woodhull, I do not believe he attempted to violate a parole. It was not only natural, but it might have been his public duty, to try to get away if he could.

Still, a president of a state Congress might not think he appeared to advantage in an account of a *frustrated* attempt to escape, in which he was cut up by sentinels. Success is very necessary to make such things go down well, and one can easily understand that it would not be a subject much dilated on by the losing party. Even admitting that General Woodhull *did* make a statement to Colonel Troup, it was probably made under the influence of such feelings as to give it very little value. If the affidavit is good for anything, it proves of itself he could not have considered himself *in danger of dying* when he gave it. This is also proved by another circumstance: General Woodhull sent for his wife, when he supposed himself about to die, and this he did not, until he was removed to a building on shore, or some days after he went on board the transport.

The death of General Woodhull is a point in American history that deserves to be thoroughly investigated, and I am not sorry that this discussion has occurred. I feel satisfied that it will relieve the memory of a gallant soldier from a most unjust and severe imputation, that has arisen from political prejudices and political intrigues. These prejudices and intrigues rest, like a blight, on this country, even at the present hour; perverting facts, misleading opinion, and having the marked effect of placing unsuitable men in places of profit and power. Under this blight we possess *two* public opinions — a whig public opinion and a locofoco public opinion. Of independent, sound, healthful, manly public opinion, there is very little — almost none; and every effort to extricate truth from the tyrants of the land should be hailed with pleasure. We get so little of that sacred quality, that there is great danger of our not knowing it when we see it. As respects the main fact stated by Judge Jones, our reasoning ought to be very simple. He has either invented it, or he has heard it. I presume no one will affirm the first. If heard, then, we are to look at his sources of information, remembering that the point was publicly discussed at the time, and that his attention was drawn to the subject. I think there can be little doubt that he has given Oliver De Lancey's explanation.

I will take this occasion to say that several misprints occurred in my last letter, the consequence of a careless manner of writing.

"Fort Neck" is spelt "Fert Neck"; the "71st" is called the "70th" regiment; in one place "Woodhull" is printed for "Onderdonk," an oversight of my own, quite likely; "all so *loudly* expressed," should read "loosely expressed," etc.[9]

Very respectfully yours,
J. Fenimore Cooper.

SOURCE: *The Home Journal*, 3 June 1848.

1. Cooper here replied to a letter by Henry Onderdonk, Jr., dated Jamaica, L. I., 8 May 1848, published in *The Home Journal* for 20 May 1848. When he wrote this letter, he had almost certainly not read Onderdonk's second letter, dated Jamaica, L. I., 15 May 1848, published in *The Home Journal* for 27 May 1848.

2. See John Marshall, *The Life of George Washington* . . . [Philadelphia: C. P. Wayne, 1804], II, 439.

3. Thompson published John L. Lawrence's letter, dated 13 February 1834, correcting Marshall's error, together with Marshall's acknowledgment, dated 21 February 1834.

4. Cooper's replies to Onderdonk contain the substance of Onderdonk's objections to Judge Jones's *History*.

5. Sir Guy Carleton (1724–1808), a former governor of Quebec, arrived in New York on 5 May 1782 to succeed Sir Henry Clinton as commander in chief of the British forces in America. Carleton was noted for his policy of clemency. (*DNB*.)

6. Cooper may have been misled by the fondness of maritime artists for representing naval heroes dying on the decks of their ships in the thick of battle surrounded by their officers and sailors, although none of the heroes mentioned here died in this manner. Perry died of yellow fever on 23 August 1819 while on a diplomatic mission to Venezuela. Claxton, mortally wounded on 10 September 1813 during the Battle of Lake Erie, lingered several weeks. Lord Nelson, carried below after his fatal wound on 21 October 1805, lived for three hours. Lawrence was taken to the wardroom after his injury, and he survived four days or until 4 June 1813. If any of the four died on a mattress on the floor, it was evidently, as Cooper argued, because this was the most comfortable position that could be contrived for him.

7. Cooper assumed that Onderdonk quoted Troup's affidavit accurately in *Documents and Letters Intended to Illustrate the Revolutionary Incidents of Queens County*, page 106, since the passage is enclosed in quotation marks with no indications of changes or omissions. In fact, as Onderdonk confessed in his second letter in *The Home Journal* for 27 May 1848, the passage had been abridged and altered for popular consumption, though Onderdonk maintained that he had not changed the meaning. The original text, as Onderdonk now furnished it, with key words in italics, read: "that *deponent* asked the General the particulars of his capture, and was told *by the said General that* . . ."

8. See *Documents and Letters Intended to Illustrate the Revolutionary Incidents of Queens County*, 104–05.

9. The errors noted here have been corrected in the text of this edition.

In a long letter dated Jamaica, L. I., 17 June 1848, published in *The House Journal* for 8 July 1848, Onderdonk summarized his arguments and sought unsuccessfully to involve Cooper in further public correspondence. The novelist's final words on the subject of the controversy were expressed privately in his letter to Onderdonk of 30 October 1849.

Part Twenty-two

"VOX POPULI"

1848–1849

"VOX POPULI"

1848–1849

Political events of 1848, the year of the Communist Manifesto, corroborated or seemed to corroborate dramatically an interpretation of "*Vox populi, vox dei*" which Cooper had advanced in his Commencement Address at Geneva College on 4 August 1841. In that speech, whose text he burned immediately after delivery, Cooper developed the thoroughly heretical proposition: "Public Opinion is a despot in a Democracy." What is commonly accepted as the voice of the people, he argued in those pre-Orwellian times, may be merely the voice of interested politicians and journalists usurping the people's authority to maintain or advance their own power; and the mass opinion so generated, whatever sanction it may advertise, is all too likely to be misguided or worthless. Since an inevitable function of political language in a republic as in a monarchy is to gain assent, the semantics of the one is as liable to abuse and corruption as that of the other. Moreover, public opinion can be so manipulated by interested groups that it will reject the truth even when accompanied by incontestable evidence. The responsible citizen, Cooper evidently tried to impress on the seniors at Geneva College, must learn to penetrate the flattery of the demagogue, to measure theoretical assertions against actual possibilities, and to evaluate conflicting political claims with an open, inquiring, critical mind.

Though he had not been in Europe for fifteen years, Cooper at once detected the fallibility of the Jacobin professions that shook the thrones of Europe in the revolutions of 1848. The insincerity or naïveté of this rhetoric might be more expertly concealed; but its intention was essentially that of the French extremist Armand Barbès, who spoke bluntly in his *Société des Droits de l'Homme et du Citoyen*: "Be united, but calm; for in this lies your strength. Your number is such that it must suffice to manifest your will, and make you obtain all you desire. It is also such that you cannot desire anything but what is just. Your voice and your will are the voice and the will of God." Rallying the multitude with their libertarian slogans, revolutionaries in France, Italy, Prussia, and Austria succeeded during February, March, and April 1848 in displacing or profoundly modifying the established political regimes; but they were uniformly unsuccessful in transforming revolutionary excitement into durable republican governments. The difficulty, as Cooper had foretold, was a fatal discrepancy between theory and practice. The people were not omnipotent: they were not even reliably republican; and the unrealistic republican programs were usually products of inexperience. By the end of the summer of 1848, reactionaries were busy canceling liberal gains; and, by 2 December 1852, when Prince Louis Napoleon Bonaparte, president of the Second French Republic, had himself proclaimed emperor, they were outwardly triumphant. Cooper erred only in supporting that the French would crown the Bourbon Duke de Bordeaux, styled Henry V, instead of turning to the son of his (the novelist's) old acquaintances Hortense and Louis Bonaparte, former occupants of the throne of Holland.

In the United States, the peculiar alchemy latent in deference to popular opinion was amusingly illustrated in the presidential campaign of 1848. Zachary Taylor, the Whig candidate, owed his popularity almost entirely to his military exploits. Inexperienced and uncommitted in practical politics, he based his campaign chiefly on his expressed desire to fulfill the people's will — without troubling to specify his conception of what that will might be. He would use the veto sparingly, he promised, for fear of interfering with the wishes of the people as interpreted by their legislative representatives. Every Democrat, urged John M. Clayton, Taylor's spokesman in the Senate, "may vote for General Taylor without disgracing or degrading himself, because General Taylor admits that the will of the majority ought to govern, and every Democrat admits the same. Every Democrat, therefore, if he be a republican, may consistently vote for General Taylor. On the contrary, no true republican can support General Cass." The Democratic candidate Lewis Cass had sinned unpardonably, said the Whigs, by stealing the Democratic nomination from Martin Van Buren who thought he had a majority at the nominating convention. Cass's own overture to the people's voice was his doctrine of Popular Sovereignty (by which the slavery issue in new territory would be decided by local plebiscite); but the enigmatic posture of "Old Rough and Ready," poised above conflict, welcoming all supporters, and avoiding all controversy, was politically impervious. Such noncommittalism struck Cooper as a confession of vacuity; and, if he had been truly cynical about popular opinion, he would have expected Taylor to win. Conversely and ironically, he placed his expectation of success on Cass, with whom he had dined and conversed in Michigan during the campaign.

943. *To Richard Bentley*

Hall, Cooperstown, May. 21st 1848

Dear Sir,

Previously to getting your last letter informing me that Mr. Newby recedes [1] I put one chapter, (1st of Vol IId Am. Ed.) into the hands of a stereotyper in this village, where the thief would never think of looking for it. As it was in progress I let it go on, and now send it to you. *This chapter Mr. Newby can not get, except from your London office.* The Philadelphia office will go on with the rest of the book, as soon as I can send the manuscript.

I shall delay the publishing according to your request as long as I can.[2] I am going west again, however, next month, and must send forward the sheets by the 1st July. The American edition might be delayed, if you wish it, until late in July, I think, without any great difficulty.

I shall send the sheets as they are ready, and a duplicate of this with them, letting you know more particularily about the time of publication.

A Republic in France is a pretty play thing, but when it comes to regular work, it will be found that the machine will require too strong a hand to keep it in motion. My own opinion is that Mons – La Martine will play the part of Monk, and bring back the oldest branch, first establishing a very liberal constitution.[3]

This is the wisest thing he can do, and it is reasonable to suppose he will try to do it. I always told Lafay[e?]tte that it would have been better had he put the duc de Bordeaux on the throne, after making a liberal constitution, and securing a liberal ministry. His objection was that the nation would not bear a member of the elder branch just then. Nations bear just what their leaders tell them to bear.

Yours truly

R. Bentley Esquire J. Fenimore Cooper

MANUSCRIPT: Cooper Collection, Yale University Library.

1. Bentley reported in his letter of 18 April that Newby had agreed at his latest confrontation not to try to pirate *The Oak Openings* (MS: YCAL).

2. "It will be well," wrote Bentley on 18 April, "to delay the publication as much as possible, for owing to the great excitement which has now been going on for two months, no books are bought, and if things continue as at present heaven only knows what the consequence will be to a great body of traders! Matters still look extremely gloomy in France, although this last demonstration of the National Guards has had already a beneficial effect. *Here* the enthusiasm displayed by all the orderly & respectable part of the population was so grand, as to put down the puny and ridiculous attempt on the part of the Chartists to disturb the tranquillity of London. If these simpletons should venture again to appear in masses, they will assuredly be well chastised. You see I have become a politician — I suppose it is because I have nothing else to do. And it is so: for in times of political excitement our branch of industry, (which especially demands the quiet & orderly proceeding of society to make way at all,) pines, and would soon have nothing else to do, but to issue political pamphlets!" (MS: YCAL.)

3. Cooper expected Alphonse de Lamartine (1790–1869), the French poet and statesman, to assist the older branch of the Bourbons in the person of the Duc de Bordeaux or Henry V to the French throne, as General George Monk or Monck, the first Duke of Albemarle (1608–1670), had assisted Charles II to the British throne.

944. *To Brantz Mayer*

Hall, Cooperstown | May 27th 1848

Dear Sir,

Your obliging letter reached me some days since, but the pamphlet has just arrived. I have waited to be able to acknowledge the receipt of the last.[1] I now beg leave to express my sense of this mark of attention.

The letters in the Home Journal are drawing themselves out in a way I did not anticipate, or I might not have written them. A forgetfulness of the past is a marked feature in the national character, I think. We live altogether in the present time, and in the future. The past is so brief, and has so little to commend it to our study, it is not surprising perhaps it should be so, but I have a veneration for old times, old names, old fashions, which may possibly arise from the conviction that I am getting to be an old fellow.

I shall take this occasion to thank you for your book on Mexico, which I read luckily, just previously to the commencement of the present war. That country seems to resemble Italy — a fine nature in the hands of a fallen people — amiable, and in a certain sense polished, but indolent and inefficient.

Very Respectfully Yours

B. Mayer, Esquire J. Fenimore Cooper

ADDRESSED: Brantz Mayer Esquire | Baltimore | Maryland POSTMARKED: COOPERSTOWN N.Y. | MAY | 30 STAMPED: 10
MANUSCRIPT: Cooper Collection, Yale University Library.

A Baltimore lawyer and historian, founder of the Maryland Historical Society, Mayer (1809–1879) had written on 8 June 1844, as corresponding secretary of the society, to inform Cooper of his election to honorary membership. On his return from Mexico where he served as secretary of the United States legation from 1841 to 1843, Mayer published the timely and popular *Mexico as It Was and as It Is* (1844), which Cooper read. Mayer was later instrumental in persuading the state of Maryland to preserve and publish its records under the auspices of the Historical Society. (*DAB*; MS: YCAL.)

1. "As I percieve by some late letters to the Home Journal," wrote Mayer to Cooper on 21 May 1848, "that you are fond of studying the minute personal details of history, I take the liberty to send you a little Revolutionary Journal of Mr. Charles Carroll [*Journal of Charles Carroll of Carrollton, during His Visit to Canada in 1776*], which I edited for our Historical Society in 1844." (MS: YCAL.)

945. *To Richard Bentley*

Hall, Cooperstown, May 27th 1848

Dear Sir,

You see what [Fagan,] the Stereotyper, says.[1] I am curious to know what *you* now say. Have you the duplicates or not? Duplicates of the first 15 chapters have been sent to you — and if you have not recieved them, they have been stolen on board ship. They often take great liberties with such packages on board packets, and I have always taken the precaution to seal those I sent myself.

I shall leave home about the 10th June, to go to Detroit, in Michigan, on the business that took me there last year. On my return about the close of the month, I shall finish the Openings, and forward the sheets. This will put the publication some where about the last of July. I have delayed it to meet your wishes.

You will see that Mr. —— Gadsall[2] is a regular thief if the package was taken from the vessel, as, if the duplicate has arrived, is most probably the case. I beg you will let me know how the fact is.[3]

Yours truly
J. Fenimore Cooper

SOURCE: Facsimile, from the holograph formerly owned by the Honorable Eleanor Eden, published in *The Autographic Mirror: Autographic Letters and Sketches of Illustrious and Distinguished Men of Past and Present Times . . .* (London and New York, 20 February 1864), No. 1, p. 27.

1. "Fagan" is excised from the sentence in the facsimile. The stereotyper's letter, which Cooper forwarded to Bentley, is unlocated; but Fagan evidently believed that the sheets of *The Oak Openings* had been tampered with aboard ship. He reported in a letter dated Philadelphia, 3 June 1848, that all his proofs were untouched, whereas "one set of which w[oul]d have been abstracted, in all probability, had any man of mine supplied Newby with sheets. It would have been superfluous and very difficult work, to have taken a set expressly for the roguish purpose." (MS: YCAL.)

2. Unidentified.

3. Bentley replied on 22 June: "The alarm about The Beehunter was unnecessary; the duplicate of the first American Volume reached me safely. The whole attempt of Mr. Newby and his friend was a disgraceful endeavour to annoy me. It is as well however, as you yourself always do, to seal the packets, because the people on board the Vessels have made free with several books sent by me to the United States." "I shall," the publisher added, "hope to publish Beehunter by the 20th July. That I trust will give me a few days prior publication." (MS: YCAL.)

946. *To Mrs. Charles Jarvis Woolson (Hannah Cooper Pomeroy)*

Hall, Cooperstown, June 1st 1848

My dear Hannah,

I am much obliged to you for your invitation,[1] but it comes at an unfortunate moment. Sue and Charlotte have just left us for Geneva, where they have gone to pass a few weeks with their aunts. As for the two others, they can not leave their mother quite alone. Some other time, when you have got as far as California, we may profit by your kind request.

As for myself, I shall leave home about the 13th or 14th, for Detroit. I think I shall go direct, but, on my return, I shall endeavour to take Cleveland in my way. I may not remain longer than a few hours, but that will enable me to see you. That there may be no missing you, I shall endeavour to send you notice when I shall be there — by telegraph, if you have one, and I believe you have.

Mrs. Campbell and Mrs. Turner are now in the house, while I am writing — They have been here about a week, and appear to be quite well.

We have a fine season. The annual June frost visited us last Wednesday, but did very little harm. I am now mowing my lawns, and your aunt, besides having made near [a] [2] hundred weight of butter (at the farm) has lots of geese, [duc]ks, turkies and chickens. I am through planting of all sorts, and we now wait to see what the summer will do for us. Your aunt and I have just come in from the garden, where every thing looks fully a forth night earlier than common — The cold weather is quite gone, and now we hope for good honest summer weather. We have melons in blossom, cucumbers nearly so, and peas fairly out. Tomatoes well in bud, and every thing looking charmingly. As for lettuce, radishes, peppergrass, spinach and asparagus, we have been exercising our teeth on *them*, nearly a month. The last fully three weeks.

Your daughter [Georgianna] has now been enough with us to feel at home here, and I hope she may often favour us with her company. I have great pleasure in seeing any descendant of my father in this house, for I think it would have given him pleasure to know that his posterity meet in this spot, where I should think they must be induced to think of its founder. I have embellished a little, but he founded the place, and it is the first man who becomes identified with any thing of this sort. I have had a good deal of difficulty in keeping possession, there being a very strong disposition in this country to make common property of any thing that takes the fancy of the public. I suppose one half of this village would gladly pull down this house, because they can not walk through the hall whenever it suits them; but I am firm, and they begin to feel that what is my property is not theirs. This feeling is what is giving so much trouble in France, just now, and which will, ere many years, drive that country into excesses that will bring it back to force. I do not mean the corrected feeling which exists here, but that which did exist before it was met.

It is amazing how many crudities circulate in this country, for want of being snubbed. The press is as cowardly as it is insolent; exactly as it bullies individuals, it succumbs to numbers. The consequence is that the people rarely hear any truth about themselves.

But I must not entertain you with such subjects. You would rather hear of births and marriages. We deal so little in these interesting events in Cooperstown that I have nothing to tell you, unless it may be that a certain nephew of yours is sadly taken with a sort of a *step*-first and second cousin of your own.[3] I leave you to exercise your wits in guessing, though I dare say Georgie has enlightened you already on the subject. I should think she might, for dancing eight or ten times of an evening is a sign that is not easily overlooked, and I think your daughter must have seen them. The parents seem very well satisfied. You are not to understand, however, that the matter is settled. I know nothing beyond my own conjectures, which are pretty strong.

Adieu — my regards to yours, and much love from all around me.

Your affec. Uncle
J. Fenimore Cooper

Mrs. C. J. Woolson | or | Woo*lst*on

MANUSCRIPT: Clare Benedict Collection, English Seminary, Bibliothek der Universität Basel. PUBLISHED, IN PART: Clare Benedict, ed., *Voices Out of the Past: Five Generations (1785–1923)* . . . (London: Ellis, 1929), 45–46.

1. Unlocated.
2. Two lines of the holograph are slightly damaged at one end.
3. Cooper presumably referred to George Pomeroy Keese, son of Georgianna Pomeroy and Theodore Keese, and Caroline Adriance Foot, daughter of Dr. Lyman Foot by his first wife Ann Treadwell Platt. The couple were married on 10 October 1849. (Albert A. Pomeroy, *History and Genealogy of the Pomeroy Family* . . . [Toledo, Ohio: private published, 1912], 454–55.)

947. *To Mrs. Cooper*

Detroit, Sunday Afternoon, June 18th 1848

Dearest,

At Fort-Plain I met Ogden, in a good disposition to move fast — We travelled all night, and reached Buffaloe about eight next morning. Our old boat the Canada, the best as to comfort on the lake, was advertised to sail at ten. At eleven she did sail, and we arrived here at nine this morning, after as pleasant a passage as was ever made. Here we are then, in the very rooms we occupied so long, last autumn, ready for action. I suppose the cause will be tried on Tuesday, and we think will be got through with next day. I do not know whether Judge [John] McLean has got here, or not, but take it for granted he will soon be here, if not already on the spot.

We went to church this morning, and heard an excellent sermon on the Trinity. I saw Mrs. [George] Mor[r]ell, and gave Mrs. [John] Chester Mary Farmer's letter in her pew. They asked us to dine with them, but this we could not do to-day.

At the falls I hear the river is passed constantly in an iron basket, and by means of an iron wire. Last week a young lady of 17 *would* go over. She got into the basket, but as soon as she found herself suspended over the cliff, she shut both eyes and made two trips, there and back again, without opening either eye for a moment. On landing she began to cry, and cried like an infant, for half an hour.

[Gerrit] [1] Smith,[2] wife, son, Dan Fitzhugh,[3] and a niece, a Miss Backus [4] were among our passengers. Mrs. Smith is so fat I did not recognize her. Altogether, we had a pleasant time of it. The night's work was fatiguing, but I was not as dull Friday, as I expected to be. [Paccand?] was in the stage, and he kept up a fire of words the whole distance. Among other things he said "Madame [*illegible*] est une *galante* femme." Has the word two meanings.

Wm. Wadsworth get no better. His wife has a child, and Miss Elizabeth remains unmarried.[5]

Tell Paul Mr. [George E.] Hand says that S'Carolina and Georgia will both go for Cass, and all Northern Ohio (the Whigs) are out against Taylor. I have no little doubt of Cass' election. He got home only on Thursday, in the night. All the north-west will be strong for him.

Tell him, also, they are getting up a wire over the Horse Shoe, and intend to take people in a basket and suspend them within feet of the cataract, in the Mists.

There, I can tell you no more. I am well. The water is good, and the country much in advance of us. Beets, peas, &c are on the tables. Peas, in abundance were on the table in Utica. Strawberries in any quantity.

Adieu, with tenderest love to all

J. F. C.

ADDRESSED: Mrs. Fenimore Cooper | Cooperstown | New-York POSTMARKED: DETROIT Mich | JUN | 19 STAMPED: 10

MANUSCRIPT: Cooper Collection, Yale University Library. PUBLISHED, IN PART: *Correspondence*, II, 589–90.

1. Cooper wrote "G[a?]errett."

2. Remembered for complicity in John Brown's raid at Harper's Ferry, Smith (1797–1874, Hamilton 1818) was a wealthy landowner, philanthropist, and reformer of Peterboro, Madison County, New York. Though his chief political office was that of representative in Congress in 1853 and 1854, his speeches and writings long were effective forces in the temperance and abolition movements. By his second wife, Ann Carroll Fitzhugh, whom he married in 1822, Smith had four children, two of whom survived to maturity. (*DAB*.)

3. See Cooper to Mrs. Cooper, 2 March 1845.

4. The niece Cooper referred to was probably the daughter of Dr. Frederick Fanning Backus (1794–1858, Yale 1813), who married in 1818 Rebecca Anne, daughter of Colonel William and Anne (Hughes) Fitzhugh, sister of the second Mrs. Gerrit Smith. The first Mrs. Gerrit Smith had been Wealthy Ann Backus, Dr. Backus's only sister. (Dexter, *Graduates of Yale College*, VI, 520–21.)

5. William Wolcott Wadsworth (1810–1852), son of James and Naomi Wadsworth and brother of James Samuel Wadsworth of Geneseo, married Emmeline Austin of Boston and had three sons. William's sister Elise or Elizabeth (b. 1815) fell in love with Cooper's friend Charles Augustus Murray in the 1830's, eventually married him in 1850 — after her father's death, and died a year later. (Henry Greenleaf Pearson, *James S. Wadsworth of Geneseo* [New York: Charles Scribner's Sons, 1913], 22–28.)

948. *To Mrs. Cooper*

Thursday evening, Detroit. June 22d [1848]

Dearest

I send this by Ogden. The summing up commenced this afternoon. I doubt if we get the charge before Saturday morning. Ogden has given much better evidence than before, clearer and fuller, but — this is Michigan. I will not predict, but I am not very sa[n]guine. Our case is certainly much better than last year, but all depends on the Judges. One, we know, *was* against us, and if he can persuade the other to the same views, we shall lose.

I am well, heartily tired of this work, and I wish I was home again. We are in the hands of Providence, and I strive to submit.

Tenderly Yours

[*signature omitted*]

ADDRESSED: Mrs. Fenimore Cooper | Cooperstown | New York POSTMARKED: BUFFALO N.Y. | JUN 24?
MANUSCRIPT: Cooper Collection, Yale University Library.

949. *To Mrs. Cooper*

Canada, off Buffaloe. Friday, June 30th 1848[1]

Dearest,

Five days trial, and no verdict, again. We have gained ground, however. Got all the law settled on our side, and see our way clear.

I am well. Went to Kalamazoo last Saturday, and left Detroit yesterday. I shall pass Sunday at Geneva, and be home on Tuesday.

Ogden's testimony is improving, though he would thrust in opinions with his facts, and it was these opinions that did the mischief.

I am in good spirits, and shall go to work as usual.

Yours tenderly
J. Fenimore Cooper

ADDRESSED: Mrs. Fenimore Cooper | Cooperstown | New York POSTMARKED: BUFFALO N.Y. | JULY 1 STAMPED: STEAM-BOAT
MANUSCRIPT: Cooper Collection, Yale University Library.

1. See reproduction on page 218.

950. *To Edward Livingston Welles*

Hall, Cooperstown | July 8th 1848

Dear Sir,

I passed through Ann Arbor, Saturday June 24th, and Wednesday June 28th, on my way to and from Kalamazoo. At that time your note was in this house, but I knew nothing of its contents. Thus you percieve that we have been quite near to each other without knowing it.

Yours &c

Master Edward Welles J. Fenimore Cooper

MANUSCRIPT: Hartwick College Library.

Though his letter to Cooper is lost, Welles (1830–1902) was obviously an autograph collector in or near Ann Arbor, Michigan. He seems to have been a nephew of Henry Woolsey Welles (1818–1860), merchant and recorder of Ann Arbor in 1851–1852. (Welles family records, Michigan Historical Collections, The University of Michigan.)

951. *To Richard Bentley*

New-York. July 18th 1848.

Dear Sir,

To-morrow, the last half of the book will leave here in the Caledonia, Capt. Leitch, (Steamer of 19th) and next day, a duplicate in the Washington. You had better publish as early as you can, conveniently, as they wish to publish here about the last of August.[1]

The draft for the balance (£150) will go forward at the same time.

I intend to get out one more tale, and I begin to think it will be the last, though there may be an exception in favour of a long cherished project, which will require time to execute — but one more tale I shall finish this season. I *think* I shall call it the "Lost Sealers." I intend it as a counterpoise, or *pendant* might be a better word, to the Crater. Scene, principally, Antarctick Ocean, and incidents very *icy*.

This book I offer on the same terms as the last. I should like an understanding that I might draw as follows: viz. Sept. 1st £100 — Oct. 1st £100, and balance in all Nov. when the book will be completed. I must get it off my hands here before our season shuts in.

Will you let me hear from you, on the subject.[2]

Yours truly

Mr. Bentley J. Fenimore Cooper

ADDRESSED: Mr. Richard Bentley | Publisher | New-Burlington Street | London | per Caledonia POSTMARKED: AT | 3 AU 3 | 1848
MANUSCRIPT: Cooper Collection, Yale University Library.

1. Burgess, Stringer and Co. published *The Oak Openings; or, The Bee-Hunter* in New York on 24 August 1848; Bentley published the novel as *The Bee-Hunter; or, The Oak Openings* in London on 14 August 1848 (Spiller and Blackburn, *Bibliography*, 153–54).

2. Replying on 3 August, Bentley postponed a decision about the terms of the next book until after the publication of *The Bee-Hunter*, warning that the new work should not be published before January. He agreed to Cooper's terms in his letter of 2 October, begging "it to be clearly understood between us that all your future drafts *must* be at *90* days' sight." As for *The Bee-Hunter*, he reported "such is the disastrous state of business, that little has been done with it in common with all recent publications. And if you will permit me to say so, the introduction of political discussion, from what I gather from many of your admirers is likely to militate against the success which the interest of the story would have otherwise insured." (MSS: YCAL.)

952. *To John Fagan*

Globe-Hotel, New York, July 19th 1848

Dear Fagan,

I forgot to ask for two title pages to deposit. Will you send them to me at Cooperstown, at once.

I also ought to have told you to send the plates, some time next week, to Burgess by the canal.[1] Letter sent back, is recieved.

Yours truly

Mr. Fagan. J. Fenimore Cooper

MANUSCRIPT: New York State Historical Association.

1. Fagan replied on 21 July: "I have forwarded the proofs of 2 titles to Cooperstown, and will send the plates of 'Oak Openings' as you direct, to Burgess & Stringer" (MS: YCAL).

953. *To John Fagan*

Globe. July. 20th 1848

Dear Fagan,

I am tired to death waiting for a person who is in the country, and I offer you as follows. Sept. 15th and Oct 15th, I shall draw on Bentley for £100s, each draft, or £200's altogether.

I will sell you these drafts, *to be held to their dates,* for 6 per cent, to be paid by my note due Sept. 4th, and balance in cash, as thus —

£200's —— $888.88
6
―――――
5333 28
888.88
―――――
$942.21
note 349.29
―――――
$592 92

As for the cash you might send half, if not ready with all, and a note at a few days for the balance. This arrangement would be a real [1] convenience to me, and I regret not having proposed it when in Philadelphia.

I enclose the drafts to save time. If you accept keep them; if not send them back *here,* where you will send the *note* and draft, if the bargain be made.[2] I am almost melted and am dying to be in the mountains – so do not delay.

Yours truly
J. Fenimore Cooper

Mr. John Fagan | Stereotyper | Philadelphia

I offer to *you,* knowing that the bills will be held, until their dates. The bills are against a new book which will go to press in about a month, and of which Bentley is duly advised.

MANUSCRIPT: Charles E. Feinberg, Detroit, Michigan.

1. Cooper inserted a superfluous "to" at this point.

2. Fagan agreed to purchase the two drafts on England in a letter of 21 July enclosing his draft for $300. He promised to send a draft for the remaining $292.90 in a day or two. (MS: YCAL.)

954. *To Samuel L. Harris*

Otsego Hall, Cooperstown, Sept 5th 1848

Sir,

Much more is *said* about the veto, than is *understood.* Properly speaking, there is no veto, in this country. A veto is absolute, and final, and places the will of the sovereign in opposition to legislation. Such was also the veto of the Polish Diet, any one member of which could veto a law. In this country, the authority of the executive extends no farther than to send a bill back for reconsideration, along with his reasons, leaving to Congress, in its collective ⟨power⟩ character, power to enact the law without the assent of the executive.

But, it is said by these late dissentients, a majority of two thirds can not be had, and this is effectually giving the President an absolute veto.

It follows from this very objection, that the President does not oppose Congress, in its collective character, but only the small majority that happens to be in favour of the law. In the face of this obvious truth, a cry is raised that the executive is counteracting the measures of Congress, regarding Congress in its collective character, when the veto is used, but disregarding that collective character when the powers of the respective functionaries come to be considered on general principles. In other words, the executive opposes *all* Congress in using the veto, but *all* Congress does not act in trying to get the two third's vote, but only the difference between that number and a simple majority!

The King of England dare not use the veto, and why should a President do that which a King dare not attempt to do?

The argument is singular were the fact as stated. What has the President in common with a King? The powers given to the first, in the Constitution, are given to be *used*, or the instrument is a puerility. Why not carry the [parallel] [1] throughout, and say that, as the King transmits his authority to his eldest son, the president should do the same!

But the reason why the veto is not used in England is so very obvious, that one is surprised any sane man should attempt the comparison. The King has, inch by inch, been robbed of his prerogative by the aristocracy, until, under the form of a ministerial responsibility, he can do nothing of himself but name his ministers. On the other hand, these ministers are so much in subjection to parliament, that *they resign when they cannot control that body*. Let what is termed a ministerial question go against the ministry and the latter retire. There is no one left to apply the veto, which requires a *responsible* agent for its constitutional exercise. Thus, when ministers lead parliament, a veto becomes unnecessary, for parliament does what the minister desires; and, when parliament is opposed, the minister gives way. It is no wonder that the King does not use the veto, in such a system. If it be liberty not thus to limit the prerogative, it is a liberty purchased at the expense of the boasted balance of the English estates.

Gen. [Zachary] Taylor quite evidently does not understand the Constitution. He is not disposed to set up his personal judgment (through an exercise of the veto) against the wisdom of Congress, except in cases in which the Constitution has been violated, or there has been careless legislation! Now, in what is his personal judgment better in judging of what is, or what is not constitutional, than in judging what is, and what is not expedient? A plain man, who is at the head of affairs, *may* form a better opinion of what is expedient, than a very clever man who is not behind the curtain; but any man, who is a constitutional lawyer, can say what is, and what is not constitutional, as well as the President. Then there is much less necessity for vetoing an unconstitutional law than for vetoing one that is simply inexpedient. An inexpedient law has all the force of one that is expedient, and must be equally executed; but an unconstitutional law has no power *ab initio,* and there is a tribunal expressly created to pronounce it of no avail. The veto is not necessary to kill it.

Washington and Jefferson, it is said, rarely resorted to the veto. This is true, and for an obvious reason. The congresses of that day were in harmony with the executives, and followed their lead. When such is the case, the veto becomes unnecessary, for laws can be passed only by inadvertency, to which the President is opposed.

But, the true argument in favour of the American veto, if veto it can be called, is this: All legislative power is in Congress, and the veto of the President is merely a check on its exercise. It is consequently a provision made *in the interest of liberty*; precisely as the power of the Senate, in the cases of appointments and treaties, is a check on the appointing ⟨power⟩ and treaty-making powers of the President. It would be just as rational, nay more rational, to declaim against the negative of the Senate, in these last cases, on the ground that it is opposed to liberty, than to declaim against the veto, for the same reason. *More* rational, because the veto of the Senate is absolute; while that of the President is merely a check.

In point of practical consequences, the use of the veto is probably more needed in this country, than the use of any other power belonging to the system. Congress has a natural disposition to be factious, regarding success more than principles, and being totally without responsibility. It needs checking far more than any other branch of the government for these two reasons.

As respects Gen. Taylor's notion of letting Congress lead the government, it appears to me that it is throwing away the principal advantage for which the office of President was created. We had such a system under the old congress, and it was found to be inefficient. Enough is ⟨given⟩ conceded to liberty when the power in the last resort is given to the legislature, and something is due to efficiency. I have a great respect for Gen. Taylor, but should he carry out his project, in this particular I apprehend it would be found that he would make his administration contemp[t]ible. All the provisions of the constitution show that the intention was to give to the president just this influence, which he seems inclined to throw away, while it secures the country from danger, by bestowing all power, in the last resort, on Congress. This is the division of authority that is most conducive to good government; an efficient executive, whose hands are tied against usurpation.

I have been amused with Mr. Clayton's [2] logic. He dislikes an exercise of power, in which one man controls the decisions of many. Now, if there be any force in such an objection, it is true as a principle, and varies only in degree when the Senate applies its absolute veto to the acts of the other house – But who is Mr. Clayton? He and his colleague represent some 100,000 souls. Messrs. [John A.] Dix and [Daniel S.] Dickinson represent some 3,000,000. What claim have the two first to a power equal to the two last? The Senators of Rhode Island, Delaware, Iowa, Wisconsin, Florida, Arkansas, Vermont, Connecticut, New Jersey, New Hampshire and Missouri have, all together, fewer ⟨people⟩ constituents than the senators of New York alone; yet they give 22 votes to our two. Whence comes this aristocratical preference? From the Constitution, as does the veto of the President. Shall one of these powers be put down by the *slang* of democracy and equality, and not the other? All this cant is unworthy of enlightened and fair-minded men.

I have little doubt that Gen. Cass will be elected; should he not be, I leave with you this written opinion – viz: – that Gen. Taylor's administration will be a complete failure, and give as much dissatisfaction to those who put him in, as to any other portion of the country –

Your Obedient Servant
J. Fenimore Cooper

Samuel L Harris Esquire | Navy Department
Occupation has delayed this reply.[3]

ADDRESSED: Samuel L Harris Esquire | Navy Department | Washington POSTMARKED: COOPERSTOWN N.Y. | SEP | 11 STAMPED: 10 ENDORSED: Recd. 14 Sep. 1848.

MANUSCRIPT: Paul Fenimore Cooper, Cooperstown, New York. PUBLISHED: *Correspondence*, II, 594–98.

Samuel L. Harris was appointed principal corresponding clerk for the Navy Department on 4 May 1846, at an annual salary of $1,500, and replaced on 1 May 1851. A file of recommendations preserved in the General Records of the Department of the Treasury (RG 56) indicates that he had been employed as a clerk in various state offices at Augusta, Maine, and that he was formerly from Portland, Maine. The recommendations insist on his Democratic political loyalty. Harris may have belonged to the Harris family described in George T. Little, Henry S. Burrage, and Albert Roscoe Stubbs, *Genealogical and Family History of the State of Maine* (New York: Lewis Historical Publishing Company, 1909), II, 972–73.

1. Cooper wrote "paralell."

2. Chief justice of Delaware from 1837 to 1839, John Middleton Clayton (1796–1856, Yale 1815) served in the United States Senate from 1829 to 1836, 1845 to 1849, and 1851 to 1857. As Secretary of State under President Tayler in 1849–1850 he negotiated the Clayton-Bulwer Treaty. (*DAB*.)

3. Harris had written Cooper from Washington on 12 August 1848: "Mr. Harris presents his compliments to Mr. Cooper, and respectfully requests his *autograph* to place in his collection, at the head of 'American Authors.'" (MS: YCAL.)

955. *To M. Wendell L'Amoureux*

Hall, Cooperstown, Sept. 9th 1848

Dear Sir,

I regret that it will not be in my power to deliver the lecture you request,[1] the approaching winter. I have nearly decided to deliver no more lectures, but my engagements are such as to admonish me of the necessity of at least abstaining from making any promises of that nature—

Your letter got mislaid, which is the reason of the delay in answering. Wishing you all success in your efforts to improve in knowledge, and sincerely hoping that your venerable town will shortly recover from the severe blow it has lately sustained,[2] I remain

Your Obl. Ser.
J. Fenimore Cooper

M. W. L'Amo[u]reux Esquire

ADDRESSED: M. W L'Amoureux Esquire | Chairman of Lecture Committee &c | Albany POSTMARKED: COOPERSTOWN N.Y. | SEP | 11 STAMPED: 5
MANUSCRIPT: The Scheide Library, Princeton, New Jersey.

L'Amoureux (1827?–1907, Union 1844) or L'Amoreaux became a teacher of rhetoric, history, and modern languages. He was a tutor at Columbia in 1868–1869, and he concluded his career as head of the modern language department and librarian at Union College. (*Union College: Centennial Catalog; The Albany Evening Journal*, 2 April 1907.)

1. Repeating an invitation of the previous year, L'Amoureux wrote from Albany on 17 August 1848 as chairman of the Lecture Committee of the Young

Men's Association of Albany to request Cooper to lecture between 1 December 1848 and 16 February 1849 (MS: YCAL).

2. See Cooper to Mrs. Cooper, 27 April 1849.

956. *To Mrs. Cooper*

Detroit. Thursday evening, Oct. 12th 1848

Dearest,

I found Ogden in the cars, and we went on very pleasantly, until evening, when we stopped at Auburn. Next day had a safe and agreeable run to Buffaloe. We did not quit Buffaloe until eleven Wednesday morning, when we sailed in the Canada. The lake was smooth as a pond, and we got here this morning a little after nine.

The case is set down for Saturday but will hardly come on until Monday. General Cass [1] has just sent us an invitation to dine to morrow, which we have accepted. I met Mrs. [John] Chester in the street looking thin, I thought, and also Wm. Baker [2] looking well.

Major Biddle [3] came across the lake with us, and I had a long talk with him.

Mr. Humphries, the husband of Fanny Comstock's protégée, is here. The child is well, and he took charge of Sabina's bundle.[4] By the way, he offered to purchase two of my lots, and talks of adding a third. If he will come a little in his price, we may agree. At all events that will be something. As for the cause I can tell you nothing. The jury is said to be good. [George E.] Hand is very well, and is very sanguine of Cass' success. Ohio is said to be safe, but there are so many false reports one can never say until all is settled.

I never was better, and hope to be home at the close of next week.

Tell Mary [Mrs. Isaac Cooper] I met Mr. Abbott [5] in the street to-day. He leaves Detroit to-morrow, to sell an 80 acre lot, price agreed on, and expects to be back in time to remit the money by me. He also said that Mr. Merrick [6] has assumed the payment of the $1500, and he expects him daily. With love to all,

yours most tenderly

Mrs. F— C— J. F. C.

ADDRESSED: Mrs. Fenimore Cooper | Cooperstown | New-York POSTMARKED: DETROIT Mich. | OCT | 13 STAMPED: 10
MANUSCRIPT: Cooper Collection, Yale University Library.

1. Cooper had probably met Lewis Cass (1782–1866), Michigan's man of the hour and her most distinguished citizen, in the 1820's. Cass was territorial governor (1813–1831), Secretary of War (1831–1836), minister to France (1836–1842), United States senator (1845–1848, 1849–1857), and Secretary of State (1857–1860). (Frank B. Woodford, *Lewis Cass: The Last Jeffersonian* [New Brunswick: New Jersey: Rutgers University Press, 1950].)

2. A carpenter of this name is listed in James H. Wellings, *Directory of the City of Detroit; and Register of Michigan, for the Year 1845* (Detroit: Harsha & Willcox, 1845).

3. Brother of Nicholas and Commodore James Biddle, Major John Biddle (1792–1859, College of New Jersey [Princeton] n.g.) was a Michigan land speculator, financier, and legislator (Silas Farmer, *History of Detroit and Wayne County . . .* [New York and Detroit: Munsell & Co., Silas Farmer & Co., 1890], 1032).

4. Frances Oathwaite Comstock (b. 1844) and Sarah Sabina Comstock (1834–1918) were daughters of Horace H. Comstock, whose wife (Cooper's niece) Sarah Sabina died in 1846. The identity of "Mr. Humphries" or "Gen — Humphreys," as he is subsequently referred to, is not clear, although Frances subsequently married a person of this name. A Levi S. Humphrey was marshal of the district, and a J. Humphreys was justice of the peace in Kalamazoo. (John Adams Comstock, *A History and Genealogy of the Comstock Family in America* [Los Angeles: The Commonwealth Press, Inc., 1949], 236.)

5. Cooper apparently referred to James Abbott (1776–1858), a prominent merchant, landowner, and officeholder in Detroit (Clarence M. Burton, William Stocking, Gordon K. Miller, eds., *The City of Detroit, Michigan, 1701–1922* [Detroit and Chicago: The S. J. Clarke Publishing Company, 1922], 1348, 1457, 1490).

6. Unidentified.

957. *To Mrs. Cooper*

Detroit, Thursday 19th [October] 1848

Dearest,

My cause was brought on yesterday afternoon, and is now on trial. Counsel are battling inch by inch. The defence wishes to exclude [Isaac] Schuyler's cross examination, in which he swears that [Sidney] Ketchum got the acceptance by fraud, and we contend for its admission. One objection filed previously to the trial has been decided in our favour. The defence fights hard. The judge seems struck with the facts, and may be with us — but there is no calculating on him. He has thrown out several ideas, some of which favour one side, and some the other. A result in such a cause must ever be doubtful, here. The defence look more grave than before, and are evidently disturbed — but.

The trial will probably terminate on Saturday, in which case

I shall leave here on Monday, and be home Wednesday or Thursday.

The democrats here are in high glee. The information is all favourable — Ohio, Pennsylvania, Georgia, New Jersey, Louisiana &c —

Mrs. Mor[r]ell and Mrs. Chester are well, and send kind regards. Gen — Humphreys, Fanny Comstock's adopted father is here, having just gained a great cause, and he has taken Sabina's bundle.

I have dined with Gen. Cass, and seen lots of people, but we have no other invitations. Oak Openings is just getting into notice, but these people are so thin skinned that they consider even a joke as an insult. On the whole, however, I think it is liked, but the election engrosses all minds.

Tell Mary [Mrs. Isaac Cooper] that Mr. Abbott is to be back to-day with some money for her. I am sorry to say that I do not hear as good accounts of him, as I could wish. I shall suspend my opinion, however, until I learn more. He has enemies, and many, or he is not the person we could wish to have in his position.

I shall not go to Kalamazoo. It would be of no use. I expect nothing from Michigan, and heartily wish I ha[d?] never heard of the state. God's will be done.

I am well, and send tenderest love to all.

J. Fenimore Cooper.

For Paul,

The defence say that the acceptance was a payment; they also say, if not a payment, it was an agreement to give time.

We say that the acceptance was obtained by *fraud*, and that fraud vitiates all contracts. That Ogden might have sued immediately after even a bargain to give ⟨in⟩ time in writing, and set up the ground of fraud. Now what he could do the endorser could do, and the last would not be estopped.

If we are right, Schuyler's evidence, and he is their witness, will be all important.

ADDRESSED: Mrs. Fenimore Cooper | Cooperstown | New-York POSTMARKED: DETROIT Mich. | OCT | 19 STAMPED: 10
MANUSCRIPT: Cooper Collection, Yale University Library.

958. *To Mrs. Cooper*

Detroit, Sunday, [October] 22d 1848

Dearest,

We commenced on Wednesday, at noon, and have not yet got in all the testimony. Every inch is fought. We have got in [Isaac] Schuyler's deposition, after a day's fight. It is very important in two respects: in throwing great distrust on [Sidney] Ketchum's testimony, and as showing fraud in procuring the acceptance. I write for Dick and Paul. We have taken the ground that, if Ketchum obtained the acceptance of Schuyler by false representations, and made a fra[u]dulent use of it in the act of passing it to us, that it so vitiates any contract to give time, that Ogden might have sued him the next day, even had the bargain to give time been in writing, and set aside the contract. What Ogden could have done, the endorsers could have done, and consequently they could not be estopped. We contended for the admission of the deposition of Schuyler on three grounds; this — that it could not have been a good contract for payment either, and that it was a cross examination. The Judge ruled it was not a cross examination in that part of it, in which he was wrong, as say my lawyers, and as I say. He also ruled that there might be a doubt whether a fraud could be set up against the ground of payment, the acceptance being available as against Schuyler and the endorsers having rights in it; but he ruled that Ogden might have set up the fraud as against a contract to give time. Of course, if he stick to this, he must so charge, and the facts will be established by a witness of the defence. Though not framed for such a purpose the deposition is very strong and full, and what is more, the witness says that he told this fact to the defendant's attorney, but he told him he did not want it in the deposition. Of course, the defence was not taken by surprise.

I do not expect a verdict, but now I do not think we shall be beaten and this winter we may set matters all right. I am well, expect to be home this week, and send love to all. Ogden is still here —

J. F. C.

ADDRESSED: Mrs. Fenimore Cooper | Cooperstown | New York POSTMARKED: DETROIT Mich. | OCT | 23 STAMPED: 10
MANUSCRIPT: Cooper Collection, Yale University Library.

959. *To Mrs. Cooper*

Detroit, Monday afternoon, Oct | [23d] [1] 1848

Dearest,

The testimony has closed — nothing new on their side, and [Isaac] Schuyler let in on ours. Morris [2] ruled out, but the point of jurisdiction, raised on both the previous trials, is now abandoned. Morris settled that much, effectually. The case stands well, I think, though I do not expect a verdict. On the question of *fraud*, I think the judge is with us, and will so charge, but no one knows. Hand sums up this afternoon, and I think the case will go to the jury Wednesday forenoon.

Ogden was drawn out by the judge, and swore much more fully than ever before, that he did not take the acceptance in payment, or on an agreement to give time.

Providence permitting, I shall be home at the close of the week. I have hopes, but they are not very lively, and I have some fears. The jury is said to be good, and tolerably independent.

I never was better, and am prepared for the worst,

Love to all —

J. F— C.

Ogden leaves me to-night.

ADDRESSED: Mrs. Fenimore Cooper | Cooperstown | New-York POSTMARKED: [DETROIT Mich.?] | OCT | 25

MANUSCRIPT: Paul Fenimore Cooper, Cooperstown, New York.

1. Cooper wrote "22d."

2. Probably James H. Morris, whose law office was in the Drews Building, on the corner of Jefferson and Griswold Streets, opposite the Capitol.

960. *To. Mrs. Cooper*

Detroit, Thursday, noon, Oct 26th 1848

Dearest,

The cause is still in progress, this making the beginning of the 7th day. It will not go to the jury until Saturday, if it do before monday. [George E.] Hand has summed up on my side, and well they tell me, especially as far as the law is concerned. I am told the Judge has said that he never understood the case until after that argument. He has stated in open court that he should abide by the law of the Supreme Court of the United States, and disregard all English, or Pennsylvania cases when they conflict. So far this is greatly in our favour, if he stick to it. But — no one can say what sudden bias his mind may take, and no one can say what the jury may think. There is one pretty strong man on the jury and he will have great influence, for or against. Half of the defence — more than half — rests on Ogden's bad manner in testifying. If asked as to a *fact*, and a material fact — he answers he don't know — has no knowledge or recollection of any such circumstance, but it *may* be so — quite likely — very possible &c. &c. Without this, the defence would make scarcely any figure. Admonitions not to argue the case for the defence were of no avail, and he has greatly weakened his evidence by puerilities of this sort. His desire to reason, and throw in cursory conjectures, when he has no positive knowledge, amounts to infatuation! The mischief is done, and no foresight could prevent it. Still his testimony on the main points of payment and time has been much stronger than it ever was before, and was drawn out fairly by the judge.

Pratt [1] has talked a day for the defendants, and with no great advantage. But Joy [2] is now speaking for them, and well and ingeniously. He sees the necessity of making a strong effort and is doing it. My counsel are in earnest, and [Daniel] Goodwin will answer to-morrow. Of the result I can predict nothing. But for Ogden's puerilities, our case would be immeasurably better than it was before — as it is, I think it much better. It is a great point gained to have the fraud practised by [Sidney] Ketchum fairly before the jury, as it now is. If I get a verdict, I shall ever regard the manner in which I got his testimony as providential. I now look back to it with wonder. It is clear, full and staggering testimony and Joy sees it. Goodwin has increasing faith in the legal effect of fraud, and the Judge has already ruled in the deposition on the same ground. For Paul's information it is this.

If Ketchum gave to Ogden an acceptance obtained by fraud, and an agreement to give time was made in consideration of such an acceptance, Ketchum could not set up that agreement though sued next day, as he could not profit by his own fraud. Did the endorsers sue him, he could not set up such a contract as against them. Equity principles must govern the case as the law that exonerates endorsers comes from equity. If sued on the note, would the chancellery grant an injunction to stay proceedings, the fraud established — We say not. Such being the law, our case is clear, since the agreement, admitting that one existed in writing, would be of no avail. I shall telegraph the result, if I beat — if beaten, or a drawn game, my silence will let you know it.

As I can not quit Detroit before Monday night, at the soonest, you need not look for me before this day week. I am well, and the weather is pleasant. I am to sup with Ledyard [3] to-night. Here, Cass' election is regarded as almost certain. The most encouraging letters are recieved from the south, which can put him in with out Pennsylvania — But Pennsylvania is thought perfectly safe for him. As for Ohio it is firm as a rock. It will not take Taylor, and it will take Cass. Connecticut, New-Jersey, Maryland, North-Carolina,[4] Louisiana, or Tennessee will, either of them, put in Cass without Pennsylvania. Now, there is a chance in each, and it will be strange if we do not get one of them. But we shall get Pennsylvania — the Canal Commissioner shows that. His patronage is double that of the Governor's, and [there?] was a close conflict for the office — All the above is for Paul.

The Mor[r]ells are well, and send their regards. Tenderest love to all.

J. F. C.

ADDRESSED: Mrs. Fenimore Cooper | Cooperstown | New York POSTMARKED: BUFFALO [N.Y.?] | OCT | 28 | [*illegible*] STAMPED: STEAM-BOAT
MANUSCRIPT: Cooper Collection, Yale University Library.

1. Probably Abner Pratt (1801–1863), lawyer, jurist, and legislator who settled in 1839 in Marshall, Michigan, home of Sidney Ketchum and the defendants in Cooper's suit in the early 1840's (*Early History of Michigan*, 534).

2. Evidently James Frederick Joy (1810–1896, Dartmouth 1833), a prominent Detroit lawyer and railroad financier (*Early History of Michigan*, 383–84; *General Catalogue of Dartmouth College . . . 1769–1925* [Hanover, New Hampshire, 1925], 148).

3. Somewhat overshadowed by his father-in-law Lewis Cass, Henry Ledyard (1812–1880, Columbia 1830) assisted Cass as secretary of legation at the French Court (1839–1842), as manager of the family's large Michigan property interests, and briefly as Assistant Secretary of State. He was mayor of Detroit in 1855. (*Early History of Michigan*, 410–11).

4. Comma supplied.

961. *To Thomas Warren Field*

Hall, Cooperstown, Nov. 4th 1848

Sir,

Your letter arrived during my absence from home, which will explain the delay in answering it.[1]

My information does not extend to the estate to which you allude, and, of course, I have no means of aiding your enquiries. On this subject I do know, however, that there is a growing and most dangerous disposition in the people to take from those who have, and to give to those who have not; and this without any other motive than that basest of all human passions — envy. How far this downward tendency will go, I do not pretend to say; but I think it quite clear that, unless arrested, it must lead to revolution[s?] and bloodshed. This State of things has long been predicted, and he who can look back for half a century, must see that a fearful progress has been made towards anarchy and its successor tyranny, in that period. Another such half century will, in my judgment, bring the whole country under the bayonet.

Your Ob. Ser.
J. Fenimore Cooper

Mr. Thomas W. Field | 112 Orchard Street | New York

MANUSCRIPT: The Henry W. and Albert A. Berg Collection, The New York Public Library.

1. Field wrote Cooper on 16 October 1848 to ask advice about recovering a large tract in the towns of Chatham and Kinderhook, Columbia County, New York, to which squatters had obtained possession about 1800. The location of Ravensnest and Mooseridge in *Satanstoe, The Chainbearer,* and *The Redskins* corresponds approximately to that of the Field family property; and Field evidently assumed that Cooper knew its history (summarized in the letter) and drew from this knowledge some of the details for the novels. "Grandfather McCoy," wrote Field, "left as agent Derrick Gose who I think is one of the characters [*Jason Newcome?*] of the dream world you have created." (MS: YCAL.) Apparently no evidence exists to upset Cooper's disclaimer.

962. *To Stephen Henry Battin*

Hall, Cooperstown, Nov. 6th 1848

My Dear Sir,

At an informal meeting of the vestry, to-day — informal in consequence of there having been no legal notice — it was unanimously agreed to give you a call. At the same time legal notices were served for a vestry meeting next Friday, when the vote will be legally taken, out of all question with the same result.

The meeting of to-day was full, all being present but Judge Nelson, who is now in town holding the circuit, and Mr. [Henry] Scott, a warden, who is sick. I saw this last gentleman myself, and

First panel: "The Savage State" or "Commencement of Empire."

Second panel: "The Arcadian or Pastoral State."

IX. *The Course of Empire* (1833–1836) by Thomas Cole.

Third panel: "The Consummation of Empire."

Fourth panel: "Destruction."

X. *The Course of Empire* (1833–1836) by Thomas Cole.

Fifth panel: "Desolation"

XI. *The Course of Empire* (last panel) and a sketch by Thomas Cole.

Study for a scene from *The Last of the Mohicans.*

(Wadsworth Atheneum)

(New York State Historical Association)

XII. Two representations of *Cora Kneeling at the Feet of Tamenund,* a scene from *The Last of the Mohicans,* painted by Thomas Cole.

he is favourably disposed towards you. I understand Judge Nelson is of the same way of thinking. Thus you may view the call as unanimous.

In accepting, you will come to a harmonious parish, and one in which the vestry is well disposed to sustain the clergyman in all his just pretensions. I was requested to communicate the circumstances to you, as I shall be in town about Thursday, or Friday (at the City Hotel, I think), but my stay may be so short as to render it inconvenient to look you up, and I have deemed it best to write you this letter.

I presume you know our terms. We give $500 per annum of salary, and the rectory. The latter is rented at a $100 a year, until April, but the current rent will go to the clergyman. These are our certain terms. A proposition was made at the meeting of to-day to give $100 to the organist from the rent of the pews, and the surplus to the clergyman – assuring to him, in all events, the $500. Our pews have sold as high as $700, or near it, and such an arrangement would give the incumbent a chance to increase his salary a little.

You will doubtless get a more formal communication as soon as the legal meeting has been held, but you may safely consider the matter as decided so far as our concurrence is necessary. Hoping that your ministrations among us may be blessed by the aid of the Divine Spirit, I remain,

My Dear Sir | Very truly yours

Rev – Mr. Battin J. Fenimore Cooper

(over)

From your conversation with Mr. [Theodore] Keese, I suppose you will accept the call. In this case might it not be useful to look about you, while in town, for an organist? One who can sing is very desirable. Such a person might pick up a living here by giving music lessons.

I have decided to leave home Thursday and shall be in town until Monday. If the Globe should be open, I shall stay there – otherwise, at the City Hotel.[1]

MANUSCRIPT: New York State Historical Association.

Battin (1814?–1893, Trinity 1839, General Theological Seminary 1842) was officially called as rector of Christ Church, Cooperstown, on 10 November 1848; and he served from 24 November 1848 to 1 August 1858. At the time of his death, he was rector emeritus of Christ Episcopal Church on Jersey City Heights. (Hurd, *History of Otsego County*, 275; *The New-York Times*, 24 February 1893.)

1. A statement on the holograph signed "Stephen H. Battin" reads: "I succeeded Dr Alfred Beach, and my salary was at once raised to $800 per annum. I baptized Mr Cooper and also buried both himself and Mrs Cooper. He was about sixty years old when baptized, having been brot up a 'Quaker.' Mrs Cooper was the Sister of Bishop De Lancey, and was also distantly connected with Mrs Battin — thro the Van Cortlandts — I also performed the marriage ceremony for two of the daughters Mrs Finney and Mrs Richard Cooper. Along with this memento should go, the letter written to me after Mr Cooper's death, by his daughter Miss Susan, at the time the Family united in sending me a pocket communion service of silver."

963. *To Richard Bentley*

City Hotel, New York, Nov. 15th 1848

Dear Sir,

Your letter accepting the terms for the new book [1] was recieved a few days before I left Cooperstown, on my last visit to this place. I have sold the book here with reference to these terms, and we shall publish in all March. By the steamer of this day, I send you vol. 1st and by that of the 20th I shall send a duplicate. My first bill (£100) will go forward early in January — the second (£100) early in February, and the third (£150) at the completion of the book.

I have changed the name to "The Sea Lions, or the Lost Sealers"; if you prefer the last for the running title, you can keep it —

I send you by the packet of the 20th a manuscript tale called the "Lumley Autograph." I think it will just suit your Miscellany.[2] It is clever, and is written by a lady of my acquaintance [Susan Fenimore Cooper], who has asked me to get it published. If you publish, you can give her such an honorarium through me as is suitable. Depend on it it is clever, and will do your magazine credit.

We have just made Rough & Ready President. Unless he go for a Tariff great disappointment, and great irritation will prevail. He owes his election to hostility to Free Trade, though I am far from being certain he is for a new Tariff.

As for Europe, Louis Napoleon, in my judgment, would do more towards bringing about a restoration than any other man in

France. His want of judgment would hasten events that I deem inevitable. Henry Vth must reign in France, and the French are for him. All this seems like a riddle, but it is not the less so.

Very truly Yours

R. Bentley Esquire J— Fenimore Cooper

ADDRESSED: Mr. Richard Bentley | Publisher | New-Burlington Street | London | England | per American Steamer | 20th Nov. POSTMARKED: AW | 6 DE 6 | 1848

MANUSCRIPT: Cooper Collection, Yale University Library.

1. Bentley's letter of 2 October. See Cooper to Bentley, 18 July 1848.

2. Bentley or his editor evidently disagreed. See Cooper to Bentley, 30 November 1845 and 18 May 1850.

964. *To Caroline Martha Cooper*

Hall, Cooperstown, Dec 7th 1848

My Beloved Daughter,

Your letter reached me last night, along with its companion, and I can not express the astonishment it produced. To me the whole thing was unexpected and new. I had not the smallest conception of any thing of the sort.[1]

And now, my child, I shall be as frank with you, as prudence will allow, in a letter. In the first place your happiness will be the first consideration with the whole family. Under no circumstances must there be coldness, alienation, or indifference. You are my dearly beloved child, of many noble and admirable qualities that I have always seen and appreciated, and you shall be treated as such a child merits. My heart, door and means shall never be closed against you, let your final decision be what it may. I say this not only for myself, but for your devoted and tender mother, who has done so much for you, and is ready to do so much more.

But that which you ask is of so serious a nature, that it can not be granted without reflection — without closer and free communications with yourself. Your visit has been a pretty long one, and you had better prepare your aunts for your return home. Paul shall come for you before the holidays — say week after next. Come as fearlessly as your own frank and generous nature will dictate, and rely on being recieved with open arms by every member of your family.

In the interval be prudent. Write no notes or letters, and give no pledges. You must hear what I have to say, unfettered; as the counsel and information of one who is still your best male friend, depend on it, and after you have heard I shall leave you to decide for yourself.

All send their love, and mother unites with me in giving this advice. I write to Mr. — to day, begging to defer an answer to his demand until after your return. I enclose ten dollars — your little New Year's gift, thinking it possible you may find it convenient. Paul will bring the means for the road.

Your most tenderly affectionate father

Miss Caroline Fenimore Cooper J. Fenimore Cooper

ADDRESSED: Miss C. M. Fenimore Cooper | Geneva | New York POSTMARKED: COOPERSTOWN N.Y. | DEC | 8 STAMPED: 5

MANUSCRIPT: Cooper Collection, Yale University Library; envelope owned by Paul Fenimore Cooper, Cooperstown, New York. PUBLISHED: *Correspondence*, II, 599–600.

Born in the Fenimore farm house near Cooperstown on 26 June 1815, Caroline Martha, the novelist's second surviving child, died at her home in Cooperstown on 10 January 1892 and was buried beside her husband in Lakewood Cemetery, Cooperstown. She was married to Henry Frederick Phinney in Christ Church, Cooperstown, by the Reverend Stephen H. Battin on the morning of 8 February 1849, in the presence of some forty or fifty persons, including the bride's family, and the father, sisters, brothers, uncle and aunt of the groom. The bride was given away by her father. The four children of the couple were: Henry (1850–1851); Susan Cooper (1852–1881), who married Jacob Sutherland Irving in 1874; Frederick (1854–1892); Charles John (b. 1856). (Cooper family Bible; Tiffany, *The Tiffanys of America*, 126–27; Anna C. Wildey, *Genealogy of the Descendants of William Chesebrough* . . . [New York: T. A. Wright, 1903], 345.)

1. The letters of Caroline Cooper and H. F. Phinney requesting consent to their marriage are lost, presumably destroyed. Cooper's shock and hesitation resulted not from any desire to prevent his daughter's marriage, but from the circumstance that Phinney's mother was Nancy Whiting Tiffany, the sister of Frederick T. Tiffany, and that the quarrel between Cooper and Tiffany had greatly complicated the relations between the two families.

965. *To Henry Frederick Phinney*

[Cooperstown, 7 December 1848] [1]

Dear Sir,

Your letter [2] reached me last night, causing in me the greatest surprise, for I had not the least suspicion of any thing of the sort. Of course I am not prepared to give an immediate answer, and least of all in the absence of the other party. Nor do I like to give the Post Master⟨'s⟩ General's clerks an occasion to edify themselves with secrets of this nature, in the event of a miscarriage of my letter. Under all the circumstances, therefore, I must ask the indulgence of a delay until next month. We shall all be on the spot, and the uncertainty will not be of long continuance. I am obliged to write now, in acknowledgement of your favour, lest your affairs should call you away from Buffaloe before my letter could arrive, and I feel that we all have a right to communicate personally with the individual most concerned in a matter of this moment, before we act.

I can not be more explicit through the mail, and remain,

dear [Sir,] [3] | very truly yours

H— F. Phinney Esquire. J— Fenimore Cooper

MANUSCRIPT: Cooper Collection, Yale University Library.

The son of Cooper's childhood playmate Elihu Phinney, Henry Frederick Phinney (1816–1875) entered the family publishing firm in Cooperstown in 1839. With its staple of histories, Bibles, and textbooks, the house flourished until the late 1840's when a series of mysterious fires, apparently set by an incendiary, led H. F. Phinney and his brother Elihu, Jr., to move the business to Buffalo, New York, in 1849. In 1853 H. F. Phinney moved to New York City to become a partner of Henry Ivison, a textbook publisher. The firm prospered as Ivison & Phinney until 1870, when Phinney withdrew because of ill health to retire to Cooperstown. (Tiffany, *The Tiffanys of America*, 126–27; Livermore, *A Condensed History of Cooperstown*, 160, 162.)

1. The place and date have been clipped.
2. Unlocated.
3. Clipped.

966. *To Anson Judd Upson*

Hall, Cooperstown, Dec. 16th 1848

Dear Sir,

I have delayed this reply from a sheer inability to answer your question.[1] I do not remember what I said in the address at Geneva, and the manuscript was destroyed, but I very well remember that the highest authority I have ever been able to get for the phrase "vox populi vox dei," was one of the English Archbishops, at a coronation sermon. Who was the king crowned, I do not now remember, but I think it was John. At all events it was a Plantagenet, and one of those who had but a doubtful claim to the throne. It might have been Henry. I have had a good hunt for my authority, but can not find it, though I perfectly well remember to have had it formerly, and to have been familiar with it.[2]

After all, I will not say that the axiom does not come from the ancients, though I can discover no authority for it there. The Latins commonly used deus in the plural, but they sometimes used [it] in the singular, when meaning a divine providence. I do not suppose that they believed in a plurality of Gods, but that their mythology was intended to be a poetical representation of the attributes of a single deity.

This country furnishes a living illustration of the truth of the axiom. It is perhaps fortunate it is so, there being great danger that the people will shortly respect nothing, but themselves. King Majority may reign as well as any other monarch, and by dint of constant struggles, it is possible that we may keep his majesty within bearable bounds. It is when one remembers who they are who give utterance to the royal thoughts that one is induced to doubt the future. Divine Providence reigns over even majorities, and the "vox dei" may interpose, after all, to save us from its miserable counterfeit the "vox populi."

Respectfully Yours

Anson J Upson Esquire — J. Fenimore Cooper

MANUSCRIPT: Paul Fenimore Cooper, Cooperstown, New York. PUBLISHED: *Correspondence*, II, 600–01. (The *Correspondence* gives the addressee's name as Anson Gleason.)

A native of Utica, New York, Upson (1823–1902, Hamilton 1843) taught rhetoric, logic, and elocution at Hamilton College from 1845 to 1870. He then served as pastor of the Second Presbyterian Church in Albany, professor of sacred rhetoric and pastoral theology at Auburn Theological Seminary, and, during his later years, vice chancellor and chancellor of the State University of New York. (The Upson Family Association of America, *The Upson Family in America* [New Haven: The Tuttle, Morehouse & Taylor Co., 1940], 171–72; *The* [New York] *Evening Post*, 16 June 1902.)

1. Upson wrote from Clinton, New York, in December 1848, to ask the source of the epigram "the voice of the people is the voice of God" and the circumstances of its first use. He could recall Cooper's employing this information in his commencement address at Geneva College on 4 August 1841, but not the information itself (MS: YCAL).

2. Cooper was almost surely thinking of the coronation sermon (1327) for Edward III, preached on the text "Vox populi, vox Dei" by the turncoat Walter Reynolds, archbishop of Canterbury. However, the Latin epigram was quoted as a familiar saying at least as early as Alcuin's *Epistle to Charlemagne* (800). It may have derived from a somewhat similar Greek expression in Hesiod's *Works and Days* (c. 735 B.C.), lines 763–64.

967. *To Winfield Scott*

Hall, Cooperstown, Jan. 3d 1849

My Dear Sir,

A young neighbour of mine, Mr. Edward Lewis Berthoud, goes to Washington to seek employment as a surveyor, if such service is to be had.[1] He thinks that Col. Abert [2] has some power in appointing to such situations, but I believe this must be a mistake. Will you permit me to recommend him to your kind offices if the army has any thing to do with the matter. The young gentleman bears an excellent character, is liberally educated, and I make no doubt would prove useful, if he could be employed.

A happy new year to you. I trust that 1849 will be a year of peace and happiness for you. The two that have preceded it will place your name in a high place on the scroll of history. The capture of Vera Cruz, the storming the heights of Cerro Gordo, the march to Mexico, and the battles of the valley make a record that would transmit far less known names to the latest posterity. You may prune your vines, for the remainder of your days.

I hope you have got the better of your attack, and that your physician will advise *mountain* air, next summer.

With best regards, | I remain very truly | Yours
Maj. Gen. Scott. | U. S. Army. J. Fenimore Cooper

ADDRESSED: Maj. Gen. Scott | Com-in Chief | U. S. Army | Washington
MANUSCRIPT: The State Historical Society of Colorado. PUBLISHED: *The Colorado Magazine*, VII (March 1931), 79–80.

An invited guest at the Bread and Cheese Club's farewell banquet for Cooper, Scott (1786–1866, William and Mary n.g.) and the novelist were acquaintances for some twenty-five years. Susan Fenimore Cooper remembered her father's bringing Scott home for dinner in their early New York years, and the two met socially in New York in later years. The defeat of the General's presidential ambitions by a fellow Whig and a military subordinate may account for Cooper's allusion in his letter to Scott's pruning his vines. (Elliott, *Winfield Scott*.)

1. On 2 January 1849 Berthoud's father wrote Cooper from Fort Plain, New York, introducing Edward (1828–1908, Union 1849) and requesting introductions for him to influential friends who might assist him to become a United States surveyor or topographical engineer. After serving as a civil engineer for the Panama railroad (1851–1852) and following his profession in Kentucky, Ohio, Indiana, Wisconsin, and Iowa, Berthoud settled in Golden City, Colorado, about 1860. He discovered the Berthoud Pass on 12 May 1861. Then, after Civil War service, he became the secretary and chief engineer for the Colorado Central Railroad Company. He published several books and articles of historical and geographical interest. (Louise C. Harrison, *Empire and the Berthoud Pass* [Denver: Big Mountain Press,

1964]; the Berthoud family Bible, The State Historical Society of Colorado; MS: YCAL.)

2. John James Abert (1788–1863, West Point 1811), lieutenant colonel of the topographical engineers from 1824 to 1838 and colonel from 1838 to 1861 (*ACAB*).

968. *To Louis Legrand Noble*

Otsego Hall, Cooperstown, Jan 6th 1849

Sir,

I did not meet Mr. Cole in Europe.[1] When he was in England and France, I was in Italy, and when he was in Italy, I was at home. My connection with Cole was very slight, and much less than I could have wished. When he brought himself into notice by his views of the Catskill, he was living not far from me in Greenwich Street, and I visited him, and he visited me. But, I went abroad shortly after, and since my return home, our residences have been so far apart, that we seldom met.

While in England in 1828, I requested Mr. Charles Wilkes to order a picture for me from Cole, and to send it to [Samuel] Rogers, the well known poet.[2] This was done. The picture, I presume, is still in Mr. Rogers' possession, though I rather think not considered one of the painter's best. My means have never allowed me to employ artists as I could wish to do, a large and expensive family requiring most of my spare cash. Had it been otherwise, I could have found great satisfaction in possessing works from the pencil of Cole.

As a man, I knew but little of Mr. Cole; but that little was greatly in his favour. He always struck me as intellectual, fair-minded, full of feeling for his art, just to others, modest and as enthusiastic as a well-regulated temperament, and a cool head would permit. Of his domestic life, I know nothing.

As an artist, I consider Mr. Cole one of the very first geniuses of the age. This has long been my opinion. ⟨, but⟩ The March of Empire [*The Course of Empire*], his best work I think, ought to make the reputation of any man. Cole improved vastly by his visit to Italy. This, however, was as an artist, rather than as a man of genius. The *thought* of the March of Empire came from within; and, so far as my knowledge extends, he might have searched all the galleries of Europe for its conception, in vain.

The series are a great epic poem, in which the idea far surpasses the execution, though the last is generally fine. As ⟨a⟩ landscapes the two first pictures are the best; as poems the others come in for their proper share. There is a sublimity about the rock on the mountain top, seen in its different aspects, but always the same, a monument of its divine origin, amid all the changes of the scene, that has always deeply affected me [3]— The criticism of this country is not of a very high order, and is apt to overlook the higher claims of either writer or artist, else [would this series?] [4] have given Cole a [niche?], by himself, in the Temple of Fame. He laboured under the great disadvantage of not having had a severe study in early youth. But his greatest draw-back was probably the want of a family, and the low prices that are given for works of art in America. The labor necessary to execute the last picture in this series, as it ought to have been, would have been immense; and probably he could not afford it.

As a mere artist, Claude [Lorrain] [5] was materially the superior of Cole. This arose from advantages of position. As a poet, Cole was as much before Claude, as Shakspeare is before Pope. I know of no painter, whose works manifest so much high poetical feeling, as those of Cole. Mind struggles through all attempts, and mind, accompanied by that impulsive feeling of beauty and sublimity, that denote genius. It is quite a new thing to see landscape painting raised to a level of the heroic, in historical compositions; but it is constantly to be traced in the works of Mr. Cole. Some of his Italian views are exquisitely true, while they are imaginative; but it requires that one should be familiar with that land of lands to appreciate them. I have heard it said, that Cole lost his originality and strength, by visiting Europe, but I regard it as a provincial absurdity. The same was said of Irving, and it has been said of me. Mr. Irving's Sketch Book, much his best work, could not have been written without a knowledge of Europe, and it is beyond dispute that two or three of my most popular works, even in this country, were written after I had been some time abroad. The truth is, that one very easily gets in advance of the public mind of America, by a residence amid the great works of the old world, and the inexperienced of this part of the world mistake their own inability to appreciate, for a fault in others.

I have heard ⟨th⟩ it said, *here,* that Cole's Italian landscapes were overcharged; copies from the old masters, and not natural. They are not American nature, it is true; but they are strictly Italian nature, and a most magnificent nature it is – one of which we have no conception. To say nothing of the Alps, many of the finest portions of which belong to Italy, your Catskill hills would be deemed tame in the Appenines. The rocks on the Shores of the Bay of Naples, in the vicinity of Castel a Mare rise nearly, if not quite two thousand feet above the Round Top. In addition to this, their shapes are infinitely picturesque. Cole has overcharged nothing in any picture I have ever seen, and it requires his perception of beauty to come any where near Italian landscape. It must be studied to be appreciated.

Nature should be the substratum of all that is poetical. But the superstructure ought to be no servile copy. The poet and the painter are permitted to give the beau idéal of this nature, and he who makes it the most attractive, while he maintains the best likeness, is the highest artist. Such, in my judgment, was Cole's great merit. His defect was want of severe early study, as is most seen in his manner of treating the human figure. This can only be done well, by those who have been well taught. Lawrence [6] drew but indifferently, as did Stewart,[7] and [John Wesley] Jarvis, who probably had more native talent than either. What Jarvis did not understand, he could not teach, and Inman,[8] who might have made the first portrait painter of his time, had some of the same deficiency. Still Inman was as near the head of his order of art, as any man.

I do not place the more laboured allegorical landscapes of Cole, as high as the March of Empire. They are very fine pictures, and there is something noble in his constant efforts to unite the moral and intellectual in landscape painting, but the first conception, I fancy, was produced most *con amore.* Not only do I consider the March of Empire the work of the highest genius this country has ever produced, but I esteem it as one of the noblest works of art that has ever been wrought. There is a simplicity, distinctness, eloquence, and pathos in the design, that are beautifully brought out and illustrated in the execution. The day will come when the series will command $50,000, in my judgment.

Some of Cole's little American landscapes are perfect gems, in their way. He never used his pencil without eliciting poetry, and feeling, exhibited with singular fidelity to nature. I mix ⟨with⟩ but little with the world, and rarely visit the exhibitions. When I did, I could tell one of these pieces as far as sight enabled me to see it. On one occasion, I remember to have been misled as to the artist, and to have stood before a little landscape that was said to have come from another hand. "Here, then, is another artist," I said, "who has caught the spirit of Cole!" After all, it turned out to be a picture by Cole, himself! No one else could paint such a picture.

Cole, like every other man of genius in this country, whose works do not directly affect the pocket, was in advance of the times. It requires a different state of society, to appreciate merit of this calibre, and it would not surprise me to learn that Cole died comparatively poor. I believe he never got an order, or patronage of any sort, from a single public body in the country. Generally, such things are reserved for pretenders, amongst ourselves. Those who are to dispense of the patronage know too little, and feel too little, to do it with judgment. One half the money that has been given to foreigners to disfigure the capitol, in the production of works that do not properly form links in the chain of American history, as connected with the arts, while they have little or no intrinsic merit, would have made [Washington] Al[l]ston, and Cole, and one or two others I could name, comfortable, if not rich. But this is not to be. A pretending but ignorant publi[c,] [9] a corrupt and vulgar press, towns composed of traders, and legislative bodies that are too ephemeral to suffer even the little that is known to become useful, are but indifferent elements out of which to create a high and intellectual civilization. We may work up something from the base, in time — are doing.

I have not written for publication, but in haste and with a long interruption, which will explain the difference in time between the date and the post mark. I wish you all success in bringing forth the virtues and merits of Cole, both as a man and an artist,[10] and remain

Sir, | Yours respectfully

Rev. L. L. Noble. J. Fenimore Cooper

MANUSCRIPT: The New-York Historical Society. PUBLISHED, IN PART: Louis L. Noble, *The Course of Empire, Voyage of Life, and Other Pictures of Thomas Cole, N.A., with Selections from His Letters and Miscellaneous Writings: Illustrative of His Life, Character, and Genius* [New York: Cornish, Lamport & Company, 1853], 224–26.

Poet, teacher, and friend of artists, Noble (1811–1882, Bristol College, Pennsylvania, 1837; General Theological Seminary 1840) ministered chiefly to congregations in New York State, at Albany, Catskill, Glens Falls, Fredonia, and Hudson. Though he published two volumes of poetry and a book on Frederick E. Church, the artist, Noble is best remembered as the biographer of Thomas Cole. (Lucius M. Boltwood, *History and Genealogy of the Family of Thomas Noble, of Westfield, Massachusetts* [Hartford, Connecticut: Case, Lockwood & Brainard Company, 1878], 144–45; *ACAB*.)

1. Noble wrote as Cole's literary executor from Catskill, New York, on 28 December 1848, to obtain Cooper's recollections of the artist, especially on Cole's first visit to England in 1829 (MS: YCAL).

2. See Cooper to Wilkes, 7 May 1828.

3. See Plates IX–XI.

4. The holograph has been injured by damp.

5. Claude Gellée (1600–1682), also called Claude Lorrain, Cooper wrote "Loraine."

6. Sir Thomas Lawrence (1769–1830).

7. Evidently Gilbert Stuart.

8. Henry Inman (1801–1846).

9. The script overran the page.

10. Noble replied from Catskill on 13 March 1849:

"It was not without design that I determined on the receipt of yours of Jan 6 to delay for a little to reply. I was so struck with the truth of your criticisms that I determined to reply as I thought the epistle deserved. I now think that no such reply is necessary — a few words are enough. I can truly say that among many letters, some from most distinguished sources at home & abroad, I have received not one of the justness & importance of your own. After some *four years* of most intimate acquaintance with the artist, & much in his study *in view to truthful criticism upon his works* — after much reflection upon his genius & work since his death, I find that you have thrown off without premeditation almost the same views in respect of him that I have formed myself. Nay, more — I find your letter possesses a leading faculty into some things that I should have entirely neglected, but now feel the importance of following out. Your letter, sir, is very valuable to me. I am much gratified that you have favoured me with it. And while I shall not give the letter itself a publicity I hope you will not deny me the privilege of frequently presenting the truths it contains. With the hope that I may at some time be permitted to make your distinguished acquaintance . . ." (MS: YCAL.)

969. *To Henry Frederick Phinney*

Hall, Jan. 9th 1849

Dear Sir,

I have conversed with my daughter, and the result is an acceptance of your proposal.

I believe it is the wish of Caroline that nothing should be

said on the subject, beyond communicating the state of things to your own family, which always includes your uncle Harry,[1] until she and you have conferred together.

Of course you will let us see you shortly, and I trust your visits, in future, will be free and as frequent as may comport with your own convenience and wishes.

Yours truly

H. F. Phinney Esquire J. Fenimore Cooper

ADDRESSED: Henry Frederick Phinney Esquire | Cooperstown
MANUSCRIPT: Cooper Collection, Yale University Library. PUBLISHED: *Correspondence,* II, 601.

1. Cooper presumably referred to Henry Phinney.

970. *To Wallace E. Caldwell*

Hall, Cooperstown, | Jan 10th 1849

Sir,

I am sorry it is not in my power to give you the information you ask.[1] My acquaintance with your part of the State is very slight, nor am I very conversant with Indian history. I would recommend Mr. Schoolcraft[2] to you, as the person [who][3] is probably most qualified to give you the precise facts you wish to obtain.

I should *think* the country of the Mohawks must have extended as far as Whitehall, though I may easily be mistaken. They were a powerful tribe, and had extensive hunting grounds. My memory goes back more than half a century, and I do not recollect ever to have heard of any people but the Mohawks between Utica and the Hudson, north of the Mohawk river, until we get near the St. Lawrence.

I regret being unable to say any more, unless it be to add that I remain your well wisher &c.

J. Fenimore Cooper

Wallace [E. Caldwell, Esqu]ire

ADDRESSED: Wallace E Caldwell Esquire | Whitehall | New York POSTMARKED: COOPERSTOWN N.Y. | JAN | 10 STAMPED: 5
MANUSCRIPT: Barrett-Eaton Collection, University of Virginia Library.

Caldwell (1819–1877), son of James G. and Eliza Blinn Caldwell of Whitehall, New York, became a well-known publisher in Brooklyn, New York (Charles H. Farnam, *History of the Descendants of John Whitman of Weymouth, Mass.* [New Haven,

Connecticut: Tuttle, Morehouse & Taylor, 1889], 508; *The New-York Times*, 26 March 1877).

1. From Whitehall, New York, Caldwell wrote, in part, on 6 January: "I wish to learn what tribe or tribes of Indians formerly dwelt in this region or this particular locality — and their fate —

"Tradition says that this town was formerly called Kah-shah-quah-n[a?] signifying 'the place where we dip fish.' Is this spelling and rendering of the word correct, & of what language or tribe is it.

"Perhaps you can refer me to some work where the desired information can be had. Still pardon me for saying that I should feel flattered in the highest degree by receiving direct from yourself *your own views* on these questions." (MS: YCAL.)

2. Cooper was conversant with the Indian researches of Henry Rowe Schoolcraft (1793–1864, Union n.g.), explorer, ethnologist, and Indian agent, though Schoolcraft's main works were published too late to have influenced Cooper's early Indian romances ("Sketches of the Life of Henry R. Schoolcraft," *Personal Memoirs of a Residence of Thirty Years with the Indian Tribes on the American Frontiers* . . . [Philadelphia: Lippincott, Grambo and Co., 1851], xxvii–xlviii; *DAB*).

3. The holograph here and elsewhere is damaged by water stains and tears.

971. *To John Fagan*

Hall, Cooperstown, Feb. 16th [1849]

Dear Fagan,

The rest of copy is on the way, complete. As yet I have recieved but three forms of the last English volume, chapters 6, 7, and part of 8, American Vol II, the mail producing [curious?] [1] delays.

I shall be at the Globe, New-York, however, by the time you get this, and hope to hear from you there, at once. This will greatly expedite matters. I shall expect you to send me there, the last Eng— vol. Preface, Title &c, in duplicate, that I may send it to England, in time for the last bills.[2]

I have a new work of considerable size — Two Vols. Octavo, I think, but may sell it to Lea & Blanchard.

It is quite likely that I shall see you in a few days.

Yours truly

J— Fenimore Cooper

Mr. John Fagan | Philadelphia

ENDORSED: From J. F. Cooper, Esq. | Feb. 16, 1849. | Has sent me the | last copy of | "Sea Lions."

MANUSCRIPT: Cooper Collection, Yale University Library.

1. Cooper seems to have written "furious."

2. Fagan's reply is unlocated.

972. *To Mrs. Cooper*

Globe, Wednesday morning, Feb. 21st 1849

Dearest Sue,

I did not suffer with the cold at all, especially in the feet. Wearing the leggings and the big boots, I had not a cold foot, all the way down. I carried Mrs. [Hamilton] Fish her letter; found them at table with [James] Stevenson, Mrs. [Daniel D.] Barnard, Miss Granger,[1] [Richard V.] DeWitt, Walter Church,[2] one of the James', and a Mr. & Mrs. Johnson, he a senator from New York,[3] and of the Stratford family, Bob Morris [4] of course. I sat down and staid a couple of hours. The Fish's all kindness, and wished me to stay with them. Christine [5] had been up, and passed a day in Albany, and sailed yesterday for Europe. By the way Mrs. Johnson said that Mrs. [Henry D.] Cruger has come ⟨up⟩ home, came up last week, passed a day at Herkimer and returned. This was all she could tell me. I fear, from the circular I got, that the scabbard is thrown away.

I met Mrs. [Gerrit] Smith's brother, [Dr. Daniel] Fitzhugh, at Albany, and we came on together, yesterday. The Senator Nicholas [6] was of his party, and we passed the day in company. The last is a sensible man, but not a first-rater. There are very few of the last, unhappily. At this house, I found [James E.] Dekay, or rather he found me, for he got in last, from Washington, where he had been to see about the Commodore's affairs, who, it seems had bought a house in W[ashington], and intended to live there. He died of dropsy on the chest, among strangers, and none of his family with him. He left home only the week before, and the Dr. says he told him he would die on the road. Die he did, and has left his affairs in terrible confusion. His widow and seven children, all young, are at the Dr's.[7]

I have not seen any one, as yet. The picture is opened, and Mr. Wight['s] [8] nails have fortunately gone through the *frame* only. *That* is a good deal injured, but the woman and the tree are both standing.

[Hamilton] Fish has a controversy with your old admirer, J. B. Scott, who is now recorder.[9] It is likely to prove fierce. His friends told me that [Thurlow] Weed was getting too much influence over him. If so I may have done good, for I gave an instance of Mr. Weed's propensity to lie, and a pretty strong one. I am afraid that Hamilton is surrounded by too many very bad men for his own good.

I bought myself a nice pair of spectacles in Albany, and am set up in that article for the present.

As for my heel, it is much the same. It has not troubled me any in travelling, and not much in walking. I shall favour it all I can. The day which was very cold and unpleasant this morning, is now (11. A. M), turning out pleasant, and I shall go into the street for a little while.

In coming down I passed through Sawpits, so altered I did not know the place. I got a distant glimpse of Rye, passing a hundred rods in the rear of Penfield's, and somewhere near [Pretty?] Land, I saw the Rye House, for an instant, more than half a mile distant. It appeared to me that we crossed Sheldrake just under the hills that lie behind Mamaroneck, crossing Sheldrake at a point a little below the Scarsdale road. There are so many changes, however, and the country was so covered with snow, and we went so fast, I could hardly recognise any thing. I did not see Union Hill, nor any other object I knew until we got to Harlem. At 27th Street we took horses, and stopped in Canal Street, near Broadway, at ½ past seven. We were nearly two hours behind our time, though we came 195 miles in about twelve hours. We experienced two considerable detentions in waiting for other trains. I paid but $4. The whole distance cost about $10 including taverns. This brings us very near New York, for the winter, but we shall be much nearer.

[George E.] Hand and [Henry D.] Cruger have both been here. The former says that, in the case of a creditor's bill it can not be resorted to until execution is returned, and that the creditor has no right to anticipate the time of return established by law. If so, I shall come home, and wait my time. Hand, however, gives us some facts of moment, and I think we shall screw Mr. [Sidney] Ketchum down so closely, as to get something out of him.

Hand dines with me to-day, and we both dine with ⟨him⟩

Cruger to-morrow. I have not been out this morning, but may take the air after dinner. Mrs. Cruger, *he* thinks, went to Albany to see the judge who was to decide her case, as she saw the Vice Chancellor, before. But the court he was on adjourned before she arrived. He came down, and gave his decision without seeing her. Since then he has consented to modify his opinion in Cruger's favour, so far as to exonerate him from the interest on his brother's bonds.

Finding nothing to do in Albany, Mrs. C[ruger] went on to Henderson. There she *took* lodgings in the porter's lodge, making a great stir about the hardship of her case. At night she prayed for him in a voice so loud as to be heard by all in the lodge. The community is much exercised with all this, some siding with, and some against her. Such is the statement of one side.[10]

MANUSCRIPT: Cooper Collection, Yale University Library. PUBLISHED IN PART: *Correspondence,* II, 604–07.

1. Unidentified.

2. Walter S. Church (d. 1890), who raised a regiment and became a colonel during the Civil War, was a land speculator who purchased much of the Van Rensselaer property (Joel Munsell, *Collections on the History of Albany* [Albany, New York: J. Munsell, 1871], II, 167; IV, 20; *The Albany Directory for the Year 1891 . . .* [Albany: Sampson, Murdock & Co., 1891]).

3. William Samuel Johnson, a lumber dealer listed in New York City directories from 1819 to 1854, was a state senator representing New York's Sixth District in 1849 (*Manual for the Use of the Legislature of the State of New-York, for the Year 1849* [Albany: Weed, Parsons & Co., 1849], 274, 307).

4. Robert Hunter Morris (1826–1865), son of Lewis Lee and Hannah Morris and grandson of Jacob Morris, was the private secretary of Governor Hamilton Fish (Lefferts, *Descendants of Lewis Morris,* Chart E, II).

5. Christine A. W. Kean married William Preston Griffin, a naval lieutenant, on 8 February 1849 (Stuyvesant Fish, *Ancestors of Hamilton Fish and Julia Ursin Niemcewicz Kean, His Wife* [New York: privately printed, 1929?], 77).

6. Unidentified.

7. Shortly before his death, Commodore George Colman De Kay, Dr. J. E. De Kay's brother, assumed responsibility for delivering, in the U.S.S. *Macedonian,* a cargo of food and clothing to the Irish famine victims. When pledges to finance the expedition were not met, De Kay advanced funds himself, expecting to be reimbursed by Congress. His sudden death left his wife Janet Halleck Drake, the only daughter of Joseph Rodman Drake and the granddaughter of shipbuilder Henry Eckford, in a difficult situation. (*DAB.*)

8. See Cooper to Mrs. Cooper, 11 March 1849.

9. John B. Scott (1789?–1854), a lawyer listed in New York City directories from 1810 to 1854, was recorder in New York from 1847 to 1849 (*The* [New York] *Evening Post,* 20 September 1854).

10. The letter is unsigned, and the manuscript may be incomplete.

973. *To Mrs. Cooper*

Globe. Friday, Feb. 23d 1849

Dearest,

I can not get the execution returned until next week, in consequence of the sheriff's officer's being ill, and I shall be compelled to remain here some time. It is not of much consequence, however, as I must remain long enough to get the Sea Lions finished. I am ascertaining the facts concerning [Sidney] Ketchum, and do not doubt that I shall have great trouble in bringing him to payment. Ask Dick to get the papers in [James S.] Sandford's case ready.

Yesterday I dined with [Henry D.] Cruger. He told me that a letter from Henderson informed him that Mrs. Cruger had ordered the materials set out for a stone house for Parson Pepper! He says he has no doubt of the fact, at all. [George E.] Hand was to have dined with us, but did not come. I have not seen him since.

My foot is much the same. I find the gum shoes a great relief to it in walking, but the necessity of using it, is much against it. I suppose it will wear off in time, and will disappear, I know not how.

The picture is at the auction store, and is exciting attention. I doubt, however, if it sell for much. It really appears quite beautiful among the daubs around it. I shall not try to sell it until next week.

I have not been up town yet. The weather is just becoming mild and good, and I trust you have it the same with you.

Ned [Myers] was here last night. He tells me that his wages have been raised, in consequence of my intercession, six shillings a day. Instead of six dollars a week, his old rate of pay, he has recieved ten and a half, all winter. This has been a great relief to him. He has had a young Ned, but he died at eight weeks old. He is now quite anxious, again, to place the eldest daughter with you, strictly as a servant and without wages, in order that she may learn something. She is near fourteen, and he praises her to the skies. She is to come and see me, next Sunday, but I have told him I can do nothing without your decision. He expects to recieve $1250 of back pension, and wishes to go to California, not to dig gold, but to provide for his family. I rather think, however, he will not go.

The Lt. Palmer [1] who made love to Mary S[hubrick?] was in this house yesterday, and sailed for England to-day, with his family, to be absent a year. He goes for his health.

Think of Hand's losing his dinner, after all. He was so long brushing &c, that I went across to Cruger's and left word for him to follow. He missed the bookkeeper, who had the message, looked into a directory, found a Cruger in Waverly Place, and gave the matter up, in despair.

Tell Dick I must get ready to try the Sandford case in April — 1st Monday, before Edmonds.[2] It seems that Mr. Hand saw a large heavy trunk in a tavern, at Detroit, enveloped in oil cloths, and directed to Sidney Ketchum. Whereupon he had it seized under his creditor's bill. He did not open it, as he had no key and applied to Ketchum for one, here. Ketchum says the trunk contains papers, deeds, letters &c. This may turn out of consequence, as Ketchum seemed much annoyed at the arrest. By getting his papers we may make important discoveries. Amariah [Storrs] is doing all he can to help me, for one of the Currie's recieved $2500 on account of Ketchum, in some interest or other, quite lately.

It is not probable I shall get home before the 10th or 12th. I think Caroline would find the Globe a good and a cheap house, considering they would have private rooms. It would not be very convenient for her, but would be quite so for Mr. Phinney. It would be necessary to make a bargain for the rooms, parlour and bed-room communicating, and they vary from $4 to $1. per day. But I will enquire, particularily, what will be the cost of living in this house, which I have found cheap — cheaper even than under the last occupant, who was not half as dear as [Francis] Blancard. I have a parlor and bed-room, with fire, in *the 4th story*, at, I believe $1.25 per day. My expenses in the house for eating will not reach a dollar to-day. I have not expended more than a dollar a day since I have been here, room and fire excepted, exclusively of a dinner to Mr. Hand.

I called to-day on Mrs. Laight, but she had gone to Maj. [Philip] Kearny's — Why, her maid did not tell me. I left the box &c, and Mrs. [William C.] Maitland has hers, also. I have not see Ned [Edward F. De Lancey]. Jim [De Lancey] was on his way to Yonkers, with his *beau pere* [Dr. Edward N. Bibby]. I have sent Fred's package to its address.

The entire lot of Grace Church is covered with a free-stone building, which has twenty seven windows towards Trinity. This large edifice has been put up since I was last down. It is intended for stores and offices, and, ere long, will produce an enormous rental.

I met Phil Van Wyck [3] in Broadway, this morning. He knew nothing of the movements of the Battins. It is possible the cold weather has kept them at New Hartford.

To-night, I am to go with Hand to call on Mrs. Ledyard.[4] I shall take the opportunity to see some of the Jays. I am afraid Fish has made a mistake in the affair of the pardon, opinion seeming to set against him.[5] I doubt if he be re-elected. He is surrounded by cruelly bad hands.

I have seen [William] Jay, his wife and children, Mrs. Bruen,[6] Eliza,[7] &c &c. I also have seen Mrs. Banyer and Miss Nancy, the latter looking very ill, the former very well. Jay, thin, old and white-headed. He keeps his colour, however, pretty well. I think the death of Mrs. Balch has shaken both.[8] Mrs. Jay looks old and care-worn. They all seemed glad to see me, and asked a great many questions. Mrs. Ledyard talked a great deal, and complained of Mrs. Baker's having had a wedding of eighty persons so soon after her brother's death.[9] She said she understood that "the judge and his sister were not on good terms!" Christine's fortune she put down at $90,000, and she is pretty good authority, in such a matter. She lives, à l'Européenne, in snug lodgings in Broadway, not far from the New York Hotel. The Bruens go to the public table, but the Jays do not. On the whole, I am not certain Caroline would not be better up town, among her friends. But, I shall enquire, and see.

As yet, I have not received a page of proof-sheets. As I must now remain to finish the book, you had better send me any English letters, reading them to see if they contain any thing worth knowing.

With love to all, I remain most tenderly
Yours — J. F. C.

ADDRESSED: Mrs. Fenimore Cooper | Cooperstown | New York

MANUSCRIPT: Paul Fenimore Cooper, Cooperstown, New York.

1. Probably James Sheddon Palmer (1810–1867), appointed midshipman in 1825, lieutenant in 1836, captain in 1862, and rear admiral in 1866 (*ACAB*).

2. A jurist, John Worth Edmonds (1799–1874, Union 1816) held many elective and appointive offices in New York City and State. He was justice of the State Supreme Court from 1847 to 1852. (*DAB*.)

3. Cooper evidently referred to Philip Gilbert Van Wyck (1786?–1870, Columbia 1807), son of Abraham and Catherine (Van Cortlandt) Van Wyck, or to Philip's son Philip A. Van Wyck (Anne Van Wyck, *Descendants of Cornelius Barentse Van Wyck and Anna Polhemus* [New York: Tobias A. Wright, 1912], 126, 171; *The* [New York] *Evening Post*, 2 August 1870; *CUOA*).

4. Henry Ledyard married Matilda C., daughter of Lewis Cass, in 1839 (*Early History of Michigan*, 410).

5. Three days after his defeat in the election for recorder of New York City, the incumbent John B. Scott imposed a discriminatory sentence on John B. Harrison, a political enemy convicted for keeping a gambling house. Of thirteen similar cases, Harrison's was the only one to carry a jail sentence as well as a fine. Persuaded that the sentence was vindictive, Governor Fish freed Harrison. (*Albany Evening Journal*, 22 February 1849.)

6. William Jay's daughter Sarah Louisa (1819–1905) married Alexander M. Bruen (1808–1886) in 1848 (Jay, *The Jay Family: A Genealogical Chart*).

7. William Jay's daughter Eliza (1823–1869) (Jay, *The Jay Family: A Genealogical Chart*).

8. Mrs. Balch, William Jay's daughter Anna, died on 5 January 1848 (Jay, *The Jay Family: A Genealogical Chart*).

9. Mrs. Baker's brother John Cox Morris died on 2 February 1849, and her daughter Christine's marriage occurred on 8 February (*The* [New York] *Evening Post*, 8 February, 12 February 1849).

ABBREVIATIONS AND SHORT TITLES

INDEX OF RECIPIENTS AND JOURNALS

ABBREVIATIONS AND SHORT TITLES

Page citations of the fiction refer (unless otherwise indicated) to the edition of Cooper's novels illustrated by F. O. C. Darley and published in New York by W. A. Townsend and Company from 1859 to 1861 in thirty-two volumes. This set, the first collected edition to incorporate Cooper's final revisions for George P. Putnam, has been the basis of most subsequent collected editions.

ACAB. James Grant Wilson and John Fiske, eds., *Appleton's Cyclopædia of American Biography* (New York: D. Appleton and Company, 1900), 6 volumes.

BDAC. James L. Harrison, *Biographical Directory of the American Congress, 1774–1949* (Washington, D.C.: Government Printing Office, 1950).

Blanck, *Bibliography of American Literature*. Jacob Blanck, comp., *Bibliography of American Literature* (New Haven: Yale University Press, 1957). Volume II.

Burke's *Peerage*. Sir Bernard Burke and Ashworth P. Burke, *A Genealogical and Heraldic History of the Peerage and Baronetage* . . . (London: Harrison & Sons, 1915).

Complete Peerage. George Edward Cokayne, *The Complete Peerage*, revised by Geoffrey H. White and others (London: The St. Catherine Press, 1910–1959), 12 volumes.

Cooper family Bible. The Holy Bible, Containing the Old and New Testaments: together with the Apocrypha . . . (Philadelphia: John Thompson and Abraham Small, 1798). In this large family Bible, measuring 10⅝" by 17⅜", the novelist recorded births, deaths, and marriages for his own and his father's families. It is owned by Dr. Henry S. F. Coper, great-grandson of the novelist.

Cooper, *The Yale Review*. James Fenimore Cooper (great-grandson of the novelist), "Unpublished Letters of James Fenimore Cooper," *The Yale Review*, n.s. V (July 1916), 810–31.

Correspondence. James Fenimore Cooper (grandson of the novelist), ed., *Correspondence of James Fenimore-Cooper* (New Haven: Yale University Press, 1922), 2 volumes.

Cruger Family Chart. Bentley D. Hasell, *The Cruger Family in America: A Genealogical Chart* (1892). Original owned by the New York Genealogical and Biographical Society, New York City.

CUOA. Milton Halsey Thomas, *Columbia University Officers and Alumni, 1754–1857* (New York: Columbia University Press, 1936).

DAB. Allen Johnson and Dumas Malone, eds., *Dictionary of American Biography* (New York: Charles Scribner's Sons, 1928–1936), 20 volumes.

De Lancey, "Original Family Records." Edward Floyd De Lancey, "Original Family Records of Loockermans, Bayard, Van Cortlandt, Van Rensselaer, and Schuyler," *The New York Genealogical and Biographical Record*, V [April 1874], 69–76.

Dexter, *Graduates of Yale College*. Franklin Bowditch Dexter, *Biographical*

Sketches of the Graduates of Yale College with Annals of the College History (New York and New Haven: Henry Holt and the Yale University Press, 1885–1912), 6 volumes.

DNB. Leslie Stephen and Sidney Lee, eds., *Dictionary of National Biography* (New York and London: Macmillan and Company, and Smith, Elder and Company, 1885–1912), 63 volumes, and supplements.

Early History of Michigan. *Early History of Michigan, with Biographies of State Officers, Members of Congress, Judges and Legislators* (Lansing, Michigan: Thorp & Godfrey, 1888).

Elliott, *Winfield Scott*. Charles Winslow Elliott, *Winfield Scott: The Soldier and the Man* (New York: The Macmillan Company, 1937).

GE. *La Grande Encyclopédie* . . . (Paris: H. Lamirould et Cie., Éditeurs, n.d.), 31 volumes.

GNR (General Navy Register). Edward W. Callahan, *List of Officers of the Navy of the United States and of the Marine Corps from 1775 to 1900, Comprising a Complete Register of All Present and Former Commissioned, Warranted, and Appointed Officers of the United States Navy, and of the Marine Corps, Regular and Volunteer* (New York: L. R. Hamersly and Company, 1901).

Historical Register and Dictionary of the United States Army. Francis B. Heitman, *Historical Register and Dictionary of the United States Army, from Its Organization, September 29, 1789, to March 2, 1903* (Washington, D.C.: Government Printing Office, 1903).

Hobart College: General Catalogue. *Hobart College: General Catalogue of Officers, Graduates and Students, 1825–1897* (Geneva, New York: W. F. Humphrey, 1897).

Hurd, *History of Otsego County*. Duane Hamilton Hurd, *History of Otsego County, New York, with Illustrations and Biographical Sketches* (Philadelphia: Everts and Fariss, 1878).

Jay, *The Jay Family: A Genealogical Chart*. Mary Rutherfurd Jay, *The Jay Family of New York: A Genealogical Chart* (Privately issued, 1935).

Jay Cemetery, Rye, New York. *The Jay Cemetery, Rye, New York* (Privately published by the trustees of the Jay Cemetery, October 1947).

Jordan, *Colonial Families of Philadelphia*. John W. Jordan, *Colonial Families of Philadelphia* (New York and Chicago: The Lewis Publishing Company, 1911), 2 volumes.

Lefferts, *Descendants of Lewis Morris*. Elizabeth Morris Lefferts, *Descendants of Lewis Morris of Morrisania . . . First Governor of New Jersey as a Separate Province (1738–1746)* (New York: Tobias A. Wright, 1907?).

Livermore, *A Condensed History of Cooperstown*. S. T. Livermore, *A Condensed History of Cooperstown, with a Biographical Sketch of J. Fenimore Cooper* (Albany: J. Munsell, 1862).

Navy *Register*. *Register of the Commissioned and Warrant Officers of the Navy of the United States* . . . (A yearly register printed by C. Alexander in Washington, D.C., for the Navy Department).

NCAB. *The National Cyclopædia of American Biography* . . . (New York: James T. White and Company, 1888–1948), 34 volumes.

PFC. Family papers owned by Paul Fenimore Cooper (great-grandson of the novelist), Cooperstown, New York.

Richardson, *Messages and Papers of the Presidents.* James D. Richardson, *A Compilation of the Messages and Papers of the Presidents, 1798–1902* (Bureau of National Literature and Art, 1896–1907), 10 volumes.

Spiller and Blackburn, *Bibliography.* Robert E. Spiller and Philip C. Blackburn, *A Descriptive Bibliography of the Writings of James Fenimore Cooper* (New York: R. R. Bowker Company, 1934).

Storrs, *The Storrs Family.* Charles Storrs, *The Storrs Family: Genealogical and Other Memoranda* (New York: privately published, 1886).

Story, *The deLanceys.* D. A. Story, *The deLanceys: A Romance of a Great Family* (London: Thomas Nelson and Sons Limited, 1931).

Tiffany, *The Tiffanys of America.* Nelson Otis Tiffany, *The Tiffanys of America, History and Genealogy* (Buffalo, New York: privately published, 1901?).

Union College: Centennial Catalog. Union University: Centennial Catalog, 1795–1895, of the Officers and Alumni of Union College . . . (Troy, New York: Troy Times Printing House, 1895).

Wethered, *Genealogical Record of the Wethered Family.* James Sykes Wethered, *Genealogical Record of the Wethered Family of Ashlyns, Hertfordshire, England, from A.D. 1400* (San Francisco: D. P. Elder & Morgan Shepard, 1898).

Wheeler, *The Ogden Family.* William Ogden Wheeler, *The Ogden Family in America . . .* (Philadelphia: J. B. Lippincott Company, 1907).

YCAL, Collection of American Literature, Yale University Library.

INDEX OF RECIPIENTS AND JOURNALS

(References are to page numbers)

INDEX OF RECIPIENTS